ARTHUR C. CLARKE

THE AUTHORIZED BIOGRAPHY

Also by Neil McAleer:

The Cosmic Mind-Boggling Book
The Body Almanac
Earthlove: A Space Fantasy
The Mind-Boggling Universe
The Omni Space Almanac

ARTHUR C. CLARKE

THE AUTHORIZED BIOGRAPHY

NEIL McALEER

CB

CONTEMPORARY
BOOKS

CHICAGO

Library of Congress Cataloging-in-Publication Data

McAleer, Neil, 1942–
    Arthur C. Clarke : the authorized biography / Neil McAleer.
      p.   cm.
    Includes index.
    ISBN 0-8092-4324-5 (cloth)
    1. Clarke, Arthur Charles,—1917-   —Biography. 2. Authors.
English—20th century—Biography. I. Title.
PR6005.L36Z77   1992
823′.914—dc20
[B]   92-24898
                                                           CIP

Unless otherwise noted, all photographs are courtesy of Arthur C. Clarke.

Copyright © 1992 by Neil McAleer
All rights reserved
Published by Contemporary Books, Inc.
180 North Michigan Avenue, Chicago, Illinois 60601
Manufactured in the United States of America
International Standard Book Number: 0-8092-4324-5

To Fred
For his faith,
encouragement, and friendship

From the great deep to the great deep he goes.
                                    Alfred Lord Tennyson

Too low they build, who build beneath the stars.
                                    Edward Young

Yet somewhere under starlight or the sun
My father stands.
                                    W. B. Yeats

CONTENTS

FOREWORD

The most vivid memory I have of Arthur C. Clarke is an afternoon some seven or eight years ago when I was walking through Beverly Hills and heard someone shouting at me from across the street.

I glanced over and there was Arthur in front of a computer shop, waving both arms.

"Ray!" he shouted, "Come here! You *must* come over!"

I crossed over to have my hand wrung off at the wrist and feel myself hustled into the computer shop by the greatest salesman in the world for toys of all sizes and shapes.

"Look here!" cried Arthur, carny barker for Tom Swift. "And here, and here!" he added.

The thing he pointed at first, of course, was the brand-spanking-new lap computer. I had never seen one before. Arthur, hearing this, launched into a spiel that would have done the president of Apple proud.

"Think," he urged. "Traveling across the world by jet, to have this incredible machine on your lap, giving you research and you giving it articles, stories, or a piece of a novel. Think!"

"I *am* thinking," I said.

I was not at that time the world's greatest flyboy. In later years, when I discovered I feared only myself and not flying, I was to jet the Concorde back and forth to Paris six times in a single summer.

Only later in life could I imagine myself with Arthur's lapdog nestled on my knees barking metaphors at my slightest touch.

But, for now anyway, here was Arthur, taking over the shop, grabbing my elbow, steering me from table to table, saying "And if you think *that* was wonderful, here's another, and yet another!"

"Arthur," I finally said, "Christmas at your house . . . ?"

"Yes?" he said.

"What must it have been like?"

"This!" he said. "Only this is better. Today, at last, I can buy most of these toys and carry them home, two under my arms and one between my legs if I have to!"

The next afternoon Arthur invited me up to his hotel apartment where his Siamese twin, the new lap beast, was permanently stuck to his fingers; an operation might be needed to separate man and machine. I don't think any encounter in my life has given me so much pleasure. The unabashed love for toys that changed the world, radiating from him, made me feel as if I were on holiday.

Of course, that has always been true. Long before my bright hour with Arthur, he had influenced the world in the best way possible. Schweitzer told us, did he not, to set a good example, someone might clone it? Arthur's ideas have sent silent engines into space to speak in tongues. His fabulous communications satellite ricocheted about in his head long before it leaped over the mountains and flatlands of the earth. Since then it has taught the world, in many languages, mainly the wild joy of playing with something that, in the main, has improved, not wounded, the nations it has shadowed and lit as it passed.

Further, I am reminded of the immense fact that Arthur C. Clarke and his demon-photographer-become-director friend Stanley Kubrick changed the aesthetics of cinema history almost single-handedly in 1968. How so?

Let me take you back to a scene in 1931. In that year, at the Regina Theater at Wilshire and La Cienega, cineasts were exercising their taste, need, and legs by lining up twenty-four hours a day to see *Dracula* and *Frankenstein*. The theater operated all day and all night for more than a year. Fantasy fanatics were arriving at

3:00 A.M. and staggering out at dawn. Why? There was nowhere else to go. Hollywood, in its sublime ignorance, refused to see the bloody writing on the cinema wall. They ignored the fantasy form frightening or science fiction form enlightening, thus ignoring the hungers of young men and women everywhere who had grown up on H. Rider Haggard, Edgar Rice Burroughs, H. G. Wells, Jules Verne, and others. These children and their hungry parents found that, save for minor exceptions (*Things to Come* in 1936, *The Mysterious Island* way back in 1929) their sci-fi heroes and their concepts hid in the balcony, where all minorities tried to survive.

There were breakthroughs in the early 1950s—*The Day the Earth Stood Still, The Thing,* and *It Came from Outer Space.* But there was no grand flurry of production activity, no wide-screen Future, until Kubrick and Clarke threw us a bone, which turned into a spacecraft, which crossed the universe and hyperventilated our lives forever. I was there at the *2001* premiere with Arthur in Hollywood. The film was a trifle long that night (it was trimmed the next week) but none of us realized we had seen something phenomenal. It not only changed history, but brought tons of money to beer halls around the world where the young clustered, babbling far into the night about what it all *meant.*

Another remembrance:

In the early 1970s, with the Viking mission to Mars ready for the grand leap, Cal Tech invited Arthur, Walter Sullivan from the *New York Times,* Carl Sagan, Bruce Murray, then head of JPL, and myself to do a Mars seminar. Said seminar turned out to be wilder than we imagined. That team of boy mechanics sparked each other so furiously that the exchange turned into a book even as the stuff poured from our mouths. We discovered, first off, that all of us had been led through space toward Mars by one author, Edgar Rice Burroughs. We made no attempt to disguise our youthful tastes. The simple fact was that we had to start somewhere with short legs, and Burroughs ran us in fevers toward Lowell Observatory photos and Schiaparelli sketches later in life.

We had a rollicking good time, with Arthur leading the team or goading us on to a shared creativity. When we saw a typescript of what we had said, we recognized we had written a book on the auditorium air. All we had to do was seize it down into type. I wrote a preface and an afterword and added a few poems before anyone could stop me. The memory of sharing such an afternoon with Arthur and the others will stay with me for the rest of my years.

Bruce Murray, our collaborator on *Mars and the Mind of Man*, came to visit me a few weeks ago. He announced that some sort of library on Mars was being planned and he asked permission to send a copy of my *Martian Chronicles* up along with copies of Edgar Rice Burroughs' *John Carter of Mars* yarns and a book to be selected from among his many by Arthur C. Clarke.

Would I mind going along on such a journey even though the Cal Tech students and faculty often speak of me as the man who put an atmosphere on Mars?

Would I mind?! I cried. My God, with Burroughs on my right and Clarke on my left? What a trip. What a forever journey!

Finally, I am reminded of the Egyptian myth that, in the hour of death, when a person begs entrance to the Beyond, the keeper of the gate asks, "In life, did you know enthusiasm?" Do I need to tell you what Arthur's shouted response will be? The gates will be knocked down and the heavens disheveled with this trumpet.

Would that I might be there to hear it.

Ray Bradbury
Paris, July 1992

PREFACE

This is the first-ever biography of Arthur C. Clarke—one of the great visionaries of the twentieth century and a man who has every expectation of celebrating the arrival of the new millennium and the twenty-first century on January 1, 2001.

After seventy-five orbits around the sun, Clarke continues to be active and productive, always involved in a dozen or more projects and championing worthwhile causes for the good of our global family. The benefit of Clarke's cooperation with this life story, and the access to interviews, letters, and other documents it afforded, far outweighs any influence his cooperation might imply or exert.

So what does "authorized" mean with respect to this biography? The truth is that nothing was ever said definitely to be off-limits by anyone who contributed information and memories to this work. It is also true that this writer never probed too deeply into Clarke's private affairs. I no more wanted to describe intimate details of a living man's private life (assuming the information was available) than he or his contemporaries wanted to read about them. If this is the compromise of an "authorized" life, so be it. All of us alive know about life's compromises. A written life is no exception.

Certainly this is a better book because of the cooperation of many people, including Clarke. I can't therefore uphold the humorously cynical view of one British biographer, Humphrey Carpenter, who has written: "While the authorised biographer generally Knows Everything, the authorised biography usually reads like a report in *Pravda*." Well, not this one.

After several requests for some stories and memories for this work, Stanley Kubrick told me that "Arthur is not an anecdotable character." This, as far as it goes, may be true, but people's different perspectives on the same person often are enlightening and help to create a more objective view. If readers also sometimes hear the unique voices of the people interviewed as they read their spoken words, then this will be the ultimate compliment to all of us.

ACKNOWLEDGMENTS

So many people helped along the way that I must first—right now—thank them all. Their names, thoughts, memories, knowledge—often their unique *voices*—are found on these pages and articulate the reason for my gratitude in concrete and real ways.

Special thanks to the following people for enlightening, lively, informative, or otherwise unique interviews: Brian Aldiss, Isaac Asimov, Ian and Betty Ballantine, Gregory Benford, Willie Blake, Robert Bloch, Russell Bowie, Ray Bradbury, John Brunner, Roger Caras, Arthur C. Clarke, Fred Clarke, John Clarke, Michael Clarke, Walter Cronkite, Lester del Rey, Hugh Downs, Daniel Drachman, Olga Druce, Fred Durant, David Fowke, Bert Fowler, Tony Frewin, Leonard Hobbs, Peter Hyams, Dick Jenvey, Dot Jones, Steven Jongeward, Kathy Keeton, David Kennard, Dick Kriegel, David Kyle, Gentry Lee, Lloyd Lewan, Lee Lubbers, Ian Macauley, Marjorie May, Marilyn Mayfield, Scott Meredith, Harry Morrin, Sam Moskowitz, Julian Muller, Kerry O'Quinn, Fred Ordway, Tom Paine, Joseph Pelton, John Pierce, Bobby Pleass, Fred Pohl, Jerry Pournelle, Eric Rabkin, Gene Roddenberry, Carl Sagan, Ken Slater, Harry Stine, Eric Taylor, Joan Temple, Pat Weaver, and Sam Youd.

For various and essential print materials, special thanks to: Ian and Betty Ballantine, Roger Caras, Arthur C. Clarke, Fred Clarke, Val Cleaver, Brenda Corbin, Michael Craven, Fred and Pip Durant, Lloyd Eshbach, Rodney Jonklaas, Laura Kapnick, Barry King, David and Ruth Kyle, Ian Macauley, Mary Clarke Maclean, Bill MacQuitty, Scott Meredith Literary Agency, Kerry O'Quinn, John Pierce, Harold Rosen, David Samuelson, Bill Temple, and Sam Youd.

For photos, videos, and other visual resources, special thanks to: Joel Banow, Willie Blake, the British Interplanetary Society, Arthur C. Clarke, Fred Clarke, Michael Craven, David Doubilet, Fred Durant, Doug Faulkner, Dean Grennell, Kathy Keeton, Robert Knecht, *Omni* magazine, Fred Ordway, Smithsonian Institution, and Frank Winter.

There have been several supportive and skillful people who also deserve my gratitude: Fred Durant, who helped get this project started; the Scott Meredith Literary Agency, especially Scott Meredith, Joshua Bilmes, and Russ Galen for their efforts on behalf of this biography over a five-year period; Tom Erickson for his assistance in printing out the thick first draft; and Anne Sweeny-Smith, Christine Benton, and Gerilee Hundt for their fresh eyes, editorial expertise, and coordination efforts.

Finally, two special people I cannot thank enough: my wife, Connie, who cheerfully shared two lives during this period; and Fred Clarke, keeper of the Clarkives, who was always there and always a great help—a true brother to me in this effort.

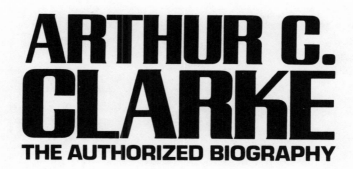

ARTHUR C. CLARKE
THE AUTHORIZED BIOGRAPHY

For when the story of our age comes to be told, we will be remembered as the first of all men to put their sign among the stars.

The Making of a Moon *(1957)*

1
NEW MOON
OVER SOMERSET

The stars were bright over Somerset in 1917. Across the English Channel, however, the skies of France were filled with the flares and artillery shells of World War I. Charles Wright Clarke was fighting in France when his first son, Arthur, was born in the seaside town of Minehead on the west coast of England. His birth date, under a waxing new moon, was December 16.

Few space cadets were born in the first decades of the twentieth century. They were a rare breed then, long before the deluge of cosmic images in film and television began to permeate our collective consciousness. But Arthur Charles Clarke was one of the early few who, before World War II, would point to the moon and stars and show us—future astronauts, engineers, scientists, and enthusiastic youth everywhere—the way. Describing his vision of the future in both nonfiction and fiction, over seven decades, he has entertained and educated us with his imaginative cosmic plots and unique view of planet Earth.

Why has Arthur C. Clarke become one of the twentieth century's most influential writers and visionaries? The answer lies in his passionate enthusiasm and energy for exploring the universe

1

around him—its celestial and terrestrial wonders and human-kind's unending stream of ideas, desires, and imaginings. Clarke has never stopped searching—for new questions and possibilities as well as answers about what the near and distant future holds for humanity. His imaginative extrapolations of science and technology have created many possible futures, most positive, that have reached millions of readers.

This quest constantly delights him. He derives great natural pleasure from what he does and who he is, and this quality comes through in his writing. All his work—books, articles, lectures, media appearances, TV series, films—is accented with a touch of personal enthusiasm, which has been an important element in attracting a global audience. Enthusiasm, optimism, and pre-science about the future—rare characteristics in his chosen genre during the century of two world wars—have set Arthur C. Clarke worlds apart.

Minehead, England, a coastal town on the Bristol Channel, was a good place for an explorer to begin his life. It was located near one of the great world ports, and a long history of maritime adventure and commerce had been witnessed from its shores. The coastline offered vistas of the Atlantic Ocean that created the illusion of infinite space, and there was the regular excitement of ships leaving their ports and beginning voyages to distant lands.

From the shores of Minehead a person could set a course for anywhere and everywhere, and that's what Arthur C. Clarke eventually did. His birthplace provided a convenient shore from which to cast off and see not just our world but other worlds as well—the moon, the planets, the stars, the galaxies—and *Homo sapiens'* future adventures among them. Arthur C. Clarke's childhood shore, with its expanses of sea and sky, helped provide him with the cosmic view of planet Earth and its place in space and time, a perspective that dominates his work and his philosophy to this day.

Mary Nora Clarke (née Willis) gave birth to her son on the morning of December 16, 1917, in her mother's house at 4 Blenheim Road, Minehead. (The address was later changed to 13 Blenheim Road because the road was extended.)

Minehead and the stone Victorian house known as Sunnyside, where Clarke's grandmother had insisted he be born, remained his home for the first few years of his life. When the First World War ended in 1918 and Charles Clarke was discharged, he bought the family's first farm. Called Beetham, it was near Chard, Somerset.

Charles Clarke was the eldest son of Thomas Clarke, postmaster of the village of Bishops Lydeard. Charles had grown up around the post office that his father had built, and that is how he came to meet Nora Willis, who had worked at various Somerset post offices and whom he married on July 29, 1915. Although his post office position had been reserved for him while he was serving in France as lieutenant in His Majesty's Royal Engineers during the Great War, Charles Clarke decided against going back to it. Like many other returning soldiers, he could not settle for confining office work after the stress and action of the war. Seeking an outdoor life, he decided to become a farmer even though he had no experience. Despite Nora's urging caution, it wasn't long before he and a partner signed a purchase contract for a farm. Unfortunately, they came up short of funds, which had to be loaned by Nora from a sum she'd inherited at age three when her father had died, and by relatives of Charles Clarke's partner.

The farm itself proved to be much worse than Nora had imagined: "The price was far too high and the house in a bad state. There was little water on the farm and in dry spells it had to be hauled for miles." With the postwar slump beginning, some of the farm's twenty cows had to be sold to pay expenses.

There was a bit of joy, however, during this difficult time: the birth of Frederick William Clarke on April 7, 1921. Nora again traveled to her mother's house in Minehead for the birth. The Clarkes now had two sons.

Finally the Beetham farm had to be sold at a loss, but Nora soon heard of a suitable farm from her mother-in-law, Elizabeth Mary Clarke, the postmistress at Bishops Lydeard. "The name was Ballifants, and I knew nothing of it," wrote Nora, "for it was away from all roads."

The word *Ballifants* was an old English family name that the place had inherited. The farm came from the 1913 breakup of the Lethbridge family estate, whose fields and their buildings became the so-called smallholdings offered to veterans and their families. Ballifants was one such smallholding. Charles and Nora applied at once, and the family moved in in 1924. The five-hundred-year-old turreted farmhouse was the center of a farm that was productive but unremarkable for the area. And it was not the land that attracted young Arthur C. Clarke but the sea.

He found it at his grandmother's home in Minehead, where the Clarke boys spent school holidays and weekends. The Minehead Beach, no more than a quarter of a mile away from his grandmother's house, became Clarke's favorite haunt. There he built battlements of sand and explored the tidewater pools among the rocks. Even today Clarke admits that the only place he ever feels completely relaxed is by the edge of the sea, "or, better still, hovering weightless beneath it, over the populous and polychromatic landscape of my favorite reef." Clarke is still actively scuba-diving at seventy-five and still loves to swim.

The Somerset coast of Minehead was Clarke's childhood shore, his dream beach, where his body and imagination played, creating ideas for his future work and prophetic visions of what life would be like—on and off the planet.

The short story "Transience," written more than twenty years later and first published in *Startling Stories*, describes a beach at three different times in geological history, over millions of years, through the eyes of a child playing there.

"Underfoot, the sand was coarse and mixed with myriads of broken shells. Here and there the retreating tide had left long streamers of weed trailed across the beach. . . .

"Beyond the sea wall and the promenade, the little town was sleeping through the golden summer day. Here and there along the beach, people lay at rest, drowsy with heat and lulled by the murmur of the waves."

That second beach is no doubt the author's childhood shore. Finally, in the far-future scene, Earth is abandoned as the solar system encounters an immense dark nebula that will eventually make the planet uninhabitable. In this last scene a boy named Bran is alone, guarded by a machine, "but he was a solitary child and did not greatly care. Lost in his own dreams, he was content to be left alone." These few words and the author's later choice of Colombo, Sri Lanka, on the Indian Ocean as home tell us more about Arthur C. Clarke than many of his interviews.

Arthur C. Clarke's return visits to the coast coincidentally provided his introduction to science fiction, through the Kille family, who lived "about three doors along at the end of the road."

One of the Kille sons, Larry, provided Clarke with his first glance at the science fiction magazines that would captivate him a few years later. It was Larry Kille's November 1928 issue of *Amazing Stories* that introduced the eleven-year-old Clarke to the genre. Its cover, painted by space artist Frank R. Paul, depicted the giant planet Jupiter dominating the sky of one of its moons, with a tropical moonscape and a cylindrical spaceship in the foreground. From the spaceship, earthlings disembarked.

The Kille family helped excite Clarke's interest in science as well as science fiction. He remembers a small room in the Kille house that was filled with the most advanced knitting machines of the day. With foot power alone, Larry Kille's grandmother produced yards of socks and sweaters. Sometimes Clarke was allowed to provide the pedal power.

"I can still hear the clicking of the hundreds of needles and the whir of the well-oiled gear wheels," he recalled. "My own interest in science owes much to the fascinating hardware that Mrs. Kille operated with effortless skill." She also loaned him books such as Ignatius Donnelly's *Atlantis, the Antediluvian World*, which Arthur naively accepted as fact when he first read it.

During the same period Clarke took up his first hobby, fossils, in part influenced by Arthur Cornish, Nellie Kille's husband. "He was an archaeologist and a very nice guy who definitely influenced my scientific interest. He gave me quite a lot of stuff, including fossils and a mammoth's tooth."

A casual gift from his father spawned a similar collection. Though Arthur was not yet seven years old when his parents moved to Ballifants, he vividly recalls riding with his father on the pony cart, known as a "trap" by the local folk. On the common of Bishops Lydeard, Charles Clarke handed his son a series of picture cards depicting prehistoric animals, which had come with cigarettes he'd just purchased. The cards—the first one depicting "a weird beast, a stegosaur"—became an instant treasure and created one of the lasting memories Clarke has of his father. They also served as visual aids for the tales of giant creatures he told to his classmates at Bishops Lydeard Elementary, where schoolmistress Maud Hanks encouraged his natural storytelling abilities.

The imagination that drove those abilities was fueled when, in the summer before his ninth birthday as Clarke recalls it, he took to the air for the first time. His mother took him flying in an aircraft owned by the Cornwall Aviation Company, Limited, of Austell. It was a British Avro 504 biplane, with its cross-wired wings and three-axis control. The passengers strapped themselves in with leather seat belts, and they heard the high-pitched singing of cross-wired wing rigging at times during the flight.

"It was a very famous type, with a skid under the two bicycle-type wheels," says Clarke. From then on he was hooked; he's been flying around the planet ever since.

It was not the integration of modern technology into his home that fostered Clarke's fascination with communications. Telephone service did not arrive at the Clarke farm until around 1930, and electricity would have to wait until after World War II. Rather, communications was a family career specialty.

Charles Wright Clarke's pre–World War I work at the post office had been as an engineer—the early equivalent of today's telecommunications engineer. "He was concerned with telephone and telegraph circuits," says Clarke. In fact his father got the contract for putting up the poles to bring the telephone to Ballifants, which paid for the phone for quite a few years. "And he had to install quite a few telephone poles to get there," adds Clarke.

Nora had worked as a telegraphist at the Taunton Post Office and learned Morse code from her mother-in-law, accumulating some valuable experience on the two common telegraphic instruments: the single needle and the so-called sounder that superseded it.

Ernest Clarke, Arthur's paternal uncle, was a post office telegraphist, and for many years his paternal aunt Zebah was the postmistress at Bishops Lydeard. So while the telephone may have come late to the Clarke farm, the post never did.

Clarke remembers having his first experience with global communication when he worked at the Bishops Lydeard Post Office in his teens.

"I was night operator for quite a long time at Bishops Lydeard, and one night there was a call from New York—very rare in those days. The call came by radio, of course; it was long before there was any telephonic cable. The operator in Taunton must have detected me listening in, and told me to unplug. I was probably weakening the signal."

Communications—post, telegraph, or telephone—may have

been a common career specialty for the Clarkes, but no one (with the possible exception of Arthur C. Clarke himself) could have foreseen how he would carry the family tradition into the future.

During the 1920s the lives of the Clarke family revolved not around communications but around farming. It was a hard life. The postwar economic slump caused real hardship, and the declining health of Charles Clarke made matters worse.

During the war Lieutenant Clarke's lungs had been severely damaged by inhalation of poison gas and by the horrible conditions of trench warfare.

Soon after the family moved to Ballifants, Charles began having violent attacks of pain, and in less than a year he was an invalid, unable to do any work on the farm. Unfortunately, like so many veterans of the war, he had signed a release whereby he lost any right to a pension.

Nora Clarke took up the full burden of providing for the family, and as her husband's physical condition worsened, she expected more help from her older children, Arthur and Fred. Siblings Mary and Michael were too young to do much work.

There were cows to be milked, eggs to be collected, clotted cream to be delivered, apples to be picked and pressed, and an assortment of animals—horses, cows, lambs, pigs, chickens, turkeys, geese, and dogs—to be fed and cared for. The beloved cairn terriers alone, sometimes more than a dozen around the farm at any one time, regularly ate substantial piles of food. But they were pedigreed and always sold for good prices. Clarke's youth on the farm instilled in him a lifelong love of all animals.

Nora did just about everything to bring in extra income, including taking in paying guests. "She used to knit gloves, string gloves I seem to remember," says Michael Clarke, who became the farmer of the family and the one to run Ballifants, now a dairy farm, "and sell them for a very small amount."

"We all had our work on the farm," recalls Fred. "If anybody wasn't doing their share, mother used to say, 'Don't let it ever be said your mother bred a jibber.' A jibber is a horse which won't do what you tell it to do—won't jump over a fence, but swings to one side instead. Or won't haul a heavy load, but puts its head down and refuses to move."

As it turned out, Nora bred no jibbers. All the children were taught to work hard, and the example set at Ballifants no doubt gave rise to Clarke's prolific literary production in future years.

Their father's long illness also left its mark on the Clarke children. Both Arthur and Fred remember seeing Charles Clarke in bed, recall taking up his medication or a hot water bottle. "I had to walk a mile," says Fred, "through fields and woods, in the dark, three times a week to get his medicine. It was probably morphine, issued only in small doses."

Charles Wright Clarke died in the hospital in Bristol in May 1931 under the ministrations of a doctor who was experimenting with mercury injections. He was forty-three years old. His eldest son was thirteen.

The loss was buried deep in young Arthur C. Clarke. At a critical time of life, when most boys turn to their fathers for self-definition, he was alone. As the eldest son, he assumed the role and responsibilities of the male head of household, and throughout his long career he has figuratively become the father to many sons, in his literary work as well as his life.

Arthur C. Clarke's personal odyssey has been motivated in part by a deep need to seek what he lost in his youth. As his fiction illustrates, there are no heights (or depths) to which he won't climb to find the missing element. His writing represents, on a biographical level, a search for his missing father and his own identity.

"More than his father had been buried today; the falling earth had covered his childhood," Clarke later wrote in his novel *Glide Path*, when Alan Bishop, the young RAF officer, attends his father's funeral. "He could never escape from its influence, for it had shaped his character irrevocably. . . ."

*He remembered his first glimpse of the Sinus Iridium,
through the little homemade telescope he had built when he
was a boy.... [I]t had given him more pleasure than the giant
instruments of which he was now the master.*

Earthlight *(1955)*

2
MOONWARD FROM
BALLIFANTS

In the midst of tragedy, life at Ballifants went on. For Nora Clarke,
there was a farm to run and a family to raise. For young Arthur C.
Clarke, there was a future to contemplate. Happily, several adults
had begun to recognize the boy's promise and were anxious to help
him fulfill it.

Remembered with great affection was schoolmistress Maud
Hanks, who may have been the first to encourage pupil Clarke's
storytelling and had the gratifying experience of seeing him blossom into a writer of world renown. Clarke kept in touch with her
until her death at the grand old age of ninety-nine.

Just before his tenth birthday in 1927, Clarke began his studies at Huish's Grammar School, five miles away in Taunton, under
a foundation scholarship from the village school. Although there
would be no money to send him on to a university, attending a
prep school would at least begin to open doors for the young man.
An all-boys' school of about 250 students before World War II
when he attended, Huish's (today known as Richard Huish College) furthered Clarke's interest in writing and science. There a
second adult saw the glimmerings of what Clarke would become.

"I recall Archie very well," says Bobby Pleass. "I started teaching him in 1931 or '32. He came into the Sixth Form [two years of preuniversity studies], where I had him for physics and math.

"I wish I'd preserved some of what we call 'scribblers'—you know, the rough book. He'd spend his time doodling, and all sorts of wonderful things were produced, things that would fly in the air and go over the sea and go under the sea—all in one vehicle."

A third person who recognized at this time what Clarke was capable of was, of course, his mother. Nora Clarke almost always put his studies first, recalls sister Mary:

"When any major catastrophe occurred, such as animals breaking out through the Heath Robinson fences, which was frequent, Mama would hastily call up her troops to round them up. Never Arthur, though—he must not be disturbed in his studies. How clever the rest of us might have been had the fences been better!"

Perhaps Nora Clarke felt her son's early adolescence was already quite demanding. He had to pedal an old postal bicycle ten miles a day to and from school. "It was made of cast iron and felt like it weighed about three hundred pounds," Clarke recalls. And that was not his first activity each day.

"That was after I delivered the mail," he explains. "I was night operator at the same time. I slept in the post office, greeted the mailmen when they came in about four o'clock in the morning, sorted the mail, delivered it, which meant riding three or four miles, and then went to school. And I managed to read about two books a day. There was no TV in those days; that made all the difference."

The moon would often rise up from the rolling Quantock Hills of Somerset as young Arthur C. Clarke bicycled back and forth. During the winter months he often cycled home in the dark, with the stars and moon illuminating his route in clear weather. Such starry evenings influenced Clarke's budding cosmic consciousness. The silent night sky above him stirred his imagination and brought forth images of the future. Men would walk on the moon someday, he knew, and later they would leave their bootprints on the red sands of Mars. Even the gulf between our sun and other stars would be bridged eventually, and their planets explored by the descendants of our species. Young Clarke was convinced that the exploration of space was inevitable. It was simply a matter of time.

When the Clarke family moved to Ballifants in 1924, the only instrument they possessed was a small field telescope that had been used in the South African Boer War. While it could spot rabbits or other game, it was not designed to observe the moon, planets, or other celestial wonders.

When Clarke was in his early teens, he constructed the first of "four or five" refractor telescopes that he aimed mainly at the moon to explore its mountains, craters, and the immense and smooth waterless seas, the maria.

"I used to collect lenses, put them in cardboard tubes (the kind used for holding maps and pictures that were about three inches in diameter and perhaps three feet long), and try different lens assemblies. I used whatever long-focus lenses I could find, such as old magic lantern lenses, and then any magnifying glass for the short-focus eyepiece."

"His first telescope," remembers his sister Mary, "was mounted on an old bicycle embedded upside down in an earth mound. He sat on a milking stool and used the wheel to move it around."

"It came as a great surprise to my friends," said Clarke, "that, with a telescope that could be made for a few cents, craters on the moon could be observed."

A few years later Clarke received a Meccano set for Christmas. After building every possible construction offered in the Meccano instruction booklet, plus a few designs of his own, he designed and assembled a tripod for his refractor that would last for the rest of his amateur astronomy days.

During his midteen years Clarke observed most nights when the skies were clear. Because his homemade telescopes were limited to twenty to thirty power at best, his observations were mostly of the moon.

"It wasn't good enough for the planets," he says, "so I concentrated on the moon. I had sketchbooks full of drawings of the lunar craters." More than once Clarke has written that he knew his way around the moon much better than he did around his native Somerset.

One of several secondhand astronomy books young Clarke bought was Robert Ball's well-known nineteenth-century *Story of the Heavens*. "I remember copying out, tracing all the star maps on tissue paper."

Clarke saw the moons of Jupiter, aligned specks of light, with one of his early telescopes, but it was not until 1941 that he finally saw Saturn's beautiful rings through an old navy telescope he bought in Wales just before he joined the Royal Air Force. "This old navy telescope was the sort that Nelson put to his eye. I took out the internal optics and put in a very short-focus eyepiece. Then, for the very first time, I could just glimpse the rings of Saturn. That was quite a revelation."

Revelation bred experimentation—and there to encourage Clarke was Bobby Pleass.

"I taught the old-style physics," Pleass says, "which was based on experimentation. The students had to experiment and find out things."

In the early 1930s Clarke's experimentation involved constructing several rockets. "He used to spend his spare pocket money in woofing up homemade rockets on his mother's farm," Pleass says.

These rocket experiments evolved from first making fireworks, which, once perfected, Clarke would set off to entertain his mother and her friends, who watched from a safe distance.

The gunpowder was made by following the recipe in his chemistry textbook, combining sulfur, saltpeter, and charcoal and mixing them with the kitchen's mortar and pestle, which his mother used to grind icing sugar for cakes.

"My hair stands on end now thinking about it," says Clarke, "but I sometimes used to grind up gunpowder in a metal tin for fuel. I was very lucky to get away with it—well, almost. One day I was mixing the gunpowder inside the house, and it caught fire! It happened in the downstairs sitting room, which was my study. I don't think it caught fire to anything outside the container. I threw it out the window before any damage could be done. It certainly did give me a fright and taught me a lesson."

Further experimentation produced the right powder mix, and Clarke decided to prepare for the next Guy Fawkes Day with homemade fireworks. By wrapping a sheet of notepaper around a pencil and gluing it down, he formed a small tube into which he packed the gunpowder. Into the gunpowder were mixed iron filings that brother Fred made in the workshop. These became sparklers.

Larger tubes, formed in the same manner around a broom handle, became fiery and colorful fountains, some of which shot into the air and sometimes emitted explosive bangs, to the delight of Clarke's siblings. After the fireworks, Clarke knew it was time to graduate to rockets.

"They were simple powder rockets," he says, "foot-long-or-less cardboard tubes, probably toilet paper cylinders—nothing really sophisticated. I'd go outside, put them in a bottle, light a match, and launch them. But they never flew very far. I do remember trying to make a rocket glider, but it didn't work. I probably had the center of gravity in the wrong place."

As his model rockets got bigger, Clarke began to add payloads. "First there were balsa wood wings, which helped them glide back to earth," Fred recalls, "and I was sent to the far end of the field to retrieve them. Later came heavier and heavier payloads, until the rocket could barely leave the ground, and [it] burst asunder at face level."

When Clarke was about seventeen, his experiments produced his most memorable early project—"the thing I'm proudest of making"—a light-beam transmitter, which used light to transmit sound.

"My uncle, George Grimstone [his father's brother-in-law], gave me a broken photocell, which came from the 'Talkie' [telephone/communications] equipment at the place he worked. He was chief engineer for all the electrical equipment at a place called Cotford, a big lunatic asylum about two miles from our farm. (He was not an inmate in the asylum as some people had deduced.)

"I took an ordinary bicycle flashlight, a carbon microphone to modulate the light beam, a couple of batteries, put them in series, and then it worked. When you talked into the microphone, the light flickered. And I aimed it at the photocell detector, the amplifier, a few dozen feet away. It worked quite well."

"When the light was shone on the photoelectric cell," recalls brother Fred, "every word could be heard in the earphones. Arthur was soon transmitting speech across the room and later across the field."

Clarke frequently enlisted his siblings' assistance. "He used to drag me in to help him," Michael recalls. "I had to hold the transmitter, aim it at him, and speak into the microphone. I can remember the apparatus was a cigar box, and a convex lens was held in the aperture by what we used to call butterfly tape."

George Grimstone was an important source of free communication supplies that helped advance his nephew's early experiments. After Grimstone installed a new telephone system at Cotford, Clarke became the lucky recipient of obsolete telephone sets, plenty of wire, batteries, and switch gear. He utilized whatever he could from all the passed-along parts and began improving the communications at the family farm. First he installed an intercom system between the kitchen and his study so that he could be told when his tea was ready. Next he wired his bedroom for wake-up calls. Finally, using the fencing wires around Ballifants, he wired the entire perimeter to determine how far a message would travel. But because the sheep kept breaking through the fence, this was not a permanent circuit.

Wireless crystal sets were also part of Clarke's early experiments in communications, and Uncle George taught him how to build them. A single shilling would buy all the necessary components—the crystal, the holder, and the coiled wire known as a "cat's-whisker." Once these parts were mounted on a wood base and connected to an aerial, all that was needed to hear live music in Somerset over the BBC was a pair of earphones. Clarke earned pocket money by building these sets for a shilling and then selling them for half a crown.

Listening was all well and good, but Clarke soon wanted to transmit as well. From one of the salvaged telephones, he took the carbon mouthpiece and built a microphone.

Fred Clarke recalls one innovative way his brother used his wireless equipment. "I remember listening to music on the wireless one evening, when the programme was interrupted with a 'newsflash' of such horror that our visitors nearly fainted. Luckily mother recognised the Somerset accent, which would have been inconceivable on the BBC in those days, and slipped out to Arthur's den. The resulting howl came over clearly, before the concert was resumed."

Sometimes things happened too fast for experimentation. Once a unique form of natural energy appeared before Clarke and Bobby Pleass at the school. They were preparing test tubes in a small room known as "the Dungeon," where the senior students (Sixth Formers) would go for private study. It was located partly below ground level under the physics lecture room. Across the ceiling of the Dungeon ran the heating pipes that came from the nearby boiler house.

"I saw this glowing globe in the air in front of us, between

Bobby and me," says Clarke. No mini-UFO, this, but a ball of fire hanging from a joint in the heating pipes. It was a ball of lightning, resulting from a thunderbolt that hit the tall boiler chimney, splitting it from top to bottom. Student and teacher both ran from the Dungeon, thinking that it could blow up in their faces at any time.

Huish's Dungeon became a significant place in Clarke's introduction and commitment to science fiction. It was here that he found, read, and totally absorbed the March 1930 issue of *Astounding Stories of Super-Science*. Unlike the mild interest he had shown in his neighbor's 1928 copy of *Amazing Stories* two years earlier, this was exciting stuff; he couldn't get enough. "My life was irrevocably changed," says Clarke. The time was right. His cosmic sails were set.

He'd spend his time doodling, and all sorts of wonderful things were produced. You know, things that would fly in the air and go over the sea and go under the sea—all in one vehicle.

Bobby Pleass, teacher

3
TERRESTRIAL INSPIRATIONS

The boy who spent his adolescence astounding his friends and family with amateur rocketry and other home inventions had a somewhat checkered career at school. Despite a love for mathematics, Clarke had to take the senior Oxford math examination, given to determine a student's preparedness for college-level courses, three times before passing. This and other occurrences belied his innate intelligence, hardly endearing him to the majority of his teachers.

"I used to fight battles for Archie," teacher Bobby Pleass recalls. "The rest of the staff would say, 'What the hell can we do with this lazy so-and-so Clarke?' He doesn't attend, and this and that and the other. But the thing was, you see, he was way ahead of them. He was always ahead of the teachers. They classified him as a nitwit, but he wasn't any such thing. I used to fight on his behalf in the staff room, discussing reports and things. I said, 'That boy's got something; you wait.'"

Why Clarke had trouble with his math exam and was often absent during his senior days at Huish's is anybody's guess, but perhaps he was spending too much of his study time designing spaceships, dreaming about rocketing to the planets, and reading anything that further stimulated his imagination.

"I read that March 1930 *Astounding* from cover to cover," admitted Clarke, "doubtless when I should have been doing geometry or algebra or (ugh) Latin, then returned it to the literary debris of the Dungeon." The cover depicted a spaceship, looking "like a cross between a submarine and a glass-domed conservatory," traveling toward a celestial body that was *supposed* to be the moon. It did not convince Clarke, however, who had put in too much telescope time observing our satellite in detail.

The cover copy displayed the featured story by the American writer of pulp adventure fiction, Ray Cummings: "Brigands of the Moon—A Thrilling Interplanetary Novel of Intrigue and Adventure."

A few days later, when he saw that no one had claimed it, Clarke decided that he would be the person to best care for this prize—this physical manifestation of his youthful fantasy life. This began his serious collection of science fiction magazines, which would grow and remain intact until he entered the Royal Air Force during World War II.

Every day Clarke would devote some of his school lunchtime to searching for science fiction magazines on the shelves of Taunton's Woolworth store. "I'd save up all my spare coppers to buy issues. I was insatiable. I couldn't bear to miss one. I used to make lists of all the copies there ever had been, so I could plug the gaps and get a complete file."

They were not easy to find, however, but were randomly scattered throughout the piles of other pulp magazines—the westerns, confessions, and detectives—that were shipped over from the United States. It was catch as catch can. Some issues, Clarke came to suspect, probably never even reached the United Kingdom, let alone Somerset towns like Taunton and Minehead.

The overseas distribution of these American pulp magazines was apparently rather haphazard, and it was commonly said that the unsold copies in the United States, the so-called surplus, reached the United Kingdom as ballast in returning cargo ships.

David Kyle, copartner of Gnome Press, Clarke's earliest American publisher, is well versed in the early history of science fiction.

"The early American science fiction magazines—*Amazing Stories*, and then the Gernsback *Wonder Stories* and *Air Wonder*

Stories, even the early *Astounding Stories*—were quite common in the secondhand bookstores in England," says Kyle. "They were not sold on the newsstands because they were secondhand copies stamped with some kind of mark, often a big purple star, to show they were secondhand. These magazines were sent over to England because they were being taken off the market in America. They were the only source of science fiction for the young English fans then.

"I don't think they were actually just used as ballast in ships, but they were tantamount to ballast because they represented such a little bit of money. The space in the hold wasn't wasted, and the shipping companies got some return for it. Probably the magazines were just bundled up and thrown on a ship. When they got to England, some dealers would bid on the lot and sort them out. What was usable was usable; what wasn't was thrown away."

This is probably why young Arthur C. Clarke found his efforts to obtain a full sequence so frustrating.

"There were heartbreaking gaps in my collection. Sometimes it took me years to assemble all the installments of a serial." On his lucky days, when he discovered a new issue he didn't have, he would buy it for what was then three pence or the equivalent of five cents U.S.

"By 1938 I think I had every science fiction magazine that had ever been published."

Clarke's devotion to his collection also brought him into contact with other science fiction fans through the correspondence columns, which proved to be a good forum for buying or swapping missing issues. While he was working at the post office before classes at Huish's, he once received an entire box of magazines he'd purchased from another fan. Another time he obtained a full set of covers from a fan who was binding his copies.

In 1934 Clarke ingeniously rigged up flash lighting for his camera and took several self-portraits in his study at Ballifants. "I had a candle and a stand with a bit of magnesium ribbon, and a bit of string," he explains. "I pulled the magnesium ribbon into the candle and waited for it to ignite." In the background, his shelves were filled with his treasured magazines. But it would be five or six more years before he acquired a complete run of *Amazing Stories* and *Astounding Stories* totaling several hundred copies—a collection that unfortunately was dispersed during the war.

Reflecting on the debated merits of these pulp science fiction magazines, Clarke later wrote, "[T]he stories brimmed with ideas, and amply evoked that sense of wonder which is (or should be) one of the goals of the best fiction. No less a critic than C. S. Lewis has described the ravenous addiction that these magazines inspired; the same phenomenon has led me to call science fiction the only genuine consciousness-expanding drug."

In the same year that Clarke read his first issue of *Astounding Stories*, a literary work was published that would have a profound influence on his future writing. The book was W. Olaf Stapledon's *Last and First Men*, which Clarke found at the Minehead Public Library during his summer vacation from school. He can vividly remember the details of his Stapledon discovery and can even visualize where he found it on the library shelf: slightly below knee level. With its time scale of some five billion years, the book did nothing less than change the boy's perception of the world and universe around him, giving him a cosmic scale of time and space, a grand and majestic stage on which to place humanity's evolution and future extraterrestrial adventures.

"No book before or since ever had such an impact on my imagination," Clarke wrote in a short autobiographical piece, "Of Sand and Stars," which appeared in the *New York Times Book Review* in 1983. Twelve-year-old Clarke was not the only one who raved about Stapledon's book. Winston Churchill, temporarily a failed politician in 1930, praised it, and the literary critic Arnold Bennett applauded Stapledon's "tremendous and beautiful imagination."

Clarke has acknowledged his debt to Stapledon many times. And there is no doubt that *Last and First Men* influenced his first novel, *Against the Fall of Night*, which Clarke began during his Huish's Grammar School days and eventually published in its first version in *Startling Stories* in November 1948.

Just as Stapledon's book covered immense expanses of time, Clarke's first novel spoke of past and future events on an immense time scale of hundreds of millions of years: "Nothing had changed: the mountains resumed their watch over the sleeping land. But a turning-point in history had come and gone, and the human race was moving towards a strange new future."

Besides his early enthusiasm for Stapledon's work and for science fiction magazines, Clarke read the classic works of Jules

Verne and H. G. Wells. But it was another new book that captured
his imagination, and Clarke remembers it well.

During a school vacation in 1931, just weeks after his father
died, Clarke found another treasure. The book was *The Conquest
of Space* by David Lasser. A young American editor in his late
twenties, Lasser edited and nurtured two of Hugo Gernsback's
early magazines, *Science Wonder Stories* and *Air Wonder Stories*,
from their inception in 1929. Gernsback, often called "the father of
magazine science fiction," has been honored by having the Hugos,
the annual achievement awards in the genre, named after him.
Lasser is also known as the founder of the American Interplanetary Society (1930), which was later renamed the American Rocket
Society because *interplanetary* was considered too far out by the
leadership. The ARS, in turn, eventually became the prestigious
American Institute of Aeronautics and Astronautics.

The Conquest of Space was one of the great finds of Clarke's
youth. "Only a few hundred copies of the British edition were
sold," wrote Clarke, "but chance brought one of them to a bookstore a few yards from my birthplace. I saw it in the window, knew
instinctively that I *had* to read it and persuaded my good-natured
Aunt Nellie—who was looking after me while Mother struggled to
run the farm and raise my three siblings—to buy it on the spot.
And so I learned for the first time that space travel was not merely
delightful fiction. *One day it could really happen.* . . . My fate was
sealed."

Today *The Conquest of Space* is considered a classic of space
literature. Upon its publication in 1931, it became the first book
in the English language to review the dreams and work of the
early rocket pioneers and to discuss the possibility of interplanetary spaceflight. In contrast to Stapledon's immense and immeas-
urable cosmic realm, Lasser's book focused on the more practical,
immediate, and accessible side of rocketry and space travel. Both
perspectives—the vast, unknowable cosmos and the practical
technology of space travel—became major and consistent themes
in much of Clarke's work.

Meanwhile, Huish's Grammar School was nurturing the fledgling writer. Almost four decades later, in 1967, Clarke included in
his volume of short stories *The Nine Billion Names of God* this
dedication:

To 'Mitty' (Captain E. B. Mitford),
who encouraged my initial scribblings
at Huish's Grammar School, 1930–36
and became my first editor

Mitty was an enthusiastic and fiery Welshman whose physical appearance Clarke compares to John Mills and Alec Guinness. Overseeing the school literary effort, the *Huish Magazine*, Mitty would gather his young editorial staff around a table about once every week to work on the school magazine. If Clarke or any of the other boys came up with a bright idea that especially pleased their English master, they would be rewarded with a toffee from a large bag of assorted favorites on the table before them.

It was in the *Huish Magazine* in the fall of 1932 that Clarke's earliest work first saw print. It appeared, however, without his byline, under the pseudonym "One-Time Sixth Former," a fictitious graduate of the school—only one of several pseudonyms Clarke used for the work appearing in the school magazine (others included "Clericus," "A. Munchhausen," "De Profoundus," and "Court").

The first piece, "Correspondence," was an imaginative two-page letter describing the difficulties of working in an extreme environment. Two more pieces on the same theme, also bylined by the fictive graduate, appeared in the magazine in 1933.

In Clarke's autobiographical essay "Of Sand and Stars," he admits that the locale for these letters, described to Huish readers as "a torrid and high-altitude Outpost of Empire (Vrying Pan, British Malaria)," was actually the moon of his imagination.

"Our houses are built on the principle of the Dewar vacuum flash, to keep out the heat, and the outsides are silvered to reflect the sunlight. . . ."

In the spring of 1936, before his graduation from Huish's Grammar School, Clarke traveled to London to take the civil service entrance exam for "executive grade" at the urging of headmaster Arnold Goodliffe, who was proud of young Clarke and groomed him for the civil service.

Clarke tested extremely well, placing twenty-sixth among the fifteen hundred others who took the exam. This allowed him to choose the branch of the civil service he preferred. Because he had scored one hundred percent in arithmetic—despite his earlier problem with the Oxford math exam—it was recommended that he join the Exchequer and Audit Department. As a neophyte in the bureaucratic channels of Whitehall in 1936, Clarke agreed.

The eighteen-year-old Arthur C. Clarke knew only a few people in London. And despite the lack of that transition to independence that many young people glean from their university years, he seemed undaunted by the prospect of leaving home.

It is highly likely that Clarke knew this was just the first step toward a future that included far horizons—and looked forward to it with unbridled enthusiasm. But his nonchalance at leaving Ballifants may have stemmed in part from the fact that he had not anchored himself to any group of individuals there.

Describing Clarke as a teenager, schoolmaster Bobby Pleass says, "Now, Archie was a loner. Don't get the impression that he wasn't a friendly type; he was friendly. But he didn't make real personal friends. He was out in his own world a lot of the time, out in the clouds, although he was still a sound member of the community, especially with his writing articles for the school magazine."

To many of his schoolmates, Clarke had the smell of the farmyard, which he carried to school on the big farm boots he wore. "Some of the kids used to complain about this," says Pleass. And that wasn't the only way young Arthur stood out. "He was made to wear short trousers by his mother, and all the other boys had long trousers. Archie didn't like that."

Sometimes the people around Clarke found his intellect and his pursuit of knowledge disconcerting—to say the least.

One childhood friend of Clarke's, Jimmy Dulborough, was devoted to making sophisticated and beautiful model airplanes, some of which would take him months to build. Jimmy would often come over to the farm and fly his splendid models in the Clarkes' open fields.

After Jimmy flew his latest model plane one afternoon, Clarke had an idea and persuaded his friend to lend his model for a worthwhile experiment—the basic piggyback approach to rocketry. Attaching one of his rockets to the bottom of Jimmy's model plane, Clarke argued, would carry the plane to a much higher altitude, and it would therefore fly a considerably greater distance.

Jimmy Dulborough was protective of his pride and joy at first, but Clarke eventually prevailed after discussing the technical aspects of his proposal. The mating of rocket and airplane was accomplished, and the countdown began.

"As the rocket rose from the ground," Fred Clarke recalls, "the flames licking out behind it enveloped the tail of the plane, and the balsa wood and lacquered masterpiece crashed like an exploding fireball in front of Dulborough's agonized eyes. We did not see him again for many months."

In contrast, some of the paying guests from London and elsewhere who spent their vacation at Ballifants became friends with the Clarkes and remained so over the years. One such good friend was Dick Jenvey, who met Clarke at the farm in about 1934, when he and a chum took a vacation there.

"My first impression on meeting up with Arthur on our first day at Ballifants was that he was a studious individual, straight ahead of his years so far as his intellectual capabilities were concerned. He showed us his book-lined study with masses of paper books, novels of space travel, with lurid covers of strange craft and filmlike figures, with ray guns spitting all over the place. Then he would inveigle us into long and learned discussions on space travel for the future, which left us with open mouths and trying to say something sensible in the bargain.

"He wanted a willing ear," Jenvey continues. "I always used to feel with Arthur it became a one-track obsession. He was so involved, so enthusiastic about his subject. But Arthur, bless his heart, had a lovely sense of fun and would never 'bore us to tears,' as he used to say.

"His sense of fun was there when he persuaded me to mount a horse in the paddock for the first time. I was never on a horse before. But according to Arthur, all I had to do was hold on to the reins, and Bobby Sunshine would do the rest. So I was told.

"Well, Arthur's smack on Bobby's rump may have had something to do with it, but Bobby took off heading toward the nearest fence, with me hanging on for dear life. How I managed to land on the other side still attached to his back confounds me. Those who watched said there was a lot of daylight between my backside and the saddle. Old Arthur, he was a real card. I just don't know how we really did click on but we did. All of us [those who came as paying guests on holiday and became lifelong friends] feel those early days really meant something to him, that a bond of friendship formed. And we never forgot it.

"But the real classic has to do with the nickname we gave Arthur. It stuck and has been accepted by him with much affection over the years. I refer to our naming him 'Scientific Sid.' This was based on his original insatiable love of science fiction, which became part and parcel of him from those early days.

"I never cease to be amazed that even now his letters and endorsements of his novels to us are always signed off as 'Sid.' His affection toward us has always included that particular name because he knows it means a lot to us.

"And for all his tremendous enthusiasm for his interests, he always knew where my interest lay. I was studying architecture, and when I qualified, Arthur sent me a book, *The Autobiography of Frank Lloyd Wright*. On the flyleaf he wrote:

"'To old Dick, against the day when I ask you to build me an airtight, meteor-proof house, with a bay window looking towards Earth. Sid. Easter. 1946.'"

It is interesting to note that the enduring friendships were with people such as Jenvey, who hailed from London, not with hometown companions. But regardless of whom Clarke was leaving behind, when he departed for his new job in 1936, he knew exactly where he was headed.

"Please could you send me particulars about your Society, as I should very much like to join it," Clarke had written to Les Johnson, the secretary of the British Interplanetary Society, in the summer of 1934 after learning about the group in a magazine. "I am extremely interested in the whole subject of interplanetary communications, and have made some experiments with rockets. I am 16, have an extensive knowledge of physics and chemistry and possess a small laboratory and apparatus with which I can do some experiments in this line."

After joining, Clarke often wrote enthusiastic letters to Johnson. "[He] became one of my liveliest correspondents, describing, amongst other things, how he had fitted dart-like wings to penny rockets and launched them off a roof."

Space cadet Clarke had found his purpose in life and was soon off to London.

I think that Interplanetary is run—and always has been run—by visionaries, poets if you like, who also happen to be scientists. Sometimes the disguise isn't very good.

Prelude to Space *(1953)*

4
EGO IN LONDON

Arthur C. Clarke was just short of nineteen when he boarded the Great Western train at the Taunton station in the summer of 1936 and left for his new government job and Paddington digs in London.

His youngest brother, Michael, then seven years old, remembers the day he left. "It is one of my earliest memories," he says. "I was standing on the porch and thought of him as being so grown up. He would have been a father figure to me, you see. I sensed an atmosphere of portent. A sense of occasion was impressed upon me, a feeling that this was something big in our family."

Clarke was excited about his future in London. "I rarely made friends at the farm, you see, so I was looking forward to seeing the whole gang of science fiction and space nuts in London, who shared my interests. That is why I was so anxious to get there. Really, the Taunton-Minehead axis was the whole of my existence before I left for London in 1936."

He had already met a few of these space cadets when they visited Ballifants, but many were friends only through correspondence. Walter H. Gillings, one such early pen pal—journalist, fanzine publisher (*Scientifiction*), and early devotee of SF, whom Clarke has called "the Hugo Gernsback of British science fiction"—had won Clarke's gratitude by supplying him with some hard-to-get science fiction magazines.

When Clarke arrived at London's Paddington Station, he headed for a small hotel nearby at 21 Norfolk Square, where his father's youngest sister, Aunt Molly, was staying. "Very talented," according to Clarke, she was nonetheless an unsuccessful actress. She was designated as the close-at-hand family member for young Clarke if he ever ran into trouble.

During Clarke's first months in London his only difficulty was adjusting to the "bedsit" in Norfolk Square that was just large enough for a bed, a sink, and a food cupboard. The modest quarters, where guests had to sit on the bed or the windowsill, were the subject of many jokes during Clarke's nearly two years there. His friend science fiction writer William F. Temple wrote the most famous joke in one of his many humorous sketches, "The British Fan in His Natural Haunts," which appeared in the June 1938 issue of what many consider to be Britain's first science fiction fanzine, *Novae Terrae*: "There is a tale that Arthur [a coeditor of the magazine] once wore a double-breasted suit for the first time and got wedged between the walls for three days."

Clarke would have liked a room larger than ten by six feet, but his initial civil service salary of three pounds a week (about twelve dollars) did not allow it—though he doesn't recall ever being actually short of money. That first job involved helping to audit accounts for the Board of Education in an office on King Charles Street, next to Downing Street. Specifically, he checked teacher pensions, for which he needed nothing more than simple arithmetic to multiply a teacher's last five years' earnings by a certain factor. This he accomplished in just a few seconds.

"I quickly realised that an auditor didn't have to get figures *exactly* right; that was the job of a mere accountant, probably cranking the handle of a mechanical calculator (though I don't remember seeing even one of those extinct monsters during my five years in the civil service). The auditor's job—as *I* defined it— was to see that the figures were approximately right—say to within one percent, or tuppence in the pound. . . ."

Clarke recalls one particular trainee-teacher file that crossed his desk, during 1937. It was, he says, "a perfectly routine case" of a young person deciding to take a new career direction and requesting a refund of money that had been deducted from his paychecks and paid into the pension program.

The file was that of Alistair Cooke, who had been awarded a two-year fellowship for graduate study in the United States and then became the BBC's film critic from late 1934 to early 1937. Clarke had heard one of Cooke's film reviews, which explains why he remembered the name and file crossing his desk before Cooke became a famous television host.

"I prided myself on having the fastest slide rule in Whitehall," says Clarke of his civil service years, "so I was usually able to do all my work in an hour or so and devote the rest of the day to more important business." That included leisurely lunch hours, pleasant walks around Green Park and St. James Park, and table tennis, which he has continued to enjoy. "We used to play table tennis at lunchtime and whenever else we could—that's how we got to know each other," says Leonard Hobbs, a civil service colleague who still keeps in touch with Clarke. "He was a ferocious table tennis player. I tell you, he was very determined to win."

On weekends, Clarke sometimes walked across Kensington Gardens to the South Kensington Science Museum, which soon became one of his favorite places. He liked to spend time in the room with mathematical machines and was impressed with the uncompleted Babbage machine.

"Today, of course, it is famous as the premature herald of the Computer Age; but in 1936 only a few specialists had ever heard of it."

Clarke also had plenty of time to think about the business of the British Interplanetary Society: spaceships and voyages to the moon and beyond.

The British Interplanetary Society (BIS) was founded in Liverpool in October 1933 by Phillip E. Cleator, an astronautical expert, and a few other dreamers with their feet on the ground. There were only fifteen members at first, and the society's prewar annual income was never more than three hundred dollars. Nonetheless, the BIS had a profound impact in anticipating and preparing for the Space Age, which began in 1957. Today it is still going strong, with a worldwide membership of about four thousand.

Its success no doubt stems in part from its unwavering dedication to its visions for the future. According to American Fred Durant, who began a lifelong friendship with Clarke in 1951, the BIS "had taken their name two years after the founding of the American Interplanetary Society. The AIS had lost some of the courage of its conviction and changed its name to the American Rocket Society. The BIS stuck by their guns, and I've always lauded them for their courage."

"The British Interplanetary Society," Clarke began one brochure in 1938, "is a Society devoted to the study of Astronautics— the science of Space Travel. Since its foundation in 1933 it has done everything in its power to convince the public of the possibility of interplanetary communication, for it believes that the conquest of space could be accomplished to-day by means of the rocket motor and known chemical fuels. The scientific grounds for this belief are indicated at the end of this leaflet, and are the results of research extending over a number of years."

Later in the same brochure Clarke waxed eloquent about the society's vision of interplanetary flight.

"Go out beneath the stars on a clear winter night, and look up at the Milky Way spanning the heavens like a bridge of glowing mist. Up there, ranged one beyond the other to the end of the Universe, suns without number burn in the loneliness of space. Down to the South hang the brilliant, unwinking lanterns of other worlds—the electric blue of Jupiter, the glowing ember of Mars. Across the zenith, a meteor leaves a trail of fading incandescence, and a tiny voyager of space has come to a flaming end.

"Looking out across immensity to the great suns and circling planets, to worlds of infinite mystery and promise, can you believe that man is to spend all his days cooped and crawling on the surface of this tiny earth—this moist pebble with its clinging film of air? Or do you, on the other hand, believe that his destiny is indeed among the stars, and that one day our descendants will bridge the seas of space?"

This was heady stuff for 1938, a year before World War II broke out. It is easy to understand why the visionary British Interplanetary Society was not taken too seriously by many people and by institutions that held more established and conservative views. Indeed, its goals of building a spaceship and sending a manned expedition to the moon were often ridiculed. Members were considered cranks by many people. The same attitude that considered rocket pioneer Robert Goddard a lunatic in the late 1920s was working against the goals of the British Interplanetary Society in the late 1930s. World War II and Germany's V2 rocket would put that attitude to rest for good.

Meanwhile, young Arthur C. Clarke kept in touch with all those who shared his enthusiasms, and much of his spare time was spent writing letters—often dozens each week. Letters in which readers enthusiastically exchanged ideas and visions about manned rockets traveling to the moon and planets were published in the early science fiction magazines. It was in the summer of 1937 that Clarke began a correspondence with another young writer, Sam Youd (pseudonym John Christopher), and shared many of his opinions and self-evaluations with him. Their letters often mentioned their favorite authors, short stories, music, and poetry. The correspondence has continued for more than fifty-five years.

In an early letter Clarke made it clear that he strongly favored stories with a scientific basis, although he still admired writers H. P. Lovecraft and C. A. Smith. In the late thirties, however, he was ambivalent about his own writing.

"I have four short stories," he wrote to Youd in October 1937, "and although I swore never to do any more story writing as it took up so much time, I fear that I shall be at it again in a very short time. I am best at short humourous stories, though what I consider my best stories have been 'straight.'"

In January 1938 he told Youd what he was reading and again tried to define for himself where writing fit into his life.

"At the moment I am reading Esnault-Pelterie's monumental tome 'L'Astronautique' which is lousy with differential equations. It takes me about a day to read a page, as every other line I run up against something that I can't integrate. Last Sunday I went out to Walter's [Walter Gillings] and he gave me a long harangue on what a wicked waste it is for me to spend my time on stuff like this when I could be setting the s.f. world by the ears—perhaps! But I shall do as I jolly well please, and there is more chance of fame in astronautics than s.f., I'll tell the Universe! That is, if one wants fame, and modesty was never one of my vices. But Walt can't understand my attitude and cannot see the 'keen, unpassioned beauty' of mathematics, the queen of the sciences, that attracts me, nor does he realise that the man who holds the equations of astrodynamics in his head will one day be worth his weight in radium. Not that I ever will, but maybe I can make it look like it."

Less than two weeks later the subject of fame and writing came up again in a letter to Youd.

"I don't want writing fame, and can see no reason to believe that I have any great literary ability. I can turn out an amusing story at times, and if I spent enough time in perfecting my style I believe that I could do better than most of the 'pulp' writers—I aim no higher than that! As I haven't the time to devote to writing seriously, I shall just put pen to paper when the mood seizes me, and no oftener. It takes such a tremendous time to write a *serious* story that I sincerely hope I don't often get the urge. At the moment, owing to the malign influence of Lord Dunsany, I am in imminent danger of starting on a rather weird scientific play. It will be a play in form only, and could never be put on the stage, as there will be direction like this:

" 'The sunlight shining through the window slowly fades over a period of about a thousand million years.' "

The intensive effort and time necessary to write good stories came across loud and clear in Clarke's letters, and he knew from experience that it was easier to criticize and tear down a piece of writing than it was to create and construct it.

"I maintain that no one should criticise stories severely until they have tried to write them themselves," he told Youd. "So until you produce a wad of dog-eared MSS from your little bottom drawer I shall not regard you as a qualified critic. Shucks!"

The fact that modesty was not one of Clarke's vices was not lost on his friends at this time. In his 1938 *Novae Terrae* sketch Bill Temple described, in his role as the jester scribe for the London science fiction fans, his first visit to Clarke's Norfolk Square room.

"For there was hardly room for the two of us, and A[rthur]'s Ego had to be left outside on the landing. A. himself generously opened the window and sat himself half outside it to allow me to look around freely."

Temple's sketch made several other humorous allusions to Clarke's "Ego." It mentioned several books Clarke possessed about the moon and then continued: " 'You B.I.S. Moonatic,' I said, 'haven't you anything else less technical?' A. replied: 'My library is at Taunton, my home-town. It contains complete sets of WONDER, ASTOUNDING, about 100 science-fiction novels and more than

100 books of pure science.' 'Darned if I'm going to Taunton (if there is such a place) to check up on it,' I said. 'So I'll have to take your word for it.' Here A.'s conscience smote him. 'Well, to tell you the truth, my ASTOUNDING collection is two short,' he mumbled. The Ego thrust its head into the room at this, and gave A. such a look of utter contempt that the poor fellow blushed.

"'A fine chance to boost yourself without being detected—and you throw it away you weak twirp!' it remarked bitterly and withdrew."

To this day "Ego" remains intact as an affectionate appellation used by Clarke's friends, fans, and himself. While from time to time a mild controversy has arisen over the origin of the name "Ego" Clarke in the early London days, Bill Temple, with good reason, claims credit as originator, and Clarke now confirms it.

"I realized *that* early," says Temple, "that Arthur was a dual personality: (1) the boaster: 'I'm the greatest!'; (2) the quiet, humorous, generous soul. Arthur *had* to prove he was a winner, to come out on top. He was born competitive."

In the 1980s Clarke initiated an "Egogram," a newsy word-processed page he sometimes sends to friends to bring them up to date on his activities.

David Kyle, Clarke's first American publisher and friend going back to the early 1950s, believes he can put the "Ego Clarke business" into its true context.

"Arthur is an enthusiast because he is interested in what he is doing," says Kyle. "But many of his acquaintances felt that Arthur talked so much because he was interested in himself, that he was into self-aggrandizement. But that is not Arthur. At any opportunity, whether he was with somebody important or whether it was just a teenage fan, Arthur would whip out his photographs and discuss something he was interested in at the time.

"Some of the other professionals, those who perhaps feel they have outgrown talking to fans, kept this label pinned on him as being an egotistical person, so 'Ego' was a derogatory term to them: Old Ego Clarke, showing off his photographs again. Yet it has sometimes been used affectionately by his friends.

"If you want to capture the spirit and essence of Arthur Clarke, you must look to his roots and relationship to fandom to understand his enthusiasm. He still has the enthusiasm of youth. Some people, regretfully, have misinterpreted this enthusiasm for blatant egotism," says Kyle.

In the 1938 sketch that started it all, Bill Temple described Arthur C. Clarke for the rather small readership of *Novae Terrae*.

"I beheld a tallish, rather clever-looking fellow (appearances are deceptive) whose eyes glinted at me through horn-rims with a condescending expression. He looks as if he hopes he looks like a scientist, does A. His hair cannot make up its mind whether it is dark or fair, is perfectly dry and sticks up like a wire-brush. . . . He's somewhat impatient and highly-strung, and says he's not, and is given to sudden violent explosions of mirth (mostly at his own jokes)."

Leonard Hobbs adds, "Arthur was pretty thin and tall in those days. He always wore glasses, and he had all his hair then—lots of wavy, light-brown hair. Even today when he speaks, he's got a little bit of a west country burr; it's rather nice actually. Just a little trace of it."

For a variety of reasons, but mostly because of his involvement with fellow space enthusiasts, the prewar London years represented the good life to Clarke.

"I can thank science fiction for that, because it was through the magazines that I got in touch with London 'fandom' and, most important of all, the fledgling British Interplanetary Society. (There was about an eighty percent overlap between the two groups.)"

Of course a move away from the Paddington "broom closet" into a spacious flat in 1938 made Clarke's good life even better. His imagination knew no bounds when it came to dreaming about space travel and manned rockets to the moon, but he desperately needed more room on Earth.

In May 1938 Bill Temple was hunting for a place to live and decided to visit his friend at his room in Norfolk Square. Temple playfully suggested that Clarke's love of space travel may have been boosted by his feeling of claustrophobia.

Both young men were members of the British Interplanetary Society and the Science Fiction Association. Both enjoyed music and aspired to being professional writers. After some discussion, they decided to pool their resources and look for a spacious flat together.

They finally found one at 88 Gray's Inn Road, Bloomsbury, a few blocks east of the British Museum and just around the corner from where Virginia Woolf lived, although no one realized it at the time. After signing a three-year lease, Clarke and Temple moved into the flat in July 1938.

It consisted of four rooms on two upper floors—plenty of space for books, friends, and meetings. The floors below the flat housed a foot clinic, a socialist press, and the International Writers' Club.

"We have plenty of space here," Clarke wrote to Sam Youd. "And it is central, so no doubt many SFA and BIS meetings will gravitate here eventually."

The two space cadets—Clarke and Temple—soon settled in. Clarke lived on the fourth and top floor (the "attic" to him), which had a kitchen and dining area, a bathroom, and a small bedroom.

The sitting room, where Temple slept, was on the floor below. Bookshelves ran along one entire wall, but there wasn't much other furniture—a few chairs, but not enough to seat everyone at the meetings; people had to catch as catch can. Temple provided a table, which was in the dining area upstairs. Although it wasn't large enough, he and Clarke attempted to play table tennis on it.

"The huge Moon photo dominated our study wall," Bill Temple wrote years later, "as the Moon itself dominated our thoughts. Number eighty-eight became the headquarters of the British Interplanetary Society, which gathered there to discuss ways and means of reaching those lunar maria."

The word spread about the new flat at 88 Gray's Inn Road, and it wasn't long before regular meetings of the British Interplanetary Society were held there.

In March 1937, the BIS headquarters had moved from Liverpool to London. At about the same time, Professor A. M. Low, onetime editor of *Armchair Science*, became the society's first chairman. He was chosen to bring some prestige to the BIS.

"He was," says Clarke, "quite a well-known popular science writer—in fact, the best-known one of his time. A lot of people, however, had some doubts about the legitimacy of his professorship because he had been affiliated with some minor institute at one time. Anyway, he was very interested in the future. Low graciously resigned later, when he thought his name was not all that good for us."

Clarke became treasurer, and Bill Temple replaced Ted Carnell (who was also editing the BIS *Journal*) as publicity director in 1938. The promotional hat was worn by everyone, of course, including Clarke, who wrote society brochures, without bylines, to educate the public, generate press coverage, and bring in new members.

Another space enthusiast, Maurice Hanson, was invited to join Clarke and Temple at the flat, and he moved in after a few months. At the time, Hanson was editing *Novae Terrae*, whose initial issue had appeared in March 1936. The October 1937 issue was the first edited jointly by Hanson, Carnell, and Clarke. Twenty-seven more issues were produced, the last being the January 1939 edition.

"Maurice came," Temple recalled, "carrying his typewriter. . . . [and] so No. 88 became the editorial offices of *Novae Terrae*, too, with Arthur and me as assistant editors. Often in the small hours the three of us would be fighting a temperamental duplicator to produce *Novae Terrae* or the BIS *Bulletin*. Or getting out copy for the BIS *Journal*, which depicted detailed plans of our proposed moonship, so similar in the event to the Apollo vehicle. (A proud moment when my own tatty copies of that *Journal* were shown on TV that momentous week when the 'giant leap' was made.)"

The meetings of the British Interplanetary Society were held every other Thursday, usually alternating with Thursday night gatherings of science fiction fans (most of whom, not surprisingly, were also BIS members).

Besides Clarke, Temple, and Hanson, the regular BIS members who often met at the flat or the nearby Red Bull pub—most in their twenties—included Ralph A. Smith, whose pioneering space art illustrated some of Clarke's earlier space books, including his very first, *Interplanetary Flight*; Val Cleaver, who was one of Clarke's best friends and would later become chief engineer of the Rolls-Royce Rocket Division and in charge of Britain's Blue Streak rocket; Jack Edwards, technical director of the BIS research effort in designing a spaceship and some of its instruments, including a "space speedometer"; and Walter Gillings.

"The meetings were often quite crazy, lots of fun and [full of] laughter," Temple recollects. "Sometimes they got side-tracked altogether. Once Ego set up his three-inch refractor telescope on its tall tripod beneath the wide skylight which covered our upper landing (and could be uncovered). It was a cloudless night with a full moon—then called 'a bomber's Moon.' And Ego focused the telescope on the moon and let us in turn examine the lunar territory which was our goal."

With the Red Bull pub next door, some of the meetings split into two factions: the teetotaler group, headed by Clarke and Hanson, who remained at the flat for the meeting; and the drinkers, including Walter Gillings, Bill Temple, and others who believed that the discussion improved with a few drinks.

Temple tells how the drinkers once rejoined the teetotalers at the flat for supper and talk until several members caught the last trains home.

"One night we returning revelers found the stairs to the flat barred by a heavy table and other flat furniture, with Arthur & Company armed with mops and brooms prepared to keep the drunks out. We stormed the barricade. Thanks to some smart rapier play by [Ted] Carnell and his rolled umbrella, we broke through. After all, the flat was *ours* too—it was everybody's.

"We staged revenge. We sent Arthur out for the fish and chips and fixed a booby trap over the door. When he entered, a large tin tea-tray fell on his head. He didn't turn a hair—and in those days he *had* hair.

"The fish and chip suppers were a ritual. Even the elegant John Wyndham (then John Beynon Harris) would eat them with us out of newspaper." The "elegant" Wyndham was of course the British SF/thriller writer who broke into bestsellerdom in 1951 with *The Day of the Triffids*.

Joan Temple, who married Bill on September 16, 1939, describes what it was like to live in the midst of the BIS: "When my husband and Arthur first moved into the flat, they had given keys to various friends, so that whenever they were in London and they needed some place to go, they could go to the flat. And when I moved in, I found it all quite amusing and sometimes quite embarrassing because I would be happily getting on with things in the flat and suddenly somebody I didn't know would come in with the door key. I never felt I knew quite who was going to turn up."

"We were a group of English eccentrics," says Bill Temple, "trying to keep alive the flickering flame of space travel research for its own sake—not for war applications, as had happened to the German Interplanetary Society now that the Gestapo had taken it over." Temple also recalls that the Germans sent a member over to investigate the work of the British Interplanetary Society, which, despite appearances, was serious.

This Nazi journalist interviewed Clarke and Temple at the

flat just before the war. They were both convinced he was a spy. Temple remembered how this "tall fellow with the quiet voice and the restless hazel eyes looked through our cuttings book and appeared very uninterested in those dealing with war rockets."

"I think we succeeded in giving the impression that we were only a bunch of fools and could be ignored," Temple later wrote.

Certainly the British Foreign Office and the Air Ministry didn't take the society too seriously, although they did sometimes respond to BIS letters. One such government response to a BIS letter about jet engines was received shortly before World War II broke out.

The letter read in part, "We note your remarks. However, we cannot seriously envisage Mr. Frank Whittle's jet engine replacing the piston engine." This attitude, says Temple, actually drove Whittle to negotiate with the German Air Force after failing to interest the British Air Ministry.

"Unbelievable?" asks Temple. "I've seen the original letter in the BIS files. The military mind, whether British or German, is always unimaginative."

This could hardly be said about the society members, who were seriously thinking about how to design a manned spaceship that would fly round-trip to the moon and were also promoting the feasibility of the idea to all who would listen.

On the fourth Tuesday of each month, the technically inclined and gifted members, about twelve in number, of the BIS Experimental Committee met to work on the general spaceship designs and to decide what, if any, system components could actually be designed, built, and tested within the modest budgetary limits of the society. It was this group that designed the BIS spaceship (and some guidance components) that got a good amount of publicity in 1939, thanks to the efforts of several BIS members.

Temple, in charge of publicity at the time, gave some good news to the membership in the March 1939 issue of the BIS *Bulletin*. The spaceship design was receiving some great publicity from large-circulation magazines such as *Time* and *Practical Mechanics*.

"The cover of the March *Practical Mechanics* depicts in glorious colour the B.I.S. space-ship roaring down towards the Moon, intent, apparently, upon landing on it upside down. Wisps wrapped around it show clearly how it is revolving, and lines streaming away from the nose show how it is cutting through the air in airless interplanetary space. The main article of the issue is a reprint from the *Journal,* H. E. Ross's description of the ship."

It was the BIS *Journal,* published quarterly and printed on glossy paper, that presented the society's serious work. The *Bulletin,* in contrast, published the lighter, less scientific articles in the typed and mimeographed do-it-yourself publishing format of the day. Technical papers and designs were produced by various specialized committees.

One such Experimental Committee meeting, held at the home of Ralph Smith in the East London suburb of Chingford, was written up by Bill Temple for the BIS *Bulletin* of September 1938:

"I fell to examining an intriguing but only partially completed model of a spaceship altimeter on the table, a heavy disc of aluminum which spun smoothly on its bearings in a framework, and soon other members came trickling in: Messrs. Edwards, Ross, Bein, Day, Bramhill, Cowper-Essex and Janser. A general discussion began, which ranged from the composition of a new steel, which could withstand thermite, to the composition of a dog's dinner. Mr. Smith, who knows only too well how these meetings persist in wandering miles from the point, called for order, and the meeting proper began. First on the agenda was the question of whether to buy four small magnets for the altimeter and alter them, or continue a so far unsuccessful search for a suitably large one. It was decided to get the four small ones if their jaws could be widened by cutting."

This inertia-governed altimeter (space speedometer, if you will) was going to get tested on the Chancery Lane Underground escalators. It never got that far, however.

At a Technical Committee meeting in January 1939, Edwards reported that the space altimeter wasn't behaving as it should. (Edwards was, according to Clarke, an eccentric genius and "the nearest thing to a mad scientist I have ever met outside fiction.")

"Sometimes when it was supposed to indicate the exact height to which it had been lifted," wrote Temple in the *Bulletin,* "the indicator shot back past zero and pretended the thing was buried in the ground. Mr. E.[dwards] pointed out how embarrassing this would be if it happened at a public demonstration. 'We could always tell them that that proves space is curved,' rapped out Clarke smartly, and everyone guffawed."

Clarke later wrote in a *Holiday* magazine feature: "The theory of the device was perfectly sound, and something similar steers every satellite into orbit today. But the engineering precision demanded was utterly beyond our means, and Mrs. Edwards put her foot down on hearing of our intention to cast lead weights in her best saucepan."

Next on the agenda for the September 1938 meeting was a discussion of an efficient, lightweight battery to heat the spaceship. Temple's description continues: "Here Messrs. Edwards and Janser started an argument on such a highly technical plane that I just sat there between them agape, and the stream of words passed over my head like a beautiful rainbow. I gathered it was something about conductivity values. Arthur Clarke made occasional interjections, which might or might not have been to the point, but at any rate showed us that Arthur grasped what was going on. Which was what Arthur wanted to show us, anyway. It all ended with Mr. [Arthur] Janser promising to hunt through his books (all 2,000 of them) to find certain tables, and perhaps consult the National Physical Laboratory on this important subject. (Wish I knew *what* subject.)"

Another piece of moonship hardware designed, built, and tested—this time successfully—by the BIS in the late 1930s was an instrument called the *coelostat*. With this optical device, a commander and crew of a spinning spaceship could observe the Earth, moon, stars, or another spaceship as a fixed image that was not spinning—a necessity for navigational purposes.

The coelostat depended on four mirrors to stop the local solar system from twirling. Two were stationary, and two were spinning. Clarke donated the spring motor of his phonograph to the project, which was begun at the Experimental Committee meeting in September 1938. First Jack Edwards made a cardboard model of the coelostat. Then, wanting to demonstrate its fundamental principles, he sent everyone searching for mirrors. The Smiths donated their compact and shaving mirrors. Wall mirrors and dressing table mirrors were also brought forth by others.

After some experimentation Edwards took the small mirror from Mrs. Smith's compact, which he wanted to use as the viewing mirror, and placed it carefully on the piano. He then asked everyone to take up a position and hold mirrors at various angles. "Soon," reported Temple, "the room was full of living statuary, standing in graceful and artistic poses, holding mirrors above their heads. Finally, after many contortions and no convincing demonstration, it was decided to build a working model of the coelostat. The meeting then broke up." But there would be other technical meetings held at the flat on Gray's Inn Road over the next few months.

"I recall," says Temple, "the dedicated BIS Technical Committee stumbling through London's wartime total blackout, spraining their ankles through tripping over sandbags, working on the instruments—the coelostat, the inertia altimeter, etc.—to guide the three-man moon rocket they'd already designed in the BIS *Journal.*"

Eventually the coelostat was built and worked well. A 1939 public demonstration at the South Kensington Science Museum was a success in every way, and generated good publicity for the society. Perhaps these "crackpots" were producing valuable scientific results after all. The original Wright biplane, on display next to the demonstration room, gave this rather modest scientific event a boost in significance.

Attendees saw a spinning disk, with affixed blurred lettering on it, on one side of the room. At the other end of the room was the coelostat, a foot-square wooden box, "looking rather like the result of a misalliance between a periscope and an alarm clock," Clarke wrote after the event.

One who looked through the coelostat at the spinning disk across the room would find the blurred lettering distinct and readable: the inscription, not surprisingly, was the acronym for the British Interplanetary Society—B.I.S. If the viewer looked at the rest of the room, however, it would be spinning. In a spinning spaceship, the coelostat could stop the twirling stars and allow the navigator to get a fix on its position.

Now all the society needed was a real spaceship, not just drawing board blueprints, in which to put the coelostat and the space speedometer. But with only membership brain power and practically no assets, the BIS would have to settle for a detailed on-paper design. The result was the "cellular" spaceship design published in the BIS *Journal* in 1939.

Armed with youthful enthusiasm and imagination, the BIS produced a realistic design. Cylindrical in shape, with its crew quarters housed in the nose, the single-stage moon rocket was designed to take three astronauts to the moon and back. The propulsion system contained main and auxiliary rockets in a honeycomb structure. These were solid propellant rockets, and the number fired would determine the acceleration. As the individual rocket tubes were fired, they would be jettisoned.

Various types of flight scenarios, rendezvous techniques, and refueling procedures for a moon journey were seriously discussed. Just as NASA would do in the 1960s to a much greater degree, the journey was broken down into several stages so that specific problems could be identified and solutions found. One moon flight scenario called for a mother ship to remain in lunar orbit and a smaller ferry craft to actually land on the moon. This anticipated the fundamental approach of the historic Apollo voyages to the moon by some thirty years.

Drawings were made of the BIS spaceship, and they were published in the *Journal* in 1939—an issue nearly confiscated by a Scotland Yard cautious in the face of Irish bombings of post offices and the gathering storm in Europe.

Returning to 88 Gray's Inn Road from a printer's shop on Theobalds Road, Clarke was carrying two parcels filled with freshly printed copies of the *Journal*—the entire edition, as a matter of fact.

"Excuse me, sir," one of two investigators said politely as they stopped Clarke, "but we're from Scotland Yard. Could we see what you have in those packets?"

"To the considerable disappointment of the detectives," Clarke later wrote, "I was not even carrying *Tropic of Capricorn* [the banned book by American expatriate Henry Miller], but when I presented them with copies of the *Journal* they very gamely offered to pay. Tempting though it was to acquire a genuine subscriber (the cash box held about $2.50 at the time), I refused the contribution; but I got them to carry the parcels the rest of the way for me."

The society's spaceship design in the *Journal* gained a fair amount of attention, even from the prestigious publication *Nature*, which made the valid point that until practical experiments were performed that supported the theories produced by the BIS, the society could not be taken *too* seriously. This prompted the membership to launch a fund-raising effort for experiments. This is how the modest funds for the spaceship's navigational components were solicited.

Clarke's immersion in BIS affairs during the late 1930s would serve his writing well in the decades to follow. All the ideas generated among society members, many of whom brought different perspectives, knowledge, and skills to the spaceflight cause, were put through the rigors of friendly debate. Clarke would use many of them in his future fiction and nonfiction writing. He was also writing fairly regularly during these London years. Besides the promotional brochures for the society and nonfiction articles for the BIS *Journal*, he was doing fiction pieces for various "fanzines," including a 1937 piece titled "Travel by Wire!" in *Amateur Science Stories* and two more tales ("How We Went to Mars" and "Retreat from Earth") for the same fanzine in 1938. He began using his nickname "Ego" as a pseudonym—sometimes with slight variations: "Ego," "Arthur Ego Clarke," and E. G. O'Brien. But he was writing much more nonfiction than fiction during these prewar years. He even found a nonfiction story market with his employer. "Into Space" was published in the Exchequer and Audit Department Association's publication, *Chequer-Board*, in October 1937.

In the piece Clarke outlines the next hundred years of space ventures. "With present-day materials and known fuels, it is possible to build a machine to leave the earth, go around the moon, and return to earth. With rather more trouble, and with the experience gained on the first flight, it will be possible to build a ship to land on the moon and return. Once we have reached the moon, going to the planets is merely a longer job, requiring practically the same amount of fuel. Out in space, distance makes little difference, for once a body has started moving, it will go on for ever unless it is stopped again, as Sir Isaac Newton observed. . . .

"Looked at logically, the conquest of space is only a matter of time, experiment—and money. It may take fifty years, it may take a hundred, it may take much less."

It took less. Some thirty-two years later, the first manned landing on the moon occurred.

The days at the flat on Gray's Inn Road were "merry days," reflects Bill Temple, "but there was a shadow over them." The storm broke on September 3, 1939, when Britain and her allies declared war on Germany. Everyone's life changed.

Maurice Hanson was the first to be conscripted into the army (he was already doing national service), and Ted Carnell took over the editorship of *Novae Terrae*, which he renamed *New Worlds*. In the postwar years it became an important magazine in science fiction.

Just days after war was declared, Bill Temple married his

fiancée, Joan Streeton. Joan Temple moved into the flat in October 1939. "We used to, the three of us, go out to supper together," Bill Temple recalls, "which required a short subway trip. Coming home, Joan and I would, being normal, take the up escalator.

"More often than not, we'd become aware of Ego racing us to the top exit via the down escalator. And he'd win. Maybe he taps into cosmic energy. I call that cheating. Joan suspected that Ego sublimated his sexual energy through ceaseless writing."

"We lived at the flat," Temple wrote later. "Arthur ignored the war and began writing his first novel, called 'Raymond.' He'd burn the midnight oil working at it, then burst into our bedroom in the small hours to declaim to us some passage of pure genius he'd just penned. It was a story he had begun in Somerset before coming to London."

"I still know exactly how it all began," Clarke said later in an introduction to the work. "The opening scene flashed mysteriously into my mind, and was pinned down on paper, around 1935. It was an isolated incident, unrelated to any plot I had been trying to develop."

The work became *Against the Fall of Night*. From its beginnings at the family farm to the time an early version of it first appeared in *Startling Stories* in November 1948, this work went through as many as six versions, its word count climbing over time. But that was not the end of it; Clarke couldn't let it go, and it was eventually published as a novel by Gnome Press in 1953. Next Clarke undertook a major revision, and *The City and the Stars* was published in 1956. Twenty years had passed since he had visualized the opening scene, and some critics believe that this marathon was worth it. Frederik Pohl, for one, considers it to be Clarke's finest novel.

The writing continued through 1940, which Clarke spent in London and then in North Wales.

"Here I sat out the Blitz," he recalled, "peacefully checking the accounts of the Ministry of Food, until I exchanged civilian clothes for RAF blue." It was early 1941, and it would be some time before Arthur C. Clarke again wrote regularly.

[T]here were great sheets of fire roaring on either side [of the runway], clouds of steam rising into the mist, and a heat like that from an open furnace beating into our faces, for we were only 100 feet from the nearest burners.

Glide Path *(1963)*

5
A PANTHEIST IN THE RAF

Even though he was deferred for the time being because of his reserved occupation, Arthur C. Clarke realized that sooner or later he'd be called up. And because of his interest in astronomy, the natural course seemed to be to learn celestial navigation and put it to use for the Royal Air Force. "I determined to go where *I* wanted to go," he wrote, "not where the random processes of the draft decided.

"I bought books on the subject by Francis Chichester (later famous as a single-handed round-the-world sailor) and studied them avidly. I then went behind the back of the civil service while in Wales and enlisted clandestinely," he said. "Without telling my superiors, I sneaked away from the civil service and just registered. That was it. . . . Then I just waited for the call-up. My call-up papers arrived a few weeks later."

On March 18, 1941, Clarke entered the Royal Air Force as an aircrafthand radio wireless mechanic/aircraftsman class II. He did not, however, relinquish his civilian independence easily.

RAF policy was to put "Church of England" on the dog tags of any inductee who had no formal religious affiliation. "I was very annoyed about this," says Clarke. "I got the man who was handling the paperwork and made them change it to pantheist." Viewing religious faith as antithetical to the scientific method and the science fiction quest, Clarke found pantheism, equating God with the forces and laws of the universe, true to his value system—and his strong individualism. Over the last fifty years he has maintained a consistent aversion to organized religion because, he says, he has never been willing to substitute faith for knowledge.

When *Playboy* interviewer Ken Kelley said to Clarke in 1986, "You don't believe in organized religion, yet a major theme in so many of your works seems to be a quest for God," Clarke agreed.

"Yes, in a way—a quest for ultimate values, whatever they are. My objection to organized religion is the premature conclusion to ultimate truth that it represents," he said, then went on to describe his unhappy Anglican Sunday school experiences as a boy, when he had to walk several miles to church, only to hear "horribly boring sermons." The children were given stamps that they had to stick in a book, and when the book was full, they were allowed to go on an outing. Young Clarke considered this a form of bribery.

"I remember doing it for a couple of months, and then saying, 'This is a bunch of nonsense, and I don't intend to do it any more.' Never went again."

After basic training, where he and thirty others were taught "how to behave without disgracing the Royal Air Force," Clarke was ordered back to London for technical training with the Air Ministry Unit. It was May 1941, just days after the last major air attack on London—the heaviest and deadliest raid of the war—took place. Clarke was one of several hundred aircraftsmen II ("the lowest form of animal life in the RAF") who were receiving training in electronics and were billeted in a partly bombed-out school building in London's East End.

"It was near Aldgate Underground Station. The ruins were still smoking, and *that* was all I ever saw of the Blitz."

The devastation was everywhere. Even Westminster Abbey, the House of Commons, the British Museum, and other historic buildings were hit by the primitive iron bombs. It was during this time that Clarke started to imagine what "*real* war would be like" and wrote some material that, after revision, would eventually become Chapter seventeen of his novel *Earthlight*, describing—for the first time—a full-scale space battle.

Fortuitously, as he had been spared some extra farm chores at

Ballifants, Clarke found himself in a position to devote extra time to study while in technical training.

"One day we were lined up on parade and inspected by the senior warrant officer," he wrote, "who selected me, of all people, to be his batman. As life on the farm had bred in me a complete indifference to tidiness and even to general hygiene, the WO's choice has always struck me as somewhat astonishing; perhaps I merely looked less moronic than the rest of the recruits."

Clarke found he could do his chores quickly—keeping this warrant officer's quarters clean and polishing his boots and brass—and used his spare time to study differential equations.

"When he discovered what I was doing," wrote Clarke, "my kindly *padrone* let me use his quarters as a study while he was bawling out squads on the parade ground."

After the technical training in electronics, Clarke was selected for training in what the Royal Air Force called *radio direction finding* or *RDF*. Hardly fulfilling his hope of being posted to a flight school and learning celestial navigation, nevertheless "it certainly sounded a lot better than the medical corps," he later admitted.

Radio direction finding was, of course, really radar, but the word and the technology were classified as secret during the war. Clarke would learn some of its secrets in the early 1940s at the Number 2 and Number 9 Radio Schools in the county of Wiltshire, on the bleak southern England moors not too far from Stonehenge. He was posted there in late September 1941.

Everyone knew that Clarke's eyes were cast upward toward the stars—that he was a member of the British Interplanetary Society and was obsessed with rockets and space travel—and this earned him the nickname "Spaceship."

"I suspect that the periods of time spent in getting his colleagues to understand were spent by Arthur in space calculations," reflects lecturer Barry R. King, who remembers Clarke as an apt pupil who outshone his fellow classmates. In fact, after the fourteen-week training course (consisting of a general electronics course and then a more specialized course on radar), Clarke became an instructor on the staff. He enjoyed teaching and eventually earned the rank of corporal in that capacity. And while he describes the Yatesbury camp's environs as "bleak and windswept," to the young instructor his new world was "wildly exciting."

That enthusiasm permeated his teaching, according to one of

Clarke's students, Harry Morrin. "One day in the canteen," recalls Morrin, "we got to talking with some of the boys who had been there longer. They said, 'Who's your lecturer?' We said, 'Corporal Clarke,' and they replied, 'Oh, you're lucky. Get him talking about spaceships. Say that rockets won't work in a vacuum or something like that.'

"Sure enough, a few nights later in class someone actually got the conversation around to it. It was about 10:00 P.M. Before long Arthur was giving us all the facts about how to get to the moon— about multistage rockets and lunar orbiters. He went on for a half an hour or so, and he had all sorts of diagrams on the board.

"Somebody asked how big the rocket was going to be, with the fuel and all the rest of it. And Arthur's answer was 'Well, somewhere about the height of St. Paul's Cathedral.'

"This turned out to be remarkably prophetic because the height of the Saturn rocket for the first Apollo mission to the moon was within a few feet of the height of St. Paul's Cathedral!

"Arthur set up a telescope in the storeroom at the end of the wooden barrack house, and I often remember being treated to a minilecture on the moons of Jupiter or the rings of Saturn."

During his off-hours Clarke took advantage of the good library on base and read technical literature on such specialized subjects as electrical circuit theory. This individual study eventually led him to write several technical pieces, one of which, "More Television Waveforms," was published in *Electronic Engineering* in November 1942. The article passed the scrutiny of the wartime censors because the mathematical formulas were presented in the context of television, not radar, the technology of which actually was derived from television.

Publication of the article, Clarke contends, helped him obtain his commission as a technical officer. Not long after publication he was called into group headquarters and questioned at length by Wing Commander Edward Fennessey (who would later become managing director of British Post Office Telecommunications). Young Clarke obviously made the grade, because soon thereafter, in early 1943, he was sent to a radar installation in Lincolnshire. From there it was on to Davidstow Moor (not too far from King Arthur's legendary coastal castle at Tintagel), the second home of the CHL (chain home low) station.

The new orders would prove a boon to Clarke's future. For the first time in his life he would be working with trained scientists, on a project involving state-of-the-art technology that would prove crucial to the Allied war effort.

Nobel Prize–winning physicist Luis W. Alvarez led the scientific team that developed the prototype Ground Controlled Approach (GCA) radar system at the Radiation Laboratory of the Massachusetts Institute of Technology in 1942. The British brass, knowing how important such a blind-approach radar system could be, arranged for Alvarez and his American team to bring the prototype Mark I system over to England for advanced testing.

Alvarez and his four-man Rad Lab team arrived at the RAF bomber base at Elsham Wolds in northeast England, not too far from the city of York, in July 1943. The testing program had the blessing of the station commander—as long as it did not interfere with his bombing missions to Germany.

The GCA equipment was mobile and contained in two truck vans weighing some twenty tons. One truck held the power plant and transmitter antennas, housed in odd-shaped structures jutting out, and had no room for personnel. The other truck was the manned control van, with the radar screens and other controls, where the actual talking down was done. Eventually the production Mark II models would be contained in only one truck.

Once the prototype system hardware was reassembled and checked out, the GCA tests began. Each day over six weeks the GCA trucks drove to the operating site near the runway. The diesel power plant was then started up, and it took about thirty minutes to warm up the vacuum tubes and align the circuits.

One passage from the novel *Glide Path*, published twenty years later and often described as Clarke's only non-science-fiction novel, describes how the GCA radar works. The words are those of Flight Lieutenant Deveraux to the protagonist, Flying Officer Alan Bishop.

"The idea's extremely simple, even if the equipment isn't. What we have is a very precise radar set, capable of tracking an aircraft to within a few feet. A controller on the ground has the information presented to him, and he talks to the pilot over the radio, telling him what course to fly in order to keep on the glide path. If the pilot obeys orders, and everything's working OK, he'll find himself over the end of the runway. The Americans call it a 'talk-down' system, which is a good way of describing it."

The Air Ministry decreed that the formal trials at Elsham Wolds had been successful but decided the system should be tested further at a bad-weather base. The MIT Rad Lab team and its support group would also train the RAF group in its operation and maintenance before leaving British soil.

It didn't take long for everyone to agree that Davidstow Moor in Cornwall had the worst weather of any place they had ever been. This was the RAF's Coastal Command, which flew bombers over the Atlantic on antisubmarine patrols.

After Alvarez passed his leadership duties on to his colleague George Comstock, the four members of the MIT group headed for Davidstow Moor in late August 1943.

It was in the fog, rain, and mist that the MIT group met the RAF team, including Arthur C. Clarke, who would eventually take over the Mark I GCA radar set and maintain it for the British. Technical Officer Clarke "found the American scientists amplifying their already excellent vocabularies over expiring transformers, and complaining bitterly that their equipment wasn't built for underwater operation. At night, when the apparatus closed down and cooled off, the all-pervading mist would creep gleefully into every cranny, depositing moisture in high-voltage circuits so that brief but spectacular firework displays would ensue in the morning." To help solve the moisture problem, electric heaters were positioned in the equipment and turned on at night.

It was also a good thing that the Americans had brought along a large supply of spare vacuum tubes because at least one was lost every day in the system, including those in the various radio sets. "I can still remember my amazement," Clarke said, "at the number of vacuum tubes in the GCA Mark I. It came to the incredible total of almost a thousand. I'd have laughed scornfully if some crazy science fiction writer had predicted that one day every engineer would have carried in his hip pocket not a Colt 45 but an HP-45 calculator—this mere handful a dozen times as complex as our Mark I. The explosion in complexity and implosion in size are two of the main parameters determining future communication technology."

In their off-hours the British and American colleagues held many enthusiastic discussions about the future.

"I do remember," says Clarke's longtime American friend Bert

Fowler, "talking about what it took in the way of thrust to get weight into orbit and about the plans and designs for a colony on the moon and spacesuits which would provide oxygen and protect you against the vacuum. Most of us, I think, were just fascinated that somebody had not only thought about these things, but had actually put numbers into them and done some engineering thinking about the problems of manned spaceflight. None of us had ever been exposed before to someone who actually thought in technical terms of getting to the moon and what it would take to live there."

Another American, Neal Jolley, was just claiming his bunk and unpacking when recently promoted Pilot Officer Clarke (equal to a second lieutenant) put his bag on the next bunk and introduced himself.

"I soon decided he must be some kind of screwball," said Jolley. "He talked of belonging to the British Interplanetary Society and took for granted rocket-launched satellites that could appear to be stationary over the Earth. We all knew that was impossible in the foreseeable future and not even worth wasting time thinking about."

Jolley's skepticism was not uncommon on either side of the Atlantic, and he was hardly the first to refer to space enthusiasts as screwballs. In fact, *crackpots* was probably the more common term in the 1940s. Had this attitude prevailed after the war, however, planet Earth might still be waiting for a chosen few of its inhabitants to walk on the moon's surface.

Figuratively and literally, Clarke was not one to keep his feet on the ground. Speaking of Clarke's favorite sport, table tennis, Bert Fowler says, "The most memorable thing about Arthur's game was that his feet were rarely on the floor. We used to kid him that the reason he won most of the time wasn't because of his talent but rather because of the way he would demoralize the opposition by hitting the ball with both his feet off the floor."

After a few September weeks of getting waterlogged at Davidstow, spending what seemed like more time maintaining the equipment than operating it, the unit moved about thirty miles to the southwest to a base on the Atlantic Ocean, not too far from Land's End—St. Evals. The unit's mission was to set up a school for training RAF crews—the controllers, mechanics, and operators— who would use the production units, the Mark IIs, which would start to arrive a year or so later. The last of the Americans were soon gone, and Clarke and his RAF comrades were sorry to see them go. "They were a grand crowd," he reflects, "and taught us a great deal. Our discussions were by no means devoted entirely to waveguides, magnetrons, and pulse techniques. We also learned some interesting songs." These were the bawdy songs and dirty limericks for which the RAF was so well known. When the GCA team had its reunion outside Boston in October 1971, the winner of the dirty limerick contest was none other than the space cadet from Somerset, Arthur C. Clarke.

Clarke now had full responsibility for the one-of-a-kind Mark I. "We were now very much on our own and could no longer run to the experts when anything went wrong—as it frequently did. It had never been intended that the laboratory-built Mark I should be used continuously, month after month, for training and for innumerable demonstrations, in a foreign country and run by people who hadn't watched it grow up from a blueprint."

Still, the RAF team always managed to get it up and working when the top brass dropped in for a look. They were impressed enough to finally approve the system for the Royal Air Force, although the road to acceptance was long and arduous.

In the beginning the pilots were against the system, and they remained skeptical for quite some time. Their attitude was understandable. The pilots, after all, were being asked to turn over control of their aircraft to the GCA radar technicians on the ground. But the hard fact that the RAF was losing more planes to the nasty English weather than to the German Luftwaffe made the GCA radar system a top priority. As the system proved itself and its reliability was demonstrated hundreds of times during the testing program, the pilots slowly, cautiously began to trust and appreciate it.

In early 1944 another classified project came to St. Evals' airfield on the Cornwall coast. It was called FIDO (an acronym for Fog, Intensive, Dispersal of), but it was more analogous to a fire-breathing dragon than a domesticated canine. By generating tremendous amounts of controlled fire and heat, FIDO was designed to burn off the fog and mist on runways and give pilots an extra margin of safety with approach and touchdown visibility. The system was meant to change, with fire and fuel and fury, local bad weather into better weather for RAF airfields.

By positioning fire-producing pipes vertically in rows for three miles along the runway and feeding them through connecting fuel lines with immense amounts of fuel (a hundred thousand gallons each hour), a colossal heater was created to burn off the bad weather with what was estimated to be ten million horsepower of heat. If FIDO did what it was designed to do, pilots could then make visual landings during the last few seconds before touch-down. In theory, by combining this system with GCA radar, any aircraft could land with complete safety in otherwise impossible weather conditions.

No one ever forgot the experience when FIDO was lit. "The scene might have come from Dante's Inferno," Clarke wrote in 1949. "[T]here were great sheets of fire roaring on either side, clouds of steam rising into the mist, and a heat like that from an open furnace beating into our faces, for we were only 100 feet from the nearest burners." And in *Glide Path*, Clarke has his protagonist, Alan Bishop, walk onto the runway and experience FIDO's full heat and fury up close.

"The hissing roar rose to a crescendo; the heat from the blazing jets battered for a moment with terrifying violence against his exposed skin. Then he was through, and the fire and fury subsided behind him. The open runway was ahead. . . . And there they fell silent, beholding a miracle.

"Like most miracles, it was a very simple one. Overhead, the stars were shining."

A combined test of the GCA radar and the fog-eating FIDO was conducted at St. Evals in early 1944. Miserable weather and zero visibility were necessary for the test. Finally, after a stretch of good weather, drizzling fog settled in at St. Evals.

One fogged-in midnight, all was ready: FIDO was lit, the GCA technicians were monitoring their radar screens in the control truck, and the pilot and station's commanding officer were on board, preparing for takeoff. Then came trouble. The search radar, which presented the big, 360-degree picture like any air traffic control system, broke down. Only the narrow, thirty-degree glide-path radar system still functioned. While there was some additional risk, it was decided that the test could go ahead with only the narrow sector of radar tracking.

FIDO roared its fire, and the aircraft took off, but it soon became lost outside the narrow active radar sector. After instructing the pilot to do a 180-degree turn GCA soon picked up the plane again and lined it up for its landing.

"The pilot was unable to land on this run: he found himself at the edge of the runway, but visibility was so bad that he could only see a single line of FIDO burners and didn't know which side of the runway he was! So the maneuver had to be repeated, and luckily the second approach was successful, despite the attempts of the FIDO-induced gale to push the aircraft off course."

These were the worst weather conditions under which the GCA Mark I was ever operated. Clarke remembers how technicians stood on the running boards of the two radar trucks and shouted out instructions to the drivers, who slowly made their way back to the hangar. This test was the prototype's last hurrah, and fire-breathing FIDO was subdued and eventually put to rest forever by a rapidly improving radar technology.

The Mark I was soon dismantled, never to be reassembled. It had, with the help of tender loving overhauls, worked exceptionally well right up to teardown day. The Mark II GCA units arrived at the newly assigned airfield in Honiley, just a few miles outside Stratford-on-Avon, too late for extensive use in the European war effort, but the new technology made the Berlin airlift a success during 1948 and 1949, with more than 270,000 flights, and it was also available and used extensively in the Pacific. And it had had a huge impact on the thinking of Arthur C. Clarke.

"Luis's brainchild," recalled Clarke in a speech given at MIT in 1976, "provided me with a peaceful environment, totally insulated from the hard things going on elsewhere—invasions and bombings and so forth—that allowed me to work out the principles of communication satellites back in 1945."

Clarke's first professional sale and payment for a short story happened near Shakespeare's birthplace, but it was probably the fact that the end of the war in Europe appeared certain, rather than a lively Avon muse, that had Arthur C. Clarke writing more.

During these GCA radar days Clarke wrote almost two dozen pieces, most of which were nonfiction. There were some notable exceptions, however. The short story "Rescue Party," with its optimistic view of humanity's future among the stars and its effective punch-line ending, was written at the Honiley airfield in March 1945, although it didn't appear in *Astounding Science*

Fiction until May 1946. This was the first story Clarke sold professionally. *Astounding* editor John W. Campbell sent a check for the then significant amount of $180.

It was 1945—Clarke's last full year in the Royal Air Force— and he wrote whenever he could. The fact that the German High Command surrendered unconditionally on May 7, 1945, allowed everyone to begin thinking about the future.

Gradually Clarke started thinking more about rockets and space travel and less about his wartime concerns of microwaves and radar. He and about a dozen other loyal members of the British Interplanetary Society corresponded with one another again and began making postwar plans. The society's public relations efforts would be much easier after the war, Clarke realized, thanks (ironically) to Germany's rocket development. No longer could people *easily* dismiss the BIS members as screwballs, nuts, and crackpots. The war proved that large rockets could be built and flown; Germany had built thousands of them toward the end of the war. But while the credibility of BIS members and their goals was less of a problem, there still was no single, motivating reason to build very expensive rockets.

The question that Clarke and his fellow space cadets were focusing on when the war ended was: How can rockets make money? Once rockets could deliver profits, plenty of money would become available to build them. Many crazy schemes were proposed, although the mail-carrying rocket schemes of the 1930s were no longer seriously considered. Then Clarke came up with a promising idea, which he developed in more detail and subsequently published. It was a system of geostationary satellites that could provide global communications.

That summer Clarke further refined and elaborated on his concept during his off-duty time while stationed at Honiley. A July 1945 excerpt from his personal journal belies the ultimate importance of the seminal piece that resulted from this work:

"Started typing out my thesis on the space station, which I'm calling 'The Future of World Communications.' I'll send it to *Wireless World* first, I think. Handed it in for censorship on the sixth. It runs to 3,000 words and four drawings."

It was Clarke's unique combination of interests during 1945— his wartime specialties of microwaves and radar and a renewed concentration on rockets and space travel—that proved essential to the genesis of "Extra-Terrestrial Relays." Published the following October, it became his most famous nonfiction article, but not until long after its initial publication.

Little did Clarke know that this single article (and a relevant letter to the editor of *Wireless World* that he'd written earlier in the year) would eventually establish his name in the science history books as the "father" of communication satellites and the visionary who foresaw the revolution in global communications.

Perhaps he did not foresee the impact of an article that would bring him numerous awards and honors because he viewed it as having been conceived in a continuum of scientific exploration by others before him. Clarke has, in fact, said that his "early disclosure may have advanced the cause of space communications by approximately fifteen minutes" and has been careful to point out possible influences. He dismisses as "ridiculous" the idea that he is somehow responsible for discovering the actual geostationary orbit itself, noting that the concept goes way back to Kepler and Newton.

Clarke has also acknowledged the possibility that a series of science fiction stories by George O. Smith—published in *Astounding Science Fiction* in thirteen installments over three years beginning in late 1942, which became known as the *Venus Equilateral* series—influenced him. When Ballantine Books reprinted Smith's stories in *The Complete Venus Equilateral* in 1976, Clarke wrote in the introduction: "It is therefore quite possible that these stories influenced me subconsciously when, at Stratford-on-Avon during the closing months of the war, I worked out the principles of synchronous communications satellites now embodied in the global Intelsat system."

Whatever the possible influences (and even minor ones have been brought forth in various essays), Arthur C. Clarke's "Extra-Terrestrial Relays" is original and historically significant. And it is interesting to note that in February 1945, some eight months before "Extra-Terrestrial Relays" appeared, *Wireless World* printed a letter from Clarke under the title "V2 for Ionospheric Research?" It pointed out that the German V2 rocket could be utilized as an important research rocket after the war and that if it were outfitted with a second stage it could reach orbital velocity.

"I would like to close by mentioning a possibility of the more remote future—perhaps half a century ahead [twenty years too late].

"An 'artificial satellite' at the correct distance from the earth would make one revolution every 24 hours; i.e., it would remain stationary above the same spot and would be within optical range of nearly half the earth's surface. Three repeater stations, 120 degrees apart in the correct orbit, could give television and microwave coverage to the entire planet."

A second typescript was written in late May 1945, although it didn't see print until 1968—just a year before *Apollo 11's Eagle* landed on the moon with its crew of two. Clarke typed up six copies of "The Space-Station: Its Radio Applications," with its nineteen neatly numbered paragraphs, on his Remington Noiseless Portable and then circulated it privately to a few friends in the British Interplanetary Society. Over the years one of these original copies found its way to the Smithsonian Institution.

After discussing the obstacles to global communications using traditional technologies, the author suggests that they all can be overcome with space stations. "All these problems [for example, how to link television systems around the planet] can be solved by the use of a chain of space stations with an orbital period of 24 hours, which would require them to be at a distance of 42,000 km [22,300 mi] from the centre of the Earth. . . . The stations would lie in the Earth's equatorial plane and would thus always remain fixed in the same spots in the sky, from the point of view of terrestrial observers."

In late June, Clarke used this "memorandum," as he calls it, as the basis for his now famous piece, whose subtitle was a question: "Can Rocket Stations Give World-wide Radio Coverage?"

The answer, of course, is yes. Clarke explains how the various problems can be solved: the rockets, the frequencies, the power requirements, and the number of "rocket stations."

"A single station could only provide coverage to half the globe, and for a world service three would be required, though more could be readily utilised. . . . The stations would be arranged approximately equidistantly around the earth, and the following longitudes appear to be suitable:

"30 E—Africa and Europe.

"150 E—China and Oceana.

"90 W—The Americas.

"The stations in the chain would be linked by radio or optical beams, and thus any conceivable beam or broadcast service could be provided."

In August 1945, just a few days after the *Enola Gay* dropped the atomic bomb on Hiroshima, Clarke received the proofs of his article. The bombing induced him to add a short epilogue predicting that atomic power would bring "space travel half a century nearer." Years later, however, he admitted that he had been overenthusiastic.

Wireless World was hardly *Life* magazine, and Clarke would have to wait until the 1950s for his work to reach larger audiences. When the satellite pioneer John R. Pierce asked his friend to write the introduction to his 1968 book *The Beginnings of Satellite Communications*, Clarke obliged. It was here that he told of how the 1945 publication of "Extra-Terrestrial Relays" was received with "monumental indifference." He could remember no response whatsoever, neither positive nor negative, to its appearance.

"[O]nce I had got the idea down on paper, I more or less lost interest in it myself. There seemed nothing more that could be said until technical developments had validated (or invalidated) the basic concept."

Years later Clarke learned that "Extra-Terrestrial Relays" had in fact generated interest in some quarters. One was the U.S. Department of the Navy, which had initiated a study on the future uses of rockets and spaceflight in 1944. Robert P. Haviland was conducting the study, and he read Clarke's article. Improved communications were vitally important to the navy, and Clarke's article was a valuable resource. In fact a formal program was begun as a result, and experts believe that this program was a major reason for the acceptance and development of artificial Earth satellites in the 1960s.

Someone connected with the U.S. Navy study or with an early RAND Corporation report gave a copy of Clarke's article to the *Los Angeles Times*, and this resulted in a science piece on the subject for a lay audience. Written by William S. Barton and published on February 3, 1946, the article was titled "Tiny 'Moons' Circling Earth Proposed as Long Distance Broadcasting Aid." While Clarke was incorrectly identified as a "Scientist Who Fought V-2 Rockets" in the subheading, the concept itself was explained accurately.

"A scientist's plan," it read, "to solve television, wireless telephone and telegraph long distance broadcasting problems by establishing, with the aid of rockets, manned radio relay stations that would forever circle the earth like tiny moons, is receiving serious consideration."

The newspaper stated that scientists in the Los Angeles area were taking the proposal seriously and considered it a real possibility for the future.

"Extra-Terrestrial Relays" has withstood the test of time. While Clarke's estimate of satellite size was off—he envisioned the relay stations as large and manned as opposed to small and unmanned due to the fact that transistors and the entire micro-electronics revolution were not foreseen in the 1940s—all the fundamental principles presented were valid.

Wireless World paid Clarke forty dollars to publish the article, and though he has never complained about the amount, he has had a lot of fun speculating about the monetary value of his communication satellite concept (how many billion?) had he been able to patent it.

Over the years many people have asked him why he made no attempt to patent his concept. The idea, he admits, never occurred to him, and he blames his own lack of imagination. He has asked himself, his readers, and his audiences if he should have published such an important paper in the open press.

After all is said and done, however, Clarke has had no regrets about the matter: "For in my heart of hearts, I believe that I've received everything that is due to me in terms of recognition from the people who really matter." He added that while others like scientists John R. Pierce and Harold Rosen have had the tough challenges and responsibilities of transforming a paper idea into real and complicated hardware systems, he has had all the fun.

The first great technological aid to education was the book. You don't have to clone teachers to multiply them. The printing press did just that and the mightiest of all educational machines is—the library.

"Electronics and Education" (1980)

6
THE PROMISE OF SPACE

Clarke's five years in the Royal Air Force had been much more stimulating and exciting than his stint auditing various government accounts, and he soon realized that a career as a civil servant was not the life he wanted. So before he was demobilized on June 21, 1946, he began thinking about how he would make a living once he resigned from His Majesty's Exchequer and Audit Department. His writing had brought in a small income, and it wasn't unreasonable to think it could be increased. Still, Clarke knew it was risky. He also knew that he had the farm to fall back on if all else failed. Then, toward the end of his RAF days, two friends persuaded him to enroll in a university and pursue an education in science.

One of these friends was fellow BIS member Val Cleaver, who, along with Clarke, worked to revive and reorganize the society after the war. Both men would serve terms as chairman during the postwar years. They shared the same interests and were the best of friends. Cleaver's wartime work involved propeller development for the De Havilland Aircraft Company. In 1946 he was invited to start a rocket division for the company, and he later became the chief engineer for the rocket division of Rolls-Royce.

The other friend and adviser was Flight-Sergeant Johnnie Maxwell of the Royal Canadian Air Force, who had been on the Yatesbury staff and had become another good friend of Clarke's. The two spent several leaves and holidays together before Maxwell returned to Canada.

Their advice to Clarke was straightforward: because of his considerable talents, he should pursue a scientific education after the war rather than continue his civil service work.

Clarke agreed and applied for one of the college grants from the British government that had been established specifically for students whose studies were interrupted by military service. Of course that meant he was not eligible.

"I was swiftly rejected on very reasonable grounds, and I do not recall being unduly depressed by this verdict," he wrote. Clarke knew what he wanted, and as a novice writer he was inured to rejection. He knew he'd shortly be accepted and enrolled in a college course of his choice; all that was required was a sustained and focused effort.

For his focus Clarke drew again from his writing experience. In November 1945 he had entered an essay contest sponsored by the *Royal Air Force Quarterly*. The essay topic, "The Rocket and the Future of Warfare," was right up his alley, and he won. (Some forty years later science writer T. A. Heppenheimer pointed out for the first time that the essential concept of mutual assured destruction was contained in Clarke's essay long before it became the policy of the United States.)

When the new Labour government came into power after the war, a young member of Parliament with a distinguished war record in the army came to prominence. His name was Captain Raymond Blackburn. "He was one of Churchill's fair-haired boys," recalls Clarke. "He was very young and had a distinguished army career." Even better, he knew something about rockets, made several references to them in his speeches, and had actually written about them. Spotting an opportunity, Clarke sent Blackburn his award-winning paper, which had been published in the spring of 1946. As a result, the two men became friends, and Clarke received an invitation to meet with the war minister.

"That was through the meeting arranged by Blackburn," recalls Clarke, "and we talked about rockets. I went to the toilet beforehand, and when I came in and greeted the minister, at that exact moment I found that the back of my shirttail had not been tucked back into my pants. I was shaking hands with the war minister with one hand and furiously tucking in my shirttails with the other. It was in the dining room at the House of Commons."

When Clarke's university grant request was turned down, he asked Blackburn for help. "In a very short time, my grant was approved," says Clarke, "and I applied for admission to King's College, London."

Housing was also a problem. Although the flat at 88 Gray's Inn Road was untouched by the Blitz, it had been in the center of a terrace. As Bill Temple describes it, "Its inner walls had become outer walls. Everything adjacent had been bombed out of existence." Added Clarke years later, "A Luftwaffe bomb had neatly excised the pub at the end of the block where we entertained so many of our friends."

Fortunately, the housing obstacle too was overcome. Clarke arranged for room and board at the home of Eric Taylor and his family on 72 All Souls Avenue in northwest London. Taylor, an artist and teacher, had been stationed near Ballifants during the war and had gotten to know the Clarke family.

"He lived with us for about two years," Taylor recalled. "He had the small spare bedroom, and it was a bit cramped, but he seemed to fit in with anything that was going on.

"Arthur was utterly and entirely immersed in his own work, incessantly pounding on his old typewriter when he was not on campus. It seemed a sort of fanatical drive to put down what was developing in his mind. He did not seem to indulge in any university fun and games in his absolute concentration on his work, and it appeared almost as if it was a race against time.

"Arthur introduced us to the then new invention—a portable radio [not a transistor radio, but one with miniaturized vacuum tubes or "valves" as the British call them], very small for the time, which he carried wherever he went. He was very fond of classical music, which was his other main interest."

Clarke's favorite music included Sergey Rachmaninoff's piano concertos, the Paganini transcriptions, and the symphonic poem *Island of Death*; Edward Elgar's *Violin Concerto* and his symphony in E-flat; and Edvard Grieg's piano concerto, one of the most popular ever written.

Clarke now also enjoys early Beatles, especially *Sgt. Pepper's Lonely Hearts Club Band*, and Pink Floyd's *Echoes*.

When he enrolled at King's College on October 7, 1946, Clarke was pursuing a bachelor of science general degree. Astronomy had been his first choice, but it was offered only at University College, which had no room.

"I had three subjects," explains Clarke, "pure math, applied math, and physics. This was the entire curriculum—a hard grind on three hard subjects. The applied mathematics that McVittie taught consisted of dynamics, statics, orbital mechanics—those are the ones I remember best—and perturbation theory. Of course, I've used that in many of my stories."

McVittie was the famous cosmologist and astronomer George McVittie, the most memorable professor Clarke had. "He taught me applied math, and I taught him about rockets!" Clarke says with genuine pleasure. "He once referred to me as one of his ablest students."

The compliment was returned in 1956 when Clarke's collection of short stories *Reach for Tomorrow* was published. In the preface McVittie's onetime student says that the story "Jupiter Five," written in June 1951, required twenty or thirty pages of orbital calculations and should be dedicated to McVittie, who taught him how to do them.

Fellow students also were aware of Clarke's intellectual powers. Says classmate David Fowke, "I was allowed to take the course in three years, coming right out of school, whereas Arthur did it in two. Interestingly enough, in spite of my having three years, I was only able to get what we call second-class honors, which is one stage down in the standard level, whereas Arthur, taking only two years of it, sailed away with first-class honors, the highest standard that can be achieved and achieved only by a select few.

"Arthur had a much quicker brain than I had. Often I would go to him and say, 'What the hell does this mean?' and he would help me sort out some of the difficulties I was having with studies. This would have been primarily in physics, which became his main interest.

"Although our degree course covered all aspects of math as well as physics, I think Arthur saw the math as something that was useful—a useful tool in developing his interest in physical things."

During his first full year at King's College, 1946–47, Clarke began his duties as BIS chairman. It was, in fact, his involvement with the British Interplanetary Society and the British Astronomical Society and his technical friendships that took up all his time when he wasn't in class or studying. As part of that work Clarke tried to bring like-minded individuals into the BIS. One of them was David Fowke, who resisted due to lack of time but did get a glimpse of Clarke's burgeoning scientific persona.

"Everybody wanted to talk with Arthur," Fowke remembers. "Even in those days he was recognized as an expert, an authority in that field, and everybody wanted to put ideas to him, sound him out, or just ask him for explanations of particular problems or aspects of interplanetary flight. People would queue up to talk with Arthur before or after he spoke. They were always keen to have him as a speaker."

Indeed it was apparently a paper he delivered to the BIS in the summer of 1946, "The Challenge of the Spaceship," which was later published in the society's *Journal* and subsequently revised, updated, and reprinted several times, that brought the great playwright George Bernard Shaw into the fold. In that paper Clarke evoked Shaw's name, and soon after giving the speech he read Shaw's *Back to Methuselah* and was moved by a closing speech that spoke of "starry mansions" and the great cosmic domain of life.

"This, I thought, showed a considerable sympathy with the ideals of astronautics," wrote Clarke, "so I sent Shaw a copy of the British Interplanetary Society's *Journal* containing my lecture— not in the least expecting a reply."

But a reply he got, in the form of one of Shaw's famous pink postcards, dated January 25, 1947.

"Many thanks for the very interesting lecture to the B.I.S. How does one become a member, or at least subscribe to the *Journal?*" Shaw asked. He then went on to present his theory on what caused Geoffrey de Havilland's experimental jet plane to crash in September 1946. De Havilland was Shaw's neighbor.

Clarke was perplexed by Shaw's theory and didn't quite know how to reply. The fact was that Shaw's main point in his letter, that de Havilland's jet aircraft "reached the speed at which the air resistance balanced the engine power and brought it to a standstill," was, said Clarke, "complete nonsense." Clarke pointed out the flawed thinking in two letters, points that he says Shaw took well, with little argument. George Bernard Shaw joined the BIS when he was ninety-one years old and continued to be an active member until his death.

Clarke's recruiting skills did not always prevail, however. One person he failed to convert was C. S. Lewis. Clarke first wrote to Lewis in December 1943, while he was in the RAF, and began writing again when he became chairman of the BIS during his college years.

In some of his novels Lewis attacked scientific humanism in general, and scientists and astronauts in particular, and praised traditional Christian values. In *Perelandra* Lewis refers to the "little rocket societies" bent on exporting the crimes of mankind to other planets.

This was enough to make Clarke see red. He wrote to Lewis, his powers of rational persuasion dominating his sense of injustice and anger—for the most part. The long letter condemned Lewis's cynical views of science fiction and interplanetary flight. This began a correspondence lasting for several years in which Clarke defended the goals of the BIS and his own dreams for the future of space travel and what he hoped would be the future cosmic adventures of *Homo sapiens*.

More than once Clarke asked Lewis to give a lecture to the BIS.

"It would only be fair to point out that your position might be somewhat analogous to that of a Christian martyr in the arena," Clarke wrote, adding that many members admired his writings even if they did not always see eye to eye with them.

Lewis declined: "I hope I should not be deterred by the dangers! The fatal objection is that I should be covering ground that I have already covered in print and on which I have nothing to add."

A face-to-face meeting was eventually arranged—probably, says Clarke, by Lewis's wife, Joy. Accompanying Clarke to the well-known Oxford pub the Eastgate was Val Cleaver.

"Val and I stayed at the Mitre in Oxford, which is a wonderful non-Euclidean building with no right angles in it, no two rooms the same," recalls Clarke. "This little guy, whose name I didn't get, was in the background. Then I found out his name was Tolkien."

"Needless to say, neither side converted the other, and we refused to abandon our diabolical schemes of interplanetary conquest. But a fine time was had by all, and when, some hours later, we emerged a little unsteadily from the Eastgate, Dr. Lewis's parting words were 'I'm sure you're very wicked people—but how dull it would be if everyone was good.'"

The second time Clarke met J. R. R. Tolkien was at the luncheon for the International Fantasy Awards in 1952. "And his publisher was there," says Clarke. "His publisher was a tiny little man. And Tolkien leaned over and said, "Do you know where I got the idea for the hobbits?' and gestured toward his publisher."

In his capacity as BIS chairman Clarke could bring in as lecturers not only those he knew would spark lively controversy but also those who had served as personal inspirations. One such speaker was W. Olaf Stapledon, whose address was entitled "Interplanetary Man." Clarke at this time was already fictionalizing some of Stapledon's themes in work that would become known in the 1950s and would launch his career in the prosperous U.S. market.

"Perhaps the final result of the cosmical process is the attainment of full cosmical consciousness," Stapledon said, "and yet (in some very queer way) what is attained in the end is also, from another point of view, the origin of all things. So to speak, God, who created all things in the beginning, is himself created by all things in the end."

Clarke's academic work load, as heavy as it was, did not preclude his writing. Several of his classic short stories—"The Fires Within," "Inheritance," and "Critical Mass," for example— with their Clarkean twists and surprise endings, were written and published during this time. So too were a variety of nonfiction articles, many of which appeared in the *Journal* and the *Bulletin* of the British Interplanetary Society.

After completing his coursework and exams for the first year of study, Clarke eagerly fell to writing. He'd made notes for a novel for more than a year, and the end result was to be his first space novel. Its writing was driven by the enthusiasm of youth, and it was completed in twenty days. Never since has he written anything so fast. In between typewriters at the time, Clarke handwrote the entire manuscript on school exercise books that had been issued by the Royal Air Force during the war. (Ironically the novel was not published until four years later, and then in magazine format; it appeared in book form in 1953.)

When he was finished, he had produced *Prelude to Space*, which contained the germs of many of the themes the author would explore over the next fifty years. A major theme is the importance of international cooperation for large-scale space expeditions, a concept central to *2010: Odyssey Two*. Another is the Stapledonian perspective in which millions of years pass before us, as in the famous opening sequence of *2001: A Space Odyssey*.

Not surprisingly, the novel was primarily a vehicle to present Clarke's ideas and convictions about the promise of space, and many autobiographical tidbits appear throughout the book. The dedication itself points to its major influence: "To my friends in the British Interplanetary Society—who by sharing this dream, helped to make it come true."

In a 1975 preface to the book Clarke places his early novel in the tradition of space pioneers such as Tsiolkovsky, Oberth, and von Braun, who wrote space fiction as a means of conveying their ideas to the general public.

"I must confess," he wrote, "that I had similar propagandistic ideas in mind when planning this book."

So be it. Many of Clarke's early visions in *Prelude to Space* have proved correct or nearly correct. Like the Apollo missions, there were three crew members aboard the novel's moonship. Although the novel's first manned moon landing didn't take place until 1977 (Clarke was eight years off in his estimate), its prediction for when an unmanned rocket would hit the moon's surface was accurate: 1959. And more than once, Clarke presented his concept of a system of communication satellites. From the then-future perspective of 1977, one protagonist gave an overview of space history: "The great radio and telegraph companies *had* to get out into space—it was the only way they could broadcast television over the whole world and provide a universal communication service."

While global communications represented the technology of unification in the 1940s, the atomic bomb was the technology of disintegration. It was this new threat of global holocaust that worried many people. Clarke was one of them, and his writing reflected his concerns.

During Clarke's college years, two of his short stories appeared in *King's College Review*. "Nightfall," better known as "The Curse" when it was first reprinted in *Reach for Tomorrow* in 1956, was initially published in the *Review* in December 1947, though Clarke remembers writing it while still in the Royal Air Force. It is a powerful story about nuclear war, filled with haunting images, the last of which is Shakespeare's gravestone and its carved epitaph sinking beneath the deadly glow of the river Avon:

> Good frend for Iesvs sake forbeare,
> To digg the dvst encloased heare
> Blest be ye man yet spares thes stones,
> And cvrst be he yt moves my bones.

Then in December 1948 the *Review* published "The Forgotten Enemy" (the advancing enemy from the north is a force of nature), which was eventually reprinted at least a dozen times in various collected stories, including *Reach for Tomorrow*.

Fantasy: The Magazine of Science Fiction published "The Fires Within" in August 1947, but for some reason Clarke used one of his pen names—E. G. O'Brien. The story concerned a dense form of life dwelling in the Earth's subterranean depths, and it may have been influenced by the 1936 discovery and proof of the existence of Earth's inner core by observing diffracted P waves.

Clarke continued to write prolifically even while continuing with a year of postgraduate studies at University College, to which he was entitled under his program.

"I decided to devote my time to astronomy in my final year," wrote Clarke, "but to my disappointment found it extremely dull. I fell into the hands of an elderly professor whose main interest was instrumental defects. He spent his entire lecture time deriving long equations showing how all the possible errors in azimuth, right ascension, elevation, declination, latitude, and longitude were related and how one could correct for them."

During the Christmas holidays, he wrote a story, "The Sentinel," that has often been called the seed for *2001: A Space Odyssey*—an idea that Clarke finds annoying. In fact ideas from several other stories were folded into the creative mix for the book and film that would come two decades later. In "The Sentinel," for example, the extraterrestrial artifact discovered on the moon was very different from the black monolith of the film and novel: it was "a glittering, roughly pyramidal structure."

"Unlike most of my short stories," recalled the author, "this one was aimed at a specific target—which it missed completely. The BBC had just announced a short story competition; I submitted 'The Sentinel' hot from the typewriter and got it back a month later. Somehow, I've never had much luck with such contests." Nevertheless, it became one of Clarke's most famous stories due to the *2001* connection.

Clarke's graduate studies in astronomy remained dull. "Luckily I escaped after a single term," he wrote. "Before terminal boredom set in, the dean called me to his office and said that he'd heard of a job that would suit me perfectly. I applied and got it; and he was right on target."

Clarke was hired as assistant editor of the journal *Physics Abstracts*, which had been published by the Institution of Electrical Engineers (IEE) since 1900. It was considered one of the primary abstracting journals in the sciences. The editor of *Physics Abstracts* and Clarke's boss was Dr. Bernard Crowther, who had studied under Sir Ernest Rutherford, the Nobel Prize–winning British physicist.

After World War II there was a tremendous backlog of abstracting work to be done, and Clarke became one of the needed reinforcements for the task of classifying and indexing everything published (in all languages) in the physical sciences. There were about one hundred abstractors in all, including some multilinguists who could tackle any subject in any language without having any knowledge of it beforehand.

"My job was to go through mountains of journals (we had cupboards-full of German and Japanese publications that had not yet been opened), and to see that everything of value was abstracted, so that it would be readily available to the world's scientific community.

"I probably had a bird's-eye view of research in physics unmatched by anyone else on Earth during this period since *every* important journal, in *every* language, passed across my desk. And the abstracts were edited there, on the way to the printer."

When the subject held a personal interest for Clarke, he occasionally would write the abstracts himself. He also contributed the heading "Astronautics" to the index system—no surprise to anyone who knew how fluent he was in the subject.

Outside work hours Clarke and his gang of about fifty fellow space cadets met every Thursday evening at the White Horse pub (conveniently located on Fetter Lane, just off Fleet Street) to exchange ideas and discuss books and stories they had read. The pub would become the fictional location for Arthur C. Clarke's humorous tall tales of science fiction written during the early 1950s and first published as Tales from the "White Hart" in 1957.

One Thursday night at the White Horse in 1950, Clarke met Mike Wilson for the first time. Wilson was an energetic young man with plenty of ideas and things he wanted to do. He was working in a London hotel as a wine steward at the time, but he had been at sea in the merchant marine. Wilson also enjoyed science fiction and got on well with the White Horse gang. Clarke and Wilson hit it off immediately, and the friendship began to evolve.

Mike Wilson told Clarke about his skin-diving experiences in the Far East during one of his voyages. Clarke became enthusiastic and decided to take skin-diving lessons, first practicing in local swimming pools and later actually renting an Aqua-Lung and diving in the English Channel. This was the beginning of their globe-trotting adventures throughout the 1950s and 1960s, their eventual business partnership, and a long-term friendship.

"I had been assistant editor for only about a year," Clarke says of 1949, "when the crucial point came when my spare-time income began to exceed my full-time income, and I realized my job was interfering with earning a living. Had this not happened, I might have spent the rest of my life quite happily at the IEE surveying the advance of physics from my Olympian height. Perhaps the deciding factor was my first book commission. Because of this outside income, I became a full-time writer."

The contract, with the British publisher Temple Press, was for writing Interplanetary Flight, a nonfiction work on spaceflight. The book evolved from a two-part article, "Principles of Rocket Flight," which was published in the British journal The Aeroplane in January 1947, and from "The Dynamics of Space-Flight," which appeared in the Journal of the British Interplanetary Society in early 1949.

"When Interplanetary Flight appeared in May 1950," says Clarke, "it was not only surprisingly successful but was quickly followed by an American edition."

The book's success actually may not have been surprising considering its uniqueness. It was the first book in the English language to present the basic theory of spaceflight with any technical detail, and general readers were not intimidated by equations because all the mathematics were put into the appendix. One reader who was a teenager then and has since acknowledged its influence on his future is Carl Sagan.

"When I was in high school," he wrote, "I knew that I was interested in the other planets and I knew that rockets had something to do with getting there. But I had not the foggiest notion about how rockets worked or how their trajectories were determined. Then I came upon an advertisement for a book called *Interplanetary Flight* by one Arthur C. Clarke. You must remember that at this time there was hardly any respectable nonfiction literature on the subject. I sent away my money and breathlessly awaited the arrival of *Interplanetary Flight*.

"It was a modest-looking book, beautifully written, its stirring last two paragraphs still of great relevance today. But the part about it that was most striking for me was the discussion of the gravitational potential wells of planets and the appendices, which used differential and integral calculus to discuss propulsion mechanisms and staging and interplanetary trajectories. The calculus, it slowly dawned on me, was actually useful for something important and not just to intimidate high school algebra students.

"As I look back on it, *Interplanetary Flight* was a turning point in my scientific development."

Clarke has admitted that he regards his first published book with "particular affection."

"Never in my wildest dreams," he wrote, "could I have imagined, when I was writing the book in July 1949, that exactly twenty years later I would be standing at Cape Kennedy, since renamed Canaveral, watching the first men leave for the moon."

Clarke's American editor at Harper, George Jones, had been a colonel in the U.S. Air Force during the war and was enthusiastic about his subjects. Jones would remain Clarke's editor for almost twenty years, and he and his counterpart in England, Jim Reynolds, later encouraged Clarke to write an even more popular book about space, which became *The Exploration of Space*. It was this book that put Clarke's name and work before tens of thousands of American readers for the first time.

Soon after the publication of his first published nonfiction book, Clarke began appearing on early television to promote science, his work, and the goals of the British Interplanetary

Society. His first appearance came about on quick notice. One spring afternoon in 1950 Clarke was being given an informal tour of the studios by a staff member, and he met the host of a science program. They had an animated discussion, and before long Clarke was invited to appear on the show, titled "The Fourth Dimension."

"He appeared on the screen for 20 minutes," reported the *Somerset County Herald*, "and his talk made television history by being the longest to be televised without any interpolations—in other words, the speaker alone had to hold interest the entire time. This Mr. Clarke did despite the abstruse nature of the subject."

Clarke used a hypothetical one-dimensional world he called Flatland and its shadowy inhabitants to describe the fourth dimension, and he illustrated his presentation with blackboard drawings and conventional models.

"As an educational experiment," wrote the editor of *Times Educational Supplement*, "the broadcast was a welcome contribution. One lesson to be learnt is that for such specialization more time is essential."

In these early days of television, faces had to be plastered with green pancake makeup so they wouldn't appear pasty white on the screen. Fred Clarke remembers Arthur, face painted green, coming home to the house he and his wife, Dot, were sharing with his brother, who had bought the semiattached Victorian brick dwelling in 1950.

"After terrifying my wife and the children, he went upstairs to clean it off and returned half an hour later with a well-scrubbed, glowing but clean face.

"The towels were not so lucky. After four repeated launderings my wife threw them away."

Clarke's persistence in leaving daily chores such as laundry to others gave him more time to think about spaceflight and the future. In the fall of 1950 he came up with what he considers one of his most important ideas. His technical piece "Electromagnetic Launching as a Major Contribution to Space-Flight" appeared in the November issue of the British Interplanetary Society's *Journal*. It described how an electromagnetic launch system could be built and applied to great benefit in the low gravity of the moon. Such an accelerator also was described several times in Clarke's fiction of the 1950s. The heroes of his young-adult novel, *Islands in the Sky*, are saved by such an electromagnetic launcher on the moon's surface; his short story "Maelstrom II" has such a launcher central to its plot; and a similar device is used as a weapons launcher in his 1955 novel *Earthlight*.

"It is also widely recognized," he wrote in the BIS *Journal*, "that interplanetary travel will not be practicable on the large scale until propellants can be obtained on the Moon, with its very low gravitational potential. . . . [A] possible long-term solution to the space-flight problem may be found in the use of electromagnetic accelerators on the Moon, launching the fuel mined there into suitable orbits round our satellite." He backed up his moon-based launch system with plenty of numbers and equations.

This basic system was adopted by Gerard O'Neill and fellow space colony enthusiasts in the 1970s when they planned their large-scale space habitats during workshops and study groups. It was called a *mass driver* during this period—"a nice name," says Clarke, "until one tries to think of a propulsion system to which it *can't* be applied." O'Neill and his colleagues worked out many of the engineering specifics and built and tested some models of the electromagnetic mass driver. It became a major element in some of their space-industrialization scenarios in the late seventies. And most experts agree that some version of Clarke's electromagnetic launcher will be an essential component of any moon base built in the twenty-first century.

The fall of 1951 was hectic. Clarke was again waging one of his in-print battles against someone who was spreading falsehoods about space and rocketry. On August 9, 1951, the *Picture Post* had published an article on space travel written by its "scientist," Derek Wragge Morley.

"It was utter nonsense," says Clarke. "He was an entomologist—an expert on ants!—not even an authority on space travel. And I wrote a letter [as chairman of the BIS] pointing out all his errors, and the idiot flatly said we didn't know what we were talking about.

"I remember one phrase he used—that step rockets had no relevance to space travel! I wrote to a number of people, including Wernher von Braun, who wrote back, enthusiastic, as one space cadet to another. It was a formal, 'Dear Mr. Clarke' letter, the first that Wernher ever wrote me."

Von Braun's reply to Clarke began, "You called on me as a

brother-in-arms in your war with the PICTURE POST and I can only hope that I shall not disappoint you. I scanned all available American press releases on rocket firings in this country, as well as our old (meanwhile declassified) reports and files from Peenemünde, in order to supply you with reliable ammunition."

Von Braun did himself proud and went on to present detailed factual information (three single-spaced pages) that refuted Morley's statements. Clarke incorporated much of this material in his letter to the *Picture Post*, which was published as "Space Travel: We Are Attacked," along with Morley's response, ". . . And Our Scientist Replies."

It appeared that Clarke had won the battle when a month later the *Picture Post* gave considerable space to review the British edition of Clarke's book *The Exploration of Space*. It was a positive review and unusual in that it was written by two reviewers: Derek Wragge Morley *and* Kenneth Allsop. The *Picture Post*, it seemed, was putting a check on Morley.

Clarke didn't meet the man who had so ably assisted him in this particular battle of wits until later in the 1950s. However, their paths crossed indirectly again in September, when Clarke chaired the Second International Congress on Astronautics, which was hosted in London by the British Interplanetary Society. The official subject of the meeting was the "earth-satellite vehicle," but the discussions covered the entire solar system and beyond. It was attended by sixty-three delegates from ten countries. Press coverage emphasized that, for the participants, spaceflight was a practical goal for the next few decades, not a figment of wild-eyed dreamers.

The opening paper, presented by Frederick C. Durant III, who went on to an impressive career in aerospace and a long friendship with Clarke, was called "The Importance of Satellite Vehicles to Interplanetary Flight," written by Wernher von Braun, who had just become a U.S. citizen but couldn't leave the country. The paper outlined a voyage to Mars, which would, of course, require a Herculean effort. Just to build and supply the "satellite station" von Braun proposed as the above-Earth launching base required forty-six three-stage rocket ships to make some 950 trips to orbit! Von Braun's scenario was ambitious, to say the least, and it was expanded and incorporated in his book *The Mars Project*, published in 1952.

Hermann Oberth, one of the three great space pioneers (along with Robert Goddard and Konstantin Tsiolkovsky), also attended. "I had him as my houseguest," says Clarke. "He stayed with us at 88 Nightingale Road during the Congress. But his English wasn't very good, and my German was even worse."

Fred Clarke recalls Oberth as the perfect gentleman at the dinner table.

Meanwhile, one of Clarke's own works focusing on Mars became his first work of fiction to be published in book form: *The Sands of Mars*, whose British edition was published in the fall of 1951.

Like many of Clarke's later novels, the book's plot, which he recalls working out while going for walks around Ash Priors during a visit home to Bishops Lydeard, has a father-son relationship as a significant element. Martin Gibson, a well-known writer, is a passenger on the first spaceliner to the early Mars colony. On the voyage he meets Jimmy Spencer, a young graduate student. It is only later in the novel that Gibson realizes Jimmy is his son from a college love affair:

"All these weeks [of the voyage], in total ignorance and believing himself secure against all the shocks of time and chance, he had been steering a collision course with Fate . . . he was face to face once more with the ghosts of his own forgotten past."

Martin Gibson and his son Jimmy would be the first of many fathers and sons separated in time and space—often forever—in the fiction of Arthur C. Clarke.

When Gnome Press first published *The Sands of Mars* in the United States in 1952, a reviewer for the *New York Times* said that the novel was "written with a quiet realism that reads more like true history than fiction."

Considering all the scientific revelations about Mars in the last forty years, the novel's science holds up quite well. Clarke has not missed the opportunity to point this out, first in a preface written in the mid-1960s and later in an introduction to the 1987 edition.

"I am agreeably surprised to find how little it has been dated by the explosive developments of the Space Age," he wrote when *2001: A Space Odyssey* was being filmed in 1966. And he was equally pleased that this was the first novel to leave the traditional Martian fantasies behind and attempt to depict the red planet with scientific realism.

After the *Mariner 4* flyby of Mars in July 1965 and the Viking landings of July 1976, Clarke did draw attention to one major error in his first published novel. The robots from planet Earth discovered that "the old image of a flat and geologically uninteresting Mars" was false. In his 1987 introduction, he quotes the novel's statement "There are no mountains on Mars" and admits that the discovery of Mons Olympus on Mars (almost three times as high as Mount Everest) has left him "seriously embarrassed." Still, considering the explosion of knowledge about Mars and other planets during the last forty years, time has been kind to Arthur C. Clarke's *The Sands of Mars*. It remains important in the literature as the first novel to incorporate and extrapolate what science knew about the planet in the late forties and early fifties.

All explorers are seeking something they have lost. . . .
                    The City and the Stars *(1956)*

7
NEW SHORES

In October 1951 American agent Scott Meredith telephoned Clarke in London with the news that the Book-of-the-Month Club had just bought the rights to *The Exploration of Space*.

"That's marvelous," Clarke said.

Then there was a pause.

"But what is the Book-of-the-Month Club?"

Clarke's ignorance did not last long. When he heard how much the book club had agreed to pay, he realized the significance of the sale.

In 1947 Clarke had begun sending stories to Scott Meredith, who already had a track record selling science fiction. "Arthur had a very modest sales record at that time," recalls Meredith, who had started his agency in June 1946, "but in those days we took on as a client anybody who had made any sales at all. He would send us everything he wrote, and we began to sell these small stories for him."

Success with the stories encouraged Meredith to go to work finding a U.S. publisher for *The Exploration of Space* after the British edition appeared in 1951. He finally struck a deal with

Harper & Row, which paid the modest sum of $1,000 for the U.S. rights. But that was only the beginning.

"The real breakthrough," says Meredith, "was our sale of *The Exploration of Space* to the Book-of-the-Month Club in the fall of 1951 for a June 1952 club selection. My recollection is that these rights were sold for around $50,000. I am virtually certain it was no less than that. So of course the sale to BOMC was a major advance for Arthur, and even though he only got fifty percent (the other half going to Harper & Row), it was still a lot of money."

It was enough, in fact, to finance the first of many trips to the United States for Arthur C. Clarke, and on April 20, 1952, he boarded the *Queen Mary* at Southampton, England, and sailed to New York. He was thirty-four years old, and, ironically, with the exception of a short trip to Paris in 1950 to attend the First International Astronautical Congress as a British delegate, previously he had traveled long distances only in his fiction.

Clarke's lasting impressions of that voyage are few, but one thing did stand out: "It was wonderful to eat real food after years of rationing," he says. And aside from winning a ship's cup for table tennis, he spent the crossing anticipating what New York City, the mecca of American book publishing, had in store for a relatively unknown British author. Both *The Exploration of Space* and *The Sands of Mars* were scheduled for U.S. publication in the first half of 1952.

It was the Book-of-the-Month Club selection, of course, that allowed Clarke to meet for the first time his American agent, publishers and editors, as well as fellow writers, fans, and new friends. And in 1952 he had little idea how unusual the selection was.

Clifton Fadiman, noted literary critic and anthologist and one of the BOMC judges, lightheartedly recalled in his introduction to *Across the Sea of Stars* that *The Exploration of Space* was chosen "in a moment of wild escapism . . . and sent out to a large, earth-bound and possibly baffled audience."

After having cocktails with Clarke at the Plaza Hotel, Fadiman described Clarke: "The Oak Room is a rather worldly rendezvous. Mr. Clarke is not worldly; he is other-worldly. He spoke of space satellites, lunar voyages, interplanetary cruises, as other men would discuss the market or the weather. As he explained how within a decade three space stations whirling in an orbit about the equator will make possible (indeed one fears inevitable) simultaneous world-wide television broadcasting, our righthand neighbor (a vice-president of CBS) went into a kind of catalepsy. . . .

"To understand a mind like Mr. Clarke's we must realize that during the last fifty years, more especially the last twenty-five years, virtually a new mental species has emerged among us. They are the men who in a real sense live in the future, men for whom the present is merely a convenient springboard."

The U.S. edition of *The Exploration of Space* got front-page reviews in such prestigious newspapers as the *New York Times* and the *New York Herald Tribune*. The reviews were all good. The *Tribune* called the book "the most important yet published in its field." Reviewer Roy Gibbons wrote in the *Chicago Tribune*: "What gives the book such charm and magnetism is Clarke's ability to reduce complex subjects to simple language," an attribute also praised by an *Atlantic Monthly* review.

No question: *The Exploration of Space* was a breakthrough popular science book. Nothing like it had ever been offered before to BOMC's subscribers. Despite this handicap, it was bought very heavily, and the BOMC connection was the first big step toward making Arthur C. Clarke famous.

Contributing to Clarke's growing status was his promotional ability. When Scott Meredith and Marty Greenberg of Gnome Press met the *Queen Mary* in late April, they took Clarke to the Roosevelt Hotel. Soon he was making the rounds of Manhattan, meeting many of the people with whom he had been corresponding and talking about his favorite subjects—rockets, space travel, and books about them.

As it turned out, the tall, lean, bespectacled man they had greeted at the dock was an excellent TV and radio guest. He appeared on "Mary Margaret McBride" and was interviewed by broadcast pioneer Dave Garroway on his innovative early-morning program called "Today."

"I was a great admirer of Arthur's fiction. I had also joined the British Interplanetary Society, and he was president. Maybe that's how we first connected," says the show's creator, Pat Weaver. "I met him several times in the States, but one of the first times we talked about our mutual interest in satellites and the interplanetary stuff. The outer space stuff was the cement. We talked, and Arthur agreed to go on 'Today.'

"He went on the show and explained his invention of the satellite service [his communications satellite concept] in '45.

This was very helpful to me because it meant that I could foresee so many of the developments that would be coming—the hardware side of the business—telecommunications and computerization and miniaturization and all the other things coming up in the new, postwar world. It was fascinating."

Weaver, later president and chairman of the board of NBC, was known for his imagination and invention. Where science fiction was concerned, however, the publishing world lagged behind. The American edition of Clarke's science fiction novel *The Sands of Mars* was much slower off the launching pad than the nonfiction space book. It eventually had three printings for a total of only eight thousand copies.

"In this period none of the major publishing companies, none of the *real* publishing companies, major or minor, were doing science fiction," explains Scott Meredith. "So several basement operations, cottage industries like Gnome Press and Fantasy Press, had sprung up, and they were started by fans of science fiction. These small presses were the only markets for science fiction novels in the early 1950s. This is really astonishing when you think about the fact that so many major houses today are publishing science fiction in large numbers. But in those days, if you wanted to sell a book, it was to someone like Gnome's Marty Greenberg for tiny little sums you had great difficulty collecting."

Meanwhile, Clarke continued on his multimedia course, which, through Scott Meredith, led him to Olga Druce, producer of the popular "Captain Video and His Video Rangers" TV show.

"I was in the first few months of producing 'Captain Video' when I met Arthur," Druce recalls, "and he was on the set a lot. The studio was in the old Wannamakers building on Ninth Street and Broadway. I didn't know a damn thing about science fiction, but I had just taken over the show for General Foods. We did five live half-hour shows a week for $6,500. Can you imagine?

"Arthur never actually wrote for the show; he wasn't the slightest bit interested in that. He was always having fun and making fun of me in a kind way. But he also inspired me. He was appreciative of what we were trying to do for the youngsters. And these five- and six-year-olds would come down to the studio, talking the space lingo of asteroids and galaxies, which I never did learn, even as the show's producer. These young kids used to come down and look around the studio. They'd seem a bit confused. Then they'd ask, 'Where's all the space?'

"Arthur was a friend of the show, and I considered him my private consultant. He was always so nice about helping me, always with a smile and always kidding in a gentle, loving way. Never condescending. He knew Al Hodge, who played Captain Video, and Don Hastings, who was the Video Ranger, and he knew some of the writers such as Jack Vance, Damon Knight, and Walter Miller.

"He helped me a lot. For example, he advised me when I wanted to have a spaceship built and nobody wanted to pay for it. He told me what to ask for, which was a big help because I had to deal with all the unions, and I had to save up enough money from my budget to pay for it. Well, we actually built the spaceship and did the first special effects for space on the air. We were also the first program to use a TelePrompTer.

"I had two painters building these effects, and Arthur used to advise them. And you know what? When Arthur did *2001* years later, he contacted these guys. I don't think Kubrick gave them a job, but Arthur remembered and contacted them and sent their names in to Kubrick. That's the kind of guy Arthur is. It's really a rare gift that he has. He has a wonderful gift of friendship."

At least one short story came out of this friendship and connection with the "Captain Video" show. It was "Security Check," first published in June of 1957 and reprinted the following year in his collection *The Other Side of the Sky*:

"His hand had gone out to the switch: the screen had filled with moving shapes—and, like millions of men before him, Hans was lost. He entered a world he had not known existed—a world of battling spaceships, of exotic planets and strange races—the world, in fact, of Captain Zipp, Commander of the Space Legion."

Though Clarke did not write for "Captain Video," he did write his first television play during the spring of 1952. "All the Time in the World" was adapted from his story by the same name, which was published in *Startling Stories* in July 1952. He wrote the TV script adaptation in one day, and ABC aired it on its "Tales of Tomorrow" series on June 13, before the story appeared.

In a rare fanzine article for this stage of his career, entitled "'Ego' Visits America," Clarke wrote up some of his American experiences. He tells of "watching the performance of my first TV play and showing unbelievable restraint when the credits didn't materialise (it later transpired that the commercial had crowded them out)."

Clarke has always been a natural and enthusiastic promoter of the many ideas that excite him. This includes his optimism about the promise of space. Whenever he's had an opportunity to speak before a group and talk about the subjects he loves, he has done so with relish.

Sam Moskowitz, editor and historian of science fiction, who was his host in Newark on one such occasion, remembers that Clarke spoke at a number of small New York meetings in the 1950s. "If he was around," says Moskowitz, "he would talk. He was a very good extemporaneous speaker, and he had a strong speaking voice. It was never hard to get Arthur to talk. He really knew his subjects. If he was talking about science, he could defend himself. And if he was talking about science fiction, he could also defend himself. So if somebody in the audience challenged him, and the guy was not right, then the person was in more trouble than he bargained for.

"One thing that impressed me about Clarke—and I had met a number of other British authors and fans—was that he was the first one to ever offer treating you to lunch or dinner. He's a very warm and friendly person. He's likable, and he's never gotten over being an avid science fiction fan.

"Arthur smiles and laughs a lot; he's always had a good sense of humor. And sometimes he's a real back slapper. He's also a great optimist and has never lost his enthusiasm. The same guy that was there when he was eighteen is still there."

Those qualities made like-minded Americans accept Clarke into the fold, garnering him invitations to "in" conferences such as the informal, unstructured 1952 Midwestcon in Bellefontaine, Ohio. Clarke and Marty Greenberg drove out from New York, bringing with them a few fresh-from-the-press copies of *The Sands of Mars* to spread around, and Clarke gave an informal talk and slide show on spaceflight based on *The Exploration of Space*.

"Arthur was accepted as one of the in group," says David Kyle, cofounder of the Gnome Press. "This is where he became acquainted personally with so many people that he had known about in America." Many well-knowns and soon-to-be well-knowns were present: Robert Bloch, creator of "Psycho"; E. E. "Doc" Smith, one of the early masters; Harlan Ellison, when he was just a kid of eighteen; and others, including young Ian Macauley, who became an instant friend. In 1952 Macauley's fanzine, *ASFO* (Atlanta Science Fiction Organization), published "'Ego' Visits America," which was just the beginning of an enduring relationship marked by mutual intellectual inspiration. In fact Clarke's juvenile adventure book *Islands in the Sky* contained this dedication: "To Ian, from an Elizabethan to a Georgian."

When he wasn't at work promoting his books, Clarke spent much of this first U.S. trip getting to know the luminaries of science and science fiction. On June 25 he flew to Colorado Springs to visit Robert Heinlein and his wife, Ginny. As Clarke remembers, their friendship had begun with correspondence following publication of *The Exploration of Space.*

"We spoke about everything under the sun," recalls Clarke, "but especially the film *Destination Moon*, which was based on Bob's novel *Rocketship Galileo*, although it was a very long way from it. We both felt very strongly about the production. It was the first attempt to show space travel realistically. A landmark film. Even now, four decades later, some of it stands up quite well, although portions of it are obviously naive. Bob and I were both crazy about it."

Released in 1950 by George Pal Productions, it had a script written by Heinlein and Rip Van Ronkel, produced by Pal, and directed by Irving Pichel. Chesley Bonestell created a two-foot-high, twenty-foot-long lunar panorama for the film that took a hundred men about two months to build. The film took a realistic, documentary approach as contrasted to the earlier space opera films like *Flash Gordon*, and for this reason it was an important film for the genre. The special effects won an Oscar in 1950.

The Heinleins were gracious hosts in their modern home on Mesa Avenue. On one side trip Clarke and Heinlein climbed Pike's Peak; on another they traveled in the opposite direction by being lowered in a bucket down to the bottom of a Colorado gold mine. It was, according to Clarke, a "wonderful visit," that transformed a growing friendship into a close one.

Clarke remembers Heinlein as "very protean. Heinlein was everything—like Walt Whitman. There were aspects of things I didn't like, but I never argued seriously with him."

Clarke's next stop, in New Mexico, was arranged by Heinlein, who had set up a visit with fellow writer and friend G. Harry Stine. Harry Stine met Clarke at the dusty airport in Las Cruces. He had just graduated from college and gotten married and was working on rockets at White Sands Proving Ground. Naturally Clarke wanted to visit the facility.

"There was no way I was officially going to get him in White Sands because he was a foreign national," says Stine. "So I took the bit in my teeth and went out and got him a visitor's pass. We drove out in my light green '52 Studebaker. He spoke English and looked like an American, and I got him the visitor's pass. I didn't take him anywhere where he could see anything that might possibly be classified. Still, if I knew then what I know now about security, I probably wouldn't have done it because I was really putting myself way out on a limb.

"We were out at White Sands for only a very short time," recalls Stine. "We remained in the headquarters area, the so-called containment area, and did not go out to the launch sites. I just didn't want to take that chance. We visited a telescope station which contained one of the rocket-tracking telescopes.

"At that time they were firing three or four Honest John missiles a day. The Honest John was a technical battlefield missile. Arthur and I saw one launched. It was launched off at an angle, and there was a lot of noise and smoke and so forth. After things died down, Arthur turned to me and said, 'Why get excited about anything that doesn't go straight up?'"

During the Las Cruces stay Clarke met many local space enthusiasts who had gotten the word that he was in town. One such enthusiast was already famous. This was Clyde Tombaugh, the man who'd discovered the planet Pluto in 1930.

"He met Tombaugh and everyone else at the base because he gave a lecture at the local section of the American Rocket Society," says Stine, "about his book, space travel, and what-have-you." Clarke was also in his second term as chairman of the British Interplanetary Society, the activities of which he would often mention to his audiences. He always managed to sign up a few new members this way.

After a couple of days Stine drove Clarke to El Paso and put him on an airplane heading west. He was off to visit California in early July before returning to New York City.

Clarke's stay in Los Angeles was hectic, and he loved it that way. He appeared on several radio and TV shows to promote *The Exploration of Space*, and he spoke to various groups, including the Los Angeles Science Fiction Society and a more scientific audience at the Radiation Laboratory at Berkeley. It was here that Clarke met Luis Alvarez for the first time, having just missed him in England during the war.

He remembers walking inside the windings of the Berkeley Bevatron while there. "I have a theory that when they switch on that magnet, San Francisco will think 1906 has happened again," he wrote in his fanzine trip summary in 1952.

The machines he saw were not confined to the subatomic microworld. Clarke also visited the great California telescopes at Mt. Palomar and Mt. Wilson.

"Probably the most dramatic moment of my entire trip came at Mt. Palomar when I went up four stories in an elevator, stepped out on to a balcony—and found myself facing the two-hundred-inch telescope," he told the fans. His guide was Fritz Zwicky, the astrophysicist who predicted neutron stars and discovered supernovae.

He also rode a bucket to the top of the 150-foot tower telescope on Mt. Wilson with Dr. Robert S. Richardson, one of the first astronomers to take space travel seriously.

An unusual honor was bestowed on Clarke when he was in the San Francisco area. Some 150 scientists and space enthusiasts gathered at an Oakland banquet of the Elves', Gnomes' and Little Men's Science Fiction Chowder and Marching Society to hear Clarke speak and to pay tribute to him for his contribution to the general public's understanding of space and its future promise. George Finigan, research chemist and society chairman, presented their guest with the third annual Invisible Little Man Award. The trophy was a base of a statue with a pair of mysterious footprints above the inscription. That was it; no statue was affixed to the base.

While Clarke's general policy is never to discuss politics or the international situation in his speeches, on this occasion he did mention that his first visit to America coincided with the Republican National Convention and wisely used this fact to discuss the future of space.

"Of course this first televised national party convention interested me," he said, "because when we get a relay chain of space stations established twenty-two thousand miles above the equator, television service can extend over the whole planet. But I did not expect the Republican party to take official cognizance of the topics the science fiction writers love to mull over.

"Imagine my surprise when convention chairman Joe Martin talked about spaceships and interplanetary travel in his opening address. After that, nothing could drag me away from the convention program. Maybe one of the elves or gnomes had got Martin's special ear in a smoke-filled room."

Clarke enjoyed some memorable visits with other writers and science fiction devotees before returning to New York. He met "Mr. Science Fiction," Forrest J. Ackerman, the genre's number-one fan, who discovered science fiction way back in 1926 with the October issue of *Amazing Stories* and has been a serious fan and collector ever since.

"He came to what is called the Los Angeles Science Fantasy Society and gave a talk one evening," Ackerman recalls. "I mainly remember his strange pronunciation of the word *moon* [as moo-un]."

A visit to Paramount Studios provided some Hollywood stars for Clarke to meet, and he had lunch with George Pal, who was producing *War of the Worlds* at the time. He also visited the set. "I saw Pal doing some of the special effects," says Clarke, "which you couldn't do nowadays. The Paramount technicians were nervously trying out the death rays, which were so important to the film."

Clarke loved the idea of seeing his own work on film, a hope that seemed likely to be fulfilled in the fall, back in England, when he met film producer William MacQuitty for the first time. MacQuitty is best known for his 1958 film *A Night to Remember*, about the sinking of the *Titanic*.

"I met Arthur in 1952 at Pinewood Studios," says MacQuitty. "I wanted to make a film of one of his stories, and eventually [many years later] we settled on his book *A Fall of Moondust*, the lunar equivalent of a submarine disaster. I failed to persuade the Rank Organization to back the film, but I formed a lasting friendship with Arthur. He had a sparkling interest in nature and was always bubbling over with challenging ideas."

Almost four decades later, in 1989, Bill MacQuitty and his wife visited Clarke in Sri Lanka and took in the sights. When they dropped by one last time to say good-bye, Clarke said, smiling, "I have news for you. Michael Deakin has just phoned from America to say that he wants to film *A Fall of Moondust*. How about that for full circle!"

"Lucky chap," said MacQuitty. "Wish I'd got it."

Lunch with Ray Bradbury was one of the highlights of

Clarke's Los Angeles visit. "Arthur came over to the house," says Bradbury. "We lived in a different place then, a little tract house over on Clarkson Road in Los Angeles, near Westwood Boulevard. So he came over to visit at our small house, and I think he was there for quite a few hours, and we had a wonderful chance to get to know one another. We had a lot to talk about.

"I think I was working on the screenplay for *It Came from Outer Space* that summer."

A photograph taken during their 1952 meeting shows Ray Bradbury holding up a copy of Arthur C. Clarke's *The Exploration of Space*. Why did Bradbury hold up (and in a modest way promote) a copy of Clarke's book?

"Because he asked me," says Bradbury, leading into a hearty laugh. "And he's a very pleasant guy. I don't consider that we're competitive. I think that we're friends."

Bradbury's last statement seems to be the consensus among the Americans Arthur C. Clarke got to know in the spring and summer of 1952. He made friends across the country—despite a few foibles.

Fred Durant, whom Clarke had met in London in September 1951, describes with affectionate amusement Clarke's June visit to the Durant home in Centreville, Virginia:

"Pip and I had been married almost five years and had an eight-month-old baby when Arthur arrived at our house in the country. Because of the temperature, Pip had poached a salmon and served it cold. Well, Arthur wouldn't eat anything cold. He was a real fussbudget.

"We ensconced him in a large second-floor bedroom. He really did live out of a suitcase, with things flung everywhere. It was a mess. And of course we did his laundry.

"Pip was busy with our baby, and about the second or third time Arthur said, 'Pip, would you get me a glass of water?' my wife replied, 'Arthur, now you come with me. Here is where we keep the glasses, here's where you turn this thing, and water comes out.' And Arthur said, 'Oh, yes, sure. I'll do it myself.' He was laughing and everything. 'That would be easier for you, wouldn't it?' It wasn't arrogance. It was the way he was brought up. Women took care of everything in the kitchen."

Arthur C. Clarke returned to England on August 1, 1952. He had launched two books and left his mark on America.

Everyone can make mistakes; it's easy to misjudge your distance when you're driving by earthlight.

A Fall of Moondust *(1961)*

8
WRITER, WITH WIFE

The American adventures over, Arthur C. Clarke returned home to 88 Nightingale Road and typed on his Remington portable for the rest of the year. Aiding him in establishing and maintaining a disciplined writing routine was brother Fred's first wife, Dorothy. The three shared the house, which remained Clarke's London base until the 1980s, and Dorothy became his secretary.

"We set aside two rooms for Arthur," says Fred Clarke. "A big room upstairs in the front of the house became his study, and a smaller adjoining room was his bedroom.

"Arthur got on very well with my wife, Dot. She was a trained secretary and did a lot of his typing. She cooked. She did all his entertaining. If anybody turned up unexpectedly to see him, there would always be coffee or a meal ready to serve. He took a very dim view of me when I let her go off with somebody else."

Fred Clarke's first wife, now Dorothy Jones, remembers Clarke's unique and enviable view of the mundane chores of daily life. "He didn't want to have anything to do with what he called the 'mechanics of life.' And so Fred and I looked after him. Fred did the painting and repair, and I did the washing, ironing, and entertained his guests and so on.

"Arthur was a very disciplined writer," says Jones. "He would get up about half past seven, get washed and dressed, and then come down and have breakfast. After having breakfast and reading about three or four newspapers, he'd say 'Right!' and upstairs to his study he'd go. By nine o'clock he'd be thumping away at his typewriter.

"The pattern was that I'd get on with chores and take him up a cup of coffee about eleven o'clock and bring my notebook along. He then dictated letters while we had our coffee. Once in a while, if I'd get sidetracked with chores, he'd come down about quarter past eleven and say, 'Dot, are we going to have some coffee?'

"Arthur, like so many of us, was a creature of habit. He used to come out of his study when his stomach called. He'd come down for lunch, but then he'd go straight up again and work till the top of five or six o'clock. We'd have an evening meal, and invariably he went back up to his study, whether he was listening to his music or reading or whatever he was doing.

"Every time he completed a book, as he got toward the end, his working pattern accelerated. He'd be up at seven, and he'd be upstairs typing at quarter to eight, and he'd still be typing at nine o'clock at night—as if he were telling himself, 'I've got to get it out.'

"The vision I have of Arthur," says Jones, "which always makes me laugh and which was always the same, was when he'd come downstairs and say to me, 'I've finished it! I've finished it!'

"And I'd say, 'Wonderful!'

"'Right. That's it. I'm not going to do anything else.'

"He'd then sort of mooch around a bit and then go off upstairs again. About an hour later, he'd come down and sort of gently kick the wall and say, 'This is terrible. I've got nothing to do. I have to go off and start another book.'

"I once asked him about inspiration, and he said, 'No, no. You go up there and work. It's a job. You go and you put a piece of paper in the typewriter and you get on with it.' And that's what Arthur did.

"He also said to me during those early days that as soon as his writing became a chore he was going to stop. So obviously it's still a pleasure to him or else he wouldn't be doing it. He may feel compelled to do it, but he enjoys it. He was never happier than when he was writing."

After the excitement and successes of the U.S. trip, there was motivation aplenty to keep his literary roll going. He settled into his second-floor study and wrote. As always, there were several in-progress writing projects. The most important, however, and the one to which he devoted much of his time, was an intense effort on a new novel. It would prove to be one of the most important he would ever write: *Childhood's End*.

Earlier in the year Clarke had begun working on Part I of the novel. His trip to the United States then took priority, and he didn't get back to work on it until late August. With the exception of his duties as BIS chairman, he wrote steadily until December. "I finished the first version on the nineteenth of December, 1952," says Clarke.

The origins of what many readers and critics still consider Arthur C. Clarke's best novel go back to July 1946, when he wrote the short story "Guardian Angel" just before he began his studies at King's College.

"I submitted it to *Astounding*, [and] it was promptly rejected by John W. Campbell, Jr.," Clarke admitted in a short introduction to the story when it was reprinted in the early 1980s. "I would like to find that letter, because I wonder if John asked whether I had borrowed my aliens from his own story, 'The Mightiest Machine.' (In a word, Yes. . . .)"

He rewrote the story in 1947 and sent it to Scott Meredith to market. After a few rejections Meredith asked James Blish, who was then working at the agency, to rewrite it. Blish did a rewrite, added a new ending, and the piece went into the marketplace for the second time. This version was sold and published in the April 1950 issue of *Famous Fantastic Mysteries*.

How did Clarke feel about Blish's ending? "I thought it was a rather good ending. But I didn't even know about it for a long time; this was rather naughty of Scott," Clarke says, laughing.

So it was in February 1952 that the story's author went back and expanded "Guardian Angel," which became Part I, "Earth and the Overlords," of *Childhood's End*. By December he had the first draft down. And in late January 1953, as he planned his second trip to the States, he continued to revise and polish the manu-script while Scott Meredith searched for the right publisher. (Some four decades later, in 1990, Clarke was still at it! He wrote a new prologue, shorter than the original, to bring the novel up to date in the Space Age that had not yet been born in 1953.)

When Clarke returned to the United States in April 1953, his first stop was New York. There his agent was in the middle of negotiations with Ballantine Books, which had been recently founded by Ian and Betty Ballantine. Their editor, Bernard Shir-Cliff, recommended that they sign up everything Arthur C. Clarke had to offer at that point. As a result the Ballantines bought *Childhood's End, Expedition to Earth,* and *Prelude to Space.* Thus began a uniquely creative relationship between publisher and author that would give birth to some important books, including a genuine classic.

"As a new house, we were evolving our own thinking on a broad fighting front," says Ian Ballantine. "We were dealing with the fact that hardcover publishers ignored large audiences. The reality was that hardcover publishers didn't know anything. When we were at Bantam before starting Ballantine Books, we sought writers who wrote about what was going to happen next. Arthur is somebody who's very interested in what's going to happen next and what he's doing next. That's why we were very much in gait with Arthur.

"My belief was that the young people had perceived how much more complex everything was than their culture gave it credit for. They wanted to stretch their imaginations. That's why they were interested in books such as *Childhood's End* and *The Lord of the Rings.*

"The editorial cliché at that time was quite the opposite: that science fiction and fantasy was something for kids. We took the opposite view and were given recognition for a broadness of interest from the community of authors. I think Arthur's work contributed mightily to that. He wasn't interested in tricks; he was instead interested in what it really would be like if you literally lived in space."

"When we started Ballantine Books," says Betty Ballantine, "we were quite determined that we were going to do science fiction in book form. Publish it seriously. So somebody had to become cognizant of what was then current. I did an awful lot of reading in the science fiction magazines, read them cover to cover, marking up every story. And Fred Pohl introduced us to several people in the field such as Fletcher Pratt and Lester del Rey. That's how we started. And the results were books such as Arthur's *Childhood's End* and Ray Bradbury's *Fahrenheit 451*—which by the way were published within just months of one another in 1953."

During his New York stay, Clarke went to his new publisher's offices on Thirty-Seventh Street to attend a meeting with the Ballantines and Shir-Cliff. The subject of the meeting was the sequence in which Clarke's next three books would be released. Each book would be published in mass market paperback and hardcover editions simultaneously—one of the many publishing innovations of Ballantine Books. The main edition would be the paperback; the hardcover, printed from the same plates, would have a more modest print run. On the back cover and in the front matter of the paperback these words appeared: "This is an original novel—not a reprint. A hardbound edition of this book priced at $2.00 may be obtained from your local bookstore." The mass paperback edition sold for thirty-five cents.

But which of the three books should be published first?

"We wanted to do *Childhood's End* first," Ian Ballantine recalls, "but Arthur didn't think we should. Arthur thought that *Childhood's End* should wait, that it was a hard book to publish.

"Betty and Bernie and I sat there and said in so many words, 'You're crazy.' We all believed it should be first because it was so important a book, an original novel that had never been published before. It made publishing sense to do a novel which had stature and some heft to it."

Everyone agreed, including Shir-Cliff, who remembers the first time he read the manuscript of *Childhood's End*.

"I was excited and nervous at the same time. It's like watching someone crossing Niagara Falls on a tightrope, and you don't want him to fall off," says Shir-Cliff. "You get to the ending, and you realize he's written himself into a very difficult spot. And you say, 'How is he ever going to bring anything off and end it satisfactorily?'"

Of the many Clarke books the Ballantines published, the only one Clarke ever had misgivings about was *Childhood's End*.

"He was of two minds about what ending he wanted," recalls Betty Ballantine. "He had written two endings. But that's the only time I've ever known him to have any doubts at all about what he was writing."

The doubts may have reflected ambivalence on Clarke's part about his novel's paranormal theme and humanity's transcendental union with the superior extraterrestrial intelligence of the

Overmind. In this respect it was not science fiction based on science, which he came to advocate and represent.

"When this book was written in the early fifties, I was still quite impressed by the evidence for what is generally called the paranormal," Clarke said. Today he admits to being "an almost total skeptic." Why? Because he has seen too many claims exposed as fakes. Says Clarke, "It has been a long, and sometimes embarrassing, learning process."

No matter; it was a powerfully used theme in *Childhood's End*, and tens of thousands of readers have been emotionally jolted by its implications in the work.

Whatever the reason for Clarke's hesitation about releasing *Childhood's End* before his other two books, he ultimately went along with the Ballantines' preferred sequence: *Childhood's End*, then the volume of short stories, *Expedition to Earth*, and then an earlier novel, *Prelude to Space*.

"Arthur was not known as a novelist at all before *Childhood's End* was published," says Shir-Cliff. "He was fairly well known in the science fiction field because he was a frequent contributor to the major magazines. This was a breakthrough for Arthur as a writer. We realized right away that as soon as we published this novel, all his work would have a much wider appeal."

In the meantime, Clarke had yet to finish the last chapter, a task he continued as he headed south, ultimately to the Tampa area. There he planned to visit Dr. George Grisinger, a great admirer of *The Exploration of Space*, who had invited Clarke to try the local scuba diving. On his way to Tampa, Clarke spent time with the Durants in the Washington area, and after publication he sent an inscribed copy of *Childhood's End* to Fred and Pip as a thank you: "With many thanks for putting me up and putting up with me while I wrote the last chapter!"

In actuality the last chapter was not completed until Clarke visited Ian Macauley in Atlanta in April.

Clarke and his young friend, Macauley, had both lost their fathers at an early age, and perhaps this visit influenced Clarke in writing the powerful scene when George Greggson says a silent good-bye to his son Jeff as Jeff leaves forever to become part of the Overmind, the transcendent intelligence into which human consciousness is absorbed.

"There was a mist before his eyes which made it hard to see.

But it was Jeff—he was sure of that: George could recognize his son now, as he stood with one foot already on the metal gangway. . . . Nor would George ever know if Jeff had turned towards them by pure chance—or if he knew, in those last moments while he was still their son, that they stood watching him as he passed into the land that they could never enter."

Speculating on how their discussions might have affected Clarke's writing, Macauley says, "We got to know one another and discussed all kinds of ideas—life, marriage, racial problems, and so on. At that time I was very concerned with the racial problems in the South. Segregation existed, and I was working against it. I belonged to certain antisegregation groups and was very active. Of course I discussed all this with Arthur. He was writing *Childhood's End* at the time, and these discussions about racial problems may have influenced him. I'd like to think that perhaps this is why he chose to make the last person on Earth [Jan Rodricks] a black person."

"It could well be," Clarke responds. "It's perfectly possible. I never met any blacks before I went to America."

On April 20, 1953, Clarke flew to Tampa to meet Helen and George Grisinger and pursue what would quickly become a favorite pastime. Equipped with an Aqua-Lung, he began to explore the Florida waters.

"I was carrying with me my first underwater camera—a Leica, in a cylindrical plastic case I'd purchased from a *Life* magazine photographer," Clarke recalls.

"A whole bunch of us went diving in Tampa Bay on a wreck—a very undisciplined bunch of divers, I might add. It was on this dive that I saw my first big groupers. Some of them got speared, I'm sorry to say.

"We then crossed Florida in George's boat, the *Ah Phooey*, with his little son, Buddy, who later became a submarine commander. We went across and all the way down to the keys, but not quite to Key West. I remember doing a little diving at places along the keys such as Marathon and Tavernier, but my big diving was in Weeki Wachee Spring, north of Tampa."

He tested his camera in the crystalline waters of the springs and there encountered his first challenging subject: "a fair-sized alligator, hanging languidly in the vertical position with its nostrils just breaking the surface. I'd never met one before, and assumed (correctly) that it wouldn't attack a strange, bubble-blowing creature heading confidently towards it. So I got half a dozen excellent shots before it became camera-shy and fled up the nearest creek.

"The Leica photographic magazine published an article and ran my alligator pictures, but the piece isn't listed anywhere. My story 'The Man Who Plowed the Sea' was a product of that period, one of the *Tales from the 'White Hart.'*"

After exploring some of the coastal waters off the keys, Clarke, Grisinger, and their group headed north and stayed over in Key Largo. It was here, on May 28, 1953, Clarke met Marilyn Mayfield, a young woman of twenty-two who was working as the social director of the Ocean Reef Harbor Club, where he was staying. Mayfield was from Jacksonville, Florida. She had been married once and had a young son, Phillip Torgenson.

The sparks flew. "It was just spontaneous combustion," says Clarke. "Electric," Mayfield adds. It all happened very fast; everyone agrees about that. Clarke wrote to Ian Macauley on June 6 after he flew back to New York City.

"Now for some news which is going to shock you to the core, but which I hope you'll be glad to hear. On the way back, up the Keys, we stayed just two days at Key Largo. And in that rather short time, I managed to get myself engaged to a simply stunning girl named Marilyn Torgenson. Incredible to relate, she's gone overboard about me, and when I got back to New York, there was a letter waiting for me with photographs, locks of hair, and 'How soon are we going to get together again?' She's flying up from Florida next week, so that we'll have a chance of getting to know each other better than we did for a few hours at Key Largo. If all goes well, we may get married before we go back to England. She's 22 years old and was married at 17, and has a little boy that's two years old."

"I was absolutely smitten on his looks," Mayfield says. "He was a dandy-looking man, and he sported a Vandyke beard. He looked stunning. The beard was red, blond and red, almost a copper color. Do you know how Errol Flynn would wear a mustache and beard contoured to his face? Well, this is what Arthur looked like. He really looked great. I was shocked rigid when he shaved it off after we were married.

"It was a whirlwind courtship. Arthur wanted me to come up there to New York and visit, but that wasn't something a young woman did in those days, go up and stay with a totally eligible man. I just couldn't do that; I would have had to leave my job and everything.

"After he returned to New York, he called me over the telephone and asked me to marry him. He just couldn't stand waiting."

Within a week of Marilyn's arrival in New York City, on June 15, 1953, she and Clarke were married.

"He didn't want anybody at the wedding," says Gnome Press's Dave Kyle. "I suggested that some of us would be happy to go down and witness the ceremony or just be there, but he wanted to keep it simple. The day before the wedding I asked him, 'What are you doing tonight?' and when he said nothing in particular, I suggested that we gather together some friends and fans from the science fiction club and have a bachelor party.

"Arthur agreed and I organized it. I got a gallon of wine, some cheese and crackers, and that was it. There wasn't much money in those days. About five of us—Arthur, Ian Macauley, Carl Olsen, David Ish, and myself—gathered in Arthur's hotel room at the Roosevelt.

"You could hardly call it a sophisticated gathering. There was nothing stereotypical about it; no blue movies or vulgar jokes. It was a chitchat situation—friendly, intimate, gosh-wow, almost juvenile—about what Arthur was doing in America and what his plans were. And we talked about science fiction and Arthur's relation to it. It didn't last long; I'd say about two hours. We all were science fiction people, and there was a feeling of being close. It's a very strange kind of brotherhood—unique and unusual.

"What we didn't talk about was marriage in general or his soon-to-be wife, Marilyn."

The wedding took place in Manhattan's City Hall. "My first publisher, Marty Greenberg, was there as witness," says Clarke. "And there was another witness, a little guy named Murray who was a sort of gofer for the Scott Meredith Agency."

"Marilyn was a strikingly beautiful girl," says Scott Meredith, "and Arthur was absolutely smitten by her. It happened so fast. He called me one day and told me he had met her. Then, before I knew it, he was married."

His brother Fred remembers him telling the family. "The day

he got married he rang Mother in Somerset and told her, 'I've just got married. This is Marilyn.' He then put her on the line. Mum was surprised and I'm sure a bit worried too. Particularly as he had only known her for less than a month."

Clarke took his new bride around to meet all his New York friends. Everyone agreed: Marilyn was a beautiful woman. Everyone was also concerned: what kind of future was there for a relationship that had gone from first meeting to marriage in less than three weeks?

Marjorie May, one of Arthur's Manhattan friends, remembers him bringing Marilyn around to meet her.

"I thought she was attractive, but I wasn't drawn to her particularly," says May. "And since he met her and married her in a matter of a few days, I thought he had married too quickly. I saw them off to England, I remember, when they were going back to live in London in the summer of 1953. I was a little taken aback that she was leaving her little boy behind with her parents. He was pretty young to leave behind."

For their honeymoon in the States, Clarke and his wife traveled to Pennsylvania's Pocono Mountains and stayed at the Mount Airy Lodge. Mayfield had worked there as social director before going to Key Largo.

"It was just a tiny little place at that time," Mayfield remembers. "I don't know how many days we stayed there, but he had to proofread *Childhood's End* when we were there. It was urgent that he do this, and I was caught up with all the old people I knew, so it didn't really matter."

After the working honeymoon the newlyweds returned to England in mid-July. David Fowke, Clarke's college friend, met them upon their arrival.

"Val Cleaver and I both went along to Heathrow to meet Arthur and his new wife when they arrived back in England. We were both interested to meet her. So we picked them up at the airport, and then we all went back to Nightingale Road and had a meal together.

"Marilyn was attractive and had a lively sort of personality. She didn't have similar interests to Arthur and would have had difficulty in keeping up with him intellectually. My guess is that he found Marilyn attractive. He also has quite a soft spot for people who have had things go wrong for them. Marilyn had been previously married and divorced. She had a small son. So here was a woman who might have been treated harshly and whose small boy needed some additional support. That's my guess."

Clarke wanted to be a father to the boy, and he anticipated having a family of his own with Mayfield. The idea of fathering, in fact, was deeply appealing to him.

"A boy needs his father," thinks the character Heywood Floyd in *2010* while he is billions of miles away from Earth on the mission to Jupiter—another example in Clarke's fiction of an immense gulf of distance and time separating father and son. In many ways Clarke tried to close that gap in his own life.

A bash was thrown for the Clarkes at the White Horse pub on Fetter Lane in London soon after their arrival, and his fellow writers and SF fans all gathered to greet and congratulate the newlyweds. Ted Carnell, editor of the magazine *New Worlds*, presented Marilyn with a beautiful bouquet of flowers.

A surprise to everyone was that Clarke made his appearance without his beard. Word was out that the North American–grown beard was not appreciated by his wife and that's why he had shaved it off.

All of his cronies playfully rubbed this in by showing up with gummed-on beards of various periods and styles—Elizabethan, Victorian, and Edwardian. Marilyn, according to witnesses, was not particularly amused.

Less than a week after their return to England, husband and wife went down to Ballifants for a weekend so that Marilyn could meet his mother and the rest of the family.

"I met his mother, and she was very pleasant and nice," recalls Mayfield. "And Arthur's sister and younger brother too."

If Nora Clarke or any other family member had real misgivings about such a quick marriage, they were not expressed during Marilyn's first visit. Meanwhile, Arthur and Marilyn were having their own misgivings. The relationship was beginning to have problems.

"By the end of a month," says Fred Clarke, "it was pretty obvious that it was a completely unsuitable marriage. Marilyn had no friends in England; she knew no one. She was a lively girl. After all, she had been a social organizer at the hotel. Her job in life was enjoying herself and helping other people to enjoy themselves. Arthur is—and I'm much the same—an unsociable animal. When we want to write or get on with what we're doing, we don't want anybody coming in and saying 'Darling I love you' or whatever, because it throws you. No matter how much darling loves me. And if you're in the middle of a complicated sentence, you're more likely to say 'For God's sake, clear off.'

"Arthur had never been to a dance in his life. He was mostly interested in high-brow music, his writing, and of course reading, two of which are silent hobbies and occupations. The last thing Marilyn wanted was lots and lots of silence.

"My first wife, Dot, took her shopping. Marilyn was always going up to Arthur and saying, 'I want some cash. I'm going to buy a dress. I'm going to buy this, I'm going to buy that.'"

In October, the *Wood Green Observer* printed an article about the newlyweds entitled "A Husband in the Clouds":

"Mrs. Marilyn Clarke, American wife of Arthur C. Clarke, chairman of the British Interplanetary Society and science-fiction writer, finds it [being married to a husband in the clouds] 'fascinating.'

" 'Sometimes when he looks at me I know he doesn't even see me. He's way up on another planet' she said."

The interviewer asked Mayfield if she was able to help her husband with his work.

" 'Yes, by listening,' she said. Although he sometimes writes all day in the 'den' upstairs without saying a word—except, perhaps, 'I don't know,' when Marilyn says, 'Here's your coffee'—he does like to talk about his work with his wife as often as possible. . . .

" 'He sits on a pouffe and types on a coffee table—sometimes I go in the room and I can't locate him at first.' . . .

"When Arthur does come down from 'his other world,' says Marilyn, 'it's wonderful. He'd give me anything I asked for.' What better person than Arthur to give her the moon?

"And, unlike some more earth-bound men, he never forgets the monthly 'anniversary' of their wedding.

"At that moment Arthur looked round the door to say hello, and disappeared up the den again.

" 'I'm going to buy him a space suit for Christmas,' said Marilyn fondly, 'with controls adjustable from earth. I don't want to lose him!'"

Behind this mask for the media, there were frequent verbal battles and sulking. Fred Clarke recalls the rising tension between them at 88 Nightingale Road.

"When Marilyn had a row with Arthur, which was quite

frequent, she'd clear out of the house and go off to Arthur's friends, the Shepherds, without any warning, and spend a night or so there. And Les Shepherd, a very nice chap, and his wife, Lynn, tried to smooth things over."

The incompatibility was not superficial; it was deep and fundamental. Clarke wrote most of the time, of course, which is why he produced so much important work in the 1950s. His young bride didn't know how to fill her time when he was busy. She soon realized that this was all very different from the free time they had spent together in Key Largo and Manhattan.

"I had no idea what a writer's life was like. At that point I was extremely unsophisticated and unworldly. Arthur was totally involved in his work, to the exclusion of everything else. He used to sit at the table—it didn't matter if it was breakfast or lunch or dinner—and he would read most of the time he was eating."

Because Mayfield already had a son, Clarke assumed that there would be children and that she would give him an heir. Soon after the marriage, however, he was shocked to learn that she could no longer bear children because of an incompetent doctor who had not properly treated a tear in her womb after the birth of her son. Clarke was particularly fond of her boy, and he thought Mayfield treated him rather badly, first leaving him in America and then later on leaving him for good with the father, more or less saying that he was the father's responsibility from then on.

"I don't think he would have ever married had he known she could no longer bear children," says his brother Fred. "He would have made a wonderful father, and he was always good with our children and enjoyed them. I remember Les Shepherd saying that Arthur used to talk with his small son about rockets and space travel. One time he explained to the boy all about the reentry of rockets, and Les realized that it was the first time *he* understood it well—and he had a doctorate in science from Cambridge! Arthur can make complex things simple so that everybody can understand them."

When *Childhood's End* was officially published in August 1953, the novel's title had an obvious relevance to Clarke's life at the time: his bachelorhood had also come to an end. As the novel appeared to critical acclaim, the marriage continued to disintegrate slowly. The consequences of a hasty, emotional decision were becoming painfully apparent.

The dedication of *Childhood's End* was telling: "To Marilyn, For letting me read the proofs on our honeymoon."

Upon publication, William Du Bois wrote in the August 27 edition of the *New York Times* that the novel was "mixed by a master's hand" and continued the accolade: "A first-rate tour de force that is well worth the attention of every thoughtful citizen in this age of anxiety. . . . This review can only hint at the stimulation Mr. Clarke's novel offers."

Basil Davenport, who had been instrumental in persuading the Book-of-the-Month Club judges to select *The Exploration of Space*, wrote a glowing review in the *New York Times Book Review*:

"In *Childhood's End*, Arthur C. Clarke joins Olaf Stapledon, C. S. Lewis, and probably one should add H. G. Wells, in the very small group of writers who have used science fiction as the vehicle of philosophic ideas. Having said that, one must hastily add that it is as readable a book, from the point of view of pure narrative, as you are likely to find among today's straight novels."

Childhood's End was an immediate success. The first printing of 210,000 copies sold out in less than two months, and another hundred thousand were printed in November. It was on its way to becoming the international classic it is today with more than fifty printings of the U.S. edition alone.

The reception of *Childhood's End* was a boon to Clarke's literary career, but his marriage was not improving. In the fall of 1953, with Fred and Dot Clarke running the household, Mayfield felt like a fifth wheel.

"Arthur's views on marriage at that time were, I think, very vague," says Mayfield. "It was almost like a hobby that he really didn't want to get into. He wanted it to be a pastime, but it mustn't in any way interfere with his work. I wanted a *marriage*. It was very difficult for me to try and adjust. Finally I could not cope with it."

The split between Arthur and Marilyn came as the Christmas season approached in 1953. A discussion about religion provoked the rift.

"I was brought up in the Presbyterian Church," says Mayfield. "God, country, all that was important in my upbringing. We were talking, and he told me he didn't believe in God and he didn't believe in Christmas. Now, that shakes your basic structure, especially if you believe and you think that everybody else does. And at that age you tend to know it all. Now that I think of it, he may have been as profoundly shocked as I was. He may have considered my belief as much a taboo as I considered his not believing. But I couldn't accept it then, and I kept waiting for God to strike him dead. I was just shocked. I couldn't come to terms with it, so I left him."

Mayfield flew to Paris in late November and then on to Miami in early December. It looked as if the marriage was over less than six months after it had begun. And when Clarke decided in January to visit the United States for the third time, it was in part to work out the details of a separation agreement. There would be no serious attempt at reconciliation; it was obvious to both of them that the relationship could not be mended.

"The marriage was incompatible from the beginning," says Clarke. "It was sufficient proof that I wasn't the marrying type, although I think everybody should marry once. We just each married the wrong person, you see."

The experience, he admits, was enough to scare him away from ever marrying again. "While we were together for only a few months before separating, we were legally married for some ten years." The marriage, in fact, was not legally dissolved until December 1964.

Meanwhile, Ballantine Books had published *Expedition to Earth*, Clarke's first published collection of short stories, in December 1953. And in the process of striving to become the first mainstream publisher of science fiction Ballantine also published that year what is indisputably one of Clarke's greatest short stories. As part of their strategy Ian and Betty Ballantine enlisted the help of author and editor Frederik Pohl.

Because the Ballantines were committed to issuing one science fiction title each month, they had to court and build strong relationships with the top authors in the genre. When Pohl suggested publishing an anthology of the best writers, Ian Ballantine went one step further and suggested that the anthology contain all original stories and that the contributors be paid better than they were by the magazines. This way they could attract the crème de la crème.

Star Science Fiction, edited by Pohl, was the first volume of original science fiction stories ever published, and it became the first such series when volumes two and three were issued later.

Arthur C. Clarke's contribution was "The Nine Billion Names of God," which ends with one of the most memorable last lines of literature: "Overhead, without any fuss, the stars were going out." It's a story of apocalypse, rendered in an ironic tone. Two computer engineers have been hired by a sect of Tibetan monks to program and run a computer to help them generate the nine billion names of God, a project they have been working on for three centuries. According to their belief, once their goal is reached, God's purpose will be achieved and mankind will have completed its reason for existence.

Their work completed after three months, the Westerners have begun their journey home when the stars blink out. Western science directly confronts Eastern religion in this famous story, and the mystic rituals prove correct. The fate of humanity is sealed, and its ultimate insignificance is dramatized up against the immense and mysterious forces of God and the universe.

Clarke had written the story during a rainy weekend in New York City, when he was staying at the Roosevelt Hotel in the spring of 1952. "It was triggered by Lord Dunsany's story about a pair of wheels run by water mills in Tibet—a pair of wheels put on the shaft of a dynamo," he recalls.

Frederik Pohl is convinced it's Clarke's best short story, and Clarke himself puts it on his top-five list, along with "The Star," "The Sentinel," "The Dog Star," and "Transit of Earth," which he considers "probably the best short story of all."

Like all of Clarke's editors over the years, Pohl enjoyed working with him. "Arthur is a very graceful and dependable writer," says Pohl. "His prose is unornamented, but it's lucid, which is a virtue I prize. I always know what he's saying."

Editor Bernie Shir-Cliff agrees: "Arthur didn't require much in the way of substantive editing because his prose was always so clean. Maybe sometimes you'd ask him to amplify an incident or something like that, but he knew what his story was about, and when it came in it was pretty well lined up."

In his dedication to the first edition of the 1955 novel *Earth-light*, Clarke wrote, "To Val/who massacred the second draft/And Bernie who slaughtered the third—/but particularly to Marilyn who spent the advance before I got to Chapter 2." Behind the humor, was there any editorial truth? When asked if he really did slaughter the third draft of *Earthlight*, Shir-Cliff replied, "I probably took out some technical descriptions he loved to do, to keep the story moving. Arthur likes to talk about things. I might say something like, 'Arthur, you've got to bring the people back in and get the plot going again.'"

When Clarke is asked about his actual writing process, he has very little to say. "You know, it's a strange thing. I don't remember ever writing anything. Not any of my books. It's a hole in my life, a big gap in my existence."

Betty Ballantine speculates on the reason for that gap: "Arthur's work is so thoroughly orchestrated in terms of pacing and tension and excitement. It must be that he does it in the back of his head somewhere.

"Arthur mastered English. He was not a great big flaming talent as a writer, but he was brilliant. His mind was so clear and logical that he could take the English language and control it and use it to express the things he wanted it to do. He had a beautiful consistency and control."

When Clarke's clear thinking was applied to a vision of the future that he had enthusiastically espoused, the result was the kind of far-reaching development that emerged from the Hayden Planetarium's Third Symposium on Space Flight.

Soon after Clarke was appointed coordinator of the May 4 event, whose topic was space travel and world thought, he began contacting scientists to speak on various topics.

"I asked who the top guy was on meteorological research, and somebody said Harry Wexler. And so I wrote and asked him to participate," Clarke recalls. He wanted Wexler to speak about future satellite applications for weather forecasting.

In 1954 Dr. Harry Wexler was the chief of the Scientific Services Division, U.S. Weather Bureau. His initial response to Clarke's letter was negative. In fact he thought it was a crazy idea. After all, the planet's weather takes place in the lower levels of the atmosphere—in the troposphere. Clarke then suggested that Dr. Wexler prove how ridiculous the idea was and make that the subject of his talk.

Wexler failed to prove anything of the sort. Instead he became an enthusiastic proponent of the concept of using satellites to forecast the weather. "Wexler's first reaction is the right one for a scientist," says Clarke, "you know, when he gets thrown some crazy idea. I challenged him, and he accepted the challenge. I admire him for it."

Thanks to Wexler's skepticism and Clarke's challenge, a new branch of meteorology was born. Harry Wexler became the driving force in using rockets and satellites for meteorological research and operations—one of the most important international endeavors of science today.

Clarke witnessed another of his visions taking shape during the same U.S. trip. One summer afternoon in 1954 he dropped by the Washington office of Fred Durant, then president of the International Astronautical Federation. Clarke's curiosity was stimulated when several highly distinguished scientists began to arrive for a meeting.

"There was Dr. Wernher von Braun, Dr. Fred Singer, Dr. Fred Whipple of Harvard Observatory, and several scientists from the Office of Naval Research. They were clearly all gathering together for the same purpose, and they all became very tongue-tied when I tried, as tactfully as possible, to discover what that was.

"Not until more than two years later did I find out that this was the first conference to initiate Project Orbiter, a confidential project of the Office of Naval Research to launch a small satellite vehicle."

Eventually, through the complex machinations of Washington politics, Project Vanguard won favor and support and Project Orbiter went into cold storage—and history.

Ironically, when Clarke and von Braun both found themselves guests at the Durant home, the subject was not satellites. "All they did was talk about skin diving into the early morning hours," recalls Fred Durant. "And Arthur indoctrinated Wernher, who became a true believer. Within a few months von Braun got his scuba certificate."

"It was Arthur who introduced me to the sport that has rapidly become my favorite—skin diving," von Braun wrote in his introduction to Clarke's *The Challenge of the Sea*, published in 1960. "I believe that man's insatiable longing for knowledge of what lies beneath the sea stems from the same source as that which prompts him to wonder whether there is life on Mars. Daily, we are learning more and more about the wonders of the sea and the solar system. But we have merely scratched the surface of both."

When Arthur sailed back to England on the *Mauretania* on

July 6, 1954, he knew his next ocean voyage would be a much longer one. By midyear, he had already decided to join his friend Mike Wilson on a diving expedition to the Great Barrier Reef in Australia.

"If you want to continue your mental and emotional growth," Clarke told an interviewer, "every so often you must surprise yourself (and your friends) by changing the pattern of your life and interests."

The Pacific and Orient SS *Himalaya* set sail for Australia from London in early December 1954.

"I can still remember watching the feeble December sun sink into the smoke of the London docks as I sailed away from winter forever. Twelve hours by jet is too short a time in which to relish such a miracle."

It's a wonderful feeling, slowly warming up as you go through the Mediterranean.

Letter to Val Cleaver, June 13, 1960

9
TOWARD
SOUTHERN STARS

Many of Arthur C. Clarke's fans and friends wondered why he decided to give up space for the sea in 1954. Wernher von Braun gave one possible reason several years later. Clarke gave another:

"I now realise that it was my interest in astronautics that led me to the ocean. Both involve exploration, of course—but that's not the only reason. When the first skin-diving equipment started to appear in the late 1940s, I suddenly realized that here was a cheap and simple way of imitating one of the most magical aspects of spaceflight—weightlessness."

The SS *Himalaya* sailed south from London, around Spain and Portugal, then headed east across the Mediterranean. In the days before the ship reached Sydney, Australia, Clarke had time to mull over his plans for the diving trip. He had a nonfiction book contract for *The Coast of Coral* in his pocket, and the adventures ahead would decide what shape that narrative would take. Clarke hoped that he and Wilson would be able to capture on film views of rarely explored seas to intrigue the armchair explorers among his readers. If all went as planned, the trip would produce the fodder for some magazine articles as well as the book.

105

But the genuine excitement came from *not* knowing what adventures and experiences lay ahead. The thrill of the unknown was calling Clarke to far horizons. And he felt a sense of freedom and hope as he left his bad marriage behind him and sailed to distant lands. It was a new beginning for his life and his work.

Clarke used the time on board to prepare for the physical rigors ahead. "A good deal of my time was spent at the bottom of the *Himalaya*'s swimming pool, hoping to improve the capacity of my lungs," he wrote. Clarke suspected that underwater breathing equipment would not be available in the more remote regions of the Great Barrier Reef, and this proved to be true.

"Eventually I was able to stay submerged for almost four minutes [closer to three and three-quarters], but then gave up out of consideration for the other passengers, who viewed my activities with increasing alarm."

It was a dangerous exercise, Clarke admits, and many divers have killed themselves in the process. It is a "trick of hyperventilation," he says, "flushing out the CO_2 in the lungs by taking deep, rapid breaths, thus inhibiting the normal breathing reflex and destroying, for several minutes, any further desire for oxygen. Hyperventilation can also produce permanent brain damage. My God, do you suppose . . . ?"

In a two-page summary of his journey sent to his buddies at the Globe pub in London (they had followed the bartender there from the White Horse), Clarke bragged that he was doing more than holding his breath. "I spent the first 3 minutes of my record dive working out plot details on my next novel, and quite forgot the passage of time. As a result I had to beat off would-be rescuers. Might have managed four minutes without that altercation."

For mental exercise Clarke spent a great many hours *again* revising his youthful novel *Against the Fall of Night*, with which he had become increasingly dissatisfied due to twenty years of scientific developments since the story was first conceived.

"In particular," wrote Clarke in his 1955 preface, "certain developments in information theory suggested revolutions in the human way of life even more profound than those which atomic energy is already introducing, and I wished to incorporate these into the book I had attempted, but so far failed, to write." The revision was major, producing about seventy-five percent new prose.

For pleasure, Clarke completed reading Tolkien's *The Lord of the Rings.* Says Clarke: "It's the only book I read three times—very readable—he's done it once and for all. But I didn't think much of his poetry in *The Lord of the Rings.*"

The *Himalaya* arrived in Colombo, the main port of Ceylon, on December 12, 1954, and remained in the harbor for half a day. There Clarke met one Major R. Raven-Hart—"a sculptor, ex–radar expert, Buddhist, s.f. fan (several GALAXY rejection slips) and author (10 books published)" according to Clarke—whom he put on his short "unforgettable characters" list.

He also met a fellow undersea enthusiast who would become a longtime friend. Rodney Jonklaas, deputy superintendent of the local zoo, was one of the world's leading underwater hunters, a man whose adventures in the waters off Ceylon were legendary. "He was hunting last year [1953] with Bill MacQuitty when a shark stole all the fish he'd shot and attached to his waist," related Clarke. "He thought it was Bill nudging him. . . ." Jonklaas was also the only skin diver Clarke had met who *never* used a snorkel: "I think he can breathe through the back of his neck."

After a brief stop in Fremantle, the *Himalaya* sailed along Australia's southern coast to Melbourne, where Clarke met up with Mike Wilson.

Wilson had left England in early 1954 and had been in Australia for ten months, making contacts in the diving and pearling business (and diving for pearls himself), acting as a film extra, and chatting it up with the ladies, leaving "at least one fractured heart in every major Australian city," said Clarke. This reputation was nothing new for the dashing, roving Wilson—only the continent had changed. "He's accumulated some stunning girlfriends," Clarke informed the Globe crowd, "one of whom is on the cover of a national magazine this week, and several of whom are probably now watching the calendar with some anxiety."

Wilson's sense of daring and love of adventure appealed to the explorer in Clarke, and most of the time Clarke viewed his friend's exploits with the same affectionate amusement with which he reported them to the crowd back in London. Still, there was no doubt that Clarke and Wilson, almost ten years apart in age, made something of an odd couple. Where Clarke was organized and prone to approach life with equanimity, Wilson was somewhat volatile—the only thing that could be predicted about the younger man was that he would behave unpredictably. Clarke, acting as the father figure, tended to have a stabilizing effect on Wilson; in Wilson, Clarke had found a comrade in adventure.

"We spent a couple of days in Melbourne and were able to greet a few of the local science fiction fans, all of whom would have been quite at home in the Globe," Clarke's letter continued. "They told us just what the Sydney fans were like; that had a familiar sound, too. . . .

"We did one very important piece of business in Melbourne," he went on. "The manufacturers of the Aussie Porpoise apparatus, which is a great advance on the Aqua-Lung, are giving us three units and their new air-compressor for nothing but depreciation charges."

A short sea voyage north, and the adventurous duo arrived in Sydney a few days before Christmas 1954. The *Himalaya* sailed through the morning mists of Sydney Harbor and passed beneath the great harbor bridge. At last—the final landing. The Great Barrier Reef—the largest coral reef on planet Earth, stretching 1,250 miles along Australia's Queensland coast—was still more than a thousand miles away, but it began to dominate their thoughts as they started planning and training in earnest for their expedition.

One Aqua-Lung and five underwater cameras were in Clarke's luggage. Wilson had brought two more Aqua-Lungs from England. So along with the loaned Porpoise equipment, they had a good start on the gear needed for their journey to the reef. The trip north, however, was still a few months away. Besides the additional preparations they had to make, they had to wait for the end of the cyclone season and fair weather.

In the ensuing months Clarke had the opportunity to accli-mate himself to diving in the Australian waters. Their boarding-house was near Balmoral Beach, a sandy stretch with a group of oddly sculptured rocks at one end; it was considered an excellent spot for beginning divers. Besides getting sunburned on Christmas Day—"something that never happened to me in England this time of year"—Clarke's new experiences included a New Year's Day encounter with his "first big shark at close quarters. I was swim-ming about thirty feet offshore," he wrote to Val Cleaver, "in one of the bays around Sydney. Visibility about 15 feet. Had just chased a small shark into the kelp when the big boy started circling me at the limit of visibility. He went around me once, with a beautiful, effortless movement. Then I swam towards him in the hope of getting a good look and he shot away. He must have been the best part of 10 feet long. I must be getting a bit blase, since all I felt at the time was 'Goody—a shark!'"

After three months of preparation, Clarke and Wilson were ready to embark on their expedition to the Great Barrier Reef. The cyclone season was over, and on March 23 the two men loaded the Chevy and began the first leg of their journey. Heron Island, one of the Capricorn group, was their destination. Oval-shaped and about half a mile long, the island is densely covered with a forest of pisonia and pandanus trees, except where clearings have been cut for the buildings. As the tides rise and fall, Heron Island undergoes a transformation. Only the small forested sand key is visible above the Pacific at high tide, but when the tide is low, the island enlarges a hundred times as the vast and flat reef becomes exposed.

"We had planned to stay . . . for no more than three weeks before moving further north along the Queensland coast," wrote Clarke. "As it turned out we stayed on Heron Island not three weeks but six."

Inclement weather was the reason for the extension. There were only four perfect days and another four that were acceptable for productive underwater work. The rest of the time it was overcast or a gale was blowing or the water was churned up and dirty. For ten days straight, the rain never ceased, and Clarke and Wilson were forced to remain in their tin-roofed hut just a few yards from the reef.

"We are just going to stick here until we have all the material we need," Clarke wrote to Val Cleaver, "even if we see no more of the Reef. So far, in about six days actual diving, we have obtained both black and white and color shots better than any I've ever seen reproduced.

"We're particularly pleased to have got from the US a dozen rolls of the new Ektachrome color film, 3 times as fast as any other on the market. Processed our first few rolls last night, with exceptional results."

In early June 1955 Clarke and Wilson packed up their thousand-plus pounds of gear, boarded the *Capre* launch vessel, and sailed back to the mainland. They would head north to the pearl-diving waters and continue their exploration of the Great Barrier Reef before returning to Heron two months later to get better photos in better weather.

"I was to see many other islands—some more beautiful and more romantic," wrote Clarke, "but for the rest of my life the words 'Great Barrier Reef' will always conjure up a certain submerged coral garden forty feet down and half a mile out from Heron Island."

Wilson and Clarke wanted to sail the entire length of the reef, but time and money prohibited this. Instead they drove back to Brisbane and then flew north in a DC-4, touching down at Cairns, the last town of any size on the coast, on June 15, 1955. The reef was a mere ten miles off the mainland at this point, but their plan was to stay a few days and continue northward.

It was another five hundred miles to their destination—the extreme northern tip of Australia, Cape York, and the Torres Straits beyond. The reef continued into Torres Straits, the body of water between Australia and New Guinea, which was scattered with many small islands.

The last leg north was flown in a DC-3. Clarke and Wilson landed on Horn Island's airstrip, which had been built during World War II. Half an hour later they boarded a launch with all their gear and headed across the narrow channel to Thursday Island.

Because it is surrounded by many other islands, Thursday Island offers protection from the open sea. The Fisheries Research vessel *Gahleru* was in port, as were a dozen or so commercial pearling luggers. The *Gahleru* would become Clarke and Wilson's home for much of their stay in the Torres Straits. On one of its expeditions the *Gahleru* pointed west toward the Gulf of Carpentaria, stopping engines off Crab Island and drifting so that the divers, including Clarke, could work the bottom for shells.

Clarke's lead weights were adjusted, and he went down the ladder into the water. Wilson held him at a depth of ten feet so he could clear his ears. Then the lifeline was played out, allowing him to sink to about sixty feet.

"I did not enjoy losing my freedom of vertical movement," Clarke wrote, "which I had always taken for granted in all previous dives I had ever made. Now I was weighted down, and had to depend upon someone on the surface when I wanted to move upward. But this could not be helped; a diver who has to walk along the bottom has to be heavily weighted; otherwise he will drift away in the slightest current."

For a while Clarke watched the helmeted divers work the bottom for pearl oysters, and then he decided to surface and get a camera. He went straight to the bottom on the second descent and experienced the reassuring click in the right ear but not the left. Immediately he was in severe pain, and no amount of blowing or yelling into his mask helped.

"Soon after I had reached the bottom there was a curious soft explosion inside my ear," says Clarke. "The feeling of pressure vanished immediately, and I was able to take notice of my surroundings once more."

The drifting *Gahleru* was dragging Clarke along the seabed. During the onslaught of ear pain he had become somewhat tangled up in the lifeline, air hose, and camera straps but had managed to unravel himself. He stayed down observing for a short while, took a few photos, and then surfaced.

"As I came back to the surface, I once again became aware of pain in my ears—and suddenly realized that my face mask was full of blood. I must have been a fairly gory sight when I removed the mask."

Wilson threw a bucket of water in his face and told him he had probably punctured an eardrum. Clarke was skeptical because he could still hear perfectly but soon realized that it was the only explanation.

Explaining how it happened in a letter to Val Cleaver Clarke wrote: "My own fault—I should have signalled. Anyway, no harm done, and it didn't interfere with visibility or hearing. It's all been quite an adventure. . . .

"Next week we go back to Brisbane and hope to arrange a trip in a whaler before going out to Heron Island again to see if the weather is better. Still hope to leave for NY on Oct. 7."

Both Wilson and Clarke would have been happy to spend a few more weeks in the Torres Straits, but pressures were mounting. "Two publishers and three taxation departments [are] breathing heavily down the backs of our necks," wrote Clarke, exaggerating a bit. Fortunately there also was some long-awaited finished business to celebrate.

"Just signed the contract for THE CITY AND THE STARS

with Harcourt Brace. (They've reversed the title. I don't feel very strongly—they both seem just as good.)" The novel that was left after Clarke had revised *Against the Fall of Night* so thoroughly became *The City and the Stars* and was published in 1956. Clarke, who usually thinks of the large scale first and the particulars second, had originally titled it *The Stars and the City*.

Their adventures in the Torres Straits over, Clarke and Wilson flew back to Brisbane, arriving on July 6, 1955. Clarke was eager to "start on the 50,000 words of COAST OF CORAL still to be done."

Later in the month the *Capre* sailed thirty miles off the coast of Queensland and delivered Clarke and Wilson to Heron Island for the second time. Luck was with them: the long spell of bad weather was just coming to an end, even if the coral waters were a bit colder.

"We now have some beautiful underwater colour shots," Clarke wrote to Cleaver on August 2, "though still no sharks . . . [photos of which were always desirable].

"The weather here has been good to excellent, with several perfect days. I've been annoyed by a cracked rib, but it hasn't interfered with diving. Did it climbing over the side with an Aqua-Lung on my back."

While the sea had dominated Clarke's life for the first seven months of 1955, some electromagnetic waves reached his wooden hut on Heron Island on July 29 that profoundly influenced his lifelong dream of space travel.

Clarke was coming in from a morning dive along the reef. He was still wet, walking along the shore to the hut and taking in the new world above the water, sensing the weather changes since he first dove under.

"I happened to switch on the radio and was transfixed by the news that President Eisenhower had authorized the launching of scientific satellites during the International Geophysical Year," he recalls.

Excited by the news, Clarke immediately thought of the 1951 meeting in London of the International Astronautic Federation, when Val Cleaver, Fred Singer, and he were thinking of ways to get the public and governments interested in scientific satellites.

After a few rounds of drinks at the Arts Theatre one night, one of them suggested that what they needed first was a snappy name for such a satellite program. After some doodling they came up with the acronym MOUSE, which stood for *minimum orbital unmanned satellite of earth*.

"In the next few months," Clarke later wrote, "Fred produced a blizzard of papers describing what MOUSE (better still, MICE) could do; his predictions were uncannily accurate, and every one of them has since come true. The publicity campaign was extremely successful, and MOUSE appeared in technical journals all over the world."

As remote as Clarke was at the time, he knew it was a historic moment for space and went to considerable difficulty and expense to cable Fred Singer: "Congratulations from the bottom of the Barrier Reef. May the MOUSE bring forth a mountain."

"I was on Heron Island," remembers Clarke. "The only contact with the mainland was the ferry coming back and forth every few days. I was very excited and rushed over to Mike and said, 'We must get a cable to Fred Singer.' I had to give some money to someone and give them the telegram, which got scrambled. By the time the cable got to Fred Singer, it was not only unintelligible, but he had to pay charges."

Clarke and Wilson were back in Sydney by late August, at which time Clarke dispatched eighty thousand words of *Coast of Coral* to his publisher. A month later, as he and Wilson prepared to leave Australia, Clarke brought Cleaver up to date on his literary affairs.

"Harper's are very enthusiastic about *Coast of Coral*, but feel that a bit too much of it is underwater and want more general adventures. I've told 'em that the contract was for an 'Underwater Book on the Great Barrier Reef,' and that in fact only 1/3rd is specifically underwater anyway. Also that all our printable adventures went into it!

"They seem in a hurry and want the photos as quickly as possible. Harcourt Brace also seem determined to let no grass grow under their feet. I had proofs of *The City and the Stars* on *airmail* paper two weeks ago, and bunged them back. For once (ahem) I am quite confident that this is far and away my best book, and you'd bloody well better like it as this time you don't have to share the dedication with anyone.

"I have *no* plans for writing in the immediate future—hurrah!"

There was also some news about what would become one of Clarke's most famous short stories. "'The Star' was sold to some obscure U.S. s.f. mag [*Infinity Science Fiction* in early 1955] for $80. None of the slicks would touch it—*Saturday Evening Post* thought it was 'blasphemous'. Let's see if it does better in the U.K."

Says Brian Aldiss, novelist and historian of science fiction, "I've always admired 'The Star' for that absolutely outrageous and grabby opening sentence, 'It is three thousand light-years to the Vatican.' I think that stands as the great opening line of all time. It acts like a kind of pun in that it creates connections between really two conflicting systems of belief—the scientific and religious. And in that way I think it embodies a great deal of Arthur's philosophy. Looked at in that light, it's not altogether different from the famous closing line of 'The Nine Billion Names of God.' Again you have the two conflicting systems. And a lot of Arthur's work is right there on that kind of crossroads."

Clarke was pleased with a good review of *Earthlight* by Francis McComas that appeared in the *New York Times* in June 1955, "saying that I am, 'beyond cavil, our ablest practitioner of science fiction.' 'Our'"? he asked his London friend.

Arthur C. Clarke and Mike Wilson left Australia in early October, and over time Clarke's Australian experiences would serve his work well. Heron Island was a central locale in his 1957 novel *The Deep Range*, and it was also used as a model, though not by name, for Dolphin Island in the 1963 adventure novel of the same name.

As their Qantas Constellation climbed out over the Pacific, Clarke and Wilson cast their eyes northward up the coast toward the Great Barrier Reef. It was one of the most unusual formations on the planet—as Clarke wrote in *Dolphin Island*, "the mightiest single work of living creatures on the face of the Earth."

Beautiful night last night. Southern Cross (a very feeble constellation) just above the front gate, with Alpha Centauri beside it. It always gives me an odd feeling to look at Alpha and to realize that's the next stop.

Letter to Val Cleaver, 1955

10
AROUND THE WORLD
TO CEYLON

The isle of Ceylon beckoned. The beautiful memory of a single afternoon there enticed Arthur C. Clarke to return, so he and Mike Wilson decided that their next underwater adventure would be in the crystal waters of the Indian Ocean. But first there was business to attend to, and that would take them around the world.

The first—and longest—stop was New York City, where all their hard-got, irreplaceable color slides and photographs were delivered to their publishers. Clarke and agent Scott Meredith also took time to hash out the 1956 publishing schedule: *The Coast of Coral* in the spring, *The City and the Stars* and a collection of short stories from the 1940s and 1950s, *Reach for Tomorrow*, in the first half of the year.

Clarke was also excited about the speaking engagements his underwater exploits had drawn. "Both Mike and I have been offered separate contracts by the Colston Leigh Lecture Agency, biggest in the world, which handles Cousteau, Mrs. Roosevelt, Joyce Cary, Ogden Nash, General Romulo, Peter II of Yugoslavia, Sir Harold Scott and a few others," he wrote to Val Cleaver. "They want me to do s.f. and astronautics; Mike will cover the underwater side."

New York proved the ideal source of equipment for the underwater expedition to Ceylon as well. Arnie Post of Richard's Sporting Goods was a tremendous help in choosing the best hardware for their needs, and it would be shipped over by the same agent who handled such matters for the Hayden Planetarium. They bought twin-cylinder Aqua-Lungs and a Cornelius air compressor, which allowed them to pump up their tanks wherever they could and gave them complete independence. They also upgraded their underwater camera equipment when Post showed them a Rolleimarin—a superb-quality underwater housing for the Rolleiflex.

Clarke and Post would go lobster fishing together in Long Island Sound when Clarke was in New York.

"We'd go diving for lobsters off the Russian Embassy in Glen Cove," says Post. "Back then lobsters were prolific in the sound. Whenever we'd go out for an hour, one diver would come up with forty or fifty lobsters. Then we'd cook them on the boat and have a royal feast."

The seven weeks in New York City flew by, and before they knew it, Arthur C. Clarke and Mike Wilson were leaving for London, just in time to miss the first winter blizzard to hit New York. It was November 20, 1955.

Weather was the dominant factor in any underwater expedition; they had learned that in Australia and had set their own deadlines accordingly. "We knew that the earlier in the year we could get to Ceylon," says Clarke, "the better our chances of success."

They also knew that dependable transportation in Ceylon was a real problem, so Clarke purchased a Landrover, which was shipped over. They also obtained an underwater motion picture camera for the film work they were beginning in Ceylon and sundry essential equipment. After shopping around, they decided that the electrically driven Beaulieu, in the case designed by Dimitri Rebikoff, the famous French underwater engineer and photographer, was the best camera in their price range.

Finally, as 1956 rapidly approached, everything was ready, and they hoped to be off before a harsh English winter was upon them.

"Our tickets were booked on the Orient liner *Orcades* for the first week in January, which seemed to be cutting it pretty fine. But we were in luck; it was still mild and pleasant when we saw the sun setting behind the cranes of Tilbury dock, and knew that the blue seas and palm-fringed beaches of Ceylon were only two weeks away."

The liner *Orcades* sailed the same eastern route to the Indian Ocean as the *Himalaya* had a year before, with a few additional ports-of-call in the Mediterranean. Highlights of the trip included Clarke's calculating what a dropped H-bomb would do to the great mass of rock called Gibraltar; his first visit to a brothel ("it went out of business suddenly in A.D. 69 when Vesuvius woke up"); and a visit with sister Mary, who was stationed as an officer nurse in the RAF at Aden, where Clarke, says Mary, "thought the colony looked like the mountains of the moon."

The *Orcades* arrived in Colombo in mid-January 1956. Rodney Jonklaas, who was then working for Ceylon's Department of Fisheries, was there to greet them. He managed to arrange his schedule so that he could guide Clarke and Wilson to the most promising underwater locations on the island—and this man knew most, if not all, of them.

Thanks to Jonklaas, they also located a promising abode on land after a temporary stay at a Colombo hotel. The flat was located in Bambalapitiya ("plain of the bamboo forest"), a Colombo suburb about three miles out of town, and came with a garage for the Landrover, which remained outside because the diving and photographic gear had priority and took up the entire garage floor. It was a bargain, wrote Clarke, "a small but pleasant apartment and a first-class cook-servant, all at an inclusive cost of about ninety dollars a month."

Somewhat sensitive to any suggestion of neocolonialism, he defends the practice of hiring servants. "In the East, of course, a servant is a necessity, not a luxury. Carolis [their first houseboy] probably saved us more money when he went shopping than we paid him in wages. The local storekeepers would have made quite a killing had we two British innocents dealt with them directly."

Clarke found cultural differences and island history encountered during his first few months in Ceylon fascinating and intellectually exciting. There were, of course, challenges to meet.

The Ceylonese place names, for example, were "terrifyingly polysyllabic" to Clarke and next to impossible to pronounce. "I mumbled for about a week before I could tell a cab driver where I lived," he says, admitting he had to practice pronouncing such tongue twisters as Illuppadichchenai and Kahatagasdigiliya.

The diversity of people and lifestyles in the Colombo streets—yellow-robed Buddhist monks, urchins selling lottery tickets, the rickshaws, the old London buses, tourists and businessmen from all over the world—added to the intrigue.

One aspect of Ceylon, however, to which Clarke could never adapt (although Wilson had no trouble with it) was the spicy food. "With my first cautious nibble, something went wrong with my windpipe, and I felt as if I were a couple of hundred feet down with a broken Aqua-Lung." He has never strayed from the basic British diet, which emphasizes meat and potatoes.

During the first half of 1956 Clarke also absorbed Ceylon's long recorded history, which went back some three thousand years and which he would later bring to his fiction, especially *The Fountains of Paradise*. He visited the ancient capital of Ceylon, Anuradhapura, located in the north-central region. It had been Ceylon's capital for a thousand years, where ninety Sinhalese kings had reigned, until invaders from India overran it and the Sinhalese built a second capital, Polonnaruwa, some sixty miles away.

Of more recent times, Clarke learned about the progressive occupations of the Portuguese, who left their religion—and much spilled blood; the Dutch, who left their architecture and law; and the British, who left their language and commerce. Only the British, who were politely asked to leave, left in a civilized way, without violence.

Ceylon's population is dominated by the Sinhalese, predominantly Buddhist, although there have been some Christian families for several generations. The second-largest group, found mostly in the northern part of the island, is the Tamils. They practice Hinduism, and some are aggressively separatist. The real and perceived grievances of the Tamils against the Sinhalese, and vice versa, have brought terror, death, and destruction to Ceylon over the past decades, and Clarke has witnessed the suffering this conflict has brought to the tear-shaped isle he has come to love.

In February 1956 Clarke wrote to Val Cleaver that he felt at peace and at home in Ceylon. He liked the people, the climate, and the cost of living.

"Mike also seems happy here, though he still gets moody and

bad-tempered from time to time. He is full of enthusiasm and ideas, and determined to make the expedition a success. However mad we may occasionally get with each other, we can't imagine not being together."

In another letter to Val Cleaver, Clarke talked about "life's ability to give one a 'come-uppance'. I'm acting on the assumption that if you work hard and produce all you can, which I am doing now, you are making the best insurance against disaster. And Mike and I are now really working together as a team, as well as making the allowances necessary for our somewhat clashing personalities! In fact, it has been a very long time since I have been so contented with life . . . pause while I wait for the roof to fall in."

Within a few days of their arrival, Clarke and Wilson loaded the Landrover and headed south. Akurala Reef, about fifty miles south of Colombo, was their first stop, and they quickly learned that the sharks off Ceylon's coast were less aggressive than those in the waters of the Great Barrier Reef.

"We had the satisfaction of seeing our first shark close-up," wrote Clarke, "and knowing that our visit to the Akurala Reef had given us results which we had never been able to obtain during a whole year in Australia."

Clarke and Wilson made the acquaintance of Jo Ebert, a leading photographer and also the shipping master for Colombo, who had a complete register, going back a hundred years, of all the sunken ships off the coast. This became a main resource for their diving adventures.

Before summer, hoping for some financial rewards as well as fun and adventure—discovering historic treasure was always a possibility—they had explored six underwater wrecks, two of which had gone down off the Akurala Reef. One of these, the *Earl of Shaftesbury*, had sunk in 1893. Nearby they also dove to investigate the *Conch*, one of the first oil tankers of the Shell Company, which hit the rocks and sank in 1903, leaving its huge spill of oil spreading over the reef.

These wrecks and others produced no treasure, but Clarke and Wilson found plenty to interest them. On another occasion they explored a Danish wreck that had gone down in 1939. The *Elsia* was a cargo passenger ship that had caught fire and been abandoned. Because it was relatively close to shore, the water was dirty and photography was out. Clarke went down to have a quick look without his Aqua-Lung.

"I took a deep breath and plunged down toward the enigmatic blur lying beneath our boat. Before I had run short of air, I found myself *inside* a ship. The *Elsia* appeared to have split open, revealing all her internal machinery. . . . Pipes and cables snaked everywhere, sometimes looking alarmingly like giant tentacles."

The next day the crew went out beyond the *Elsia* to the Rala Gala Reef (also known as Wave Rock because of the ten-footers it creates). The water clarity was amazing. "It was the first time I had ever encountered visibility of over a hundred feet in the open sea," says Clarke. Soon after Jonklaas speared his first pompano, Clarke and Wilson got their cameras ready, expecting sharks, which immediately appeared, although most of them were small and camera shy—with one notable exception.

"I was relaxing twenty feet down when I saw a large shark coming straight toward me, almost on a collision course," wrote Clarke. "I quickly whipped the camera up to my eye, praying that my air would hold out until the shark reached me. . . .

"At the last minute he swerved to my left; I clicked the shutter and then realized that I was completely out of air." Clarke came up gasping, but he had gotten his photograph, and the shark was not seen again.

They spent four hours in the water off Rala Gala Reef that spring afternoon. When they returned to the coastal village of Weligama, Wilson and Jonklaas wanted more fish for dinner and headed out in the bay. But Clarke was bushed and did not want to contradict his basic philosophy of water activity.

"The whole secret of underwater sight-seeing—and indeed of diving in general—is summed up in what is known in physics as the Principle of Least Action," wrote Clarke. "Never exert yourself unnecessarily: the universe doesn't."

As the sun set, Clarke practiced what he preached by relaxing on the veranda of the Rest House at Weligama Bay, overlooking the curving shoreline, commonly agreed to be one of the most beautiful spots on Ceylon's coast.

"The scene was so peaceful and so completely relaxing that I was able to enjoy it without the feeling—from which professional writers are seldom free—that I really ought to be working on something, it didn't matter what. For an hour or so I had escaped from the tyranny of the typewriter, and that was an achievement well worth the journey to Ceylon."

Becoming further assimilated, Clarke learned in Weligama to wear a sarong—the traditional native wraparound garb for males: "a simple tube of cloth about four feet long and seven feet in circumference." He took an immediate liking to its convenience and comfort and henceforth advertised its benefits by sometimes wearing one during his world travels.

Clarke and Wilson had been away from Colombo for almost two weeks, and on their way back they stopped at the small town and harbor of Galle, which according to some historians of the Bible is the Tarshish of the Old Testament, where Solomon's ships were provisioned as they set forth to find riches of gold and ivory.

In more recent history, all the sunken wrecks in the Galle harbor were dramatically exposed when an extraordinary event occurred: in August 1883 all the water drained out of the harbor in a matter of minutes. It was caused by a powerful wave moving west, originating more than a thousand miles away, and formed by the cataclysmic volcanic explosion of Krakatau in the Pacific off Java. Because of Galle's sheltered location on the far side of Ceylon, relative to Krakatau, no devastating tidal wave returned; instead it came like a swift, smooth tide, once more covering the many shipwrecks on the harbor floor.

But there were more than ancient wrecks to explore. In fact, on March 5, 1956, the Greek freighter *Aenos*, carrying six thousand tons of manganese, struck Rala Gala Reef north of Galle and went down. The crew was rescued by local fishermen, who then proceeded to loot the bridge and boat deck—the only portions of the ship not submerged.

Five days later Clarke and company arrived on the scene with their diving equipment to see what they could bring up from beneath the waves. The diving conditions were not ideal, however, because the flow from the nearby mouth of the Gintota River muddied the water, and the monsoon winds were getting stronger. Because rough seas were still battering the *Aenos*, they decided to skin-dive and not use the Aqua-Lungs, which would have been a disadvantage and potential risk.

They brought up two wooden chests filled with tools, some water or coffee pitchers, and other souvenirs.

In addition to all his coastal adventures, Clarke was always writing—along the way and even more intensively when they stayed at their flat outside Colombo. *The Reefs of Taprobane* documented these months in Ceylon and was published in 1957. Its magnificent color plates were the product of the Rolleimarin/ Rolleiflex camera equipment purchased in New York.

"I realized that I now had the background for a whole novel, which was written in Ceylon during the spring of 1956 and published the next year," Clarke relates. The novel was *The Deep Range*, and its theme was ocean farming and whale ranching. It was dedicated to Mike Wilson, who more than anyone else shared these wanderlust years with Clarke: "For Mike who led me to the sea."

Like several other Clarke novels, *The Deep Range* had its start as a short story. This one was written in 1953 and appeared in the third volume of Frederik Pohl's *Star Science Fiction* series.

Visions of meetings with his editors in New York City in the summer were starting to pop up unexpectedly in Clarke's head, pushing him to produce as many words as possible during the spring. "How the hell does Simenon do it?" he wrote to Val Cleaver.

A May 25 letter, this one to Ian Macauley, delivered surprising news: "Have made up my mind—I'm settling in Ceylon and commuting once a year to the U.S."

As he explained to Val Cleaver, "The contrast between here and England is fantastic, and it's strange to feel free after all these years. Maybe a couple of months a year in Ceylon will be all I can take—will need the remaining 10 to recover."

It was about this time that Arthur met Hector Ekanayake, a young Sinhalese who would become the flyweight champion of Ceylon in the fall of 1956. He was the youngest flyweight ever, and his age kept him out of the Olympics.

"Hector was working at a U.S. agricultural show in Colombo I happened to visit," says Clarke. "His father, a police inspector, got him a temporary job there."

Over the next few years Ekanayake helped with miscellaneous projects around Clarke's place and would sometimes accompany him on trips. He eventually learned the underwater business and helped Clarke and Wilson on their local adventures. The friendship grew steadily throughout the fifties and sixties. Ekanayake has stayed by Clarke's side, more a family member than a mere friend, for almost forty years.

As summer 1956 approached, Ceylon was caught up in a general election. The outcome, to the surprise of many, was that the pro-Western government lost to the left-wing nationalistic one. This brought forth a controversy over the national language. During the election campaign both parties agreed that English should be replaced with the majority language, Sinhalese. But the minority Tamils, making up about one-sixth of the population, objected. The antagonism between the Sinhalese and the Tamils, often erupting in violence and death, has continued ever since. Clarke hoped that his newly chosen home would not be "spoilt by silly politicians and unruly mobs."

At this time film director David Lean and his crew were in Ceylon shooting *The Bridge On the River Kwai*. It didn't take Mike Wilson long to show up on the set location when he heard about the shoot.

A member of the film company recalls that this strange character walked onto the set one morning wearing a white marine cap. He walked up to the Columbia representative, introduced himself, and told him that he represented the *London Times* and wanted to cover the shooting of the film.

The man from Columbia said that he would let him know in a few days. He then immediately cabled London for verification. The reply: they had never heard of Mike Wilson.

The six months Clarke had spent in what had become his home had been productive ones. *The Reefs of Taprobane* and *The Deep Range* would become his fifteenth and sixteenth published books, and as he left for London he looked forward to two weeks of leisure to catch up on life's miscellany.

He also had his next trip to the United States to look forward to. Scheduled to receive a special honor, he spent his last few days in London polishing the keynote speech he would deliver at the World Science Fiction Convention. Then he flew across the Atlantic Ocean once more.

The rising rocket appeals to instincts older than reason; the gulf it bridges is not only that between world and world—but the deeper chasm between heart and brain. . . .

"L'enuoi," First on the Moon *(1970)*

11
SPACE AGE DREAMS

The 1956 World Science Fiction Convention was held at the Biltmore Hotel in New York City during the first few days of September—Labor Day weekend. Held annually since 1939, the event boasted a higher attendance than ever before. Mass paperback publishing undoubtedly was partly responsible for the convention's drawing power, but so was the fact that science was catching up with the visions of science fiction. The United States had announced its plans to launch an artificial satellite in 1955, although no one knew that Sputnik and the Space Age were just two years away. David Kyle, chairman and organizer, had named Arthur C. Clarke as the guest of honor.

"This was the first time that a non-American was chosen," says Kyle. "And I also pushed and helped put together the bid that took the convention out of North America for the first time, and the following year, in 1957, it went to London."

Novelist Robert Bloch was toastmaster. "It was certainly one of the first large Worldcons," recalls Bloch, "with between one and two thousand people attending. The large turnout was very impressive. And I do know Arthur met many, many people because this was one of the first conventions that began to attract large numbers of professional writers from all over the country. The whole affair was just beginning to be a little bit tainted by commercialism. More dealers were showing up. More editors. More publishers. It began to lose its fannish connotations."

There was corporate participation too. People from the Martin Company of Baltimore, prime contractor for the navy's Project Vanguard, attended, bringing with them a model of the three-stage Vanguard rocket vehicle. Clarke was at the beginning stages of his nonfiction book *The Making of a Moon,* and the Martin people gave him an open invitation to visit Baltimore and tour their facilities and interview managers.

"I hope to sit on their doorstep for a week or so, picking their brains," he wrote to Val Cleaver.

The new tenor of the convention had little effect on the behavior of those in attendance. Mike Wilson, for one, was as sociable as ever. "I was fast asleep," says Clarke, "and there was a knock on the door. It woke me up. I went and opened the door, and there was this small boy outside; it was Harlan [Ellison]. And he said to me, 'Will you please ask Mike Wilson to leave my girl alone?' And I said, 'Certainly, Harlan. Good night.'"

With that Clarke went back to sleep.

Recalls Robert Bloch, "I do remember remarking to Arthur that when this thing was finished, after the way the fans had been behaving, we had to change the name of the hotel from the Biltmore to the ReBuiltmore."

At the banquet dinner on Sunday evening, Clarke didn't get to speak "until past my bedtime." He was sitting in between Bloch and cartoonist Al Capp, so at least things were lively. They joked back and forth for about four hours.

Isaac Asimov was also on the dais, but he wasn't laughing.

"I had a kidney stone," said Asimov. "Worse yet, the stone managed to get itself into a position where it activated the 'I have to urinate' button. I had warned people who were organizing the convention that I would be periodically leaving the dais and explained why. Arthur was guest of honor, and when he got up to speak, I was determined *not* to leave the dais until he was through, lest the audience assume that I was demonstrating my disapproval of what he was saying. I turned slightly green, therefore, when he rose with something like thirty sheets of paper."

Science fiction enthusiasts, Clarke told his audience, were unique: "No other form of literature arouses such passionate loyalty as does science fiction." And true enthusiasts, he continued, always combine a sense of wonder and mental flexibility. Clarke went on to defend the genre against its critics, whose unconscious logic was all too often "I don't understand what all this is about, and therefore it's nonsense."

Clarke also had some criticism for science fiction. There was "a great deal of what one can only call ugliness in much modern science fiction," he said. He complained about regrettable trends in the field, "a cult of irrationality [which] has been gaining ground . . . the cults of colliding planets, of airborne crockery [UFOs], and of reincarnated colleens [Bridy Murphy]." Clarke's primary objection was "that thousands of people are prepared to believe these things *on the sort of evidence that has been put forward*." He then cited an example of how many eyewitnesses came forward to confirm a UFO sighting that was a deliberate hoax.

He voiced his concern about the "antiscientific bias of some current writing" and about the emphasis on wars and other negative futures, even though science fiction is still a "basically optimistic and inspiring form of literature. . . ." His plea was for science fiction writers and readers to be more responsible to real science and in educating the public.

"Our society can only continue to exist if there is a revolutionary upgrading of technical and scientific education in the very near future—by which I mean before the end of this century."

Those gathered at the Biltmore were, said Clarke, "trustees of a future which we will never see, but which our thoughts and actions will inevitably shape. . . . it may seem fanciful to imagine that what we write can affect the future, but that is the literal truth. Who can doubt, for example, that the world's acceptance of space-flight is due to the countless works of fiction on this theme. . . . I am quite sure that by writing about space-flight we have brought its realisation nearer by decades. Perhaps even more important, we have helped the public to appreciate what it will mean when it comes."

No one there could have imagined that the Space Age was just over a year away and that it would be the Russians who would officially give birth to it.

After the convention Clarke began the lecture tour that would keep him busy for the rest of 1956 and the first two months of 1957. It was the first of the multistate speaking tours that he would go on through the seventies. Although it would help to make Clarke an important educator and disseminator of ideas, it was not all glamour and glory. In his first appearance, in York, Pennsylvania, he could not help noticing that "there was one lady in front who kept on looking at her watch."

In between the nearly two dozen talks given in thirteen states before the end of 1956, Clarke returned to New York whenever possible. He stayed at Manhattan's Hotel Chelsea, famous for literary guests such as Brendan Behan, Dylan Thomas, Mark Twain, Thomas Wolfe, Eugene O'Neill, and Arthur Miller. Quickly discovering that the residents of the Chelsea could provide local color or anecdotal material whenever his stories needed it, Clarke from then on made it his home base when he was off the lecture circuit or passing through New York City.

During January and February of 1957 Clarke traveled as far as Vancouver, Washington, taking pleasure in the American trains he rode and all the reading time his travel provided. He also enjoyed being invited to stay at the home of fellow writers and well-known science fiction fans such as Ted Thomas, a Pennsylvania attorney whose hobby is science fiction.

"He was giving lectures in my area," remembers Thomas, "so I suggested that he stay with us if he wanted. That way he'd have a base. We met at the first Milford Science Fiction Writers Conference.

"Well, I got his book, *The Exploration of the Moon*, with drawings by his friend R. A. Smith [published in 1955], because I had an idea to write a story. It was one of my very early stories, and its title was 'A Far Look,' which was soon published in *Astounding*.

"What I did to write this story was to assume that everything Arthur and his artist friend said about the moon in their book was gospel. And I had gone through that book, annotating and making notes in the margins, and used them to develop a storyline.

"Now even to this day, I don't know why I did it, unless it was an attempt to be funny, but somewhere toward the end of the book, Arthur had written something about the 'colour' of something. He of course spelled it the English way. And I put a note next to the margin, 'Can't spell color.'

"Well, what happened was, when Arthur was staying with us at the apartment, I said, 'Here, use my desk. I've got to go to the office all day.' He had some writing to do. So he was at the desk working, and there was a bookcase right alongside it. He looked up and saw his book there. He pulled it out, and then got intrigued, as you can imagine, with my notations in the margins of his book. So he's reading these things along, and in the meantime my wife is out in the kitchen doing dishes. And really, she takes the story from there.

"There she is, minding her own business doing dishes, and all of a sudden Arthur is in the kitchen, holding this book, steaming.

"'Doesn't he know that in England we spell colour c-o-l-o-u-r?' he told her. My wife of course had no idea what all this was about. But after I came home from work, we finally got it straightened out and all had a good laugh over it."

The last few years of Clarke's life had been tumultuous. He had been married and then quickly and permanently separated. He had traveled around the world for the first time. And he had made enough of a name for himself that he was sought to speak on both science fiction and science; he had become a self-proclaimed "unemployed prophet."

During that period, 1953 to 1956, Clarke had written fifteen scientific tall-tale short stories. Finally published in 1957, *Tales from the "White Hart"* was his most fanciful collection of fiction. The stories were set in a fictitious London pub that was closely based on the White Horse, where Clarke and all his friends met to discuss science fiction and space travel. Harvey Purvis, the teller of these tales, was certainly a fictive conglomerate of many personalities, but some of the other characters were real, as were their names. Clarke's prewar roommate, Bill Temple, was mentioned a few times, and Clarke even put himself into one story—"What Goes Up."

Ken Slater, a science fiction fan and patron of the White Horse, remembers the pub meetings well enough.

"Anybody new that came to the pub was always told to ask Arthur to tell them about rockets, you see. Which they would do and then sit back for the short lecture. After Arthur broke into the short lecture, then we'd always strongly advise the newcomer to ask, 'Look, what does the rocket push against?' Which immediately brought forth from Arthur the long lecture, you know, the five-guinea version. That was a standard put-on at the White Horse, because if you ever got Arthur on rocketry, you could sit back and let the bar listen for up to a couple of hours."

British writer John Brunner remembers going to the White Horse for the first time.

"It must have been in the summer of 1952. I was a callow seventeen-year-old, going on eighteen," says Brunner. "I had just made my second sale to an American magazine and earned a thousand dollars out of my first year as a professional writer. And I celebrated by going to the London Science Fiction Circle at the White Horse. Among the people who were there was Arthur Clarke. Also there were Charles Eric Maine, Bill Temple, Sam Youd, and others.

"What I remember mainly about that evening, though, was the fact that I was in the presence of people whose work I had frequently read in magazines and in one or two cases in book form. And they were very polite to me. I just came back thinking, 'Wow, I've just met these people. They're selling writers. And I'm one too. Gosh.' A terrible thing to happen to a teenager, of course.

"That the circle members took to meeting regularly at the White Horse on Thursday evenings was a tradition that goes back a very long way, to the time when science fiction had to be paid for in dollars because there was so little of it about. American magazines were extremely hard to find. People would go and literally trade books and magazines they'd read for ones they hadn't.

"The landlord [Lew, to whom *Tales* is dedicated] was such a popular character that when he moved to another pub the entire London Science Fiction Circle moved with him. And that's how we moved to the Globe in Hatton Garden," says Brunner.

Clarke fictionalized this real move at the conclusion of the last story in *Tales*: ". . . we all followed Drew lock, stock and barrel—particularly barrel—to his new establishment . . . the 'Sphere.'"

The critics called the book "hilarious," "wholly delightful," "high diversion, amusement and amazement," and a "light and frothy conglomeration of side-splitters." Readers might use one of Clarke's favorite phrases to describe it: "great fun!"

"The Songs of Distant Earth," a short story that would gestate and become a novel more than two decades later, was Clarke's other major piece of fiction for the first year of the Space Age.

"For some reason, at the beginning of that momentous year a phrase lodged in my mind and wouldn't go away; it echoed round and round my skull as persistently as the last movement of Sibelius' 2nd Symphony."

The phrase, of course, was "The Songs of Distant Earth," and it raised a question that helped to define Arthur C. Clarke the writer. Was it possible, he asked himself, to write a completely realistic story using an interstellar—as opposed to a merely interplanetary—background?

The query was based on the scientific fact that "we are 99.99 percent certain that it will always be impossible to travel faster than light, which means that journeys to even the nearest star systems will take decades." The answer was yes, a hard science fiction story about interstellar travel *could* be written; and not just a story but a complete novel.

This question is important to Clarke because it is the basis for his primary commitment to science fiction as opposed to fantasy—and *his* definition of both. *Stars Wars* (and Clarke, like everybody else, loved it as entertainment) could have its characters and spaceships jump from star to star as fantasy, but the story was *not* science fiction.

"Now, I like fantasy every bit as much as science fiction," he says, "but I recognize the distinction between the genres. . . . Fantasy is something that couldn't happen in the real world (though often you wish it would); science fiction is something that really could happen (though often you'd be sorry if it did)."

Appropriate to the historic significance of that year, 1957 was more of a nonfiction year for Arthur C. Clarke. He worked hard that year on two nonfiction titles for Harper & Brothers: *The Making of a Moon* (published in mid-1957) and *Voice Across the Sea* (issued in the latter half of 1958).

That both of these books were out of print at the beginning of the 1990s had only to do with their topicality and relevance to the last half of the 1950s. In fact Clarke came to realize that his fiction would, with few exceptions, outlast his nonfiction, from the long-term perspective of his complete corpus. In the 1970s he deliberately devoted his creative time to novels, avoiding any nonfiction contracts that were not collections of earlier works.

When Clarke began writing *The Making of a Moon*, he had no

idea that *Sputnik 1* would be launched in October, just a few months after the book's publication and before the first Vanguard rockets made America eat humble pie by exploding on their launching pads or soon after. In fact, when a year earlier Clarke and Anthony Boucher discussed the theme "1956 looks at 1984" on a CBS program called "Conversation," the possibility of a satellite launching as soon as 1957 was not even raised.

In *The Making of a Moon*, Clarke wrote what was sensible and relevant nonfiction in early 1957: a history of the U.S. Earth satellite program and Project Vanguard, just one scientific endeavor of many planned for the International Geophysical Year (IGY), which officially ran from July 1957 to December 1958. In the final analysis, *The Making of a Moon* still holds up as good prehistory of the Space Age.

The other Harper nonfiction title Clarke wrote in 1957, *Voice Across the Sea*, was a history of the first telephone cable across the Atlantic, which was completed and christened in 1954. Another midcentury history, this book had the advantage of not being immediately outdated by the rush of technological events. It would be more than two decades before fiber optic cables began to dominate land and sea communications lines.

When history was made on October 4, 1957, Arthur C. Clarke was in Barcelona, attending the International Astronautical Federation conference.

"I was woken up by a call from the *London Daily Express*," says Clarke. "It was a complete shock; I had not anticipated it in the least. But I knew it would change the modern world.

"I then called the rest of the British delegation, and I didn't get to sleep again for the rest of that night."

Catching most of the world off guard, the Russians had successfully orbited *Sputnik 1*, the world's first artificial satellite.

Fred Durant recalls that the news was slow to reach Spain: "The head of the Soviet delegation was Leonid Sedov. We saw him at the airport on Saturday afternoon [the day after the event], and we knew nothing about the launch because in Spain under Franco they didn't allow British papers in until they had been censored or reviewed. So a lot of us didn't know about it until later, when people came in from England and the States with the news.

"We saw Sedov that evening at a reception and of course

congratulated him. We also sent a cablegram of congratulations to the president of the Soviet Academy of Sciences."

Clarke had a good laugh at the same reception: "I'll always remember what one of the Russian delegates said during a conversation. It really struck me. When I mentioned *Sputnik 1* weighed about 150 pounds, she said, 'It can't be that big. *Pravda* must be wrong.'

"Back then, you rarely heard Russians say *Pravda* was wrong. Of course it was even heavier [184.3 pounds]."

*I seem to be regarded as the philosopher of spaceflight—
that's what they're calling me.*

Letter to Val Cleaver, February 23, 1959

12
THE SPACE CIRCUIT

After the United States failed twice in launching its Navy Vanguard satellites, the alternative Jupiter-C rocket successfully
placed America's *Explorer 1* satellite in orbit on February 1, 1958.
It was Clarke's friend Wernher von Braun who led the U.S. Army
team in its successful Jupiter-C launch.

While the space race was just beginning to fire up between
the superpowers, Arthur C. Clarke was on the road again in America, delivering some forty-eight lectures in fifteen states, in the
first three months of 1958, this time about a subject close to his
heart—Earth satellites.

Holiday magazine featured a Clarke piece about his road tour
in its October issue: "U.S.A.: A Spaceman Rides the Lecture Circuit." Wrote Clarke, "In my 1958 season, thanks to the unexpected
co-operation of the Kremlin, I started my tour not merely one up
but two up on my audiences. Both Sputniks were circling the
Earth when I delivered my first talk on satellites; gone forever,
consequently, was the opinionated little man in the front row who
was quite sure that space travel was impossible—because no one
had ever done it before. Sometimes I miss him; it used to be more

fun when there was at least one person in the audience who thought I was crazy, and didn't hesitate to say so."

Clarke spoke anywhere he was invited, including business associations, universities, women's clubs, churches, libraries, YMCAs, and so on. In his *Holiday* article he asked himself why he hadn't yet been invited to a prison and speculated that "perhaps the subject of spaceflight is considered too escapist."

After a dozen or so lectures Clarke usually knew what questions were coming, what issues would be raised. In early 1958 it wasn't difficult to anticipate this most frequently posed query: "Why didn't we put up a satellite first?" There were several reasons, of course, not the least of which was Washington politics, but it *wasn't*, Clarke emphasized, because the Russians had the expertise of more German rocket scientists. Rather it was the United States that got the leading rocket men after World War II.

The subject of "flying saucers" or UFOs also aroused debate at most of Clarke's lectures. Clarke was both "astonished" and "disturbed" by the extreme interest. "My pleas for sanity and skepticism were often not well received by the devotees of this new religion," he says.

No stranger to UFOs, Clarke has seen far too many to believe in them as ET spaceships. His lecture approach to this subject was to describe several of his sightings—all extremely credible and initially mysterious—and then explain what they were proved to be. Three examples he often gave audiences: a line of brilliant silver disks along the horizon was actually seagull wings acting like mirrors reflecting sunlight; what looked like an aerial jellyfish or silken cloud in the late summer sky was actually a mass of sunlit gossamer threads discarded by spiders; a flying object, spitting sparks and flames, was a burning golf ball ejected from a burning trash can by its own highly combustible and energy-torqued rubber bands. And he had more. He presented them all objectively, giving detailed sightings and thorough explanations. But there were always some true believers who refused to be convinced by his rationality.

"On one occasion," says Clarke, "a lady from the audience asked me if I believe that those who claimed to have met men from flying saucers were liars. She sat down rather abruptly when I replied, 'Yes, madam'; not until a little later did the chairman gleefully inform me that her husband had authored one of the best known of the sacred writings."

Clarke did not hesitate to make his opinion known. After participating in a special symposium called "Britain Enters the Space Age: A Discussion on Guided Missiles and Space Travel" in England on April 14, 1958, Clarke chatted for a while with Prince Philip. Later he wrote rather mysteriously in an essay, "I recklessly jeopardized my place in the future honours list by getting into a brisk argument on the subject [of UFOs] with royalty." Actually, it may have been less than an argument. "I expressed surprise that he seemed to take UFOs seriously," Clarke recalled, "but at least I made it to the honours list after all." (Clarke refers to his honor of personally receiving the Commander of the British Empire award from Queen Elizabeth in October 1989.)

Clarke himself sighted a "classical" flying saucer on October 17, 1958, when he was flying up the coast of Italy aboard KLM flight 826 on his way to Geneva. The aircraft was at an altitude of about ten thousand feet, and it was a bright, hazy day. Clarke was looking at the coastline below, waiting to see Naples and Vesuvius.

"I became aware that a brilliant oval of light was keeping pace with the aircraft a few thousand feet below. It appeared quite solid, though its edges were hazy and seemed to pulsate slightly; they also had a bluish tinge rather like that of a mercury arc. It was impossible to judge its size or distance, but I had the impression that the object was halfway between the aircraft and the ground. Sometimes it was so brilliant that it hurt the eye to look at it directly."

He watched the UFO for at least ten minutes. It was a solid disk, with no transparency at all, and its shape and size were constant as it kept station beneath the aircraft. Other passengers also saw it; several even took photographs of it. Clarke wouldn't take his eyes off it, and he finally won the wait.

"I was able to keep it in sight until it disintegrated and slowly faded from view, like a cloud breaking up beneath the sun. By that time there was no question of its identity.

"It was a mock sun, or 'sun dog,' caused by the presence of an invisible layer of ice crystals between the aircraft and the ground."

This was another good sighting to describe to his lecture audiences. He also imparted his humorous rule for UFO observers:

"It's not a spaceship unless you can read the Mars registration plate."

The lecture circuit had one major surprise for Clarke: nowhere did he find religious opposition to the idea of space travel.

Was it because his audiences were generally well educated and pro science and research to begin with? Probably. But had there been some aggressive attacks from the overzealous believers, Clarke would have replied with his commonsense perspective: there was no basic difference between exploring the solar system and universe and exploring planet Earth.

Even Pope Pius XII stated formally that the exploration of space, once the means of doing so had been discovered, was fulfilling mankind's God-given potential. Clarke called the pope's address "brilliant" and wrote, "It is hard to believe that anyone, whatever his religious faith, can seriously disagree with this argument. Any path to knowledge is a path to God—or to Reality, whichever word one prefers to use."

The main theme of Clarke's lectures in the 1950s (and many thereafter) was that an immense revolution would be taking place within a decade—or certainly no more than a generation. "We are living, I told audiences from New Hampshire to New Mexico, in a moment unique in all history—the last days of Man's existence as a citizen of a single planet."

Clarke then created an analogy that became famous when the *Eagle* landed on the moon a decade later and Armstrong and Aldrin left their historic bootprints in the lunar soil. Wernher von Braun gave a variation on Clarke's analogy to the media: "What is happening now is nothing less than the next stage in evolution, comparable to the time, perhaps a billion years ago, when life came out of the sea and conquered the land."

The concept was similar to one written by the great Russian space pioneer Konstantin Tsiolkovsky, which Clarke confesses he was unaware of at the time he wrote his aeonic view: "The Earth is the cradle of Mankind—but you cannot live in a cradle forever."

By May 1958 Clarke was back in Colombo, Ceylon. He'd settled in to a new address, 20 Rheinland Place, which he ended up sharing with Mike Wilson, Hector Ekanayake, and at times Rodney Jonklaas. Clarke apparently did not find company a distraction—perhaps the opposite—because he habitually gathered a few people around him, and in the spring of 1958 he was on a disciplined but less prolific writing schedule again. "I feel that I have now lost my amateur status, as my 21st book comes out this autumn," he wrote to Sam Youd. ". . . Now that I've accumulated this stock-pile, my aim is less writing and more thinking."

During the summer of 1958, major violence erupted in Ceylon—the first of many internal conflicts Clarke would witness over the years. Radical separatists attempted to overthrow the government of Prime Minister W. R. D. Bandaranaike, and there was bloodshed.

"About 200 people have been killed in riots," he wrote Youd, "and there has been a lot of property damage. Until this week [July 10, 1958], there has been a rigid curfew, but that has now been relaxed and things are generally calming down. But it does make one doubtful whether to invest much in the place."

Clarke was stuck in the middle of *Glide Path*, his war novel, in mid-August, but some of this frustrated energy was going into a new business enterprise with Mike Wilson. Their venture would seek out work on salvage operations, surveys for government agencies, cleaning of dam outflow "tunnels," and the like.

"We are just floating (if that's the word) Clarke-Wilson Associates, diving consultants," he told Youd. "Mike's already done one survey job on a wreck in the Maldives, about 400 miles west of here. He has brought back some fabulous close-ups of sharks feeding. They have bad table manners."

His partner's underwater photography was getting recognized; Wilson won second prize in an international competition in Italy. He also shared authorship with Clarke on a nonfiction juvenile book, *Boy Beneath the Sea*, that was published in the fall of 1958.

In September Wilson met a beautiful girl named Elizabeth. One night after a small get-together with friends at Rheinland Place, he took her home by cab.

"As he was leaving her place," Clarke wrote to Youd, "he was attacked by four thugs who bashed him on the head with an iron bar and gave him some nasty scalp wounds which put him in hospital for several days. The man behind the attack was Liz's dad, a very wealthy doctor and by all accounts a nasty piece of work. Mike has retaliated in the most effective manner—by marrying Liz. . . . (The entire family is on Mike's side, inc. Elizabeth's Scots mother, so it's only a matter of time.) Meanwhile all sorts of underground campaigns are in progress to smuggle her clothes out of the house past the old man's guard."

Liz was now at Rheinland Place, running the household, and she and Clarke got on well together. It was just the two of them when Wilson left in September for his underwater film lecture in the United States. By the time he returned, Clarke would be on the road again, sharing his visions of the future with diverse audiences and trying to finish *Glide Path* and write some shorter pieces in between stops.

As 1958 came to a close, the United States aimed and launched three Pioneer spacecraft toward the moon. The Pioneer program grew out of the International Geophysical Year and was inherited by NASA from the Department of Defense. *Pioneer 1, 2,* and *3* failed to reach destination moon, but they did send back useful data on the atmosphere and radiation belts.

Clarke knew it would not be long before a Russian or an American spacecraft crash-landed on the lunar surface.

"I'm getting quite reactionary in my old age," he wrote to Youd as he approached his forty-first birthday in December 1958. "I think it's rather a pity that we'll soon look for the last time on the virgin moon."

Before the New Year arrived, Clarke had flown the Atlantic once again. After taking care of business in the New York area, he traveled to Concord, Massachusetts, to spend the Christmas holidays with the Durant family. A few days after Christmas, Isaac Asimov (then at Boston University) and Arthur Kantrovitz (an executive at Avco Corporation and Durant's boss) came for dinner. It was a wonderful evening of talk, Durant recalls, most of which was dominated by these two big names in science fiction.

"Kantrovitz was a brilliant physicist, but he knew nothing about science fiction," says Durant. "While Arthur and Isaac threw out ideas back and forth across the room, I can remember Kantrovitz's head just going from left to right, left to right, as if he were watching a tennis match. He was utterly stunned with the brilliance and exciting concepts of these two. And Arthur Clarke would say, 'You can have that one, Ike.' And Ike would say, 'All right, here's one for you. . . .'" The two great egos of science fiction were one on one, having a great old time.

Back in Manhattan at the Hotel Chelsea, Clarke prepared for his 1959 lecture tour, whose major lecture themes were the promise of the Space Age and the benefits of communications and weather satellites. To a Michigan audience in January 1959 he predicted: "Should the Soviet Union launch a concentrated rocket program, men will be on the moon within the next ten years." The timing was right, but the country was wrong. It was the "concentrated rocket program" of the United States that won the historic triumph in the summer of 1969.

In his travels Clarke spent time with a diverse range of people, from the Beat poets to Jacques Cousteau.

Clarke recalls that it was A. C. Spectorsky, the *Playboy* editor, who "asked me to be on a panel protesting local censorship of *Naked Lunch*. I had never heard of Burroughs or the Beats, but it sounded fun. I took part and met Ginsberg, Corso, and so on."

The famous Chicago attorney Elmer Gertz, who fought the legal battle for Henry Miller's *Tropic of Cancer* in the United States, was the man who arranged the January panel.

Wrote Gertz, "I was to preside, but I suddenly recalled that my daughter was to be graduated on that very night. I had to turn over the task of chairing the meeting to someone, and I chose Clarke. Everyone told me later that he was convulsively funny. He was like a Bob Hope of the intellectuals."

In February, Clarke also had the pleasure of spending a weekend with Jacques Cousteau, whom he described to Sam Youd as a "fascinating but tense type." The occasion was a big skin divers' convention. The latest project in Cousteau's life, Clarke learned, was his sea farm in Monaco. During their discussions Clarke raised the possibility of Cousteau's writing a short introduction to his book *The First Five Fathoms*.

The end of Clarke's lecture tour for the 1959 season brought him a surprising personal revelation. During the question-and-answer period at one of his last talks, a young lady asked Clarke why he liked Ceylon so much.

"I was about to switch on the sound track I had played a hundred times before," says Clarke, "when suddenly in my mind's eye I saw those two beaches—both so far away. Do not ask me why it happened then; but in that moment of double vision, I knew the truth.

"The chill northern beach on which I had so often shivered through an English summer afternoon was merely the intimation of an ultimate and unsuspected beauty—the Platonic ideal, as it were, of a childhood dream. Like the three princes of (how appropriately!) Serendib, I had found far more than I was seeking.

"Six thousand miles from where I was born, I had come home."

And that's exactly where he was going on March 20, 1959. After a brief visit to London, he would fly back to his tropical dream—the isle of Ceylon.

There were no major crises to face upon his arrival home in mid-April. Mike and Liz Wilson were "very happy and domesticated," he wrote to Val Cleaver, and Hector Ekanayake, who would become one of Clarke's most trusted friends, was "speechless for a few hours, but now going great guns & much less shy than last-year." There was a new pet squirrel in the household—"a baby squirrel 5" long (incl. tail!)"—and the monkeys, Clarke noted, were not as friendly as they were before he left for the States.

Soon Clarke was busy preparing for a diving and filmmaking expedition with Mike Wilson and Rodney Jonklaas off Ceylon's south coast. Their destination was the Great Basses Reef. Almost wholly unexplored because of the rough weather found there ten months of the year, the reef promised to yield a bounty of firsts to document in print and on film. After cutting, much of this film would become a twenty-five minute tourism promotion movie for the Ceylon Tea Board, *Beneath the Seas of Ceylon*.

The two good months on the reef are March and April, but even this period is not always reliable. In April 1959, however, luck was with the Clarke team, and they had almost perfect weather for their week of diving and photography.

Thanks to an arrangement with the Imperial Lighthouse Service, they stayed at the Great Basses lighthouse, ten miles out in the Indian Ocean, and used that as their base. They got to the lighthouse aboard the service's powerboat, the *Pharos*, whose uniquely experienced crew knew how to navigate the treacherous waters and unload people, gear, and stores at the lighthouse under all but the worst conditions.

The surge of water made it impossible to do any exploring close to the reef, and so, with their heavy equipment, they had to struggle to reach calmer waters a few hundred feet away, fighting the powerful currents and pulling their rubber dinghy and tanks behind them.

"But," wrote Clarke, "the struggle was worth it. Beneath us was a fantastic fairyland of caves, grottoes, coral-encrusted valleys— and fish in such numbers as I have never met anywhere else in the world. Sometimes they crowded round us so closely that we could see nothing but a solid wall of scales, and had literally to push our way through it."

Besides a rainbow-rich variety of small tropical fish, the waters were filled with eagle-rays, turtles, angelfish, three-hundred-pound tuna, groupers, and sharks. The sharks near the Great Basses Reef were easy to photograph once a fish was speared and its blood spread into the sea. The challenge was to get the rare photos of sharks with one or two divers in the same picture. This was tried by taking up certain positions relative to the speared bait.

"We had sharks all around us—two nine-footers fought over a fish just six feet away from me as I lay on the sea bed," Clarke wrote to Val Cleaver. "But despite all our efforts, Mike couldn't get me and the sharks in the same picture."

Perhaps the creatures they saw most were a family of three groupers who often came out of their caves to see what the intruding divers were doing. Groupers, also known as *sea bass* or *sea perch*, come in many varieties and sizes—some over one thousand pounds. The heavy in this particular threesome, however, was only 150 pounds, with the others weighing in at about seventy-five and forty pounds.

By handing a speared fish to the big member of the grouper family Jonklaas began an underwater friendship, and soon the three groupers all had names, from large to small: Ali Baba, Sinbad, and Aladdin. The groupers gratefully accepted the free food that Jonklaas could obtain much easier than they could. In return they would pose for the still and movie cameras. It became a good working relationship, and Jonklaas trained and fed the actors.

"Usually Ali Baba swam up from the cave," said Jonklaas, "which he regarded as his own private castle, while Sinbad had already joined us from his own territory a few yards to the lee. Aladdin was last on the scene and usually performed his actions after the larger two had had their fill. It was because of this that he displayed such amusing actions of haste, jealousy, and peevishness."

Cameras ready, Jonklaas began the action by spearing a fish. Once the gun was discharged, the grouper swam quickly to the struggling fish. "If I missed (which was fairly often)," said Jonklaas, "the expression of bewilderment displayed by the disappointed grouper was remarkable."

Three nonunion actors who didn't have to remember their lines—what more could the movie crew desire? Wilson was able to shoot sixteen-millimeter color footage of the underwater adventures of the groupers, as well as the shark activity.

"Writing the script, doing some of the camera work, and producing sound effects in the bath was an interesting experience," Clarke admitted before lapsing into a tongue-in-cheek hyperbole, "and quite helpful when I had to do the same sort of thing, on a slightly larger budget, with a fellow named Stanley Kubrick."

But Clarke's first meeting with Kubrick was five years in the future. There were several more books and modest regional movies to be produced before then.

The quiet life—that's what Clarke hoped to lead for the rest of the year; quiet with a lot of hard work. Besides all the book contracts he had to fulfill, he and Wilson were building up their underwater consulting business, Clarke-Wilson Associates, and work was coming in.

Hector Ekanayake began working full-time for Clarke-Wilson Associates in May 1959, and Rodney Jonklaas also left his job at that time. Along with Wilson, they were ready to take on whatever underwater work came their way. One of their first jobs together was to survey underwater obstructions for the Fisheries Department.

Soon after returning from the Great Basses Reef, Clarke began working hard on a juvenile book for Harper & Brothers, which he was supposed to deliver in early June. When published in the spring of 1960, it became *The First Five Fathoms: A Guide to Underwater Adventure*, "with Mike Wilson" added to Clarke's name as author. The book also boasted an introduction by Jacques Cousteau.

After the manuscript and photographs were sent to the publisher, Clarke immediately began his twenty-fifth book, "about all the possible ways of exploiting the sea, " which was due to Holt, Rinehart and Winston before the end of 1959. This was *The Challenge of the Sea*, published in 1960. This one had an introduction by Wernher von Braun.

As if that weren't enough, Clarke still had *Glide Path* to complete. He was hard at work on it again in September 1959, completely rewriting and retyping it.

"The first draft was partly an aide-mémoire to myself," he told

Left: Lieutenant Charles
Wright Clarke, circa
1917.

Below: Wanderlust at an
early age. A two-year-old
Arthur C. Clarke begins
his travels.

Above: The Clarke family in the late 1920s, when their father was ailing from war wounds. Clockwise from top: Arthur, Nora, Michael, Mary, and Fred.

Right: Clarke's beloved collection of science fiction magazines are on the shelves behind him.

Above: Group portrait of British Interplanetary Society members at a meeting in July 1938. Left to right: H. E. Ross, J. H. Edwards, H. E. Turner, Robert C. Truax (holding rocket), R. A. Smith, M. K. Hanson, and Arthur C. Clarke. (Courtesy Smithsonian Institution)

Left: Clarke's official Royal Air Force portrait, circa 1940.

Above: Clarke in front of his childhood home, Ballifants, in the mid-1940s.

Below: At the Midwestcon in Bellefontaine, Ohio, May 1953, where Clarke met many fellow writers for the first time. Left to right: Robert Bloch (author of Psycho*), Harlan Ellison, Evelyn Gold (wife of Horace Gold, who founded* Galaxy *magazine), and Clarke. (Courtesy Dean A. Grennell)*

Left: The newlyweds, Arthur and Marilyn, leaving the United States for England, June 1953.

Below: Clarke's underwater adventures in Australia and Ceylon changed the direction of his life and work. Here he discovers a huge propeller from a wreck off the coast of Ceylon.

*Above: Clarke and
Wernher von Braun at a
meeting in New York
City, 1966. (Courtesy
Smithsonian Institution)*

*Right: Clarke and Alan
Watts met at the
Chelsea Hotel in 1971
for a series of
discussions that became
a Playboy interview.*

Left: Clarke and Stanley Kubrick on the 2001 set in 1966. (Courtesy Fred Ordway)

Below: Most of the spaceship scenes in 2001: A Space Odyssey were shot inside this forty-ton, thirty-eight-foot centrifuge.

Right: On the moonscape set of CBS studios during the Apollo 15 coverage, August 1971.

Below: At the CBS anchor desk with Walter Cronkite and Wally Schirra.

Val Cleaver, "and I'll probably only use about half of it." That estimate was not far from the mark. By the end of September he had written twenty thousand words of new text.

At the end of October Clarke moved into a new house in Colombo. Its address was 47/5 Gregory's Road.

"Our new house is a beauty," he wrote to Cleaver in late October, "47/5 is a common local convention. It means that 47 is a lane and we are the 5th house in it. Actually we are at the end of the lane, nicely secluded. As soon as possible I'll take some shots of it, but photography has been out of the question while the darkroom is being installed."

Clarke was settling in once more: "I hope to be here right through 1960, repairing my shattered finances (if possible)."

I was scared to go on with the story as my brain was racing too fast and I thought I'd better stop. Very odd feeling.
                                    Letter to Val Cleaver, October 17, 1960

13
DOWN TO EARTH

"If worse comes to the worst, we may be wiped out at any minute."

So wrote Arthur C. Clarke to Val Cleaver in mid-1960. His financial situation, he told his friend, was too complicated to describe, but it came down to the fact that he was getting taxed heavily in Ceylon and elsewhere. All the earnings he had brought into Ceylon were not wasted, he explained, but had gone into the house, the VW bus, the diving gear, and cameras and motion picture equipment. And the underwater work that Clarke had financed, now called Submarine Safaris to clear up any ambiguity about what the company did, was proving to be an unpredictable source of income.

"The worst of it is," wrote Clarke at the time, "having to run around seeing lawyers, accountants and govt officials leaves me completely exhausted for writing, though I have been able to get off several pieces recently. So it's a vicious circle."

So far 1960 had not been a stellar year for Arthur C. Clarke. Ironically, it kicked off a decade that would witness the realization of many of Clarke's dreams.

When New Year's Day 1960 was celebrated, no one knew how

momentous the coming decade would be. Not even Clarke cared to predict when the first man would orbit the Earth, set foot on the moon, or descend almost thirty-six thousand feet beneath the Pacific Ocean to the bottom of the Challenger Deep—all near-future events. (The last was accomplished in early 1960 by Naval Lieutenant Don Walsh in the bathyscaphe *Trieste*.) Clarke was thinking and writing more about the far future—beyond the year 2000—than the current decade. He was beginning to write speculative essays that would become *Profiles of the Future*.

Clarke's most important new magazine market in the 1960s was *Playboy*, for both fiction and nonfiction. The May 1960 issue ran "I Remember Babylon," about possible abuse of the coming communications satellites. The story was unique in that the author himself was one of its two main characters, and the first scene at the Soviet Embassy was based on an actual event. Clarke even gave passing mention to Mike and Elizabeth Wilson, who were attending the fictional embassy gala, and *Playboy* ran a color photo of the threesome with the piece.

"Mixing fact and fiction was a deliberate experiment," he told Val Cleaver in April. So was sending a message in the story, even though Clarke usually agrees with Samuel Goldwyn that people with messages should use Western Union. "[I]t was written in the pre-Telstar days, with the deliberate intent of making the U.S. public think seriously about communications satellites," he wrote. "I didn't take any moral attitude," says Clarke. "In fact I was probably licking my chops at the idea of such programs."

Gene Hartford, the American character in the story, planned to launch an independent communications satellite in orbit and broadcast pornography and other decadent programming direct to American homes. Said Hartford, "We'll be using America's own decadence as a weapon against her, and it's a weapon for which there's no defense."

"Only a few years after *Playboy* published this cautionary tale," wrote Clarke, "I was watching the launch of *Early Bird* by closed-circuit TV at Comsat headquarters."

In August 1960, just three months after the story's publication, the *Echo 1* satellite was launched. This huge aluminum-coated balloon was the precursor of communications satellites. While it was rather primitive and could only passively bounce off signals (unlike the *Early Bird*, which could receive, amplify, and retransmit them), it nevertheless marked the beginning of the communications revolution. Millions saw it as a bright star arcing across the night sky—a true symbol of the new Space Age.

A week after the launch, the Bell Telephone Laboratories announced that they had made the first transatlantic wireless code transmission via *Echo 1* from Holmdel, New Jersey, to Issyles-Moulineaux, France.

That this new technology could be abused was an extremely important message at the outset of the Space Age. Thirty years later, as the 1990s began, several lawsuits were filed against an American company that broadcast X-rated pornographic programming direct to satellite dish owners who subscribed to its service. Clarke's story foresaw such problems even before *Telstar 1* telecast the first TV images across the Atlantic in 1962.

The diving expeditions of the late 1950s as well as current financial struggles had definitely cut into Clarke's literary output. Although life was made a bit less chaotic by the new house on Gregory's Road, which offered some badly needed extra space, the new surroundings didn't help Clarke overcome his difficulties with the autobiographical World War II novel. "GLIDE PATH abandoned indefinitely," he wrote to Val Cleaver. "After 4 months solid work I sent the MS to Scott, who NBG'd [No Bloody Good'd] it. . . . Now I want to forget it completely, so I can leave my subconscious to decide what to do."

Nor was he hopeful about the progress of *Imperial Earth*, a novel first conceived in the early 1950s: "Doubt if I'll ever do it now. Put it aside for several years anyway. (I've written 3,000 words of it in 5 years!) . . .

"I seem to have lost all interest in novels, & know better than to try to force the matter. It'll come when it will come: if it doesn't, I could hardly care less. I've always enjoyed essays & short stories much more, and now I'm beginning to feel I'm a fool to write anything else both from the financial & the influential point of view.

"I know all the arguments in favor of novels, and *hope* I'll do one again sometime. But I've several years' accumulated backlog of story and article ideas I want to work through: that should take most of this year, & when I'm fed up with short pieces I hope I'll feel like tackling another major work. I have the "Breakthroughs in Science" book [*Profiles of the Future*] half-promised to Harper, but intend to write that in article form anyway.

"Also the economics of novels doesn't make any sense—unless you land a movie sale, or are a Nevil Shute." (Shute was a British mainstream writer, best known for his 1957 novel *On the Beach*, which became a film starring Gregory Peck, Fred Astaire, and Ava Gardner in 1959. He commanded high rates.)

Besides the better pay for magazine articles than books (comparing initial income and number of words written), the large audiences for magazines such as *Playboy* and *Holiday* (about one million each at that time) appealed to Clarke. He knew he could never reach that many people with a book—at least not in the first few printings.

Clarke was obviously discouraged. In fact his letters show that his attitude about his work and life in early 1960 was basically down; it appeared that he was going through some kind of midlife crisis.

The ultimate sign of trouble was when he confessed to Cleaver, "I've largely lost interest in SF. . . ." For anyone who had ever experienced Clarke's genuine, unwavering enthusiasm, this attitude was a shock and could be explained only as a temporary aberration—a rare downer in his outlook that no doubt would turn upward. The only question was "When?" and the answer was rather noncommittal when Cleaver asked his friend how he was feeling in April.

"It varies in a way which doesn't seem to have a definite period and probably depends on what I've eaten," Clarke replied. "Sometimes I feel on top of the world and full of energy; at other times everything is too much bother. I was cheered by your remark that I looked thinner in the photo—then remembered that it was taken four years ago!"

One drain on Clarke's energy was the details of the diving business, which he ended up handling because Wilson and Jonklaas were both almost equally "hopeless at accounts." When he was able to write, however, Clarke worked on short stories such as "Summertime on Icarus," which he hoped to bring together in a short story collection. The author considered it a suspense-action story, "quite a tough piece full of technicalities (though all explained) about a man trapped on Icarus at perihelion and doomed to be cooked at dawn." When the *Saturday Evening Post* hesitated to buy it (although it didn't reject it), Scott Meredith promptly sold it to *Vogue* and told Clarke, "This will shake the *Post* to the core."

Clarke's reduced prolificacy was not improving his financial status, and current political events in Ceylon threatened to make matters even worse. In late July, Mrs. Sirimavo Bandaranaike was elected prime minister, and the change in government put the demand for the underwater and other services offered by Clarke and cohorts very much in doubt.

"It will be some weeks before we see how things work out," Clarke updated Cleaver, "but we now have to face up to the fact that we may have to close down here at a moment's notice.

"The awkward thing is that this has happened just when we were about broke and the overdraft was due for repayment. If the bank won't extend it, we've had it and will have to sell up."

A month later: "All hell has broken loose here, and we are too exhausted and upset to even think, let alone write. We have run into all sorts of snags, personal and financial . . . not to mention political."

For the first time, one of Clarke's books was turned down. It was *Glide Path*, and it was finally rejected after two major rewrites.

The news really threw Clarke.

"That means I've gambled several thousand dollars and lost; I'd been relying on that to pull us out of the hole," he told Val Cleaver. "I could have earned at least ten thousand dollars in the same writing time."

A few months later the book would be rejected by Clarke's British publisher, Gollancz, as well. Despite the reader's opinion that "the wartime atmosphere is excellent," it was pronounced stale and passé.

There was still hope, of course, that a few other things would break right. Several diving jobs could come through at any time, allowing Ekanayake and Jonklaas to pull their own weight in the underwater diving, salvage, and tourist business.

"And any moment, of course, I may sell something to Hollywood! But the big trouble is that we have absolutely no reserve to carry us over the sticky patches."

At least one good thing was coming out of all the troubles: Clarke was losing weight from all the stress. And ultimately his problems forced him to return to his customary writing pace.

"I decided to do a short story to make some money quickly, and it just blew up in my face," he explained to Cleaver. "I am working from 7:30 am to around 9 pm on it, have canceled all lectures etc and have only been to a movie once in the last month."

The man who had lost all interest in novels earlier in the year was fifty thousand words into a new one by mid-October—a novel he hadn't even thought of six weeks earlier.

"I am in a slight stupor at the moment," he wrote to Cleaver on October 17, 1960, "having written 3,500 words of the novel yesterday, much of it in a kind of automatic frenzy."

For most of September, October, and November, Clarke wrote nonstop. *A Fall of Moondust*, without a contract or even the interest of a publisher, was completed by November 21, 1960.

Perhaps it is symbolic that the passengers and crew of the novel's Dust-Cruiser *Selene* are buried alive beneath the moon's surface. *A Fall of Moondust* is a survival story, conceived when its author himself was struggling to survive.

The stress in the household produced by financial woes had slackened by fall 1960, probably because everyone finally understood that there were no quick fixes; solutions to their problems would take some time. Meanwhile, less stress meant fewer disagreements and arguments in the Clarke household. And besides Clarke's confidence in his new novel, the Colombo premiere of Mike Wilson's first film, *Beneath the Seas of Ceylon*, was a success: "Almost 1,000 turned up and many were unable to get seats," Clarke told Cleaver. There was the hope that a sale of extra copies to the Ceylon Tea Board could provide financial assistance.

At the end of 1960 there were a few more uplifting notes. Harcourt Brace offered a contract for a second anthology, *From the Ocean, From the Stars*, which included two novels (*The Deep Range* and *The City and the Stars*, and his collection of short stories, *The Other Side of the Sky*). This produced an unexpected check, and Scott Meredith had collected another one from Gnome Press. "These two cheques," Clarke wrote to Cleaver, "have saved our bacon—for the time being—but I don't like having to rely on unexpected windfalls."

Clarke now focused his efforts on *Indian Ocean Adventure* for Harper & Brothers, which was already two months overdue—a fact that had been weighing on Clarke's mind since he already had his advance. The book was about the fall 1959 expedition to Great Basses Reef and wasn't going to involve that many words; it was completed on New Year's Eve. That obligation fulfilled, Clarke found another burden lifted when it was decided that the underwater business would be handed over to Rodney Jonklaas.

Business and financial matters seemed to be looking up when sadness descended on the Clarke household. The baby that Mike and Liz Wilson had been expecting, a girl, was stillborn on December 23. Mike was terribly upset and became very ill the next day with a kidney infection and was delirious for some time. He was too sick to pick up his wife at the hospital, so Hector Ekanayake brought her home. "She's pale but composed," Clarke told Val Cleaver, "and said to me, 'The growing-up process finished yesterday.' She spoke for them both."

The same day the bad news came from the hospital, Clarke received a cable from William Jovanovich, president of Harcourt Brace, saying, "new novel [*Moondust*] superb repeat superb. I am anxious to publish as soon as feasible." Scott Meredith said it was Clarke's "greatest book yet."

"Keep your fingers crossed," he told Cleaver in a letter he wrote on Christmas Day. "This book may pull us out of the hole."

*It was one of the unforgettable moments of a lifetime, for I
knew then that I was staring at something that very few
men have ever seen—genuine, honest-to-goodness treasure.*
The Treasure of the Great Reef *(1964)*

14
SILVER LININGS

Writing *A Fall of Moondust* had been an act of will that was
Arthur C. Clarke's way of regaining his confidence as a writer. Still
basking in the euphoric afterglow of its enthusiastic reception at
the beginning of 1961, he carefully laid out his next ten book
projects.

"I am pretty firm in my resolve to write only what I *want* to
write, *and* I'm sure is worth writing," he wrote to Val Cleaver.

High on the list was *Breakthroughs in Science*, which would
be first published in England in late 1962 as *Profiles of the Future*,
Isaac Asimov having preempted Clarke on the use of the original
title.

"Have done about 12,000 words, but it involves a great deal of
research that is impossible here, and I think I can only complete
it in London and NY," he wrote to Cleaver. "At the moment I am
having a lot of fun dealing with some of the false prophets of the
past, to put the reader in the right frame of mind."

Clarke knew this project involved much more than adding
some new essays to old ones. "I think this book may be my most
important non-fiction since EoS [*Exploration of Space*]. I hope to

151

finish the rough draft by the middle of the year." That goal was much closer by mid-March, when he sent off some twenty-five thousand words to Scott Meredith for possible serialization rights.

Meanwhile, Mike Wilson's filmmaking projects, which he was able to focus on now that Jonklaas had taken over the underwater business, were beginning to pay off. The Ceylon Tea Board paid eighteen hundred pounds for the first ten prints of the twenty-minute-long *Beneath the Seas of Ceylon*, his first production venture. If the board ordered a few more copies, the project soon would be in the black.

What had started out as a hobby with the purchase of their first movie camera soon became a way of producing income for the business partnership in underwater work. Believing that Wilson's talent should be encouraged, Clarke financed the filmmaking ventures. Both he and Wilson did the script writing and other production chores.

The second moviemaking venture was scheduled for spring 1962, and Wilson was in a big hurry to complete it.

"Reason is," Clarke told Cleaver, "that Cousteau arrives here mid-March with about 15 tons of gear, including his diving saucer. We look forward to helping him as far as we can, but Mike is determined to finish his first 35 *mm* colour movie and to get it off to market before Jacques can trump him. The amount of work involved in preparing scripts and equipment is fantastic.

"The film will be a 15 minute fantasy about a small boy who finds a genii in a bottle and gets his wish—an Aqua-Lung. The underwater sequences [off Great Basses Reef] will involve the boy and our pet giant groupers (who we hope will remember us from last year)."

With both Clarke and Jonklaas otherwise occupied, it was up to Wilson to find some great on-location swimmers. Two teenage American boys, Bobby Kriegel and Mark Smith, who were both first-class swimmers and divers, were perfect.

"They lived in the water," says Dick Kriegel, Bobby's father, who was a training officer at the U.S. Operation Mission in Ceylon at the time. "And they got to know Mike Wilson in the summer of 1960 while they were skin-diving out in Colombo Harbor. Mike then began training the boys in the use of scuba-diving equipment in the fall of '60. They were doing snorkeling with a face mask and breather, and he trained them in scuba diving.

"By the time they went down to Great Basses in March of 1961, the boys were like ducks, very confident. They were excellent swimmers, and they had become competent divers. They were trained for the open sea and the more treacherous waters of the Indian Ocean."

"After a very few lessons," wrote Clarke, "Mike was confident that they could tackle all ordinary underwater jobs quite safely, and wouldn't lose their heads in an emergency."

The film's script was not complicated (it starred one boy and some fish), and Wilson wrote it for Mark Smith, who was smaller and looked younger than Bobby Kriegel. It is Mark who dreams that he is exploring the sea in the film and then wakes up to discover his dream has come true.

Wilson and his two young apprentices loaded up the Volkswagen bus and headed south to the Great Basses Reef, arriving at the village of Kirinda on March 12, 1961. This is where they could catch the power launch, *Pharos*, that would take them to the lighthouse.

The trio did a lot of diving and underwater filming during the next week. They would jump off the edge of the reef and swim out some hundred yards to where the groupers were. They towed a large inner tube behind them, with the cameras and Aqua-Lungs attached. Once on location they anchored this temporary dock and got to work on their underwater set.

Sinbad, Ali Baba, and Aladdin were still there after two years, and as long as they were well fed they cooperated for the camera. A big shark was seen at a distance, but it was not aggressive and caused no alarm. Only a less-than-friendly grouper chased them once. Another time their friendly film star Sinbad got greedy and tried to swallow Mark's arm up to the elbow. No real harm done, though. Sinbad's small teeth left a few minor scars, that was all, and Mark was proud of them—his battle scars from the deep.

The weather was good most days, and Wilson was getting the film he needed. On March 22 the sea was calm. It was too calm for photography because there was no current to clear away the sand in the water. Since no filming was possible, Wilson and the boys decided to explore another reef about a thousand feet away from the lighthouse. This became a vacation day; without their gear they were just underwater tourists. The free time was a pleasure, the new territory exciting. They explored for a few hours.

"They were thinking of turning back when Mike spotted something on the sea bed that he had been looking for, in vain, for many years," Clarke wrote later. "It was an old cannon—a very tiny one, only about two feet long—shining brightly in the sunlight as if it had been lost only yesterday." Wilson knew that, depending on how the ship had hit, there might be more of the wreck on the coast side of the reef.

"After we got to the other side, the first thing we saw was a shiny cannon [swivel gun]," recalls Bobby Kriegel, "about two and one-half feet long, sitting on the edge of a big canyon; and it was worn smooth by the water. . . ."

The wreck's wooden hull probably had long ago decayed and vanished, but they knew—even without that—there must be more to discover. They made a second dive in the afternoon. This time they brought their Aqua-Lungs; they could stay down longer on the seabed and explore more thoroughly. Soon they found a five-foot cannon, two huge tangled anchors, and a massive pile of twelve or more large iron cannons.

"Mike was hitting everything he saw with his knife," says Mark Smith. "Then Mike came over to us and showed us the cannon, and Bob pointed out something shining right near it. Mike examined it and then yelled . . . 'Silver!' underwater with his mouthpiece on!" The first Indian Ocean treasure ever recovered had been found.

Wilson and company returned to Colombo four days later on March 26, 1961. Clarke had just sent half the manuscript of *Profiles of the Future* to Scott Meredith and was taking a breather, relaxing and reading Lawrence Durrell's *Alexandria Quartet*. He had finished *Balthazar* and found it "brilliant and amusing."

When Clarke asked Wilson and the boys how it had gone, they mumbled a few noncommittal words as they staggered into his office carrying a battered tin trunk. Wilson locked the door behind them.

"Look at this," he said mysteriously, throwing open the lid of the trunk. Clarke gazed into the trunk and saw two small bronze cannons.

"My God, you've found an old wreck!" Clarke cried as Wilson lifted out the guns to show him what was underneath.

"At first I thought I was looking at dirty lumps of coral," says

Clarke, "about the size of coconuts. Then I realized just what those lumps were; and I was too astonished to say anything."

Clarke bent down to pick up one of the lumps of coins; he could hardly lift it. Beside the lumps there were also hundreds of loose coins, and all had Arabic letters on them.

After the initial excitement subsided, they discussed their plan of action and decided to contact their lawyer and inform the boys' parents.

Later that evening Clarke's adrenaline was still flowing. "Well, Mike has done it at last!" he wrote to Val Cleaver. "I'm too excited to go to bed, and this letter will probably be a bit incoherent. You may even think I'm drunk or pulling your leg!" He then went on to summarize the treasure story for his friend. "We've always dreamed of this, and never found anything but busted-up tankers. Mike says there's more where these came from. I've just weighed the lumps and they come to 115 pounds. So I'm sitting here in my office with a hundredweight of treasure at my feet, wondering if it's all a dream, and what will happen next! . . .

"We've been doing a lot of research: the coins are Persian, c. 1650, pure silver, so the lot Mike's brought back is worth more than 500 pounds [$1,500 U.S., approximately] if melted down."

The next day they invited the Kriegels and the Smiths over to inform them about the find.

"We got a telephone call from Arthur," recalls Dick Kriegel, "and he said, 'Can you come over?' So the Smiths and my wife and I went over to his house, which was all shuttered up. It was almost like we were going into a dungeon. It was very quiet . . . kind of funny. Mike Wilson was there when we came in the house, and Clarke was excited. He can often be almost droll, almost casual about most things. But this time he was really excited.

"He said, 'Listen, what you're going to see, don't say anything about it. You must not discuss this with anybody. Just leave it right here with us.'

"So we went in, and he had a great big wooden chest. They opened it up, and it had about five or six large chunks of gray stuff. It was silver, congealed bags of silver coins, estimated at about thirty pounds and probably one thousand coins in each one. They were Arabian coins and had apparently been minted on the east coast of India and were being shipped back to Arabia.

"Of course Arthur says, 'We can't let it get out of here. I've got to check with the Ceylonese government to find out what possible claims they may have on the treasure. Also I want to make sure that the Smithsonian gets a share of this and the right story on it. I think that this is something that we can write and make a very exciting story about.'"

The treasure of the Great Basses Reef consisted not just of silver coinage; it also held at least one unwritten book by Arthur C. Clarke: *The Treasure of the Great Reef*, published in 1964.

The Muslim coins, research soon determined, were rupees that were minted at Surat (in northwest India) in 1702 during the reign of Mughal emperor Aurangzeb. During the eighteenth century these coins were common currency for a large area of Asia. Because all of the coins bore the same Muslim date and appeared to be brand-new, it was most likely that the ship carrying them had come directly from India. And since all the large clumps contained exactly one thousand coins, they had obviously been packed in bags of that number, but the bags had disintegrated long ago.

"The Smithsonian is quite interested and would like to buy one of the lumps which weighs some 25 lbs," Clarke wrote to Cleaver.

There could have been many more silver lumps of treasure beneath the waves of Great Basses Reef, and the group decided to mount an ambitious expedition the following spring, in 1962.

While the treasure continued to provide most of the excitement around Gregory's Road (even though it was a closely guarded secret), the literary side of Clark's life also provided uplifting news from time to time. When Gollancz published *The Other Side of the Sky* in England two years after the U.S. edition first appeared, Victor Gollancz himself praised the volume on the press release: "This is a superb book. I am inclined to think that 'The Star' may be the finest short story I have ever read."

Russia and the United States, meanwhile, were making the ancient dreams of spaceflight actually fly. On April 12, 1961, Yuri Gagarin was strapped into the *Vostok 1* spacecraft mounted atop Russia's A-1 rocket and roared into orbit. He became the first human in history to orbit planet Earth and witness two sunrises in just under two hours.

"Well, the Russians have certainly done it now!" wrote Clarke.

"The Mercury people must be feeling sick, however much a brave face they put on it. And if they kill one of the US astronauts, it will be exactly like the Vanguard situation again. I hope Major G took some nice snaps with his box brownie. Doesn't he look like Lindbergh!"

Less than a month later, Alan B. Shepard, Jr., rode his *Freedom 7* spacecraft on a successful suborbital flight, America's first manned spaceflight.

Clarke wrote to Val Cleaver: "I was pleased that the Americans got their first astronaut back safely—although slightly overshadowed by Yuri, it's still a fine feat, and I feel they've earned some success. I'm glad to see, however, that there is no disposition to claim that it's bigger than it is."

Clarke heard Shepard's flight on the shortwave, although not very clearly. "Hope it shames the Russians into being more forthcoming," he wrote to Cleaver.

Russian rocketry and its impressive feats appeared to be on Clarke's mind in June, when he had an "incredibly vivid dream."

"I was going through Russia on a bus, and we passed within a few hundred yards of one of their launching vehicles," he wrote to Cleaver. "It was a couple of hundred feet high, three or four stages (come to think of it, the original stimulus was probably that recent photo of the SATURN mock-up—I've just realised that). But it was apparently made of overlapping boilerplate, with the rivets quite prominent!

"But the funniest thing is that the next incident (after a friendly argument with a Russian soldier sitting beside me, who rather objected to my intense use of binoculars as the bus drove past the rocket) was a meeting with you in which I carefully described the beast, and we decided that I *hadn't* dreamed the whole thing!!!! Work that one out. . . ."

Dreams of spaceflight and of treasure were coming true in 1961. What else could a writer hope for? A bit of peace and quiet would have suited Clarke just fine.

In early summer he told his friend Sam Youd that, because of Wilson's growing filmmaking business, there were as many as ten people in the house at one time. Then there were the five dogs, including his beloved Laika, who often curled up by Clarke's feet. And there was more.

"Mike and Liz got married the other evening—in the eyes of

the church," Clarke wrote to Youd in June. "They've also adopted a little boy, a month old.

"All is quiet here at the moment (except for the baby), despite anything you may have read in the UK press. There has been trouble, but only on a very small scale, in limited areas."

Still not clear of his cash flow crisis, Clarke was working "like a galley slave," he wrote to Cleaver, putting in fifteen or sixteen hours a day at the typewriter. "I've been turning out about two articles or short stories a week as I have to get together at least $3,000 *above* normal income to make the US trip possible."

Before leaving for England and the United States, Clarke became quite upset by news he received from his brother Fred.

"I'm sorry to say that my brother and sister-in-law have separated," he wrote to Sam Youd, "and Dorothy has gone off with my little nieces, of whom I'm very fond and was looking forward to spending some time with this summer. Luckily they're still in Wood Green and I hope to see them all. This has been a great blow to the family—the Clarkes do not seem too successful at their marriages. The casualty rate is now 50%."

Clarke had not left Ceylon for two years, so he was eager to see friends and family in England, talk to his agents, editors, and publishers on both sides of the Atlantic, and see his aerospace colleagues at two conventions in the United States.

After spending most of August in London and Somerset, he had almost four weeks at New York's Hotel Chelsea before the conventions began: the International Astronautical Congress in Washington and then the American Rocket Society's "Space Flight Report to the Nation" in New York. Among the many people he saw in New York during September was Hugo Gernsback, the pioneer editor and publisher who coined the term *science fiction*.

"We met at his Fourteenth Street office and went out for lunch. I remember his Old World charm (and that he never owed me for any stories). Later he wrote complaining that I'd used the phrase *orbital post office* in an article on communication satellites without crediting him for its invention: he gave a reference to his first use. I shot him down in flames by pointing out it was used *earlier* in *Profiles of the Future*—which was dedicated to him! He apologized handsomely and sent me his amusing Christmas min-imag to the end of his life."

In late September it was on to Washington, D.C., for the Twelfth International Astronautical Congress. Almost four years before the first commercial communications satellite was launched in April 1965, Clarke predicted that "by the end of this century all terrestrial calls may be local calls and may be billed at a flat standard rate"—an idea he would use again in *2061: Odyssey Three*. His speech also described the information age of the last quarter of the twentieth century and the inevitable future of the global village as it would be in the 1990s: "no dictatorship can build a wall high enough to stop its citizens listening to the voices from the stars."

Clarke spent a lot of time at the congress with the Soviet expert on astronautics L. I. Sedov. After having seen the Soviet film *With Gagarin to the Stars*, Clarke said to Sedov, "Pity the rocket you see at the end of the Gagarin film isn't G's [Gagarin's]." Sedov's nonplussed reply: "Well, from a distance all big rockets look the same."

Back in New York in early October for the American Rocket Society's big conference, Clarke was "flattered and shattered" to be asked to participate in both the U.S. and USSR space program reviews that would be televised. (Security excluded Sedov or other Russians from participating.) The panel had the biggest audience in the society's history, perhaps in part because Clarke went out of his way to generate controversy. He even asked General Bernard Schriever, head of the U.S. Air Force missile program, how to begin integrating the U.S. and USSR space programs—this when the space race was still escalating!

Also at the conference was Vice President Lyndon B. Johnson, and the final result of Clarke's brush with Johnson was that the White House asked Comsat to coordinate arrangements for televising live the 1964 Olympic ceremonies from Tokyo to the United States.

"He [Johnson] gave a speech," says Clarke, "and someone passed on to him the suggestion I had made in an earlier meeting that we ought to get Syncom ready in time for the Tokyo Olympics. I think that's what triggered that chain of events."

That someone was Dr. William Pickering, director of the Jet Propulsion Laboratory, who was in the front row of the audience when Clarke was moderating a panel discussion. Pickering liked the idea so much that he indeed did pass it on to Vice President Johnson.

The signals ultimately were sent via *Syncom 3* and the U.S. Navy earth station at Point Magu, California. Not as many people saw the historic broadcast as had been hoped because the networks did not want to upset their existing program schedules and advertising commitments. This event, however, heralded the new era that would officially begin when *Early Bird* started commercial operation in April 1965.

After a brief stay in London, Clarke returned to Ceylon to round off the year by meeting the first man in space, Yuri Gagarin.

The most famous man in the world in 1961, and the first man to leave it, Gagarin arrived in Colombo aboard his own four-engine jet on December 6. There was major publicity for his arrival, and his schedule was crowded.

"I was walking back to my house in the Colombo suburb where I still live," wrote Clarke. "I'd just been playing table tennis at the local athletic club and was about to cross the main road. Suddenly a police escort came in sight, followed by a car containing a group of dignitaries. . . .

"My gaze locked on to a single figure, and instantly there flashed into my mind a phrase that was used more than a hundred years ago, when President Lincoln was assassinated: 'Now he belongs to the ages.'

"That was my first glimpse of Yuri Gagarin; I never guessed how soon, and how tragically, the same quotation would apply to him." (Colonel Yuri Gagarin died in the crash of a jet trainer on March 27, 1968, some eight months before *Apollo 8* made its historic flight around the moon in December of that year.)

Because of Gagarin's tight itinerary, Clarke managed to speak only briefly with him after a public lecture. He then asked him the same question he had asked Professor Sedov: "Why doesn't your film show your rocket?" Gagarin's answer was somewhat more forthcoming than Sedov's:

"Well, when we can destroy all our war weapons, then we'll be able to show it."

They chatted a bit longer, with the help of an interpreter, and Clarke saw him as "a cheerful, friendly, and in no way unusual young man, quite untouched by destiny."

Before he left, Clarke gave Gagarin a copy of *Indian Ocean Adventure*, knowing that all the men in the first groups of cosmonauts and astronauts had an interest in underwater exploration.

Several weeks later, after Gagarin had completed his international tour, Clarke received a signed copy of his hero's autobiography. It read, "To Arthur Clarke, this souvenir of our cosmic voyage and our meeting in Ceylon—Y. Gagarin."

I was convinced that my spine was being slowly bent back-wards until it was about to snap. In other interludes, I was dying of thirst while being buried in desiccated dust.

Treasure of the Great Reef *(1964)*

15
PARALYSIS

"[A]t the end of February I conducted an unsuccessful experiment to see if two objects could occupy the same space at the same time. One was a doorway and the other my head."

Thus wrote Arthur C. Clarke in May 1962, three months after fate took a rather uncompromising stand and left his entire future in question.

It happened on the last day of February, while he was shopping in Pettah, the Colombo bazaar.

"Leaving one store, I misjudged the height of a doorway and crashed the top of my head against the lintel," Clarke wrote months later. "It took me a few minutes to recover, and I had a painful scalp wound; but I felt none the worse. After I stopped cursing, I got on my motor scooter, drove three miles home, played several vigorous games of table tennis, and ate a hearty dinner—my last for many months."

That night he became violently sick, but he believed that it was some kind of temporary stomach ailment. His condition didn't improve. Still, he didn't think it necessary to call a doctor and spent a few days in bed, convinced that his body would rally and destroy the mysterious intruder. It didn't happen.

Finally the doctor was called, but by the time he arrived, Clarke was in trouble. "I was almost completely paralyzed and could barely breathe," he wrote.

He vaguely remembers being carried to the hospital, where he remained delirious for several days.

"A plastic collar fastened round my neck gave me the worst nights I have ever endured, for I was convinced that my spine was being slowly bent backwards until it was about to snap. In other interludes, I was dying of thirst while being buried in desiccated dust (I can still taste the dust)."

When Clarke finally came out of his delirium, he had no strength or body control whatsoever.

"Though I could just move one arm and one leg, I could do nothing with them. The greatest feat I could achieve, after long deliberation and careful planning, was a slow roll from my back on to one side. . . .

"Although I could breathe without much trouble when perfectly relaxed, the slightest exertion left me gasping. I could not speak more than two or three words without panting for breath. Having my face washed was a frightful ordeal; I could barely endure the brief passage of the suffocating sponge over my nose." He wouldn't be seeing the Great Basses Reef soon—that was certain.

Clarke spent six weeks in a private hospital, helpless and unable to feed or bathe himself. In mid-April he was carried home, but he was wholly dependent on Hector or one of several male nurses to help him move. The prognosis was unclear. All that his doctors had been able to tell the patient was that his debilitation was caused by a spinal injury resulting from the blow to his head.

With Clarke's prospects for a full recovery uncertain, the planned moneymaking ventures and adventures remained on hold, while ongoing projects continued to drain the coffers.

Mike Wilson's adventures in Technicolor moviemaking were costing Clarke a bundle, as was their custom-built boat for the now-canceled Great Basses expedition. Wilson had convinced Clarke that the boat was an important investment for the return expedition to Great Basses and its treasure and for the future of their underwater business. The boat's name was taken from Mike Wilson's two-hour Sinhala movie *Ran Mutu Duwa* (*Island of Pearls and Gold*). But by the time immediately before the accident, says Clarke, "it was not clear whether the movie was going to pay for the boat or the boat for the movie." Three months later, of course, nothing was paying for either.

The contract delivery dates with Harper & Brothers to write two books about the treasure had to be amended. Clarke and company wouldn't see Great Basses and the treasure again until 1963 at the earliest. The additional advance money paid upon delivery of the manuscripts and photographs therefore was delayed.

Still, Clarke was determined not to let this bad luck keep him down. And while he was still extremely weak, he noticed a gradual improvement. At least he could sit, propped up in a chair, with some help.

"My slow but steady recovery was like a new birth; for all its worries and unpleasantness, it was a voyage of discovery I am glad to have made," he later wrote. "There was the day when I could sit up in bed unaided; there was the day when I could reach the bathroom by myself; there was the day (a good deal later) when I could *leave* the bathroom by myself; there was the day when I could rise from a chair using both arms, then one arm, then *no* arms. And finally I was able to walk, with the aid of two sticks, for as much as a dozen yards."

By late July, Clarke still had only about half his normal strength, but at least he could walk, with the aid of crutches, for considerable distances. Because of his dramatic improvement— from complete helplessness to self-propulsion—he was no longer terribly worried about his health prospects. And he gives much of the credit for this turnaround to a single timely event that occurred in mid-April, when he was still lying helpless in bed.

The news came by telegram that he had won the tenth Kalinga Prize for science writing, which was administered by UNESCO. This prestigious annual award, given for the popularization of science and donated by Biju Patnaik, the Indian statesman and industrialist, brought Clarke a much-needed one thousand pounds and put him in the distinguished company of Bertrand Russell, Sir Julian Huxley, George Gamow, and others—a valuable psychological boost.

Hoping to be well enough to attend the ceremony in New Delhi in the fall, he continued to work on his physical recovery and on the reading and writing that his illness had permitted him.

"It's been a weird experience," he wrote to Sam Youd, "and has just chopped a couple of months out of my life. But doubtless I'll be able to use it in due course as I was able to do a lot of reading and think of a lot of plots." One of them matured into an adventure novel for youngsters, which Clarke began writing in the summer of 1962 and finished in less than two months. Called *Dolphin Island*, it drew on his rich experiences on Heron Island, the rest of the Great Barrier Reef, and the coast of Ceylon.

"I wrote a couple of pages every day in pencil," says the author, "propped up in my chair—and got my secretary [Pauline de Silva] to type them out while I could still remember what the squiggles meant. *Dolphin Island* went very smoothly, but when it was finished I felt rather sad. I could not help thinking that it was probably my farewell to the sea, which had given me so many strange, wonderful, and exciting experiences."

In *Dolphin Island* the character Professor Kazan becomes a mentor to the young adventurer Johnny Clinton:

"Though he never stopped to think about it, the island had become the home he had never known, and the professor a replacement for the father he could scarcely remember." Once again, a son finds his father in Clarke's fiction.

The novel, with its vivid maritime depictions and its good pacing and suspense, wasn't just a good read for Clarke's intended audience. Even today it is enjoyed by people of all age groups.

While Clarke was working on his health and his writing, Mike Wilson had been working on *Ran Mutu Duwa*, a treasure adventure movie. It was a much more ambitious project than the short tourist promotion film, *Beneath the Seas of Ceylon*. As the Colombo premiere drew near in the early summer, Clarke was hoping that the movie would establish Wilson as a big name in the Asian film industry.

What they got was a Ceylonese success. Clarke wrote, "*Ran Mutu Duwa* turned out to be a smash hit, and its catchy songs were soon blaring out of every radio. Within a few months it had been seen by a million people—a tenth of the population of the country—and had created a great reservoir of good will for us. Wherever we went, members of our diving team who had played parts in the movie were recognized and cheered (if they were Good Guys) or hissed (if they weren't)."

By the fall of 1962, the film, the first Sinhalese color movie, had broken all records for Ceylon and was running in twelve cinemas. It helped pay for the new boat along with the cameras and other costly equipment. Clarke had no illusions, however, about its becoming an international commercial success.

One triumph followed another. After a six-week visit with family and friends back in England, Clarke winged to India for the first time to receive the Kalinga Prize. On the way he saw the great Himalayas flash with lightning storms. In New Delhi, the man who had been paralyzed a mere six months before managed to stand while giving an impassioned acceptance speech that extolled the virtues of science fiction and pronounced that the hope of a better future "lies in science combined with wisdom and foresight."

The year 1962 was ending on an up note: Clarke came home to the news that *Dolphin Island* had been chosen by the Junior Literary Guild. He knew he still faced a long convalescence, and he put himself on a regimen that called for limited physical exertion and the usual unlimited mental activities, writing for *Playboy*, *Holiday*, and the *New York Times Magazine*. In between bouts of productivity he had time to mull over the news he had received after consulting a specialist while in England: his paralysis had been caused not by a blow to the head but by polio.

The sea had begun to shape his life and thought, as it must that of all men who try to master it and learn its secrets.

The Deep Range *(1957)*

16
RETURN TO GREAT BASSES

When Arthur C. Clarke's *Comet* aircraft landed in London on August 12, 1962, he had no idea what the British physicians he had agreed to see would tell him. By the time he left for India, he wasn't sure what to believe.

The British doctors who examined Clarke disagreed with their Ceylonese colleagues, who had assured Clarke that the bang on the head had caused his paralysis. Their diagnosis: he had polio.

"There is not much that a mere patient can do when the experts disagree," Clarke said at the time. "I would have preferred polio, which was likely to gain me more sympathy than my own carelessness."

Nonetheless, Clarke chose to go along with the Ceylonese diagnosis. "I became seriously ill in February as a result of a spinal injury," he wrote to Sam Moskowitz in October. "Later diagnosed as polio. But the original verdict seems correct."

Whatever the ultimate cause of his paralysis had been, Clarke's main goal for 1963 was to recover sufficiently from his ailment to make the trip to the treasure wreck he had missed in the spring of 1961:

"By the beginning of March—exactly a year after the accident," Clarke wrote, "I had made up my mind that I *would* go to the Great Basses."

Ten months after the paralysis struck him down, Clarke was still weak. His doctors had anticipated a slow recovery, and his body proved them correct. Basic arm movements continued to be difficult for him in January 1963, so he began working out to build up his strength.

"I did not expect that I would be able to dive," he says, "but I was sure that I could watch operations without getting in the way." Discovering that he could manage an Aqua-Lung and breathe comfortably under water gave him the incentive to keep up his exercise regimen. Concurrently he found it mentally uplifting to see his 1945 vision become hardware: on February 14, 1963, *Syncom 2* was launched, becoming the first artificial satellite to go into a geosynchronous orbit.

Clarke looked even further ahead in *Profiles of the Future*, published in the United States early in 1963. Critics placed Clarke and this book in the tradition of English futurists and considered *Profiles* a pioneering effort in future studies, confirming the author's opinion that it would be his most important nonfiction work since *The Exploration of Space*. The book, wrote Isaac Asimov, gave "all of us a chance to raise our eyes from the ground and to contemplate the scenery ahead." Fritz Leiber viewed it in a historical context as "a splendid introduction to the devices and concepts which the science-fiction writers of the past half-century have been exploring with controlled imaginations."

It also had an impact on Gene Roddenberry, creator of television's "Star Trek." "I read *Childhood's End*, of course, and was mightily moved by it," said Roddenberry. "And I should say that *Profiles of the Future* was the next most important Clarke work in my life because a great deal of what I did on 'Star Trek' was guided by that." It is, in fact, difficult not to think of the famous Roddenberry line "Beam me up, Scottie" when reading Chapter 7 of *Profiles*, "World Without Distance," about teleportation.

Profiles of the Future was not a narrative listing pie-in-the-sky predictions. "All attempts to predict the future in any detail appear ludicrous within a few years," Clarke wrote in an updated introduction in 1983. "This book has a more realistic, yet at the same time more ambitious, aim. It does not try to describe *the* future, but to define the boundaries within which possible futures must lie." *Profiles* offered the best of rational speculation based on the limits of natural laws and discredited any loose imaginations that cast aside the truths and methods of science.

As a bonus, readers were presented with Arthur C. Clarke's First Law. (The Second and Third Laws were later pulled out of the text and given the status of "laws.") The revised 1984 U.S. edition then mentioned all three for the first time, although on different pages. Here they are, gathered together:

Clarke's First Law: "When a distinguished but elderly scientist says that something is possible, he is almost certainly right. When he says it is impossible, he is very probably wrong."

Clarke's Second Law: "The only way to find the limits of the possible is by going beyond them to the impossible."

Clarke's Third Law: "Any sufficiently advanced technology is indistinguishable from magic."

In the middle of March, the weather for the south coast looked good. Mike Wilson, Rodney Jonklaas, and two boatmen sailed *Ran Mutu* out of Colombo harbor and headed down the coast. Arthur C. Clarke, Hector Ekanayake, and the others followed by land a few days later, with all the additional equipment in tow.

The small harbor of Tangalle was the protected anchorage closest to the reef, and the land and sea parties met at a rest house on the water's edge of the small bay where *Ran Mutu* anchored. Their jumping-off point to the Great Basses, as on their earlier trips, was the fishing village of Kirinda some forty miles farther along the coast. But the weather turned bad, and they had to remain at Tangalle.

When the weather did not improve in the next few days, it became clear that it was a waste of time and money for the entire team to remain. Clarke and Wilson returned to Colombo, while Jonklaas and the two boatmen remained behind to watch over *Ran Mutu* and the equipment.

Back in Colombo, Anne Wilson was born to Elizabeth and Mike in late March. Then an unexpected letter arrived on April 1 from Peter Throckmorton, the archaeologist who discovered and excavated a Bronze Age trader off the Turkish coast that had last sailed in about 1300 B.C. His letter asked that he be notified if anything of historical importance became known off the coast of Ceylon.

Clarke and Wilson immediately cabled Throckmorton, taking the long shot that he might be free and able to join them. Before long he answered that he was free and would be coming.

Soon after Throckmorton's arrival in early April, they received reports of good weather on the south coast and set off once more in their quest for the silver beneath the sea.

After more frustrations, including a broken exhaust pipe that was none-too-easily repaired, the *Ran Mutu* finally arrived safely at Kirinda with Wilson, Throckmorton, and the two boatmen aboard. They rendezvoused with the shore party—Clarke, Ekanayake, Jonklaas, a cook, and a photographer. The treasure waited only ten miles offshore.

When *Ran Mutu* headed out to the reef the next morning, Clarke climbed the small hill overlooking Kirinda Beach and set up his 3½-inch Questar telescope.

"Though Mike had pressed me to come, I was not aboard. The boat was already crowded, and this first day I decided to stay on land. I was still extremely weak, and if anything went wrong I would only be in the way." Clarke thus became the unofficial onshore observer on the first day of the expedition to the treasure wreck. He even wrote an "aide-mémoire" on communications satellites while on Kirinda's shore. Requested by UNESCO, its purpose was to provide guidelines for a special 1963 Geneva conference on space communications called by the International Telecommunication Union. It was reprinted several times as "The World of the Communications Satellite," making its most popular appearance in Clarke's 1965 volume of essays *Voices from the Sky*.

Clarke could see *Ran Mutu*'s canvas awning ten miles out in the Indian Ocean, and while she looked submerged in the boiling surf, he knew that this was an illusion of perspective. The boat was actually anchored a few hundred yards away from the harsh surf of the reef.

Meanwhile, Wilson and Throckmorton had located the wreck, but Jonklaas had to turn back because of a defective regulator.

"I very quickly recognised the plateau where we found the second bronze cannon two years previously," said Wilson, "and led Peter right to the spot. I swam the whole length of the wreck with

Peter, showing him the cannon, the anchors, and finally the place where we'd found the silver."

After replenishing their air, they went down again.

"We dived around a bit," recalled Wilson, "and since we had such a long swim, about two hundred yards, through very hard conditions, we didn't feel much like carrying anything back with us. We had a very good look at the site, made some measurements, drove some pitons in, left some equipment on the spot, and we came back with Laza [a boatman] in the dinghy around the reef to the *Ran Mutu*."

The second morning Clarke was aboard *Ran Mutu* when she sailed to Great Basses Reef. It was April 14, 1963. He didn't feel strong enough to handle an Aqua-Lung, so he decided to don flippers, face mask, gloves, and weight belt and do some snorkeling while staying attached to the rubber dinghy stationed not too far from the wreck site. The water was clear, and he could see his cohorts at work below.

"Mike was chipping away," Clarke wrote, "with hammer and chisel, at the half-exposed cannon, while Peter was swimming along the wreck unrolling a tape measure. He was engaged in the very difficult but important operation of mapping the site, by measuring the distance between the numbered metal tags he had wired to prominent objects such as anchors and cannon."

No significant new finds were made that morning, Wilson confirmed during a midday break aboard the *Ran Mutu*. "I think we got most of it last time. There doesn't seem to be much more," he said.

Was this possible? Clarke wondered. No treasure left?

After a snack of hot cocoa and cookies, Wilson and Throckmorton made their second dive to the wreck. Later still, about midafternoon, Throckmorton continued his systematic investigation while Wilson and Jonklaas paddled one of the rubber dinghies over to visit the lighthouse.

Throckmorton was alone when he got lucky. He found the mother lode.

"There's at least a ton there," he told Clarke on the *Ran Mutu*, having rowed back to tell his exciting news and fill up on air.

Clarke's face lit up. He was excited. The expedition was worth it after all. He couldn't wait to break the news to Wilson and Jonklaas when they returned from the lighthouse.

"I was greeted with that grin that Arthur gets when he's happy about something," said Wilson.

As soon as Clarke told him, he grabbed a new lung and headed back to the reef to find Throckmorton and get directions to the mother lode!

Besides the many coin masses (once bags of silver coins that had congealed together) they brought up a 331-pound bronze cannon with the help of Throckmorton's Port-A-Lift balloon, which became a powerful lifting tool when inflated under water. Other items brought up included wooden pistol stocks, rusty hand grenades, a copper serving plate, cannonballs, a bronze pestle, and so forth. Throckmorton's further investigation indicated that it was a twenty-two or twenty-four-gun ship, much larger than they'd originally thought.

Their last dive on Great Basses was on April 21, and Clarke went along. Snorkeling near the surface, he could clearly see the activities below. Wilson and Throckmorton had found still more silver, "a couple of lumps as big as your head."

"I had a perfect bird's-eye view of the salvage operation," says Clarke. "I was watching something which, I suppose, not more than a handful of living men have seen—the lifting of treasure from the seabed, at the actual moment of discovery."

The next day the divers drove back to Colombo. All the salvage from the wreck had to be classified, photographed, and preserved in a manner consistent with good archaeological methods. This had to be done quickly with Throckmorton's expert guidance because he had to return to Greece and prepare for yet another expedition.

Clarke's priority was to weigh the accumulated silver from the 1961 and 1963 expeditions. It came to about 350 pounds of silver coins, including the clump that went to the Smithsonian.

For the lump donated to the Smithsonian, Clarke received a tax credit of about three thousand dollars—"the only money I ever got from it," he says. The rest of the ten or so lumps recovered, worth a total of thirty to fifty thousand dollars in the early sixties, were distributed as souvenirs among friends.

The accumulated treasure remained in a chest in Clarke's office while the research into the ship, its origins, and its cargo continued and while the legal aspects of the discovery in international waters were clarified and confirmed.

In late April, Clarke's experiences still fresh, he began work on a new book, *The Treasure of the Great Reef*, which documented the discovery of the only known sunken treasure from the original Taj Mahal family.

During a London stay later that year Clarke took some of the treasure to the British Museum. Says brother Fred: "On Friday, September 13, I took Arthur to meet Dr. Walker at the British Museum to identify the coins. As we went down the long corridors, they had to unlock and lock again several sets of doors as we went through them, arriving finally in the room which held all the silver.

"We showed them one of the big lumps of silver coins; they had never seen anything like that. They were able to identify the rupee coins, but they had never seen the half rupee coins, one of which Arthur donated to the museum."

Also, while Clarke was in London, the mass media beckoned. On September 10 he went to the BBC studios and filmed an episode of "The Sky at Night" (a long-running classic of British television) with host and friend Patrick Moore, who introduced Clarke as the man who first put forward the concept of a communications satellite in 1945.

Clarke bravely made some forecasts at the end of the program. The first flight around the moon, he predicted, would be made in 1967 (he was a year early). The first manned moon landing he put at between 1970 and 1972 (just six months off), although he qualified it by saying that "there is a chance that it will come earlier—perhaps even in 1968." The first flight around Mars (1980) and the first landing there (1990) were far from the mark (assuming he meant manned missions and not the unmanned Viking spacecraft of 1977). His forecasts of a lunar base (1975) and Mars base (about 2000) were too optimistic, extrapolating as he did from the tremendous "space race" momentum of the early sixties that resulted from *Sputnik 1*.

What's important here is that Clarke's 1963 short-term forecasts, those within ten years, were generally accurate; those beyond a decade were less often accurate. Clarke had proved a point he'd made almost ten years earlier in *The Exploration of the Moon*: ". . . the further we try and see into the future, the more our prediction will depart from reality when it comes about."

One thing Clarke could be sure of was that *Glide Path* would finally be published that fall. While preparing his body for the

Great Basses trip, Clarke had also revised the novel for the third time. With the help of Julian Muller, his editor at Harcourt Brace, Clarke's thirtieth book and his only autobiographical novel to date was rewritten in an acceptable form. Clarke felt a tremendous sense of relief whenever he was able to put a book behind him. The publication of this novel offered more relief than usual.

In the offing were potential forays into the film medium. Toward the end of 1963 "major" interest in *Childhood's End* was being expressed, but this was hardly the first time. There had been talk of a film version of the 1953 novel for a decade. And a small option was being offered for *A Fall of Moondust*.

More than twenty-five years earlier, Arthur C. Clarke had been a founding member and secretary of the film club at his grammar school, and his memories of the film shows he helped to arrange are still vivid. "*Metropolis* was one film that I arranged to show, and I can remember screening it," he recalls. "I can still remember cycling back through the dark after seeing *Frankenstein* starring Boris Karloff."

Because of that long-nurtured love of the medium, Clarke's failure to break into movies rankled. He closed a November letter to Sam Youd by saying "Meanwhile I remain the most successful writer in the world who's never had a movie made."

One day we shall meet our equals, or our masters, among the stars.

2001: A Space Odyssey *(1968)*

17
THE GENESIS OF
2001: A SPACE ODYSSEY

That tens of thousands of people still carry vivid images in their minds from the great film *2001: A Space Odyssey* more than twenty years after it first appeared on the screen is proof of its lasting artistic power. Even today its influence is seen frequently in new films, television programs, and advertising in several media. Some of the classical music adapted to its sound track is now all but universally associated with the future. And film giants Steven Spielberg and George Lucas both have acknowledged its influence on their movies with cosmic and extraterrestrial themes.

The famous collaboration between Stanley Kubrick and Arthur C. Clarke on the film classic *2001*, and the novel upon which the film was based, began by chance. It was one of those lucky connections.

"I was having lunch with Stanley at Trader Vic's," recalls Roger Caras, who was then working for Columbia Pictures. "It was just as *Dr. Strangelove* was coming out [February 1964]."

"What are you going to do next?" Caras asked Kubrick.

"You'd laugh," Kubrick said.

"No, I wouldn't. What are you going to do?"

"I'm going to do something on ETs," Kubrick said, looking to see if Caras knew what that meant.

"That's fantastic," said Caras. "As a matter of fact I'm doing a radio show on extraterrestrials tonight."

Caras eventually asked Kubrick who the writer was going to be, but Kubrick didn't know yet.

"I'm reading everything by everybody."

This, Caras knew, was the thorough way Kubrick approached his projects. He'd pick the top twenty-five science fiction writers, have his assistant pull together everything they'd ever written, and read it.

"Why waste your time?" Caras asked. "Why not just start with the best?"

"Who?" Kubrick asked him.

"Arthur C. Clarke," Caras replied.

"But I understand he's a recluse, a nut who lives in a tree in India some place," said Kubrick.

Roger Caras put that rumor to rest. "Like hell. He's not a recluse or a nut. He just lives quietly in Ceylon."

When Kubrick asked Caras if he knew Clarke, Caras told him of their 1959 meeting, when Clarke spent a weekend with Jacques Cousteau in Boston. "It was like a meeting of kindred souls," says Caras of that introduction, "and we went on from there."

"Jesus, get in touch with him, will you?" Kubrick asked. Caras said he would, and he recalls his cable's wording as

STANLEY KUBRICK—"DR STRANGELOVE," "PATHS OF GLORY," ET CETERA, INTERESTED IN DOING FILM ON ET'S. INTERESTED IN YOU. ARE YOU INTERESTED? THOUGHT YOU WERE RECLUSE.

Clarke replied rather promptly:

FRIGHTFULLY INTERESTED IN WORKING WITH ENFANT TERRI- BLE STOP CONTACT MY AGENT STOP WHAT MAKES KUBRICK THINK I'M A RECLUSE?

Roger Caras passed the information on to Scott Meredith, who then began to define the first stages of the project with Clarke and Kubrick. That was the last Caras would hear of Kubrick's ET film project until well into 1964.

Scott Meredith had met Stanley Kubrick in the early 1960s, when he sold him the film option rights to a novel by one of his clients, Peter George.

"*The Red Alert* was a voice-of-doom novel," says Meredith, "which was published by one of the small paperback publishers. We sold *Red Alert* to the movies in June 1959 for one thousand dollars. This was a little motion picture deal for a very minor book. Just an outright deal. It then went through three or four different hands. This fellow sold it to that fellow for the same thousand dollars, and this fellow sold it to someone else. None of these people could get financing to make a film. The final owner came to us in the early 1960s and said that he couldn't find the money to make the picture. He wanted us to represent him and wanted us to sell the film option rights once again.

"We resold the rights for thirty-five hundred dollars on behalf of the owner to a small company which became Polaris Productions—Stanley Kubrick's company. That's how I first met Stanley," says Meredith. "And the film that evolved out of Peter George's novel became *Dr. Strangelove*—rather a famous film. A serious book became a satire on the screen."

After Meredith learned of Clarke's interest in Kubrick's next film project, he called and discussed things with Kubrick, who suggested that the next step was to select some of Clarke's stories that could be considered resources for the screenplay. Kubrick then wrote to Clarke directly in Ceylon.

Clarke received Kubrick's letter in March 1964.

"He wanted to do the proverbial 'really good' science fiction movie," wrote Clarke. The letter went on to describe Kubrick's main interests in confronting the question of extraterrestrials.

"(1) The reasons for believing in the existence of intelligent extraterrestrial life. (2) The impact (and perhaps even lack of impact on some quarters) such discovery would have on Earth in the near future."

The letter further aroused Clarke's interest in the project. He had seen Kubrick's *Lolita* and was impressed by it. "Kubrick is obviously an astonishing man," he wrote to Caras. And everyone was talking about the just-released *Dr. Strangelove*, although Clarke hadn't seen it yet.

Clarke wanted to meet with Kubrick and discuss the project further the next time he was in the States. "By a fortunate coincidence, I was due in New York almost immediately, to complete work on the Time-Life Science Library's *Man and Space,* the main text of which I had written in Colombo." Before the trip he searched through his published fiction for ideas that could be used in the film.

"I very quickly settled on a short story called 'The Sentinel,' written over the 1948 Christmas holiday for a BBC contest. It was this story's idea which I suggested in my reply to Stanley Kubrick as the take-off point for a movie. The finding—and triggering—of an intelligence detector, buried on the Moon aeons ago, would give all the excuse we needed for the exploration of the Universe."

The original story did not win or place in the BBC contest when it was written in 1948. But Clarke's rule is never to throw any writing away, so he had filed one copy and eventually sent another on to Scott Meredith to sell. Two years later it was sold to the magazine *Ten Story Fantasy* and was published in the spring of 1951 under its original title, "Sentinel of Eternity." Then it found a new life in 1964 and became *one* of the sources for the extraterrestrial theme of *2001: A Space Odyssey.*

"I am continually annoyed by careless references to 'The Sentinel' as 'the story on which *2001* is based,'" said Clarke. "It bears about as much relation to the movie as an acorn to the resultant full-grown oak. Considerably less, in fact, because ideas from several other stories were also incorporated. Even the elements that Stanley Kubrick and I *did* actually use were considerably modified."

Besides the differences in the extraterrestrial artifact itself, its location was different. Instead of Mare Crisium in the book, it became Crater Tycho, which Clarke considered the "most spectacular of all lunar craters." Tycho had the additional attraction that it actually can be seen from the Earth at full moon.

Clarke traveled from Ceylon to New York via London in April 1964. During his brief visit to London he saw *Dr. Strangelove.*

"I was happy to find that it lived up to the reviews," he said later. He also believed the film's "technical virtuosity" bode well for the even more ambitious cinematic space epic that was gestating in Kubrick's mind.

On April 22, Arthur C. Clarke met Stanley Kubrick for lunch at Trader Vic's in the Plaza Hotel. Clarke describes him as a "rather quiet, average-height New Yorker," not yet sporting the full beard that he had during the making of *2001*. He had little or no color in his cheeks, Clarke noted, because he was very much a night person—a fact that would become apparent in their working relationship.

It was immediately obvious to Clarke that Kubrick had already absorbed a tremendous amount of science fiction and general scientific fact. The director grasped new ideas, no matter how complex, almost immediately, and his creative curiosity seemed to encompass everything.

"We talked for eight solid hours about science fiction, *Dr. Strangelove*, flying saucers, politics, the space program, Senator Goldwater—and, of course, the projected next movie," recalled Clarke.

"Even from the beginning, he had a very clear idea of his ultimate goal. He wanted to make a movie about man's relation to the universe—something which had never been attempted, much less achieved, in the history of motion pictures. Stanley was determined to create a work of art which would arouse the emotions of wonder, awe, even, if appropriate, terror."

The two men met often and talked extensively during the spring of 1964. Clarke remembered, "I was working at Time-Life during the day and moonlighting with Stanley in the evenings, and as the Time-Life job phased out, Stanley phased in. We talked for weeks and weeks—sometimes for ten hours at a time—and we wandered all over New York. We went to the Guggenheim and to Central Park, and even to the World's Fair. We talked at Stanley's apartment, in restaurants and Automats, movie houses and art galleries. We considered and discarded literally hundreds of ideas. Besides talking endlessly, we had a look at the competition."

There was none, of course, according to Kubrick. In Clarke's opinion there had been several good ("or at least interesting") early science fiction movies. His list included *Destination Moon* (the collaborative effort of his friend Robert Heinlein and producer George Pal), *The Day the Earth Stood Still*, *Forbidden Planet*, *The Thing*, and *War of the Worlds*.

One of the technical advisers on *2001*, Frederick Ordway, remembers Kubrick commenting on several occasions that, for all his brilliance, Clarke was totally mesmerized by what Kubrick considered grade B or grade C science fiction movies. It was incredible to Kubrick that Clarke, who was so precise and so knowledgeable, would go see a horrible black-and-white science fiction film and just sit there like a school kid.

Needless to say, Kubrick was very critical of all the old science fiction films the pair screened. Even the classic H. G. Wells film *Things to Come*, which Clarke persuaded Kubrick to watch, didn't fare too well under Kubrick's critical eye, although it did influence *2001* and was listed in the credits.

By May 1964, after seemingly hundreds of hours of talkathons, the two men agreed that "The Sentinel" was good material and could be used. At first they thought of the story's extraterrestrial artifact as a climax rather than a jumping-off point. When they decided that the discovery of the artifact buried on the moon would be up front in the story line, Clarke reviewed his backlist of published stories for more ideas.

He came up with six additional building blocks for the novel and the screenplay: "Breaking Strain," "Out of the Cradle," "Endlessly Orbiting . . . ," "Who's There," "Into the Comet," and "Before Eden."

An early working title for the film, used privately by Kubrick and Clarke, was *How the Solar System Was Won*. Kubrick next proposed a rather unorthodox approach to producing the screenplay. He and his agent, Louis Blau, had to show the top brass at Metro-Goldwyn-Mayer something of substance to get their commitment to finance production. But Kubrick disliked movie scripts and wanted to present the backers with something completely different.

"He proposed that we sit down and first write the story as a complete novel," wrote Clarke. "That way, before embarking on the drudgery of the script, we [could] let our imaginations soar freely by developing the story as a novel upon which the screenplay would eventually be based. We would generate more ideas this way, Stanley thought, and give the project more body and depth. Though I had never collaborated with anyone before in this way, the idea suited me fine."

Clarke never considered the novel to be anything but independent and self-contained, even though it was written as the basis for the film proposal and later the screenplay.

"In theory, therefore, the novel would be written (with an eye on the screen) and the script would be derived from this. In practice the result was far more complex; toward the end, novel and screenplay were being written simultaneously, with feedback in both directions. Some parts of the novel had their final revisions after we had seen the rushes based on the screenplay based on earlier versions of the novel . . . and so on."

Although the novel *2001: A Space Odyssey* has gone through some fifty printings and has sold three million copies since publication in July 1968, its complex and intricate relationship to the film is often simplified and even erroneously stated. "A novel by Arthur C. Clarke based on the screenplay of the MGM film by Stanley Kubrick and Arthur C. Clarke," reads the back cover copy of a recent printing.

"I felt that when the novel finally appeared it should be 'by Arthur Clarke and Stanley Kubrick, based on the screenplay by Stanley Kubrick and Arthur Clarke'—whereas the movie should have the credits reversed. This still seems the nearest approximation to the complicated truth."

But in the spring of 1964 the writing of the novel had not even begun. Clarke and Kubrick continued to brainstorm.

"Stan's a fascinating character—I've been living with his family, very nearly, ever since reaching NY," Clarke wrote to Sam Youd. "Working with him 6–8 hours a day *after* my stint at TIME-LIFE, where I have a lovely office on the 32nd floor."

At this early stage both men envisioned the film as "a kind of semidocumentary about the first pioneering days of the new frontier." That concept was soon left behind.

The first projected schedule calculated by Kubrick for all the work was "hilariously optimistic," Clarke recalls. His time estimate for all the various project tasks, from writing the story to editing the film, added up to about two years.

Clarke reluctantly accepted the fact that his planned return to Ceylon would have to be postponed until enough work was completed for the all-important one-shot proposal for MGM. It was at this time that he and Kubrick came to an agreement.

"We shook hands on the deal during the evening of May 17, 1964," wrote Clarke, "went out onto the penthouse veranda [Kubrick's penthouse off Lexington Avenue] to relax, and at 9 P.M. saw, sailing high above Manhattan, the most spectacular of the dozen UFOs I've observed during the last twenty years."

Clarke had persuaded Kubrick in their initial conversations

that UFOs were simply that—unidentified flying objects—and had nothing to do with outer space and extraterrestrials. "Stanley was in some danger of believing in flying saucers," he explained. "I felt I had arrived just in time to save him from this gruesome fate." And now here he was, with Kubrick as a witness, staring at a UFO that he couldn't quickly explain.

"I can still remember, rather sheepishly, my feelings of awe and excitement," says Clarke, "and also the thought that flashed through my mind: 'This is altogether too much of a coincidence. *They* are out to stop us from making this movie."

Kubrick and Clarke both continued to stare at the bright object. It appeared to come to rest at the zenith, remain in that position above Manhattan for about a minute, and then sink down to the north.

It looked like a brilliant satellite to Clarke, yet the listing of satellite passes in the *New York Times* included no such transit at nine in the evening.

Clarke kept on arguing that there was a simple explanation, but he couldn't come up with one. Reluctantly they contacted the Pentagon (reluctantly because the air force was still smarting from Kubrick's acclaimed satire on the military, *Dr. Strangelove*). They even filled out and submitted the standard sighting form. Besides the Pentagon, Clarke contacted his friends at the Hayden Planetarium and gave them all the relevant details of the sighting. They fired up their computer, and shortly thereafter the mystery was solved.

What they had seen was indeed what Clarke had first suspected: a satellite. It was a transit of the huge *Echo 1* satellite, the hundred-foot balloon, with its highly reflective aluminum surface, that had been launched in the summer of 1960. Why the *New York Times* hadn't listed this spectacular appearance, yet had listed two less impressive ones that occurred later the same night, was anybody's guess.

In May, Scott Meredith and Louis Blau began working out the details of a formal legal agreement for Clarke's participation in the *2001* project. This was some eight months before Kubrick had any solid backing from MGM.

"We signed the agreement for Arthur's six stories," recalls Meredith, "on the twentieth of May, 1964. We got ten thousand dollars for the option on these stories, including 'The Sentinel.'

"By the twenty-eighth of May, 'The Sentinel' had been picked, and we signed an agreement for Arthur to write a treatment based on it for thirty thousand dollars—fifteen thousand dollars on commencement of principal photography and the other fifteen thousand dollars on completion.

"Now the 'novelization' deal, as it was thought of at the beginning, was really a collaboration. Arthur did all the writing, of course, but Stanley was feeding him ideas every day. The book was a sixty-forty deal, with Arthur getting sixty percent and Stanley forty percent. That's continued to this day, of course. The book has made millions; we keep sending Arthur checks and Stanley checks. Everything continues to operate because it's a worldwide deal. It must be published in at least forty countries, and every time a license runs out in one of these countries, we relicense them.

"Stanley made a deal with MGM for the financing of *2001* on January 14, 1965. He called it 'Journey Beyond the Stars' at that time. For the novel, our original deal was with Dell to do it as a Delacorte hardcover and a Dell paperback."

Kubrick and Clarke continued their brainstorming sessions throughout the film production. They usually met at Kubrick's place while in New York, but sometimes at restaurants nearby. In early summer 1964 they were plotting and discussing several possible endings for *2001*. They had ideas aplenty, but they also had a dilemma. How should they depict extraterrestrials in the novel and film? One or more of the crew members would come into contact with them, but what would they look like?

Familiar with the book *Intelligent Life in the Universe* and considering him "one of the first reputable scientists to take the subject seriously," Clarke decided to give Carl Sagan a call and solicit his ideas. He and Kubrick invited Sagan to have dinner with them at Kubrick's New York penthouse. Sagan was just short of thirty years old and was then an astrophysicist at the Smithsonian Astrophysical Observatory in Cambridge, Massachusetts.

"They had no idea how to end the movie," wrote Sagan. "That's when they called me in to try to resolve a dispute. The key issue was how to portray the extraterrestrials that would surely be encountered at the end when they go through the Star Gate. Kubrick was arguing that extraterrestrials would look like humans with some slight differences, maybe à la Mr. Spock. And Arthur was arguing, quite properly on general evolutionary grounds, that they would look nothing like us. So I tried to adjudicate as they asked.

"I said it would be a disaster to portray the extraterrestrials. What ought to be done is to suggest them.

"I argued that the number of individually unlikely events in the evolutionary history of man was so great that nothing like us is ever likely to evolve again anywhere else in the universe. I suggested that any explicit representation of an advanced extraterrestrial being was bound to have at least an element of falseness about it and that the best solution would be to suggest rather than explicitly to display the extraterrestrials.

"What struck me most is that they were in production [some of the special effects, at least] and still had no idea how the movie would end.

"Kubrick's preference had one distinct advantage, an economic one: He could call up Central Casting and ask for twenty extraterrestrials. With a little makeup, he would have his problem solved. The alternative portrayal of extraterrestrials, whatever it was, was bound to be expensive."

How the film and novel actually would end remained an open question. In fact more than two years later, in September 1966, Clarke was completely rewriting the ending of the novel for what he hoped would be the last time. But in mid-1964 it looked as if the ETs would be suggested rather than depicted, and Clarke had much work ahead of him.

"Just bought a ream of paper and start work in ten minutes (I hope) on the new novel, which Stanley Kubrick bought a month ago," he wrote to Sam Youd on June 19. "I'll be stuck here (or in Hollywood, ugh) for the next year or so, though I hope to commute back to Ceylon occasionally."

Clarke also wrote, "Stanley installed me, with electric typewriter, in his Central Park West office, but after one day I retreated to my natural environment in the Hotel Chelsea, where I could draw inspiration from the company of Arthur Miller, Allen Ginsberg, Andy Warhol, and William Burroughs."

The Chelsea offered many distractions, but Clarke did his best to avoid them. He wholly dedicated himself to researching and writing the novel that would be used to convince MGM to back the film. He produced an average of one thousand to two thousand words a day during the summer and into the fall. Typing on an old gray Smith Corona in Suite 1008, he subsisted for the most part on tea, crackers, and liver pâté.

"Every other day Stanley and I would get together and compare notes," Clarke has said. "During this period we went down endless blind alleys and threw away tens of thousands of words. The scope of the story steadily expanded, in both time and space."

Says Roger Caras, "Arthur and Stanley were very interesting foils. There was some slight conflict in that Arthur goes to bed very early. Arthur gets very tired, and typically nine to nine-thirty is his bedtime. Stanley goes to bed about three in the morning and sleeps till about three in the afternoon. That presented problems sometimes. But when their times meshed, they were terrific foils."

Clarke recalled, "The merging of our streams of thought was so effective that, after this lapse of time, I am no longer sure who originated what ideas; we finally agreed that Stanley should have prime billing for the screenplay, while only my name would appear on the novel."

During the latter half of 1964 the ambitious theme of a space odyssey began to emerge—what Kubrick referred to as a "theme of mythic grandeur." The universe was depicted as a vast cosmic ocean upon which mankind would sail, evolve, and discover new worlds. It represented the last ever-expanding frontier for mankind's exploratory voyages.

In Clarke's 1958 book of essays, *The Challenge of the Spaceship*, he concluded with a poetic envoi that captures the essence of what he and Kubrick were exploring in *2001*:

"Across the gulf of centuries, the blind smile of Homer is turned upon our age. Along the echoing corridors of time, the roar of the rockets merges now with the creak of the wind-taut rigging. For somewhere in the world today, still unconscious of his destiny, walks the boy who will be the first Odysseus of the Age of Space. . . ."

"We set out," wrote Clarke, "with the deliberate intention of creating a myth. The Oddysean parallel was in our minds from the beginning, long before the film's title was chosen."

As early as 1965, Clarke went around quietly saying that there was a surprise in store for Metro-Goldwyn-Mayer executives. "MGM doesn't know it yet, but they've footed the bill for the first $10,500,000 religious film."

Ultimately it was the mythic elements in *2001* that created all the controversy and assured its status as a classic in film history.

But in 1964 Stanley Kubrick had his worries. The robot probe *Ranger 7* impacted on the surface of the moon on August 1, and both he and Clarke stayed up late to see the TV close-ups. The reality of what these space probes could discover got Kubrick worrying about the *Mariner 4* space probe and what it might find as it flew by Mars in July of 1965. What if signs of life were discovered on the red planet? Such a discovery could wreck their story line.

"This was typical of Stanley's ability to worry about possibilities no one else would think of," wrote Clarke. "He always acts on the assumption that if something *can* go wrong, it will; ditto if it can't."

Later on, once MGM had committed to the film, Kubrick actually tried to insure the studio against the risk of extraterrestrial life being discovered. He consulted Lloyd's of London but dropped the idea when he found out how much the premium would be.

"Stanley decided," wrote Clarke, "to take his chance with the universe."

During October and November both men were grappling with the material that would become the evolutionary sequence that begins both the novel and the film. Background research included Clarke's reading Louis Leakey's *Adam's Ancestors* and Robert Ardrey's *African Genesis*. Clarke also spent time with Dr. Harry Shapiro, director of the anthropology division at the American Museum of Natural History in New York.

The day before Christmas, Clarke was at his Smith Corona, laboring on what he believed to be the final pages of the first draft. He wanted to have them ready as a Christmas present for Kubrick. When his partner read them, he was delighted with the last chapters. "We've extended the range of science fiction," he told Clarke. And so their grand myth was further defined as the New Year approached.

It was Clarke's belief, fleeting though it was, that the novel was essentially complete then and that the screenplay would be developed from it in a rather straightforward way.

"In reality," he says, "all that we had [as 1965 began] was a rough draft of the first two-thirds of the book, stopping at the most exciting point. We had managed to get Bowman into the Star

Gate but didn't know what would happen next, except in the most general way."

The early draft of the manuscript combined with Stanley Kubrick's track record, then rated excellent with the recent success of *Dr. Strangelove,* were all Louis Blau needed to sell the project to MGM.

"I took the treatment that they had," recalls Blau, "and presented it to MGM to read. They had a two- or three-day deadline during which they had to come back to me, and that's how I made the deal. Stanley never uses a traditional screenplay like some directors who want to know all the stage details. Instead he keeps working up to and through his shooting to make sure it's better all the time."

The executives at MGM decided to finance the film, to the tune of six million dollars.

Less than two months later the final title was chosen. "Stanley selected *2001: A Space Odyssey* in April 1965," says Clarke, "and as far as I can recall, it was entirely his idea."

This future date evolved naturally during the hundreds of hours of discussions in 1964. The space activities above Earth and the discovery of the extraterrestrial artifact took place in the year 2001—a setting thirty-five years in the future when MGM decided to finance production. The date was far enough away in time to ensure that the film's future realism wouldn't be undercut by reality.

Fred Ordway, one of the two principal astronautic advisers (along with Harry Lange) whom Kubrick contacted at Clarke's suggestion, remembers *2001* coming up as a potential title.

"Stanley asked me if we should say 'two thousand and one' or 'twenty oh one' like we say 'nineteen oh one,'" says Ordway. "And we decided that 'two thousand and one' sounded better. We often wondered among ourselves whether the fact that the film was called two thousand *and* one would have an influence on the English language when we got into the twenty-first century."

Revision of the novel continued throughout the spring of 1965, and entire chunks of text, earlier thought to be essential to the final plot, were discarded as the story line constantly changed. As Clarke revised and wrote new sections, Kubrick began directing the film project—hiring the staff, initiating design work, negotiating agreements with actors and technical people.

"My primary job was still polishing the novel," wrote Clarke, "though I was constantly involved in technical discussions with the artists and production staff."

In March, Clarke stood his ground when Kubrick attempted to bring Dr. Poole back from the dead after computer HAL killed him off.

"I'm afraid," he scribbled in his notebook, "Stanley's obsession with immortality has overcome his artistic instincts."

When most of Part III was ready for typing in May, Clarke was again encouraged. He had also completed the "Universe" chapter and the "Floating Island" sequence, both of which were later cut from the novel. At the same time, Clarke realized how much of the material he'd abandoned earlier could be incorporated into the final version.

Kubrick assembled the preproduction team in New York during the first half of 1965. It included his assistant from England, Ray Lovejoy, artist-designer Tony Pratt, secretary Judy Minoff, technical advisers Ordway and Lange, executive producer Victor Lyndon, art director Tony Masters, Masters's associate John Hoesli, and artist-designer Richard P. McKenna.

Roger Caras also reappeared on the scene in the spring. "One day the phone rang and it was Arthur," he says. "I said, 'Hey, Arthur, when did you get in town?' And he told me that he had been in the city for nearly six months, working on the new project.

"I spoke to Arthur for a few minutes, and then Stanley came on the phone. 'Do you want to come to England with us and make a movie?' he asked. It was a Sunday night, about eleven-thirty, which is late for Arthur. I called over to my wife and said, "'Jill, do you want to move to England?' And she said, 'Sure.'

"So the next day I resigned from Columbia Pictures after ten years and prepared to move to England with Arthur and Stanley and the rest of the team. I had become the director of publicity for *2001: A Space Odyssey*."

A telling fact about the relationship between Clarke and Kubrick is that Kubrick began setting down conditions from the beginning—not that that surprised anyone who knew him. Even Clarke admitted that, as far as the film was concerned, Kubrick had "total control." "He knew exactly what he was doing," says

Clarke, "and he was absolutely right. I have tremendous regard for Kubrick. He's a genius—there's no question about that. A force of nature."

"In plain fact," says Roger Caras, "Stanley Kubrick is probably the only person in the last forty years that Arthur has had to take a back seat to. Kubrick is the more famous of the two; Kubrick is much more the forceful personality of the two. Kubrick says yes, Kubrick says no; it is yes or no. Arthur says yes, Arthur says no; it is maybe. Arthur is so easily coerced by people he likes because he's so kind. Stanley's nowhere near as generous or as softhearted, although he is a kind man."

Clarke and Kubrick had what Roger Caras called a good "cerebral marriage." They stimulated one another with a constant flow of ideas and challenges during their creative conversations.

"Arthur became very fond of Kubrick," says Fred Ordway. "They seemed to get along quite well together, and it was a tremendous and exciting experience for Arthur."

And frustrating. There was no way the novel could be completed before the film was finalized. Clarke made changes, then more changes. The only certainty appeared to be additional changes. Once Clarke jokingly suggested that they push the release date back to 2002 or later.

Both the novel and the screenplay were in a state of flux when the preproduction team began moving to England in the summer of 1965 to prepare for actual filming. The design and research work that had been completed in Manhattan, as well as some of the special effects footage used in Commander Bowman's final voyage through space and time, was packed up and sent to the MGM studios at Borehamwood just north of London.

Clarke left Manhattan in late June and returned to Ceylon after more than a year away. He remained there for the month of July before traveling to London and rejoining Kubrick and the film company. As he always did while in London, he stayed at 88 Nightingale Road with his brother Fred and Fred's second wife, Sylvia.

The production company had expanded dramatically since its move from New York. The art department had graduated from preliminary sketches, drawings, and models to actually constructing the large sets. Once in Borehamwood, Clarke's time was "equally divided between the apparently never-ending chore of developing ideas with Stanley, polishing the novel, and almost daily consultations at the studio."

In early September 1965 Kubrick was thinking about a major story change. He wanted to substitute the planet Saturn for Jupiter as the destination for the spaceship *Discovery*. Kubrick's desire for the change was based on aesthetics—the beauty of Saturn's rings and the many spectacular special effects that could be created as the spaceship flew among them. He asked technical adviser Fred Ordway to research the ringed planet.

"I prepared the memo," says Ordway. "Kubrick was delighted, and Clarke backed the change with great enthusiasm. Arthur then brilliantly wrote Jupiter out and Saturn in. Everybody got excited about the change—except the special effects people, who went ape."

Eventually this major change proved to be too much for the special effects group, which was already under tremendous pressure. Douglas Trumbull, who was in charge of special effects, got his way—no Saturn.

For the film, therefore, Jupiter remained the destination planet for spaceship *Discovery*. But Clarke retained Saturn as the destination planet in the novel, and this became one of the major plot differences between the book and the movie.

In fall 1965 the ending of *2001* was still unapparent to Clarke and Kubrick. Both men were searching for a memorable conclusion to their mythic journey.

In late August, Clarke had "suddenly realised how the novel *should* end, with Bowman standing beside the alien ship." Kubrick was not convinced, however, and the search for an ending continued through September and October.

"The ending was altered shortly before shooting it," said Kubrick. "In the original there was no transformation of Bowman. He just wandered around the room and finally saw the artifact. But this didn't seem like it was satisfying enough, or interesting enough, and we constantly searched for ideas until we finally came up with the ending as you see it."

On October 3, during a telephone conversation with Kubrick, Clarke was presenting his latest ideas for an ending, and one of them clicked.

"Bowman will regress to infancy," Clarke suggested in an

essay, "and we'll see him at the end as a baby in orbit. Stanley called again later, still very enthusiastic. Hope this isn't false optimism: I feel cautiously encouraged myself."

Two days later, after much creative brooding, Clarke came up with a logical reason for Bowman's appearing as a baby at the end of the film. "It's his image of himself at this stage of his development. And perhaps the Cosmic Consciousness has a sense of humor. Phoned these ideas to Stan, who wasn't too impressed, but I'm happy now."

In the novel the Star-Child detonates the nuclear weapons orbiting planet Earth. This concept actually went to the shooting-script stage but was finally nixed. Kubrick and Clarke agreed that it was too similar to Kubrick's ending in *Dr. Strangelove*.

By mid-October, Kubrick had decided to kill off the entire crew of *Discovery*. Only Commander Bowman would survive. This was drastic, Clarke thought, but it also seemed right somehow. "After all, Odysseus was the sole survivor," he noted.

Even at this late date, with filming only weeks away, Kubrick was seriously considering major changes that, if pursued, would have had serious ripple effects throughout the entire production effort.

Fred Clarke remembers Kubrick calling Clarke late one night toward the end of October.

"Stanley had decided to change the type of drive used on the spaceship to what we call the ion drive. This was a new form of propulsion, which he thought might be used in the year 2001. But Arthur said that the production crew had been building the space-ship set for three months using the old system and that the new ion drive would mean an entirely different spaceship design."

There were other spaceship sets besides the interplanetary *Discovery*. One was the Earth orbit ship, *Orion III*, which Clarke visited in November with Kubrick and the design staff. His presence in this case may have been unfortunate, however—at least for the short run. During the visit to this set he "happened to remark that the cockpit looked like a Chinese restaurant. Stan said that killed it instantly for him and called for revisions." Clarke noted, "Must keep away from the art department for a few days."

December came, and Kubrick was under mounting pressure to start filming before the end of 1965. The growing tension was felt by everyone. Fred Ordway believed that Kubrick, under the circumstances, became less friendly to everyone working around him. Ordway, as technical adviser, brought in design recommendations from U.S. industry for equipment on the sets, but Kubrick often was not satisfied.

"Many design aspects of the vehicles in the film changed regularly," says Ordway. "It became impossible at times to finalize anything. And we were faced with the fact that the screenplay had a definite tendency to change rather rapidly."

All of this was the price of Stanley Kubrick's creativity—fighting his way through chaos toward the new unity, smithing a contemporary celluloid myth.

The New Year was only days away, and everyone involved in the film was under the gun. Clarke worked right through the Christmas holiday, including December 25, and sent the fresh manuscript pages over to Kubrick the next day.

"He called to say that he didn't think much of the dialogue," wrote Clarke. "I agreed."

This was the first indication that the screenplay dialogue was a problem for Kubrick and that he would solve it in an innovative way—by getting rid of much of it and substituting silence and music.

But he couldn't get rid of the shooting schedule.

While most of the film was shot at the MGM studios in Borehamwood, the first days of shooting were done at Shepperton-on-Thames, six miles southwest of London, because it was the only studio in England large enough to build the huge excavation site (which was 150 feet in diameter) in the moon's Crater Tycho. Kubrick had no flexibility at all with this sequence; the set had to be torn down by January 7 to make way for another production. Time to shoot or die.

Arthur somehow manages to capture the hopeless but admirable human desire to know things that can really never be known.

Stanley Kubrick

18
A COSMIC CLASSIC

Filming of *2001: A Space Odyssey* began on December 29, 1965, at Shepperton.

"About a hundred technicians were milling around," Clarke wrote in his diary. "I spent some time with Stanley, reworking the script—in fact we continued through lunch together. I also met the actors, and felt quite the proper expert when they started asking me astronomical questions. I stayed until 4 P.M.—not actual shooting by then, but they were getting near it. The spacesuits, back-packs, etc. are beautifully done, and TMA 1 [Tycho Magnetic Anomaly 1 Excavation] is quite impressive—though someone had smeared the black finish [of the monolith] and Stanley went on a rampage when I pointed it out to him."

The black rectangular monolith was not the easiest prop to move. It was a three-ton block of Lucite (the largest piece ever cast), which was later painted black and hauled onto the excavation set by a crane.

Roger Caras, director of publicity, was on hand for the first day's shooting on the moon set.

"There was a scene where the scientists come walking down

the ramp into the excavation," Caras recalls. "Stanley wanted a dolly shot with the camera in front of them, backing down as they walked down the ramp.

"Well, the SuperPanavision seventy-millimeter camera is a big, heavy machine, and the operating cameraman couldn't do the shot the way Stanley wanted it because the slope was steep and the ramp was made of corrugated steel, which was too rough for the dolly wheels.

"Stanley was going to get the shot he wanted despite the problems. He decided to shoot the scene himself. He took the SuperPanavision camera, hand-held it, had two or three people behind him to guide him and keep him from going over backwards from the weight of the camera, and he walked down the ramp backwards. Stanley physically shot the whole scene, taking over the operating cameraman's job."

"He's one of the rare filmmakers who can do it all," says Louis Blau. "He knows the duties of everybody from the lowest grip or electrician on up to the cameraman and the art director—and everybody else."

While Kubrick was handling the camera, Clarke was still writing. He wrote the dramatic confrontation with HAL, the 9000 computer, on January 8 and knew immediately that he was producing one of the most exciting scenes in the book.

"I got quite scared," he said at the time, "when the computer started going nuts, being alone in the room with my electric typewriter." These emotions were transferred from print to film in the powerful scene showing HAL's slow death. Film critic Andrew Sarris later praised its emotional power in the *Village Voice*: "I have never seen the death of the mind rendered more profoundly or poetically."

Clarke and Kubrick managed to resolve most of the remaining plot questions during a long discussion in mid-January. By January 17 Clarke had completed the first draft of the last chapters. He felt that the end was in sight but cautioned himself that this would be the third time he'd felt that way.

A few days before Clarke returned to Ceylon for six weeks, in early February 1966, he viewed a demonstration film that Kubrick had produced for the MGM executives.

"Stan spliced together a few scenes to give the studio heads some idea of what was going on," he recalled. "He used Mendels-sohn's *A Midsummer Night's Dream* for the weightless scenes and Vaughan Williams's Antarctica Symphony for the lunar sequence and the Star Gate special effects, with stunning results. I reeled out convinced that we had a masterpiece on our hands—if Stan could keep it up."

Despite his busy filming schedule, Kubrick still had time to request more work on the novel and screenplay. He cabled Clarke in mid-March and requested some "poetic Clarkean narration" on HAL's breakdown. Clarke wrote it and sent it off the same day, but it turned out to be another rush job that was never used.

Clarke considered his final draft of the novel finished in early April, before he flew from Ceylon to Lawrence, Kansas, to speak at the University of Kansas centennial celebration. His host was Professor James Gunn, a fellow science fiction author, and he would be in the distinguished company of friends such as Buck-minster Fuller and Pat Weaver.

"I met Arthur at the airport," says Gunn. "And one of the publicists who was working on *2001* also met him there. We had dinner at the downtown airport. He showed us some production stills he had brought along with him, and he showed them with considerable pride. Arthur was glowing about the film. He thought it was going to be a great film.

"But he was complaining a bit also, irritated that Kubrick would not let the book be contracted. He wanted to get it out at the time the movie was released. And he was unhappy that Ku-brick would not let him release the manuscript and get his portion of the proceeds.

"I remember he was still suffering from the consequences of his variously diagnosed disease which caused his paralysis. He was still having some trouble breathing when he exerted himself. When he gave his speech, he did pause to breathe a few times, and he used his stool to sit on as I recall."

Toward the end of his speech Clarke speculated about the future of "ultraintelligent machines" and the possibility that any advanced extraterrestrials might be nonorganic. "[This would] make them highly suited for interstellar flight because machines don't mind waiting around for thousands of years. They don't mind vacuum conditions; in fact they probably prefer them. They don't mind high accelerations. So if we do have any visitors from space I suggest they won't come in spaceships, they will be space-ships."

Besides strongly anticipating his 1973 novel *Rendezvous with Rama*, this portion of his Kansas speech also presents a plausible rationale behind the decision not to depict the extraterrestrials in the film or novel *2001*.

Without doubt, the question of the book's publication was very much on Clarke's mind at this time. He had to have some kind of resolution.

"I cabled Stanley to say that I was heading back to London to make final arrangements for the publication of the novel. He replied, 'Don't bother—it's not ready yet.'"

But Clarke *was* bothered. He desperately wanted to get the book into the marketplace because he had been working on it for almost two years and still had not received a publisher's advance. Kubrick's discouraging words did not stop him. He flew to London after his Kansas engagement, still hoping to persuade Kubrick to move on the book.

When Clarke arrived back at the studio on April 19, 1966, Kubrick was directing the camera work inside an immense centrifuge that had been built specially for the film. The lamps and other hardware bolted to the centrifuge, designed to be stationary, were always in motion during shots. This caused a variety of problems, including falling hardware. It was, says Clarke, "a portentous spectacle, accompanied by terrifying noises and popping lamp bulbs." Because of its complexity, the centrifuge challenged the director, the actors, and everyone else on the set. It involved the most difficult work of the entire film, and Kubrick fell behind schedule.

"Stanley came in during a shooting break and himself raised the subject of publication date," says Clarke. "I asked him if he were deliberately delaying publication of the book until the film was out, so that it would not appear that the film was based on the book. He made a genuine protestation that he was not up to that. He said that he believed that the book needed further work and that he did not then have the time to read it. He also explained that the general release of the film would not be until late in 1967 or even 1968. And when it did first open, it would be running only in a few Cinerama houses, which would give us some more breathing space."

It was, as Clarke put it, "Stanley's way," and not much could be done about it, although he kept trying to convince Kubrick, right into early summer 1966, that the manuscript should go to the publisher and the publishing process should begin.

"I maintained that *I* was the writer and he should rely on my judgment; what would he say if I wanted to edit the film?"

Finally, in June, Kubrick suggested a compromise that Clarke knew was at least a step in the right direction. Kubrick promised to read the manuscript and give Clarke a list of improvements he wanted. He kept his word in July by sending a long memorandum of queries, observations, and constructive criticism about the manuscript. The memorandum was nine pages long. This was enough for Scott Meredith to begin negotiating a contract with Dell/Delacorte Press.

But two months later nothing had really changed. "I gather that there has been a friendly meeting between Louis [Blau] and Dell," Clarke wrote to Sam Youd in September. "They have agreed to wait but I can't afford to. Altogether apart from the fact that I still don't know when and if I'll ever get any part of the novel advance (Stan talks of delivery in February!), I have *lost* about $15,000 in commissions I've had to turn down while working on the revisions."

Clarke was fighting for his financial life because of the delayed book contract. He was in debt and had to borrow money.

In December 1966 he wrote to Sam Youd that the book contract was still in limbo and everything depended on Stanley's cooperation. "He keeps promising he will send me his [final] revisions but I have received nothing and I don't know what the situation is."

"It was," said Clarke, "a very sad period for me. When Stanley finally approved the book for publication two years later [1968], not a word had been changed. There seems to be a right way to do things, a wrong way, and Stanley's way."

Originally Kubrick had indicated to Dell that it might get an approved and signed contract in February 1967, but there was no news from him that month. He wasn't answering the cables Clarke sent. Dell, however, decided to go ahead and send a contract to Scott Meredith.

"The president of Dell at that time was a lady named Helen Myer," says Meredith. "We finally made a deal with her for a $65,000 advance in the spring of 1967. (This amount was less than originally agreed to because of the delays.) Stanley took all those years to work on the picture and the script and wouldn't OK Arthur's script because he kept changing the picture."

When the Dell contract was received by Scott Meredith on April 28, 1967, and then forwarded to Kubrick for signature, he didn't sign it. His reason for the delay, as before, was that he was not yet completely satisfied with the manuscript and wanted to make additional revisions when his schedule permitted.

Dell eventually got tired of waiting for the novel *and* the film, which would give book sales a healthy boost. By mid-1967 corporate patience had run out.

"The *2001* novel contract is cancelled," Clarke wrote to Sam Youd in June 1967. "I've never had a penny. Dell spent about $10,000 setting galleys, publicity, etc. . . . Stanley refuses to release it until he has tinkered with the dialog . . . & he's too busy to do so! As a result, I'm $50,000 in debt. . . ."

Says Scott Meredith, "In 1968, when we were ready to go again, I went back to Dell, but Helen Myer wasn't interested."

It's not surprising that Kubrick felt his schedule did not permit work on the manuscript at that time. One of his goals for *2001* was to take special effects in film to new heights, making them look completely realistic. Therefore it took him a year and a half to shoot the many scenes, and the special effects cost $6.5 million out of a $10.5 million total budget. The film ended up going over budget, and the release was delayed.

"I had to invent new techniques all the time," related Kubrick. "It was necessary to conceive, design, and engineer completely new techniques in order to produce the special effects. We ran through 205 special-effects shots. The last ones were arriving in Hollywood as the negative printing was being done."

One of the most expensive and important pieces of hardware for the final film was the forty-ton centrifuge, which was capable of rotating at a variable speed of up to three miles per hour. This rotation speed had nothing to do with creating artificial gravity as it would have in space, of course, but rather gave Kubrick an entire new range of photographic effects for the interior of the *Discovery*.

A British firm, the Vickers Armstrong Engineering Group, designed and manufactured the centrifuge to order at a cost of three hundred thousand dollars back in the mid-1960s. It took six months to build only one of eleven used for filming *2001*. No soundstage had seen anything like it before; it looked like a heavy-duty Ferris wheel located in the middle of an airplane hangar.

The centrifuge was thirty-eight feet in diameter, and its exterior was densely covered with cables and lights. Its interior was eight feet wide. Two large ducts at either end brought in the air-conditioning. Everything had to be bolted to the floor, both the set constructions (computer console, medical dispensary, shower, recreation area, and five hibernation "beds," called *hibernacula* in the film) and all the camera and lighting equipment.

Camera work in the centrifuge began in March 1966, but because this set was so unusual and complex, there were many difficulties and delays. Kubrick had originally planned to shoot the main scenes in 130 days, but shooting in the centrifuge slowed down progress and added about a week. It was slow work because all the cameras and lights had to be rearranged for each new sequence, and each time this took hours to accomplish.

The centrifuge set was also dangerous, and the fire hazard was real.

"When the actors were inside," says Roger Caras, "they were sealed in. They went in through the bottom, and then the trapdoor was closed. There was a fire department rescue unit on the set at all times. They would have dry runs and rehearsals of how to get the actors out should anything catch on fire.

"There was a lot of electricity and flammable set elements like wood and plastic. Had there been a fire inside that machine, it could have been a flash fire like the one in *Apollo 1* that killed the three astronauts.

"There were special bolts, strategically placed, which could be hit with sledgehammers and cause the actors to drop out. The actors were always on the bottom of the centrifuge, you see. The camera moved and the machine moved, but the actors were always at the bottom, only about four or five feet above the soundstage.

"Another thing. All the lighting inside traveled with it. So all the spotlights, although they were designed to be relatively stationary, were going upside down and around on the merry-go-round. This did something weird to the filaments, and the bulbs kept exploding. Everyone on the set had to be under shields, including Stanley, because the goddamn bulbs were exploding and showering the stage with glass.

"During one shoot (maybe the jogging scene) the camera, which was traveling around inside the centrifuge, tore loose and fell thirty-odd feet to the floor and nearly killed the actors in there. It was a dangerous set."

Another innovation on the centrifuge set was closed-circuit television. Kubrick installed the system so he could see what was going on inside and direct the activities without actually being sealed in with the actors, although he sometimes was. A large console was located to one side of the centrifuge, and there were three television receivers and six microphones among all the switches, levers, and lights.

Kubrick spent an enormous amount of time, money, and energy making sure everything was scientifically feasible. Even all the dials and gauges in *Discovery* and the other spacecraft had the benefit of expert advice for their design, and many were never even seen in the final film. There also were sixteen rear-screen projectors mounted on the exterior of the centrifuge. When filming began, all of them were synchronized and feeding images to the interior set. They activated all the screens in the command module and projected various information onto each of them.

Jeremy Bernstein, science writer for the *New Yorker*, visited the centrifuge soundstage in March 1966 and was overwhelmed by the strange structure and the dozens of varied activities going on. After being led to the trapdoor at the bottom of the centrifuge, he peered into the brilliantly lit interior and saw Kubrick staring into the huge camera's viewfinder with complete concentration.

"Keir Dullea, dressed in shorts and a white T-shirt and covered by a blue blanket, was lying in an open hibernaculum on the rising curve of the floor. He was apparently comfortably asleep, and Kubrick was telling him to wake up as simply as possible. 'Just open your eyes,' he said. 'Let's not have any stirring, yawning, and rubbing.'"

When one of the lights burned out and had to be replaced, Kubrick noticed Bernstein for the first time, staring at the furniture of *Discovery*'s dining quarters bolted to the top of the centrifuge. He assured him that it was well secured and invited him to climb in.

Derek Cracknell, the film's assistant director, then handed a Polaroid to Kubrick through the trapdoor.

"Here's your Polaroid, Guv," he said. Why did Kubrick need a

Polaroid? Bernstein wanted to know. Kubrick explained that he and Geoffrey Unsworth, his director of photography, had figured out a correlation between how the lighting appeared on the Polaroid shots and the setting on the movie camera. This allowed him to check for subtle lighting effects on his color film.

When Bernstein asked Kubrick if it was usual for directors to become so involved in the details of camera work, Kubrick simply answered that he had never seen another film director work.

The burned-out light was replaced, Keir Dullea climbed back into the hibernaculum, and Kubrick and his crew went back to the wake-up scene. For this scene the centrifuge was not rotating. After Kubrick relinquished the SuperPanavision seventy-millimeter camera to his cameraman, they filmed Dullea waking up. He simply opened his eyes.

Standing in for HAL, Kubrick fed his actor the lines that expressed good morning greetings and asked what he wanted for breakfast. Director and actor repeated the scene five times. Kubrick was finally satisfied that he had it right and climbed out of the centrifuge.

He was immediately surrounded by a lot of people, one of whom told him an animal trainer and his animal were waiting outside. Kubrick went outside to speak to the trainer and inspect a giant black pig that was to appear in one of the prehistoric scenes that began the movie. Kubrick approved the black pig.

The director answered several other questions, gave some directions, and then climbed into his private blue trailer located on the set.

"Maybe the company can get back some of its investment selling guided tours of the centrifuge," Kubrick lightheartedly told Bernstein. Smile or not, this was a sure clue that some of the MGM money men were starting to grumble.

During a trip back to the States in late May 1966, Clarke met with some nervous MGM executives and attempted to reassure them about Kubrick's budget-busting production. But his principal reason for the visit—besides having to leave England periodically to avoid higher income taxes because of his status as a British citizen who had an official residence abroad—was to fulfill general promotional and public relations duties.

In 1966, MGM had commissioned a promotional short, *The Making of 2001*, that was to be shown to film distributors and leaders in high-tech industries who could lend expertise or some other form of support to the production. Clarke was one of its stars, and scenes of him and Tom Buck of *Look* magazine were shot at the Grumman Corporation plant in Bethpage, New York, during his visit.

The film was produced by Craven Film Corporation and had no connection with the later book, *The Making of Kubrick's 2001*, edited by Jerome Agel and published in 1970. It was the first indication to the outside world of what Stanley Kubrick had been doing since *Dr. Strangelove*.

"It is the year 2001," begins the promo film's narrator. "You are on your way to a space station on routine business. You have been traveling less than an hour and have remembered to call your office. Now you transmit your thoughts across space electronically.

"You receive your answer transmitted directly to the built-in television screen in your case. This is but one example of what life will be like in the year 2001."

The Making of 2001 then goes on to interview Frederick Ordway and Harry Lange, who talk about everything they are doing to "ensure the scientific integrity of the film." Ordway names major corporations such as IBM and GE that have been consulted regularly.

When Clarke and Buck are shown in front of NASA's Lunar Excursion Module (LEM) at the Grumman plant where it was being built, Clarke addresses the camera. "We're in the final assembly building of the LEM, which will take two American astronauts down to the surface of the moon. And in *2001* Stanley Kubrick and I have set ourselves several objectives. We hope to relate to the public the wonder and beauty and promise of the new age of exploration which is opening before the human race. We want to convey the message that perhaps our Earth is not the only abode of life. Our sun which shines on this planet is one of a hundred billion circling in the Milky Way. How many of those shine upon our equals or masters out there in the depths of space? That's a question that *2001* asks and seeks to answer."

The promotional film proved to be more talkative than the movie itself. As the filming of *2001* progressed, the screenplay's dialogue became less and less important to Kubrick. He was, after all, trying to visualize for his audience an experience that was beyond words. Less than a third of the final film has dialogue (forty-six minutes out of a total running time of 141 minutes), and approximately a half hour goes by before the first words are spoken by a receptionist aboard *Space Station V* to Dr. Heywood Floyd: "Here you are, sir. Main level, please."

"I tried to work things out," said Kubrick, "so that nothing important was said in the dialogue and that anything important in the film be translated in terms of action."

This goal, itself controversial, evolved over time as the writing and filming progressed. The lead actor, Keir Dullea, who played Commander Bowman in the film, certainly noticed the change.

"Any similarity between the script I first read and the movie is purely coincidental," Dullea says. "All I saw was a science fiction story with a very visual approach."

Ray Bradbury thought the film's dialogue "banal to the point of extinction."

When an interviewer told Bradbury that this was probably intentional on Kubrick's part, Bradbury replied: "I hope not. I'd like to believe Kubrick is more intelligent than that. I just think he's a bad writer who got in the way of Arthur C. Clarke, who is a wonderful writer."

Asked in 1989 if his opinion had changed in two decades, Bradbury said no. "If I could write the dialogue, then I would write scenes for the actors up front before you kill them. Then you've got some friction going, you've got a plot going for you, and you've got an antagonist. I would make more of a contest all the way along with HAL.

"I love the film—that's why I criticize it," says Bradbury. "I've seen it six times just to check my feelings. The film is still too long.

"I could go in and edit that film for him tomorrow," continues Bradbury, "and make it into a better film, except that what is missing is humanity. There are no sympathetic characters. The Popsicle people whom HAL kills off, you never find out who they are, so you don't care.

"But the film is historically important and broke ground as far as space travel is concerned. The photography is glorious, and the music, and we'll never forget the excitement of seeing it for the first time for the good parts."

Stanley Kubrick explained his position regarding the dialogue to the *New York Times*: "There are certain areas of feeling and reality that are notably inaccessible to words. Non-verbal forms of expression such as music and painting can get at these areas, but words are a terrible straitjacket. It's interesting how many prisoners of that straitjacket resent its being loosened."

Fred Ordway argued strongly for using voice-over narration in the "Dawn of Man" sequence, which became the prologue, as well as in the final scenes in the film.

"I thought it was excellent dialogue prepared by Arthur, and I think it would have added immensely to the film," says Ordway, "but Kubrick didn't want that. And of course Kubrick knocked out a lot of dialogue that was already there. Originally the stewardesses and the pilots were talking, but Kubrick knocked it out and put music over. Apparently his purpose was to keep it almost a silent film. But a lot of people in the audience would have been less mystified about the film's meaning if the dialogue and narration had remained."

That the meaning of *2001* would be less mysterious, of course, went against Kubrick's and Clarke's intent—at least in retrospect.

"This is what makes *2001* so unique," said Clarke. "It poses metaphysical, philosophical, and even religious questions. I don't pretend we have the answers. But the questions are certainly worth thinking about.

"*2001: A Space Odyssey* is about man's past and future life in space. It's about concern with man's hierarchy in the universe, which is probably pretty low. It's about the reactions of humanity to the discovery of higher intelligence in the universe."

Stanley Kubrick says, "I don't like to talk about *2001* much, because it's essentially a nonverbal experience. It attempts to communicate more to the subconscious and to the feelings than it does to the intellect. I think clearly that there's a basic problem with people who are not paying attention with their eyes. They're listening. And they don't get much from listening to this film. Those who won't believe their eyes won't be able to appreciate this film."

As the film evolved, music became more important than dialogue and replaced it.

"Stan and I used 'Carmina Burana' [a so-called scenic cantata] a lot for atmosphere during writing," Clarke once wrote to Sam

Youd. "We tried to hire [Carl] Orff, but he was too old to tackle a major new project."

The film opened with Richard Strauss's powerful *Also Sprach Zarathustra*, which led into the prehistoric "Dawn of Man" African sequence. All action shots in the sequence were filmed in England in the fall of 1967 with a large-scale front-projection system of African transparencies thrown from in front of the screen. This was another innovation first used in *2001*. It was invented and described by science fiction writer Murray Leinster in the mid-1960s, and Clarke was impressed when he first saw it demonstrated.

"I can still recall my amazement when Stanley first showed me the principle of front projection in the MGM Studio at Elstree," wrote Clarke. "We stood at one end of the set, facing the huge screen of retro-reflective ('cat's-eye') material covering the far wall. Stanley lit a match—and its image came straight back at us, its brilliance apparently undiminished after a journey of more than a hundred feet."

Later in the film, Johann Strauss's waltz "The Blue Danube" became the sound track for the famous evolutionary jump to the space station vista. Kubrick chose Herbert von Karajan's interpretation of the piece.

"It's hard to find anything much better than 'The Blue Danube' for depicting grace and beauty in turning," said Kubrick. "It also gets about as far away as you can get from the cliché of space music."

His choice again of Richard Strauss's *Zarathustra* for the music bed toward the end of the "Dawn of Man" sequence, when Moon Watcher appears to understand how he can use the bone he holds, is another powerful moment in the film, signifying that an evolutionary leap is about to take place.

Clarke remembers when the last scene in the "Dawn of Man" was filmed, the one in which Moon Watcher smashes the animal skulls and then throws his bone weapon up into the air. It was the only scene in *2001* that was filmed on location and not in the studio. The location, however, was only a few hundred yards away from the studio in a nearby field.

"A small platform had been set up," says Clarke, "and Moon Watcher (Dan Richter) was sitting on this, surrounded by bones. Cars and buses were going by at the end of the field, but as this was a low-angle shot against the sky they didn't get in the way—though Stanley did have to pause for an occasional airplane.

"The shot was repeated so many times, and Dan smashed so many bones, that I was afraid we were going to run out of warthog (or tapir) skulls. But eventually Stanley was satisfied, and as we walked back to the studio he began to throw bones up in the air. At first I thought this was sheer joie de vivre, but he started to film them with a hand-held camera—no easy task.

"When he had finished filming the bones whirling against the sky, Stanley resumed the walk back to the studio; but now he had got hold of a broom and started tossing *that* up into the air."

This was the creative genesis of the memorable transition from twirling bone to similar-shaped spaceship—what Clarke has called "the longest flash forward in the history of movies—three million years."

Kubrick had planned twenty-six weeks to shoot the main scenes, and even though the shooting in the centrifuge had delayed the schedule for about a week, the principal shooting of live action such as the Moon Watcher scene had been completed during the first six months of 1966.

There was still a tremendous amount of postproduction work, however, to be finished. The intricate, time-consuming, and all-important special effects needed to be designed and filmed. Most of this work was done during the last half of 1966, all of 1967, and the first few months of 1968.

Clarke was not at the MGM studios every day that he was in England. He often worked at his London residence, 88 Nightingale Road, and communicated by phone with Kubrick and other members of the production team. He also traveled during this period, returning to Ceylon and visiting the United States before heading back to England just in time to celebrate his birthday—"(ugh!) my 50th!!!"

With the New Year came the release of *2001*. At long last the cosmic film odyssey was about to go public. And it was likely that the book would follow!

"I feel pretty relaxed about all this & can now take it or leave it," Clarke told Sam Youd.

Stanley Kubrick wasn't so lucky. Even after he returned to the United States in early 1968, special effects work continued. And after some advance screenings, Kubrick had additional cutting to do. In fact he cut the film by nineteen minutes in the spring of 1968, just before its general release.

This was not the first time Kubrick had made last-minute cuts on a film after he'd gotten initial audience reaction. He'd also cut *Dr. Strangelove* and *Paths of Glory* just before they were generally released.

When preview audiences saw the original uncut version of *2001*—which ran two hours and forty-one minutes—it was not uncommon to hear people criticizing it as too long and boring.

"Stanley also sensed it was too long," says Roger Caras. "He hadn't seen the film complete with music and sound effects until about a week before it opened. But he couldn't decide on the cuts until he observed a live audience and could get an idea of the squirm factor. He walked up and down the side aisles and across the back endlessly during the screening to see where they were squirming—and that's where he made the cuts."

After the premieres in Washington, New York, and Los Angeles, which took place during the first four days of April, Kubrick cut the original print on April 5 in New York City. He made all the cuts himself; no one asked him to.

"Stanley sat up all night doing the trimming in the basement of the MGM Building on Sixth Avenue," recalls Caras. It took thirty individual cuts to make up the nineteen minutes, and they came from several different scenes, including the "Dawn of Man," *Orion III* spaceship to orbit, *Space Station V*, exercising in the centrifuge of *Discovery*, and Poole's (actor Gary Lockwood's) space pod exiting from *Discovery*.

"There was a whole sequence in the space station that was cut," says Caras. "A village square inside the station, with shops and a playground with children running around—that came out. And Gary Lockwood's 'breathing' sequence outside the spaceship, before he was killed by HAL, was greatly shortened."

Kubrick did not believe that the cuts made a crucial difference: "I think it just affected some marginal people. The people who like it like it no matter what its length, and the same holds true for the people who hate it."

The film *did* provoke extreme reactions—from both the general moviegoing public and professional film critics. There seemed to be no middle-of-the-road response. Some critics, however, after seeing the movie a second time, changed their opinion from negative to positive. This was, if not unprecedented, at least rare in the world of film criticism.

After the first Washington, D.C., press preview of 2001, Clarke overheard someone say, "Well, that's the end of Stanley Kubrick." Several days later, at the world premiere, he overheard another cynical prediction from an MGM executive. It was April 2, 1968, the day that President Johnson announced he would not be seeking another term. The executive, thinking of then MGM president Robert H. O'Brien, said, "Well, today we lost two presidents."

"The most remarkable thing about 2001," Clarke said, "is that it is doing so well without any concession to popular taste. Kubrick never once said, 'Let's not let the popcorn set get away.' It's so uncompromising that people realize it deals with much bigger issues than science alone."

The New York critics were, as a group, less kind than reviewers in Washington and Los Angeles, although Penelope Gilliatt of the *New Yorker* wrote that "*2001: A Space Odyssey* is some sort of great film, and an unforgettable endeavor." Less kind was Renata Adler writing in the *New York Times*. "The movie is so completely absorbed in its own problems, its use of color and space, its fanatical devotion to science-fiction detail, that it is somewhere between hypnotic and immensely boring."

John Lennon of the Beatles was one who thought it was hypnotic. "I see it every week," he said (facetiously?).

One cynical critic made the tongue-in-cheek suggestion that the film was produced so that *Life* magazine could have a major photo spread article at the time of release—which it did.

The film, said *Life*, "dazzles the eyes and gnaws at the mind." The article went on to summarize and explain the movie as well as inform readers about the complexity of creating some of the scenes and special effects.

Generally *Life* was kind to 2001, as well it might be, considering the fact that it had its own special screening on March 29, 1968—before any of the special press previews for the VIPs and film critics in New York and Washington.

Why such favored status? The reason probably dates way back to spring 1964, when Clarke and Kubrick were brainstorming the project. During one of their sessions they asked Albert Rosenfeld, *Life*'s science editor, to join them at Kubrick's apartment.

"They were plotting their movie," said Rosenfeld, "and Kubrick was bouncing ideas off Clarke, who sat there, a mild, scholarly-looking man, full of facts and crinkly with humor. . . .

"My own audience participation had come about mainly because at that stage of incipient planning and brain-picking, the two thought that, as *Life's* science editor, my brain might yield some stray, useful bit of information."

Working out to be mutually beneficial, it also yielded some invaluable publicity in a major magazine four years later. Although *Life's* coverage was neutral, controversy over the film raged in other quarters.

Wrote John Allen in the *Christian Science Monitor,* "Whenever the thunder of critical controversy rips through the air, one thing is certain: Lightning has struck. Stanley Kubrick's *2001: A Space Odyssey* is just such a bolt of brilliant, high-voltage cinema."

The *Chicago Daily News* critic, Sam Lesner, was one of the critics whose opinion changed after seeing the film again.

"I have seen Stanley Kubrick's mind-bending, maddening, awesome, debilitating, demoniacal, dehumanizing, and miraculous extraterrestrial fantasy-drama twice. At first I thought Kubrick had flipped his lid. Now I believe he is a genius."

For each word of praise there was another of criticism. One particularly nasty review came from Pauline Kael, writing in *Harper's.*

"It's fun to think about Kubrick really doing every dumb thing he wanted to do, building enormous science-fiction sets and equipment, never even bothering to figure out what he was going to do with them. In some ways it's the biggest amateur movie of them all, complete even to the amateur-movie obligatory scene—the director's little daughter (in curls) telling daddy what kind of present she wants. It's a monumentally unimaginative movie."

Rumor had it that Kubrick flew into a rage once or twice after seeing reviews such as this.

Clarke, on the other hand, was having fun with all the controversy. In fact he sometimes added to it. Soon after the film's release, he made a statement about *2001* that disturbed the MGM executives. "If anyone understands it on the first viewing, we've failed in our intention." When asked what he thought of Clarke's statement, Kubrick said he disagreed with it.

"I believe he made it facetiously," said Kubrick. "The very

nature of the visual experience in *2001* is to give the viewer an instantaneous, visceral reaction that does not—and should not—require further amplification. Just speaking generally, however, I would say that there are elements in any good film that would increase the viewer's interest and appreciation on a second viewing."

Clarke rejects Kubrick's characterization of his comment as "facetious." Wrote Clarke, "I still stand by this remark, which does not mean one can't *enjoy* the movie completely the first time around. What I meant was, of course, that because we were dealing with the mystery of the universe, and with powers and forces greater than man's comprehension, then by definition they could not be totally understandable. Yet there is at least one logical structure—and sometimes more than one—behind everything that happens on the screen in *2001*, and the ending does not consist of random enigmas, some simpleminded critics to the contrary. (You will find my interpretation in the novel; it is not necessarily Kubrick's. Nor is his necessarily the 'right' one—whatever that means.)"

Of all the praise *2001* received during its first six months in the theaters, Clarke was most flattered by a comment from Alexei Leonov, the Russian cosmonaut and first man in the world to leave his spaceship and "walk" in space. Clarke met Leonov in Vienna in August 1968. The occasion was the United Nations Conference on Peaceful Uses of Space. It was also the European premiere of *2001: A Space Odyssey*.

After seeing the film Leonov remarked, "Now I feel I've been in space twice."

Neil Armstrong, the first man to set foot on the moon, saw the movie before *Apollo 11* blasted off from Earth in July 1969. "It was a particularly fine production," says Armstrong, "with exceptionally accurate portrayals of spaceflight conditions and visual effects."

The *Apollo 8* astronauts—Frank Borman, James Lovell, and William Anders—who made the first, history-making circumnavigation of the moon in December 1968, saw *2001* before they departed Earth.

After seeing the film, Anders had an idea for his upcoming *Apollo 8* mission. "I remember thinking at the time I saw the picture that it might be worth a chuckle to mention finding a monolith during our Apollo flight."

"I have never quite forgiven Bill Anders for resisting the temptation," says Clarke.

It was not until July, a few months after the film's release, that the novel *2001* was actually published. Clarke had to wait until spring, just before the film went into general release, for Kubrick to approve its publication, and in fact it was only days before the release that Scott Meredith was able to resell the book.

Says Meredith, "The only one who showed a certain amount of interest was Sidney Kramer, president of New American Library. Sidney said, 'I'm interested, but I'm not sure, and I've got to see the film.'

"A preview was arranged, not just for Sidney but for various people in New York. About a week before that, MGM had told me that it was the consensus of opinion that the picture was a disaster. Some of the people at MGM actually thought that *2001* would put them out of business, since it had gone way over budget. They thought they might lose every penny. They obviously didn't understand the picture, which was so different from previous space operas. New American Library, of course, heard about this and kept vacillating about whether or not they ought to do the book at all.

"Finally I took Sidney to the preview. During the intermission we walked out to the lobby to stretch our legs and have a Coke. I turned to him and said, 'Well?' And he said, 'Goddamned if I know.' Of course, I wasn't sure myself. It was so very different from what one would expect.

"So we went back in and saw the rest of the picture. When we came out again, Sidney asked me what I thought. 'Sidney,' I said, 'if you don't buy this book, you're totally out of your mind. This is going to be a classic—the movie and the book.' I talked a blue streak, telling him he'd be making the mistake of his career if he didn't do the book.

"He then said to me, 'OK, I'll buy it, purely on your recommendation, because, I'll tell you the truth, I don't know what the hell this picture was all about!'

"So we made a deal with New American Library for $130,000—less than the original one with Dell that fell through [but more than the second Dell deal, which also fell through]. It wasn't a record breaker, but it was a very good solid deal. And that was *2001*, the novel."

The publication date came two years after Clarke had completed the final version of the manuscript. It had been a frustrating period, but that was over. Now, during the raging controversy over Kubrick's movie, Clarke was having a wonderful time on the lecture circuit and promotion trail. All the talk, of course, was about the film, but that helped sell copies of the book.

"I always used to tell people, 'Read the book, see the film, and repeat the dose as often as necessary,'" said Clarke.

Book reviewers were generally kinder to the novel, which was almost always seen in relation to the film. The *New York Times* said that "all of it becomes clear and convincing in the novel." The *Washington Post* praised "Clarke's conception [which] soars and takes you along, stretching your imagination as only good fiction can do." The *Post* also said that "[t]he book does something that the Stanley Kubrick movie cannot: It leaves the vision to your imagination—and an awesome vision it is."

Physicist Freeman Dyson, of the Institute for Advanced Study in Princeton, liked the novel and urged others to read it: "After seeing *Space Odyssey*, I read Arthur Clarke's book. I found the book gripping and intellectually satisfying, full of the tension and clarity which the movie lacks. All the parts of the movie that are vague and unintelligible, especially the beginning and the end, become clear and convincing in the book. So I recommend to my middle-aged friends who find the movie bewildering that they should read the book; their teenage kids don't need to."

The desire of befuddled fans to make sense of the film helped book sales. Many buyers agreed with Herbert Kenny of the *Boston Globe*, who said that "since the motion picture has its baffling moments, a perusal of the book will help, and indeed, the motion picture helps elucidate the book."

During the novel's first year of publication, there were more than one million paperback copies in print. As a result, many of Arthur C. Clarke's other books enjoyed increased sales. During the following year, 1969, three more printings of *Childhood's End* were published. The name Arthur C. Clarke became known to large numbers of people outside the science and science fiction communities. His reputation was now international.

The film *2001* was nominated for four Academy Awards, including best picture. The controversy surrounding the movie was good for the box office, but it didn't help win best-picture votes. The film received one Oscar—for special effects.

"It was a major breakthrough in motion picture production and technology—a good twenty years before its time," says Roger Caras. "Everything we've seen since with special effects was born in *2001*. No one dreamed that a film production could go to such heights of technical brilliance."

Ray Lovejoy, Kubrick's editor on the film, emphasizes *2001*'s influence on other filmmakers: "The film inspired a tremendous number of filmmakers. George Lucas was certainly inspired by *2001*. Lucas actually took an ad out somewhere when *Star Wars* first came out, when everyone was praising its special effects, which said that *2001* is still the champion of them all.

"I also did *Aliens* with Jim Cameron," says Lovejoy, "and *2001* is the reason Jim went into film. I've met a lot of American technicians who've said exactly that—that this film inspired them to follow the careers they did in the film industry.

"The film never dies. It's inspired so many people, and a lot of directors that I've worked for have said, 'God, you know, *2001* is the reason why I started in films.' And there's a lot of credit to Arthur for that as well. It was his story, after all."

Clarke was bitterly disappointed that the Oscar for best screenplay went to Mel Brooks's *The Producers*. He attended the award ceremonies at the Dorothy Chandler Pavilion in the spring of 1969. "I tore up one of the best speeches of thanks never delivered. When I ran into Mel Brooks years later, I snarled: 'Mel— you stole my OSCAR.'" But Mel Brooks made the perfect reply, Clarke recalls. "He said, 'You're a genius.' That, of course, instantly put things right!"

On another occasion, Clarke mildly insulted the Oscar judges, with a twinkle in his eye, implying that they lacked basic discrimination: "*2001* did not win the Academy Award for makeup because the judges may not have realized the apes were actors."

How does Arthur C. Clarke view the *2001* phenomenon that boosted his reputation worldwide and eventually brought tens of thousands of readers to his other work?

His agent, Scott Meredith, puts it this way. "Ginger Rogers has made seventy-three pictures, and nine of those pictures were with Fred Astaire. She is so identified with the Astaire pictures that she hates the very mention of them.

"You have the same situation with Arthur and *2001*. When I'm interviewed, and they ask about famous clients, and I mention Arthur Clarke, they say, 'Oh yes, the *2001* man.' Well, of course he's a lot more than that. It's easy to understand why *2001* isn't Arthur's favorite book."

"My favorite work, my best work, is *The Songs of Distant Earth*," said Clarke in 1989. "*2061: Odyssey Three* is much better than *2001* or *2010*. *2001* is not a very good book. It was written entirely to make a movie and was really nothing more than a glorified screenplay."

Many of his millions of readers would disagree with him and defend *2001*, the novel, as a worthy work in its own right.

What did Stanley Kubrick have to say about his onetime collaborator?

"As an artist," said Kubrick, "Arthur's ability to impart poignancy to a dying ocean or an intelligent vapor is unique. He has the kind of mind of which the world can never have enough, an array of imagination, intelligence, knowledge, and a quirkish curiosity which often uncovers more than the first three qualities."

*We could—with great expense and difficulty, it is true—
reach the moon even with today's technologies.*
                    The Exploration of the Moon *(1954)*

[T]hey stood looking up at the stars and the waxing Earth.
                                    Earthlight *(1955)*

19
THE LUNAR AGE BEGINS

As the film *2001: A Space Odyssey* played to awestruck (and often baffled) audiences, Arthur C. Clarke was actively promoting the real promise that spaceflight and its advanced technologies held. Four years had gone into the making of *2001*, the film and the book, during which time the U.S. space program, with its vast resources and pool of talent, had developed, built, and tested the hardware that would fly men to the moon.

Despite President Kennedy's May 1961 speech, no one knew that we would actually put a man on the moon by the end of the decade. But in 1963 Clarke had made a prediction for the event that was only six months off. True to form, his near-future forecasts were on target; his far-future prophesying varied. In his BIS years, for example, Clarke and his British associates were making fairly accurate predictions about lunar landings, but by the 1950s Clarke was pessimistic.

"When I published my first space novel [*Prelude to Space*] in the early 1950s, I very optimistically imagined a lunar landing in 1978," wrote Clarke. "I didn't really believe it would be done so soon, but I wanted to boost my morale by pretending that it might happen in my own lifetime."

Clarke was even more conservative in response to a survey taken in 1953, when he was one of sixty-five scientists and writers asked to predict the date for the first manned flight to the moon or another planet. His prediction was 1985.

"He never thought we would land a man on the moon in the sixties," says Thomas Paine, NASA's administrator during the historic flight of *Apollo 11*. There were two things that almost everybody missed. "First, nobody foresaw the scale of the effort that would be required. If you think back on all the science fiction in the twenties and thirties and forties there was always an inventor who went out to his garage, fiddled around with some gunks and goos, and miraculously invented a propellant or an antigravity device so that he and the neighbor's daughter could fly to the moon in something he put together over the weekend. So it was always a very small-scale effort based on a highly inventive breakthrough.

"On the contrary, spaceflight turned out to be a very large effort that required a great deal of organization and coordination of whole industries and economies.

"The other thing that everybody missed, however (and I think the two are related), is the fact that by the 1960s two of the world economies—the Soviet Union and the United States—would be quite large enough to afford this at around one or two percent of their gross national products. This and the fact that these nations decided to compete is what would propel us to the moon.

"The hardest point for people today to realize when trying to predict the settlement of Mars in 2020 or so," says Paine, "is how enormous the world's gross national product is going to be by then."

Because of *2001*, Arthur C. Clarke's reputation was ascending. Consequently so was the demand for him on the lecture circuit. He spent most of the second half of 1968 on the lecture trail in the United States and England, speaking in more than a dozen major U.S. cities before pursuing a similar hectic schedule across the Atlantic.

These speaking engagements and Clarke's increased fame helped him gain some degree of support from more than a dozen aerospace corporations for a ninety-minute film called *The Promise of Space*, which was the initial project of Spaceward Corporation. That organization had been founded in 1966 by Clarke, Thomas Buck, and Thomas Craven, with whom he'd worked on the *2001* promo film. Its purpose was to educate the public, primarily through television films but also through various related projects, about the benefits of space exploration and other inventive science programs. The first film would lead into six other shorter complementary films concentrating on specific subjects such as health, communication, and education—all of which were to be written by Clarke. The lead film would be adapted from Clarke's nonfiction book of the same title, which was published in 1968, the same year that *Apollo 8* made its historic circumnavigation of the moon and the year before the first moon landing. *The Promise of Space* covered the dreams and achievements leading up to the Space Age of the 1950s, the early Apollo program of the 1960s, and the future promise of space exploration into the 1970s and beyond.

While corporate backing made it possible to produce footage for the lead film, in the end Spaceward failed to win the support of a major television network.

"*The Promise of Space* was dead in the water by the early seventies," says Michael Craven, who now heads Thomas Craven Films. "The networks controlled everything then. Independent film producers had little chance of selling their productions to the networks, and Spaceward's first film never won network backing."

By the fall of 1968, life on the road was starting to wear Clarke down. It was time, he knew, to head for home base. In October he returned to his Indian Ocean paradise for some badly needed rest and relaxation.

In doing so Clarke had passed up one of the most enticing perks of his growing renown: an invitation to witness the launch of *Apollo 8*.

"I am sitting glued to the short-wave radio following the progress of Apollo 8," he wrote to Tom Craven from Ceylon on the day before Christmas. "I wish I could have been in the States—it must have been a wonderful thing to watch on TV. Still, I will see it later and even more ambitious shots." This was the beginning of the Lunar Age, and still Arthur C. Clarke's adopted island paradise received no television.

A local newspaper reporter came out to interview Clarke, who saw yet another golden opportunity to educate the public. He turned on his radio, and "Voice of America" came through loud and clear with coverage of the historic first circumnavigation of the moon by a manned spacecraft.

"How many people have powerful radios to pick up these transmissions?" Clarke asked the journalist. "If not for this, I would be unable to sit in my garden, listen to the radio, look up into the sky, and hear the voices of the astronauts speaking from outer space."

And what of television? Clarke went on to say that television would come to the underdeveloped countries through communications satellites. A year later, in 1969, *Intelsat III* began service over the Indian Ocean region. This established the Earth's first global communication system, its messages traveling at the speed of light. The entire planet was finally served with just three satellites in geostationary orbit—the same system that Arthur C. Clarke had first envisioned in 1945.

"Television is of tremendous educational value for countries that lack experienced teachers, for a few good teachers could educate classes of millions through the medium of television. That is why I always stress that television *must* come to countries such as India and Ceylon."

The journalist was left with a Clarkean vision of an evolving global communications network—mankind's nervous system, linking together the entire human race.

Although he had called a halt to travel for the time being, Clarke's views on the future were in too great demand to allow him to be idle. Besides working on the script for the ill-fated film *The Promise of Space*, he was writing a synopsis for a nonfiction film about the Apollo project for Time-Life/MGM.

"This was going to be a major production, and I wrote the screenplay," recalls Clarke. "Then Time-Life/MGM got a divorce, and the whole thing fell through."

In late January, he played host to Jeremy Bernstein, the *New Yorker* science writer, who'd come to Ceylon to do a profile on him for the magazine. It was Clarke's opinion that Bernstein had gathered enough material for a whole book. The piece, entitled "Profiles: Out of the Ego Chamber," appeared in the *New Yorker* in early August 1969, just weeks after the successful *Apollo 11* mission that landed men on the moon. It was the most complete overview of Clarke's life and work that had yet appeared. Appropriately it honored his decades-long vision at one of the great moments in history.

Clarke seemed similarly gratified by the attention he received at the World Science Fiction Symposium and film festival held in Rio de Janeiro in spring 1969.

Wrote Frederik Pohl, "The SF Symposium was only an added afterthought to a major world film festival, and the city was full of superstars and starlets." Among the writers there were Poul Anderson, Forrest J. Ackerman, A. E. van Vogt, Robert Bloch, Brian Aldiss, and J. G. Ballard.

"Clarke seemed to have a bully good time there," says Sam Moskowitz, historian, editor, and longtime fan of science fiction. "And why not? They were feeding him *and* feeding his ego."

Among the international film notables present was the famous German director Fritz Lang, whose masterpiece *Metropolis* Clarke recalls screening back at Huish's Grammar School. Lang's 1929 film classic *Woman in the Moon* (*Frau im Mond*) invented the rocket countdown to create a dramatic plot device.

"The most vivid memory of Rio de Janeiro," says Clarke, "is meeting Fritz Lang. He was a very old man then and had a black eye patch.

"I'll tell you who else was there," Clarke continues. "George Pal. George Pal who made *Destination Moon, War of the Worlds,* and all those great space films. That was the last time I saw dear old George."

During the spring and fall of 1969, when he didn't have other commitments, Clarke resumed the speaking engagements that not only supplemented his book royalty income but, just as important to Clarke, made possible a vital exchange of ideas with his audience. Imbued with his infectious enthusiasm, these events drew admirers from many fields.

When Clarke gave a lecture on astronomy in Arizona in the first half of 1969, Gene Roddenberry, the creator of "Star Trek," traveled from Los Angeles to hear him.

"That was an indication of my respect for him," Roddenberry said. "I went there just planning to be a member of the audience. I not only met this great man, but was persuaded by him to continue my 'Star Trek' projects despite the entertainment industry's labeling the production an unbelievable concept and a failure. Arthur prophesied at this time that when humans walked on the moon it would cause a revolutionary change in attitudes toward space."

In fact, Roddenberry in large part credited Clarke with saving his career.

"Arthur literally made my 'Star Trek' idea possible, including the television series, the films, and the associations and learning it has made possible for me.

"At the time I wasn't getting a lot of assignments because of the so-called failure of 'Star Trek.' It was a case of develop a separate or additional income or begin to lose my house and insurance policies and all of that. Arthur got me in touch with Bill Leigh [Clarke's lecture agent] and encouraged me to make use of the lecture platform.

"I visited the lecture bureau in New York City, and Bill senior said, 'Arthur tells me he thought it would be amusing if you recounted some of your adventures in television land.' And you know, I had the feeling that television was not something that Leigh was close to. The feeling I got was 'If Arthur recommends you, of course we shall try to handle you.'

"So I went out on my first lecture. Leigh, of course, had no way of knowing that the college students were really gung ho for 'Star Trek.' And instead of a hundred people showing up, two thousand did! The auditorium was not large enough, and so I spoke a second time for those who couldn't get in the first time.

"I then began lecturing regularly, and there was more money in it than the Leigh agency had predicted. This continued for a number of years, to steadily increasing audiences as 'Star Trek' became more and more popular.

"Over the years, Arthur and I have gotten even closer. He's been very helpful to me in the *Star Trek* films that I've done. He's backed me. When Paramount started to do a *Star Trek* film about religion and finding God in the galaxy, I wrote to Arthur. He in turn wrote to Paramount and said he thought it was nonsense. You know, it's one thing for me to say something to Paramount, but when Arthur Clarke says it, that's stronger."

Gene Roddenberry's "Star Trek: The Next Generation" holds a distinct record.

"It's the first time a show has ever come back to television and been a success," said Roddenberry. "And I give many thanks to Arthur for helping."

When Gene Roddenberry died in the fall of 1991, Clarke wrote: "There is a sad irony in the fact that he entered *The Undiscovered Country* just when the eagerly awaited movie of that name was about to be released.

"At a dark time in human history, 'Star Trek' promoted the then unpopular ideals of tolerance for differing cultures and respect for life in all forms—without preaching and always with a saving sense of humour. We can all rejoice that Gene achieved professional success and world respect. What must have given him even greater satisfaction is that he lived to see so many of his ideals triumphantly accepted.

"Few men have left a finer legacy. *Enterprise* will be cruising the Galaxy for centuries to come."

I still have in my mind the image of that beautiful ship going up; and it's curious, although it's three miles away, it seems enormous. . . . In my memory I can only see the rocket filling the sky, although of course I know it was only a fairly small visual image.
                    Arthur C. Clarke to Walter Cronkite, July 16, 1969

20
MAN ON THE MOON

Arthur C. Clarke had been thinking seriously about going to the moon for more than a quarter of a century before the *Eagle* landed in the Sea of Tranquillity on Sunday, July 20, 1969. Thus there's an existential justice in the fact that he helped to cover the historic launch and moon landing of *Apollo 11* for CBS News with Walter Cronkite.

This was not the first time that Clarke had worked at CBS with Walter Cronkite. In 1967 CBS produced "The 21st Century," a series of documentaries about the future. Clarke was the leadoff expert on "The Communications Explosion," the first program in the series, which aired on January 29. He described the many possible wonders of satellite communications, including his prediction of a search and rescue function, using SOS signals and directional satellites, that could save thousands of lives every year. Just such an international search and rescue satellite system now exists (SARSAT-COSPAS, initiated in 1982) and has indeed saved more than a thousand lives. Clarke also discussed the future of direct broadcasting from communications satellites on the same program.

"Then you'll be able to tune in to Russian, Chinese, European broadcasts, TV direct, wherever you are. Well, the effect of this is going to be tremendous in both directions. It means that we can talk to the Chinese and they can talk to us, and nobody on either side can stop it."

Walter Cronkite recalls, "I'd known of Arthur through his books and other writings and his general reputation before he was on that program. So he didn't come to me as an unknown character. I think our producer, Burton Benjamin, actually decided that he should be on that broadcast with us, and I was delighted that we could work it out."

Clarke joined the CBS Apollo coverage team for three moon-landing missions: the historic *Apollo 11*, which took Neil Armstrong and Buzz Aldrin to the moon, in July 1969; *Apollo 12*, which flew in November 1969; and then the flight of *Apollo 15* in July–August of 1971. (He was too busy writing in 1970 and the first half of 1971 to cover *Apollo 13* and *Apollo 14*.) Clarke also helped out on *Apollo 10*, the so-called dress rehearsal mission above the moon, which flew from May 18 to May 26, 1969.

Dick Hoagland, a science adviser for Walter Cronkite and the CBS team, remembers one of the planning meetings in late June or early July 1969 before the *Apollo 11* mission began:

"We were sitting around this long conference table with producers, technicians, Robert Wussler (executive producer of the *Apollo 11* coverage), Arthur, and me. In this particular meeting we were looking at some footage of the astronauts from Houston. We were talking about how we could demonstrate on TV how the moon landing, in fact all the Apollo missions, was going to affect humanity. Everyone there knew how expensive model work was and how those kinds of costs were constantly discouraged. How did we show the future—that was the challenge.

"Then Arthur had an idea. 'I know how,' he said. Everything got quiet, because Arthur was respected. He didn't talk a lot, so when he spoke, everyone listened. Even the technicians knew this guy was something different.

"Arthur said that for twenty-five dollars he could come up with a visual thing. His suggestion: Take a model globe of the moon and cut a hole in the bottom. Then punch little holes in it, one where Tranquillity base will be, for example. Then put a light bulb inside, and people will see the future cities of an inhabited moon. He demonstrated how elegantly simple his vision had been and how it could be adapted to television.

"Arthur was respected even if he was not fully understood. He's quite ingenious."

An estimated half million people had come to Cocoa Beach and the surrounding areas to view the launch of the great *Saturn V* rocket. The press site, with some three thousand people, had never been more crowded. Eventually it was estimated that six hundred million people or more (one-sixth of the world's population at the time) watched as *Apollo 11*'s lunar excursion module, the *Eagle*, landed on the moon's surface and its commander, Neil Armstrong, later became the first human being to step foot in the powdery lunar dust.

The CBS News coverage, an unprecedented forty-six hours over a period of eight days, was titled "Man on the Moon: The Epic Journey of *Apollo 11*." Besides Walter Cronkite and Eric Sevareid, the other major on-camera people included CBS News correspondents David Schoumacher, Heywood Hale Broun, Ike Pappas, and Ed Rabel. Apollo astronaut Walter Schirra, Jr., and Arthur C. Clarke were the two regular guest commentators. Clarke, billed as "one of the leading space visionaries," appeared on camera about twelve times during the *Apollo 11* coverage.

Launch day arrived. Lift-off of the gigantic *Saturn V* finally came at 9:32 EDT, Wednesday, July 16, 1969. None of the hundreds of thousands of witnesses who came to experience the launch would forget the deafening roar and the brilliant, all-but-blinding flame that descended from the great rocket as it climbed into the sky.

At the moment of lift-off the CBS News studio at Cape Kennedy (since renamed Canaveral) was quiet and almost empty. Only Walter Cronkite, former astronaut Wally Schirra, producer Joan Richman, and a few other people remained inside. Everyone else, including Clarke, went outdoors to watch the launch.

G. Harry Stine, a science adviser for CBS, was with Clarke just moments before takeoff.

"It was down to about T minus three minutes on the launch," says Stine. "And Arthur said, 'I'm not going to stay inside for this.' I agreed. So we went outside, just the two of us, and stood side by side in front of the CBS studio building, and we watched *Apollo 11* leave for the moon. That was a thrill. Arthur didn't say anything;

I didn't say anything. We watched it disappear in the sky and then went back to work. We were only outside for about a minute."

Clarke remembered something else: at some point the tears started coming. "I hadn't cried for twenty years. Right afterward, I happened to run into Eric Sevareid, and he was crying too," says Clarke.

Inside the studio Cronkite saw the giant rocket lift off the pad three miles outside his window, but his view was cut off as soon as it cleared the tower. He then looked at the monitor to follow its upward flight. Producer Joan Richman remembers lying on the floor, flat on her back, so that she could continue to see *Apollo 11* as it arched over the Atlantic Ocean on its way to space. And ex-astronaut Wally Schirra was down on his hands and knees, his face pressed against the window glass, following Saturn's ascension.

For the first few seconds after the launch Walter Cronkite was speechless. Then he exclaimed, "Oh boy, oh boy, it looks good, Wally. Building shaking. We're getting the buffeting we've become used to. What a moment! Man on the way to the moon! Beautiful!"

Later, Clarke joined Cronkite on camera, and they spoke about the launch and mankind's future in space.

"I've got you back here in the copilot's seat with me, I'm pleased to say," Cronkite said to Clarke. "What are your observations on the flight of *Apollo 11* up to now?"

"Well," said Clarke, "it is one of the most thrilling things I've ever seen. I still have in my mind the image of that beautiful ship going up; and it's curious, although it's three miles away it seems enormous, it seems as though it's only a few hundred yards away. Where it rises, the rest of the landscape vanishes. In my memory I can only see the rocket filling the sky, although of course I know it was only a fairly small visual image."

Copilot Clarke went on to speculate about the near future and what developments we might expect in the next ten years.

"We've got to see the development of reusable spacecraft," he told Cronkite and the TV audience, four years before the Space Shuttle program was announced by President Nixon in 1972. "I mean, spectacular and beautiful as the *Saturn V* is, it's a fantastic way of doing the job. It's like the *Queen Elizabeth* sailing with three passengers and sinking after the maiden voyage, except that the *Saturn V* costs more than the *Queen Elizabeth*. We've got to have spaceships that we can use over and over again as often as we use a conventional airliner. The reusable space transporter is the next thing which we have got to get."

About three hours after the launch, spaceship and crew were over Australia preparing to fire their third-stage engines, which would thrust them out of their Earth orbit on their way to the moon.

Commander Neil Armstrong verified a successful third-stage firing shortly after noon. "Hey, Houston, *Apollo 11*. This Saturn gave us a magnificent ride." They had reached a velocity of 35,579 feet per second. Neil Armstrong, Buzz Aldrin, and Michael Collins were curving toward their rendezvous with the moon. The seven-hour launch-day broadcast ended at 1:15 P.M., and most of the CBS team began packing for their return flight to New York City. Four days would pass before the human drama again would rise to a crescendo, and then, with a round-the-world sigh of relief, two men would land on the moon.

"Lunar Day," as CBS referred to Sunday, July 20, was the day the *Eagle* would set down on the lunar surface. The network planned for thirty-two hours of continuous coverage, anchored in New York City's Studio 41 (the network's largest), and it included guests, remote interviews, and simulations from all over the United States, as well as the reactions of people from all over the world. The film bank was the most extensive ever compiled. It contained 140 separate pieces, one of which was a science fiction film narrated by Orson Welles. Altogether, close to one thousand people were involved in the "Lunar Day" coverage.

The set design in Studio 41 was, some people opined, as far out as the event being covered. A painting of our Milky Way galaxy was the background behind Walter Cronkite's anchor desk, which was built twenty-four feet above the floor. Why so elevated? Because an important assistant, "a second HAL" computer, was built below to help support the anchor with visuals.

Dick Hoagland explains: "To help marshal the overwhelming video and background data that we felt Walter eventually needed to tell the lunar-landing story to the television audience, we created a programmable, monstrous 'electro-optical device.' Walter and all the guests and consultants who participated were ultimately assisted by this system, which could be loaded with a variety of film clips and stills, all on motion picture film—exactly like the display screens in the original *Discovery* spaceship of *2001*. But the real capper was that all those on camera from the anchor studio at Broadcast Center in New York physically did the broadcast sitting on the top of 'HAL!'

"Walter and his guests discussed the epochal events evolving a quarter of a million miles away from atop this megalithic throne. The thing was *huge*. The screens faced outward, directly under them, allowing the audience to see what was projected, mixed, inputted, et cetera, as background to the discussions occurring 'up on top.'

"Even if Arthur was aware of all this—the fact that he was broadcasting from the summit of a semiintelligent multiscreen projection system—I doubt whether he was ever made aware that this Rube Goldberg device behemoth was deliberately created in the image, and specifically named in honor, of his HAL."

Joel Banow, who was in charge of simulations and special effects, originated the idea and named the unit HAL.

"I wanted to graphically put information on the screen pertaining to many aspects of the mission," says Banow. "Because of the movie *2001*, I got into a dialogue with Doug Trumbull, the creator of special effects for the film, and after lots of discussions and many trips out west, our HAL evolved."

CBS then hired special effects wizard Trumbull to design and develop this complicated visual display system to be used for its moon coverage.

"HAL was essentially a library of motion picture film," says Banow, "and we determined what the images were. What made it different was the grouping of eight sixteen-millimeter film projectors, high-speed data film projectors that worked together in an electromechanical system. You could project one frame at a time, or ten, eighteen, or twenty-four frames at a time to create moving images.

"It was like programming a computer. What we did was program a roll of film with words and numbers. Each projector had the same images. You could project an eight-word sentence, for example—one word from projector one, another word from projector two, and so forth. And all of them were projected by front-screen projection, similar to what was used on Kubrick's famous centrifuge set.

"We were also able to superimpose any kind of graphic onto

the television image at any time. During launch, for example, we'd do altitude, and each frame would be another five thousand feet. We'd do the same thing for velocity and have the frames ready to call up and superimpose. And it also gave us the capability to animate alphanumeric information.

"There were one or two spots in the show," Banow recalls, "where Walter would throw a question to HAL, and we'd type out the answer, which would appear on the screen. And I programmed a lot of words and phrases into HAL like 'How are you, Arthur?'" Clarke, of course, was in his glory, talking about what he loved best.

Before the moon landing on Sunday, July 20, Clarke also had an opportunity to argue the issues surrounding the lunar landing. In an interview conducted by correspondent Harry Reasoner, Clarke, one of the foremost proponents of a manned space program, defended the Apollo missions and future space exploration, while Kurt Vonnegut, Jr., a so-called black humorist, made the case that resources should be used to solve problems on planet Earth. Their exchange never got hostile.

Reasoner spoke of the many people who questioned the vast expenditures of the Apollo program and asked Clarke if he often faced this attitude.

"Yes," Clarke replied. "I'm always running into it. Of course, anything one does could be done better in some other way. If you build a school, it means you can't build a hospital. There's always a question of priorities. But I think in the long run the money that's been put into the space program is one of the best investments this country has ever made. Because you're going to get back a so-called spin-off, which NASA's always talking about, which is important, but not as important as the real thing. This is a down payment on the future of mankind. It's as simple as that."

"Well," said Vonnegut, overlooking Clarke's last point, "I've been interested in this spin-off for a long time. I've been led to believe that the ball of my ballpoint pen and Teflon were spin-offs. And now I find out that Teflon was a spin-off from World War II. So that only leaves the point on my ballpoint pen."

The ballpoint pen, Clarke replied, existed before the space program, at least its terrestrial version. He was right; it was patented in 1938 by Lazio Biro, a Hungarian.

"But the real spin-offs are going to be largely in the next

decade or so," Clarke emphasized. "Many of them haven't really come into use. But the spin-off is going to be more knowledge rather than hardware. The ability to do new things which we weren't able to do before. Because the space program uses such an enormous technology, it's going to really revolutionize life and make it much easier all over the world."

The same evening, Neil Armstrong and Buzz Aldrin landed on the ancient moon dust after a dramatic descent. A television camera broadcast live from the moon's surface and captured the bouncing moon walks and the deployment of experiments. Tens of millions of people from all over the planet were enthralled. Arthur C. Clarke was one of them. He had dreamed of this moment for most of his life.

"When the *Eagle* landed, I was sitting beside Walter and Wally in the New York CBS studio," he recalls. "I wasn't on camera at that moment. For me it was as if time had stopped."

Recalls Cronkite, "I'd had as long as NASA had had to prepare for the landing. And at the moment it happened I found myself speechless. It was just so overwhelming that all I could say was 'Oh boy' I believe. It was just the exaltation of the event coming through in our voices and our appearances more than any descriptive material we had."

Hours later, during the moon walk, Clarke noticed one of the studio technicians sitting in front of a TV monitor. The words "Live from the Moon" ran across the bottom of the TV screen as the two ghostly figures, Armstrong and Aldrin, went about their lunar explorations. What astonished Clarke was that the technician was ignoring the historic events taking place on the monitor before him. "He was reading the racing reports in the newspaper"—Clarke chuckles—"during this live coverage from the moon. I still have the photograph."

Later, the mind-boggling moon walk over, Cronkite discussed the future of space with Clarke and fellow writer Robert Heinlein.

When asked, Heinlein wouldn't predict any specifics of future space exploration, but he was convinced that it was going to be done in a big way, going out to all the planets and eventually to the stars.

"We're going out indefinitely," said Heinlein. "There's just one equation that everybody knows: $E = MC^2$. It proves the potentiality whereby man can live anywhere where there is mass. He doesn't have to have any other requirement but mass, with the technology that we now have. And this human race will do so."

Clarke agreed. He then went on to express once again his vision of global unity, his United Nations of the World, which he had been espousing and hoping for since the 1940s. "And when they do go out, just as when they came to this country, they'll forget their original nationalities. We're going to see them going out into space as nations which will develop new ideas. And I do hope that this great lifting of the spirit which we've all experienced today will make a change in morale and help this country get away from the defeatism of the past."

It wasn't until 3:15 the following morning that Clarke left the CBS studios and returned to his hotel room. Sleeping quarters for Cronkite had been arranged in one of the dressing rooms off the studio, so he remained close at hand as David Schoumacher took over the anchor for the remaining early morning hours. HAL's film bank gave some wonderful programming to the minority of Americans who were not asleep. At 8:00 A.M. the international reaction was covered, including that of U.S. troops overseas. Correspondent Don Webster interviewed the GIs in Vietnam.

As the world continued to celebrate, the *Eagle* lifted off from Tranquillity Base in the early afternoon of July 21. While the long rendezvous process took place between the *Eagle* and *Columbia*, the CBS television audience was treated to a special film narrated by Orson Welles. Titled a "History of Space Journeys," it included clips from a variety of films, such as a 1902 French movie version of *A Trip to the Moon* by Jules Verne, some footage from Fritz Lang's German film *Woman on the Moon*, clips from Buck Rogers and Flash Gordon films, and scenes from George Pal's *Destination Moon* and Kubrick's and Clarke's *2001: A Space Odyssey*.

The great and authoritative voice of Orson Welles concluded his narration. "Now the moon has yielded, not merely to man's imagination, but to his actual presence. But for the science fiction writers and filmmakers, there remain other challenges to pose to man."

Walter Cronkite and Arthur C. Clarke, at the anchor desk, spoke about the short film they had just seen.

"It really is remarkable how close all of this came to reality," said Cronkite. "The only thing they didn't seem to contemplate was that the United Nations was going to be in the act, and we would have a space treaty. We wouldn't be claiming the moon. But in a sense we did, in claiming it for all mankind, as opposed to claiming it for the United States itself."

"I wrote about that trend twenty years ago," Clarke said, "in my first lunar landing novel [*Prelude to Space*]. I coined the phrase 'We shall take no frontiers into space.' And I think that's the way it will be."

Cronkite then asked Clarke what was next for science fiction writers. Would they still write space stories, or would they write about earthbound concerns—for example, biological problems?

"You know," said Clarke, "it's a fallacy to imagine, as some stupid people do, that because we've been to the moon, that's the end of science fiction. The more we discover about space, the more possibilities there are for really long-range and yet soundly based science fiction. . . . I'm looking forward to the next few years, when I absorb all this, to do my best science fiction."

Clarke had a chance to absorb *Apollo 11* while back on the U.S. lecture circuit during the fall of 1969, before returning to New York City in mid-November. There he again served as Walter Cronkite's copilot, this time for the CBS News coverage of *Apollo 12*, the second manned mission to the moon in 1969—and in all of history. The *Intrepid* separated from *Yankee Clipper* and landed on the moon's Ocean of Storms on November 19. Charles "Pete" Conrad and Al Bean worked on the moon, while Dick Gordon watched over the mother ship in moon orbit. A few months later they would be on a world tour together, and when they reached Ceylon and its beautiful tropical shores they would be hosted regally by Arthur C. Clarke.

A unique gathering took place at CBS during the *Apollo 12* coverage. Dick Hoagland remembers Walter Cronkite, Arthur C. Clarke, Wally Schirra, a scientist by the name of Paul Gast, and himself together in the green room of Studio 41.

"Paul Gast was like an Arthur Clarke of the hard science world," says Hoagland. "He had little vials of real lunar material with him, and I remember we all stood in a circle, like a druid circle—Walter, Arthur, Wally, Gast, and I—and we held these vials with ancient moon soil in our palms, soil that was 3.8 billion years old and had been brought back from the moon just a few months before on *Apollo 11*. We didn't need to say anything."

"What the railroads and the telegraph did here a century ago, the jets and the communications satellites are doing now to all the world."

State Department Speech, August 1971

"In the long run, the Comsat will be mightier than the ICBM."

The Promise of Space (1968)

21
JETTING FOR THE FUTURE

The grueling schedule Arthur C. Clarke had kept during the last months of 1969 had worn him down, and he was ready to settle in at home for a few months to await the new decade. After giving a speech called "Beyond Babel" at the UNESCO Space Communications Conference in Paris in December, he was happy to be leaving the winter chill for the tropical warmth of his adopted island, Ceylon. The address had focused on the future of telecommunications and was a positive vision of the future, ending with Clarke's frequently expressed hope of unifying the peoples of planet Earth through advanced communications systems. It was the right message for the UNESCO conference and for the holiday season.

Despite leaving Europe on that positive note, Clarke was exhausted, and he became ill upon his return to Ceylon.

"I had to check in to the nursing home for several days," he wrote to Tom Craven in mid-January, "but there was nothing wrong with me except the flu, and though I am still rather shaky I am slowly recovering."

Shaky or not, he began writing one of his favorite stories, "Transit of Earth." Perhaps stimulated by the astounding advances made by the space program just months before, the story was based on astronomical fact. It was hard science fiction, the type of story Clarke liked and for which he is so well known.

In theory a person on Mars could actually observe the black disk of planet Earth moving across the face of the sun at certain future times. Clarke admitted that, even in his college days of applied mathematics, predicting such an astronomical event was beyond his powers of computation. He gave credit to Jean Meeus, a Belgian astronomer, who computed and predicted such a transit in a scientific paper published in 1962. The story's basis in fact was reinforced when, a few years later, the Salt Lake City Planetarium presented a successful dramatization of it.

A couple of months later Walter Cronkite's two-time "copilot" was delighted to hear from the American Embassy in Ceylon that the three *Apollo 12* astronauts were planning to extend their stay because of Clarke. The fact that he and Hector Ekanayake were planning to take them skin diving in the beautiful coastal waters of northeast Ceylon no doubt influenced their decision.

As they were preparing to go down and explore an old wreck in Trincomalee Harbor, Clarke handed astronaut Alan Bean one of the underwater cameras.

"I begged him: 'Alan—*please* don't point it at the sun.'" Clarke was referring to the time on the moon's surface when Bean had accidentally pointed the TV camera at the sun, destroying it and making it unusable for the entire mission.

The jest didn't fly. "He did not seem much amused," says Clarke.

Nonetheless, they had a wonderful time on the diving expedition. "They liked it so much," wrote Clarke, "it was a job to get them back on the plane."

Speaking engagements kept Clarke from participating in coverage of the next Apollo mission. Clarke wrote that he was "sick to have missed covering *Apollo 13* with CBS TV, but enormously relieved that they got back even without my help."

During the same month that *Apollo 13* took place, the official book on the historic *Apollo 11* moon mission, *First on the Moon*, was published. Clarke had been chosen to write the epilogue, "Beyond Apollo," which he'd done during the summer of 1969. It closes with one of his most famous quotes, which is often repeated with slight variations:

"For it may be that the old astrologers had the truth exactly reversed, when they believed that the stars controlled the destinies of men.

"The time may come when men control the destinies of stars."

Following the *Apollo 13* mission, NASA administrator Thomas O. Paine organized a meeting that included Arthur C. Clarke.

"President Nixon asked NASA to give some thought to where we would go after Apollo," says Paine, "and so I authorized a retreat at NASA's launch center out on Wallops Island. We got together about two or three dozen people who were carefully selected to be long-range, imaginative, creative thinkers.

"Arthur was invited because he had shown a remarkable ability over the years to identify what was going to be terribly important in the future.

"I have a nice picture of Arthur standing there with von Braun, George Mueller, Neil Armstrong, and all the bright lights from NASA."

Clarke remembers meeting Neil Armstrong for the first time.

"It was on the way to this NASA affair. I was boarding a private bus in Washington, and when I stepped into the bus I saw him. He was sitting quietly in the bus next to the NASA public relations man, on one of the aisle seats just ahead of me. I'm afraid I gaped like a schoolgirl seeing her favorite film star or rock idol. . . . A slow, embarrassed smile spread across his face; and the senior NASA official sitting next to him, whom I'd completely ignored, said rather testily: 'Hello, Arthur—I'm here as well!'"

Later during the conference Clarke asked Armstrong about the controversial missing *a* so many people had failed to hear in his historic words upon stepping on the moon: "That's one small step for *a* man, one giant leap for mankind." Even Mission Control's audio recording had failed to pick up the article *a*.

Armstrong's somewhat exasperated reply was "That's what I *intended* to say, and that's what I *thought* I said."

Clarke next flew halfway around the planet to Japan. The 1970 International Science Fiction Symposium, held in Tokyo, was his destination. It was a less formal occasion for Clarke—especially at the beginning. Writer Frederik Pohl recalls who was there.

"I represented the U.S.," says Pohl, "Judy Merril Canada, Brian Aldiss England, and Arthur the world in general. There were also four Soviet writers—Yuli Kagarlitski, Eremy Parnov, Vasili Zaharchenko, and I don't remember the other one's name—and of course several dozen Japanese ones, and we lectured in Tokyo, Osaka, and various other points along the way. The World's Fair was on at that time, and we also toured the fair.

"The Japanese arranged an evening event after we arrived," recalls Pohl, "where all of us were expected to either give a little talk or perform in some way. We were invited to make fools of ourselves. It was an icebreaker and worked very well. I remember that Arthur did a sort of Polynesian dance for them."

"They did put us up on the stage," says Clarke, "and I was real embarrassed. I have no talent in the performing arts."

One of the Japanese present, a professor of physics and engineering, had designed a rocket train.

"We saw a film of this rocket train," Clarke recalls, "a very small-scale model of it, and the thing took off the track and went flying in all directions. Brian Aldiss or I (I can't remember which) christened it the 'Kamikaze Express.' The inventor was a distinguished Japanese aeronautical engineer. I think he was the guy who designed the Zero—one of the famous wartime fighters.

"Anyway, I went around telling everybody this was the Kamikaze Express. To my great embarrassment, the next day this guy came up to me, pointed to me, and said, 'Ha-ha, Kamikaze Express! Ha-ha, Kamikaze Express!' This was the inventor himself who had heard the name. He seemed quite amused, but I was embarrassed."

"We were looked after by Japanese writers and translators," says Brian Aldiss. "Our chairman was an illustrious man by the name of Sakyo Komatsu. He's a very powerful man, indeed, in the circles in which he moves.

"On one occasion, we were taken to stay for the night at a hotel on Lake Biwako. Very, very pleasant. And everyone was relaxing after a rather hard day, and we persuaded Arthur to have a little dry sherry. And he seemed to be enjoying himself. But finally he looked at his watch, and he said, 'Well, it's ten o'clock, and I have a golden rule that at ten o'clock, no matter how good the company, I go to bed.' And with that, he got up, said his good night, and went up to bed. And I couldn't help noticing that he had only half-finished his little dry sherry. I was interested to see that he only wanted a sip or two, of society as it were."

In a December 1970 letter to Sam Youd, Clarke examined what he did want from life. He told his friend how difficult it was becoming to leave his adopted homeland despite the political and economic problems in Ceylon. "Besides this house (where I have a library—all my books, at last—cameras, telescope, computer)," he noted, "I have a very nice brand new place on an unbelievably beautiful bay 70 miles S with a coral reef outside the front door. . . .

"I guess I am lucky—everything of mine is in print, except the very early non-fiction space books, which have been absorbed by later editions. The fiction goes on for ever. Even my 1947 *Prelude to Space* has just come out with a post-Apollo preface, encapsulating it like Jules Verne. This is one of the reasons I'm writing no more non-fiction . . . at least for a few years.

"I could have retired years ago if I was content to live reasonably and not commute round the world twice a year. I have to get out of Ceylon 6 months in the year as the tax situation is impossible—there's no treaty with the US or UK. I can't pay tax in *three* countries . . . hence my mobility. Anyway, I like lecturing, and since *2001* I've become a minor cult hero on campus."

Earlier in the year, in "a dialogue on man and his world" with philosopher and theologian Alan Watts, commissioned by *Playboy*, Clarke delved more deeply into his outlook on the cosmos.

"I have a long-standing bias against religion that may be reflected in my comments," Clarke told Watts near the beginning of their three-day conversation. He could not forgive religions for the atrocities and wars over time, he said, focusing more on this subject than in other interviews.

Many people "confuse religion with a belief in God," he went on. "Buddhists don't necessarily believe in a god or a supreme being at all, whereas one could easily believe in a supreme being and not have any religion." Elsewhere Clarke has said that any valid theology must await our contact with extraterrestrial intelligences.

"Fundamentally, I'm an optimist, and I believe that the future is not predetermined, that to some extent we can determine our own destiny. By thinking about the future and its possibilities, we do have a chance of averting the more disastrous one. This is why I believe that the interest in the future that is so common now is a good thing. There are suspect ways of looking at the future of course—astrology, divination, that sort of thing."

Arthur C. Clarke's concluding words were: "The purpose of

the universe, Alan, is the perpetual astonishment of mankind." To which Alan Watts responded, "That's as likely as any other purpose I've ever heard about. . . ."

Ever looking forward, Clarke spent the beginning of the new year writing his rather long short story "A Meeting with Medusa" for one reason: "Over the previous decade I had accumulated some fifty thousand words of short stories and needed another fifteen thousand to make up a complete volume."

The Wind from the Sun, published in 1972, became that volume, and "A Meeting with Medusa," which won a *Playboy* editorial award as well as the Nebula Award from the Science Fiction Writers of America, was the final story.

" 'Medusa' was," says Clarke, "the last story I ever wrote before concentrating entirely on novels."

Much of the rest of 1971 was spent on compelling space matters, but trouble was brewing at home. Clarke's beloved tropical island, still officially known as Ceylon in 1971, underwent a political crisis while he was on a spring lecture tour in the United States. On April 4, 1971, several thousand insurgents (members of the People's Liberation Front) attempted to take over the country. This was at a time when the "island of 13 million people appeared reasonably contented under a government which had been elected by a large majority," Clarke wrote later. The well-trained insurgent force attacked many of the provincial police stations and easily overwhelmed them. Arms and ammunition were stolen, and the rebels continued their fight and were able to control some rural areas for short periods. Many people were killed.

There had been some signs of unrest, but the government was caught off guard by this violent revolution. "It appealed for help— which promptly started to arrive from a remarkable variety of sources," wrote Clarke. "The countries which rushed to the aid of Ceylon included the United Kingdom, the United States, India *and* Pakistan, the United Arab Republic, Yugoslavia—and China. Ceylon is a land without enemies; however, she frequently exasperates her friends."

Within a few weeks the bitter fighting ended. Fifteen thousand rebels and suspects were rounded up and put in prison camps, eventually to be released. Those identified as PLF leaders, however, were brought to trial. There were many executions.

"Most of them appear to have been young idealists and left-wing extremists, dissatisfied with the progress that the government they had helped to elect had made towards solving its social problems," he wrote later. The country had more or less returned to normal by the end of 1971, but periodic problems and bloodshed have continued right into the 1990s.

The causes of the turmoil are complex and arise from deep religious, racial, and socioeconomic divisions. Even the official language of Sinhala, spoken by the Sinhalese majority, has caused vehement protest and violence by the minority Tamils. Hatred and distrust have dominated for far too long, and many observers are pessimistic that the cycle of violence will stop anytime soon. In some respects the strife can be compared to the ongoing violence in Ireland.

While Clarke was in California on the western leg of his lecture tour, he visited his old friends Robert and Ginny Heinlein. He also stopped at the North American Rockwell plant and saw the mock-ups of the space shuttle and an early design version of a space station.

Shortly thereafter, Clarke wrote a letter to the editor of the *New York Times*, and it was printed under the heading "Space Shuttle: Key to Future," on May 22, 1971. After stating that "many of the solutions of our present social and environmental problems lie partly in space" and citing the tremendous benefits of an educational satellite project in India, Clarke brought forth the example of the fifty-million-dollar Orbiting Astronomical Observatory, which failed soon after it reached orbit because of a minor circuit defect.

"A man with a screwdriver might have been able to fix it," Clarke wrote to the editor, anticipating the first satellite repair in orbit by more than twelve years. "As our application satellites become larger and more complex, space shuttles will be essential not only to orbit them, but to carry the technicians who must check, service, and repair them." Arthur C. Clarke went on record and cast his vote for the space shuttle about half a year before President Nixon announced that the nation and NASA would proceed with the shuttle program.

Two months later it was on to New York to cover the *Apollo 15* mission with Walter Cronkite on July 30 and 31—the two days during which astronauts Dave Scott and Jim Irwin landed the lunar module *Falcon* on the moon and explored seventeen miles of its surface, thanks to a lunar roving vehicle, never used before. One of the craters they drove past they named Earthlight after Clarke's 1955 novel.

This was the longest Apollo mission to date, more than twelve days, and Clarke flew to Houston and the Johnson Space Center for the splashdown coverage. He got the complete VIP tour of the facilities, including Mission Control and various training facilities, and had dinner with astronauts Joe Allen and Phil Chapman.

Allen was a longtime fan of Clarke's and had read several of his books as a youth. More than once he acknowledged that Clarke had had a major influence on his decision to become an astronaut. "When I was a boy," Allen wrote to Clarke, "you infected me with both the writing bug *and* the space bug but neglected to tell me how difficult either undertaking can be."

Next month, at the U.S. Department of State, Clarke's influence, this time on worldwide communications, was celebrated again. The affair was hosted by Secretary of State William Rogers, and another prominent guest was Mamie Eisenhower. The first voice ever beamed to Earth from a communications satellite had been that of her husband, President Dwight Eisenhower, in December 1958.

"We are here," said Rogers, "to sign a constitutional instrument, a permanent charter, for man's first international cooperative effort in space. I doubt that even the most optimistic of prophets, even Arthur C. Clarke, would have predicted in August 1964 that on this seventh anniversary of the establishment of the international arrangements for Intelsat, we would be gathered here to sign the definitive arrangements for an organization of eighty nations, an organization which already has in being global satellite systems interconnecting people on six continents."

This agreement created an international partnership in telecommunications and brought Clarke's dream of a united family of man one step closer to reality.

"Do we have the imagination and the statesmanship to use

this new tool for the benefit of all mankind?" Clarke asked the audience. "Or will it be used merely to peddle detergents and propaganda?

"I am an optimist; anyone interested in the future has to be. I believe that communications satellites can unite mankind. Let me remind you that, whatever the history books say, this great country was created a little more than a hundred years ago by two inventions. Without them, the United States was impossible; with them, it was inevitable. Those inventions, of course, were the railroad and the electric telegraph.

"Today, we are seeing, on a global scale, an almost exact parallel to that situation. What the railroads and the telegraph did here a century ago, the jets and the communications satellites are doing now to all the world.

"I hope you will remember this analogy in the years ahead. For today, whether you intend it or not, whether you wish it or not—you have signed far more than just another intergovernmental agreement.

"You have just signed a first draft of the Articles of Federation of the United States of Earth."

Thanks to such advances in communications, the world was indeed shrinking. And so was the solar system.

The *Mariner 9* spacecraft was nearing its November 1971 encounter with Mars; it would be the first to orbit the red planet and would send back thousands of photos. Fittingly, Arthur C. Clarke was en route to the Jet Propulsion Laboratory in Pasadena, California, where he would join his old friends Ray Bradbury; Carl Sagan; Bruce Murray, then head of the lab; and Walter Sullivan, of the *New York Times*, to discuss Mars. The fact that a planetwide dust storm obscured the planet's surface as the robot spacecraft approached left plenty of room for the imagination in the JPL discussions.

Walter Sullivan was moderator for the conference, and he introduced everyone, including Clarke, who began by paying tribute to early science fiction writers like Edgar Rice Burroughs, Stanley G. Weinbaum, Percival Lowell, and H. G. Wells, all of whom contributed to the myth of Mars.

"It was Edgar Rice Burroughs who turned me on," wrote Clarke, "and I think he is a much *underrated* writer." He went on to make some comments about Lowell, the man who believed that

Mars had a sophisticated network of canals and got a lot of other people to believe it too. Arthur referred to Lowell as "our Boston brahmin."

"Whatever we can say about Lowell's observational abilities, we can't deny his propagandistic power, and I think he deserves credit at least for keeping the idea of planetary astronomy alive and active during a period when perhaps it might have been neglected."

Clarke then told the audience about his recent visit to Lowell Observatory and how he'd actually looked through Lowell's twenty-six-inch telescope. "He's buried right beside it; his tomb is in the shape of the observatory," he said. "Whatever nonsense he wrote, I hope that one day we will name something on Mars after him."

Clarke would make no predictions about the real Mars that *Mariner 9* would reveal once the vast dust storm abated. What was important to remember, he said, was that "the frontier of our knowledge is moving inevitably outwards.

"We're discovering, and this is a big surprise, that the moon, and I believe Mars, and parts of Mercury, and especially space itself, are essentially benign environments—to our technology, not necessarily to organic life. Certainly benign as compared with the Antarctic or the oceanic abyss, where we have already been. This is an idea which the public still hasn't got yet, but it's a fact.

"I think the biological frontier may very well move past Mars out to Jupiter, which I think is where the action is. Carl [Sagan], you've gone on record as saying that Jupiter may be a more hospitable home for life than any other place, *including* Earth itself. It would be very exciting if this turns out to be true.

"I will end by making one prediction. Whether or not there is life on Mars now, there will be by the end of this century."

Clarke admits to being somewhat embarrassed by this prediction, which was made when the United States was flying Apollo missions to the moon and the vice president of the United States was suggesting a Mars mission as the next step in space exploration. "I hope we get to Mars by 2020," Clarke now says. "This is not a technological question; it's entirely a political one." In March of 1992 he wrote, "Mars is the next frontier, what the Old West was, what America was 500 years ago. . . . Everything you need is on Mars."

Ray Bradbury remembers the JPL conference. "Every single person there had had his life changed by Burroughs," says Bradbury. "We all discovered that we had grown up on Edgar Rice Burroughs. The chemistry between Walter Sullivan and Arthur and Carl Sagan and myself and Bruce Murray was so wonderful that at the end of a day of talks and lectures and what-have-you, it all fell together. Somebody said, 'By God, we've got a book here.' It was so fabulous that it turned into a book."

Besides the transcript of the discussion, the participants added their more considered thoughts a year later, after the dust storm had subsided and the cameras of *Mariner 9* sent back images of the real Mars with all its wonders. The book, *Mars and the Mind of Man*, was published two years later, in the summer of 1973.

The dreams of childhood had been far surpassed by the reality of adult life.

The Fountains of Paradise *(1979)*

22
SET OF THE SAILS

On December 19, 1972, the last men to visit the moon in the twentieth century returned home to planet Earth. As the *Apollo 17* astronauts Eugene Cernan, Ronald Evans, and Harrison Schmitt splashed down in the Pacific, one of humanity's most daring adventures was coming to an end. The great Apollo voyages to the moon were over.

Post-Apollo apathy reigned supreme, signaling the abrupt U.S. retreat from the moon. For most people the thrill and drama of *Apollo 11* could never be repeated, and most space missions, manned and unmanned, were treated with a ho-hum attitude. Few people recognized that a vigorous space program was a powerful and important driver of cutting-edge technology that would benefit all sectors of the economy—a point that Arthur C. Clarke continued to make on the lecture circuit.

In the early 1970s Americans were preoccupied by domestic and international issues, and championing the cause of space exploration was an increasing challenge. Clarke readily took up the gauntlet. He had never been intimidated by controversy, and he found his speaking engagements gave him an outlet to expound on his nonfiction interests.

In March 1973 Clarke found himself, to his surprise, oppos-
ing Saul Bellow on the issue of art versus science. Clarke was at
the Smithsonian Institution's National Museum of History and
Technology to deliver a lecture, "Technology and the Limits of
Knowledge," in a series entitled "Technology and the Frontiers of
Knowledge." Because the lectures were spread out over a year, the
five lecturers—Daniel Bell, Edmundo O'Gorman, and Sir Peter
Medawar in addition to Bellow and Clarke—were not together to
exchange views. And it was only later, when Clarke read the
others' speeches, that he learned that Saul Bellow had publicly
taken a poke at him.

Bellow, in his lecture "Literature in the Age of Technology,"
took exception to a passage in one of Clarke's essays, "The Mind of
the Machine," which appeared in *Report on Planet Three and
Other Speculations*. He quotes Clarke, out of context, from an
admittedly speculative essay, a portion of which concerns itself
with the possibility of intelligent machines creating art.

"It has often been suggested that art is a compensation for the
deficiencies of the real world; as our knowledge, our power and
above all our maturity increase, we will have less and less need for
it. If this is true, the ultra-intelligent machine would have no use
for it at all.

"Even if art turns out to be a dead end, there still remains
science. . . ."

Bellow should have quoted the rest of the sentence: ". . . there
still remains science—the eternal quest for knowledge, which has
brought man to the point where he has created his own successor."

Said Bellow, "This statement by a spokesman of the 'victorious'
party is for several reasons extraordinarily silly. First it assumes
that art belongs to the childhood of mankind, and that science is
identical with maturity. Second, it thinks art is born in weakness
and fear. Third, in its happy worship of 'ultra-intelligent' machines, it expresses a marvelous confidence in the ability of such
machines to overcome all the deficiencies of the real world. Such
optimistic rationalism is charming, in a way. . . ."

Bellow associated Clarke with a group of "power-minded
theoreticians" and ascribed to him "the confidence of the great
simplifier." The novelist then went on to put hypothetical words in
Clarke's mouth.

"Mr. Clarke says in effect, 'Don't worry, dear Pals, if art is a dead end, we still have science. . . . Thinking machines will give us all the wisdom and joy we want, in our maturity.'"

But of course Clarke didn't say that at all. His essay was designed to get readers thinking. It was qualified by *if*s and "[i]t has often been suggested. . . ." For whatever reason (perhaps for purposes of debate), Bellow was overreacting, and Clarke did not bother to make a move in his own defense. Of course he couldn't have done so; neither was there when the other presented his lecture. When Clarke's essay was reprinted in *The View from Serendip* in 1978, however, he at least referred to Bellow's criticism:

"I count it as a noble (and possibly unique) example of my self-restraint that, though I had the last word [his lecture came after Bellow's], I refrained from comment.

"And still do."

There were many, of course, who agreed with Clarke's views. One longtime admirer was astronaut Joseph P. Allen, who would later fly as a mission specialist on the first operational flight of the space shuttle in November 1982. In a letter Allen told Clarke that of all the lectures he had heard, he had "enjoyed none more than the one which you delivered for the Smithsonian Institute in March.

"You put into words the thoughts and ideas which I flirt with on occasion, but am never quite able to pin down in such an efficient and straightforward way. Thank goodness you devote some of your energies to helping the scientists and technologists themselves, not to mention everyone else, understand better what they are about."

Another example of helping people understand was the April 1973 publication of *Beyond Jupiter: The Worlds of Tomorrow*. This beautifully illustrated book was in the tradition of the classic *Conquest of Space*, published in 1949, which presented the unique space art of Chesley Bonestell and the text of rocket expert and science writer Willy Ley, Clarke's old friend, who had supplied him with science fiction magazines during World War II. In *Beyond Jupiter*, Clarke and Bonestell combined their words and artwork to describe the historic voyages of *Pioneers 10* and *11* to the outer planets *before* the spacecraft made their planetary encounters. In the book's concluding paragraphs, Clarke wrote about these first interstellar robots, saying, "We should build them well, for one day they may be the only evidence that the human race ever existed."

Ironically, Kurt Vonnegut had paid dubious tribute to Clarke and his interest in the destiny of *Homo sapiens* in his short story "The Big Space Fuck," published in 1972 in *Again, Dangerous Visions*. Wrote Vonnegut, "The ship was named the *Arthur C. Clarke*, in honor of a famous space pioneer." The spaceship's mission was to impregnate the universe by carrying eight hundred pounds of freeze-dried jizzum to the Andromeda galaxy. The mission was "to make sure that human life would continue to exist somewhere in the universe."

Clarke's advocacy of worldwide communications, in contrast, engendered little controversy. In an address called "The Last Revolution," given in Washington, D.C., in March 1972, Clarke explained how satellite communications were rapidly changing the world: "The TV coverage of President Nixon's China trip was in some ways as significant as the visit itself. It marked the crumbling of the last communications barrier on this Earth. *The wiring of the global electronic village is now complete.* [Italics added.]

"But not all the fittings are yet installed," he went on. "When they are, the world will be changed beyond recognition. How many of us can remember the age before the coming of radio? Already, it is hard to recall life without television. Yet the changes wrought by radio and TV are trivial compared to those that are coming. This fact is so overwhelmingly obvious that it is almost impossible to grasp it."

Referring to a recent trip to India, Clarke told his audience, "I was standing on a lonely hilltop in Ahmadabad, beneath the sixty-foot dish of the Experimental Satellite Ground Station—one quarter second, via synchronous orbit, from Calcutta and all other cities of India. As I am sure you know, in 1974 the satellite ATS-F will be parked over the subcontinent for one year, and for the first time it will be possible to televise information on health, improved agriculture, family planning, into the remotest villages, to millions who can neither read nor write."

Arthur C. Clarke, born to a post office family, was the messenger for the future.

As much as he enjoyed the immediacy of speaking to an audience, Clarke never strayed far from the print media. Keeping the vow he had made in late 1970, he limited his writing mostly to fiction.

The exception was *Report on Planet Three and Other Speculations*, but even that, including work mostly from the 1950s and 1960s as well as some reprinted speeches, required little new nonfiction writing.

Three other collections of Clarke's works—all of them fiction—were published in 1972, and these too consisted mainly of work done in the preceding decades. There was *The Lost Worlds of 2001*, which brought together all the chapters or segments that had been cut from the novel *2001*. Victor Gollancz, Clarke's British publisher, issued *Of Time and Stars: The Worlds of Arthur C. Clarke*, a collection of short stories that included several early classics and was distinguished by a J. B. Priestley introduction:

"From the first he seems to have fallen in love with space, and as soon as I met him I was aware of his genuine tremendous enthusiasm. (He is also a great gadget man, and if a robot had served lunch I would hardly have been surprised.) It must be this enthusiasm that gives him such an astonishing air of youth, suggesting a man in his thirties and not already in his middle fifties."

Priestley dropped the age down even more when he wrote about his visit to Ceylon and described Clarke as a man with the "heart and mind of a boy of sixteen." When Sam Youd quoted this, Clarke quipped, "Actually, nineteen is nearer my mark."

Perhaps that trait and a statement Clarke made in the preface of the third collection of short stories published in 1972, *The Wind from the Sun*, explain how Clarke spent much of his time during this period: "I was tempted to give it the subtitle 'The Last of Clarke'—not through any intimations of mortality (I have every intention of seeing what *really* happens in the year 2001), but because I seem to be doing less and less writing, and more and more talking, traveling, filming, and skin-diving."

In April 1973 Clarke flew to St. Thomas, U.S. Virgin Islands, to participate in a conference of the Sea-Space Society—the two major interests in his life.

George Mueller, then NASA's administrator for manned spaceflight, describes what happened while he, Clarke, and about fifteen others were snorkeling off the island:

"I was down around ninety feet. And Arthur came swimming down, free-diving, waved to me, and then leisurely swam up to the surface. It was about that time that one of my buddies saw that he was in trouble and went over to help him."

Clarke had been diving all morning, going down, joining the other divers, and then going up again to get a breath of air. Clarke remembers, during one dive in the afternoon, taking a photo with his underwater camera of several divers swimming over a wreck below him.

"That was very nearly the last photo I ever took," he says. "And I remember saying, 'That's enough for today; this will be my last dive.' Which it almost was.

"It was a beautiful calm day, lovely day, clear water. I went down. Then on the way up, within ten feet of the surface, I suddenly got vertigo, spinning around in the water, absolutely helpless. My inner ear had gone.

"I had a life jacket, but I couldn't find the rip cord. And then I thought I should try to inflate it, but of course that was ridiculous because I was out of breath. And then I could just feel the beginning of panic; luckily I didn't get there. I hit the quick-release button on the weighted belt, which fell off, and then I popped up instantly to the surface. There were a couple of guys on a life raft only a few yards away. They got me onto the raft, then back to land, and they rushed me to the hospital. It was the narrowest escape I ever had."

George Mueller swam over to help the two already helping Clarke. "We finally got him back on board, but he was unable to move. He had to be carried because the vertigo was so bad. We took him into the local hospital, and he stayed there overnight. The next morning there wasn't any apparent problem, and so we got him on an airplane and sent him off to New York City."

The experience apparently didn't dampen Clarke's spirit of adventure. In June, at an IBM convention in Acapulco, Clarke tried some paragliding over the Pacific: "I went up a hundred meters or so, towed not by a boat but by a jeep on the sand! My most vivid recollection was the discomfort when I hit the ground again—the sand was red-hot. But it was great fun, and I'd like to do it again."

"It was exhilarating," says Walter Cronkite, who attended the convention and who also took to the air. "But more of an amusement park experience than anything very extraordinary. It didn't require any great athletic skill or anything of the kind. It was a fun ride."

A few weeks later Clarke told one interviewer how much he loved the experience. "'I'm arranging to have all the parachute equipment sent to Ceylon. People there will be simply amazed!'"

Clarke's next destination was the Caribbean to see the total eclipse of the sun. On June 23 he boarded the *Cunard Adventurer* for a special cruise, with a full educational program and various scientific activities planned for two weeks. There were 550 passengers on board to learn and to see the eclipse in the open Atlantic on June 30. Wally Schirra and Rusty Schweickart were the two astronauts on board, and another dozen experts in the various sciences were on hand to give lectures. Clarke gave two lectures, each of which had two parts: "Life in the Year 2001" and "The Promise of Space."

Kerry O'Quinn, program director for the cruise, later to become publisher of *Starlog* magazine, remembered hearing the first lecture.

"I stood in the back of the large cabaret theater (converted into a lecture hall)," said O'Quinn, "and listened as he told an entranced audience his predictions—how communications satellites would bring wonders to the underdeveloped peoples of our planet. He spoke of children in remote parts of India and Africa seeing television for the first time and having their minds fired with curiosity and new possibilities. He spoke of electronic education putting an end to illiteracy, to hunger, and even to war. He spoke of hope for the future, through science and reason.

"As I stood there and listened, his words touched me profoundly. I heard the thinking of one of the great minds of our century, and I found myself infused with admiration and inspiration.

"I also found myself crying, it was such an emotional experience.

"Afterwards I went and had a little talk with him and told him that he had brought me to tears. From then on, instead of being Mr. Clarke, he was Arthur. From that moment on we became soul mates."

O'Quinn remembered one evening when astronaut Schirra and Clarke were sitting at the same table: "Unknown to us, the two of them were either the world's best or worst punsters. The entire dining room would hear either gales of laughter or loud groans periodically coming from that table. This was a personal contest between Arthur and Wally as to who could make the worst pun. They did it constantly, and everybody would groan with delight."

The *Adventurer* found clear weather in the Atlantic for the eclipse on June 30.

"It was a wonderful eclipse," said O'Quinn. "It was one of the longest ones possible on Earth—almost seven minutes long at its maximum off the coast of Africa. For the *Adventurer*'s location in the Caribbean, it was not at its maximum duration, but was more like five minutes long.

"Arthur and I watched it together from the bridge with the captain, who invited us up. The captain also tried to stabilize the ship against rocking. Tripods, cameras, and telescopes covered the decks of the ship. We arranged to pass out special glasses for people to view the eclipse. And Arthur had brought along some eye patches which we could put over one eye. He's always prepared. He had a pocketful of them and passed them out to those of us who were on the bridge. This way we could watch the partial phases, but the one eye with the patch would already be night-adjusted when totality begins, just after the bright flash of the diamond ring effect occurs and before the sun's corona suddenly appears and shines out in all directions around the black disk of the moon. Then, once totality begins, you would put the patch over the other eye and let it become night-adjusted.

"It's one of the most spectacular celestial events that the solar system offers," said O'Quinn. "And there was very much a feeling of love and companionship among all the people that were on board the ship. A kind of bonding takes place when you share a rare experience like this."

The *Adventurer* anchored in San Juan, Puerto Rico, on July 4. Before flying back to New York, Clarke visited the huge radio-radar telescope at Arecibo, whose great antenna dish has made so many important discoveries and has been used in the search for extraterrestrial life. After the telescope's great dish received a new surface a year later, in 1974, a powerful radio transmission was beamed toward one of the densely packed globular clusters in our galaxy, some twenty-five thousand light-years away. A reply may come in A.D. 51,974.

Back at the Chelsea Hotel, Clarke gave an interview to Alice

Turner, then at *Publishers Weekly* and later the editor at *Playboy* who bought some of his stories. The talk turned to *Rendezvous with Rama*, Clarke's first novel in ten years, which had recently been published and was receiving excellent reviews, and his love of science fiction.

"Science fiction is often called escapism—always in a negative sense," Clarke said. "Of course it's not true. Science fiction is virtually the only kind of writing that's dealing with the real problems and possibilities; it's a concerned fiction. It's the mainstream that escapes from these things into small anxieties—away from fact, away from things that threaten or enrich our lives.

"It's hard to define science fiction these days, especially since the mainstream seems to be moving in that direction. Traditionally, it's been a form that offered a good story, and I suppose you could call that escapism, in a positive sense. C. S. Lewis, who wrote it himself, said, 'The only people who think there's something wrong with escapism are jailers.'"

And what of the current state of science fiction? Turner asked.

"We know so much more now that we don't have to waste time on the petty things of the past. We can use the enormous technological advances in our work. Vision is wider now, and interest has never been deeper."

Rendezvous with Rama was an example of this wider vision. The book won several awards in 1973—the Hugo, Nebula, John W. Campbell, and Jupiter awards for best novel of the year.

There were accolades galore, including compliments from other big names in the field of science fiction. Isaac Asimov, Robert Heinlein, and Frank Herbert all had praise for the novel. And John Leonard of the *New York Times* judged *Rama* as "storytelling of the highest order" and praised its "sense of wonder and breathless suspense." Continued Leonard, "Mr. Clarke is splendid. As a superior intelligence spins a strange spider-culture out of its bowels, we experience that chilling touch of the alien, the not-quite-knowable, that distinguishes SF at its most technically imaginative."

Julian Muller, Clarke's editor at Harcourt Brace Jovanovich, says, "I had a spectacular time with *Rendezvous with Rama*. It was one of the most intriguing books I had ever dealt with. Arthur's invention in terms of plotting was so extraordinary. And there's almost an explosion of invention in *Rama*. Just the capacity to be able to create that world—it staggers me to think that anyone could. Arthur not only created that kind of image in his own mind, but he was able to articulate it brilliantly."

Muller recalls that the novel's last line caused a stir: "*The Ramans do everything in threes.*"

"It provoked an enormous amount of mail and much discussion around publishing circles because it obviously suggested a trilogy. And when I spoke to Arthur about it, Arthur said, 'No, it just seemed like a good way to end it. I had no intention of doing a trilogy.'"

When *Rama II* was published sixteen years later, there was good reason to believe that Clarke's intention had changed.

*I have always been more interested in the spectacular possi-
bilities of the distant future, and not the practical problems
of the day after tomorrow. . . . [I]f you take me seriously,
you'll go broke—but if you don't take me seriously enough,
your children will go broke.*
                    *Speech to U.S. Congress, Committee on Space
                    Science and Applications, July 1975*

23
FROM SRI LANKA TO TITAN

As Arthur C. Clarke approached the age of sixty, he began to truly
reap the rewards of his life's work. He was clearly established as an
authority on space exploration and the future of science and
technology, receiving invitations to conferences such as that held
in October 1974 by the Smithsonian and NASA at the Auchin-
closs summer house in Rhode Island to discuss the future of space
with the likes of Wernher von Braun, Margaret Mead, and Alistair
Cooke. His visions of the future, predicted in his younger years,
were rapidly becoming reality. Clarke's dream of a global village
seemed more plausible every year. And his prolific output of ideas,
expressed in fictional and nonfictional vehicles, had finally put
financial difficulties far behind him.

It could never be said that Clarke was one to rest on his
laurels. He has always seemed, in fact, to have a difficult time
resting at all—at least in any fashion recognizable by the rest of
the human race. Still, the culmination of much of his work over
the years did seem to allow him a less frenetic pace, one that saw
him focusing on home and family during the years 1973 to 1975.

One event that helped facilitate his slightly revised lifestyle was his finally becoming a permanent resident of Sri Lanka in June 1975. More than two decades had passed since he first set foot on his beautiful tropical island, and to avoid heavy taxation he had been forced to leave the country for half of each of those twenty years on lecture tours and other business.

But after the mid-1970s travel would become more of a choice and pleasure for Clarke thanks to the "Clarke Act," which went into effect in 1976 and allowed approved guests to live in Sri Lanka without paying local income tax. It also allowed them to bring in a car and a boat and household effects. In anticipation of the act, Clarke had begun to establish nonresidency in the United States and residency in Sri Lanka during 1974. The need to stay out of the United States for eighteen months to deestablish himself, in fact, had been his reason for declining the invitation to the Smithsonian/NASA conference.

"I could begin to enjoy a civilized and leisurely life, in the one place I really wanted to be," Clarke recalls. Unfortunately that hope was only partly fulfilled, what with the political unrest that continued to plague his chosen tropical island even after Ceylon became the Republic of Sri Lanka in 1972.

Two years before becoming a permanent resident, Clarke had bought a large new home on Barnes Place in Colombo from Lady de Soysa, the mother of the bishop of Colombo; it was, in fact, the Anglican bishop's residence. Tom Craven later described it as "neo-Somerset Maugham with great square rooms equipped with ceiling fans that stir the moist Colombo air." Quite a change from the much smaller home on Gregory's Road where Clarke had lived for about ten years and a big step toward making Sri Lanka his permanent home.

"It will be hell for a few weeks," Clarke wrote to Tom Craven on November 18, 1973. "Right in the midst of the moving to the new house now." A couple of weeks later, Clarke gave Craven an update.

"We have moved and have been cut off from the outside world for two weeks. The house is huge and we are still finding our way around, as well as unpacking 15 years junk. To complicate matters we had to fire a houseboy this morning (so we're struggling along on four—you'll weep for us) and we've just had a cable saying that Hector's German girlfriend's mother arrives from Munich in two hours, not tomorrow as expected. . . ."

Hector Ekanayake's youngest brother, Leslie, was a tremendous help in bringing order to chaos at Barnes Place, and he eventually went on to skillfully manage the large household—no small feat for a young man of twenty-six. Over time Clarke developed a fatherly affection for Leslie. Leslie personified "simple goodness" to Clarke.

A few days before Christmas all were still trying to bring order to their new home.

"Still fighting to get the mansion operational—there are about three sets of workmen here at any given time, but at least the elevator is working and water flows intermittently. We had our first dinner party here a couple of nights ago—my guests were Bill MacQuitty and his family."

Nine months later, with the new home settled, Clarke was host to Hugh Downs and his wife, Ruth, during their five-day visit to Sri Lanka. Downs, a pioneer broadcaster with fifty-plus years in the business, hosted NBC's "Today" show for ten years, from 1962 to 1972, and had Clarke as his guest several times during his tenure. Both Clarke and Downs have been actively involved in the National Space Institute (now the National Space Society) since it was formed in 1975, and Downs has been president of the organization since its early days. His memories of that 1974 trip give an interesting view of the land that Clarke had made his home.

"We went up to Sigiriya," Downs recalls, "and Arthur showed us something on one of the frescoes on the vertical rock walls, where they've got steel staircases going up the side. We saw this painting he spoke about, of a woman holding a box, with a kind of latticework (it looked like a grille), a round thing up to her ear. For all the world, it looked like a transistor radio, and Arthur pointed this out to us."

Clarke mentions this in the "Sources and Acknowledgments" section of his novel *The Fountains of Paradise*, which was published in 1979.

"The attendant is clearly *listening* to the mysterious hinged box she is holding in her right hand. It remains unidentified, the local archaeologists refusing to take seriously my suggestion that it is an early Sinhalese transistor radio."

Downs also remembers getting his picture taken while playing a double-reed instrument next to a basket that held a big cobra.

"I sat down cross-legged in front of this basket," he says, "and honked out a few notes on this guy's instrument. The cobra came up and weaved and everything. After I finished, I found out that this cobra hadn't been milked recently. (They usually milk the fangs to make sure there's not much venom.) If he hadn't liked what I was playing, I'd be dead now. Fortunately the snake didn't dislike my few notes."

On another jaunt Clarke and Ekanayake took the Downses east to Trincomalee and showed them the beautiful coast and their oceanfront diving operation, Underwater Safaris.

"Arthur was not diving because he had been ill and was recovering," says Downs. "He and my wife, Ruth, sat in the boat and had a long talk while Hector and I went diving. We went down quite a ways and saw some interesting ruins, some ancient columns from a temple that had fallen into the ocean. There wasn't much in the way of coral growth or anything, but it was a very interesting ocean.

"He also took Ruth and me on a river not far from his house where we saw the 'flying foxes,' a species of bat there. The damn things are the size of a dog—a small dog with wings. Arthur pointed them out to us. Bats of any size bother my wife a bit, and when we saw these monsters hanging on the trees like Dracula, she put a grip on my arm, and I thought her fingers were going to go through to the bone.

"I had never seen anything like them before, or since, in any other part of the world. They were like something out of *The Wizard of Oz*."

The large Barnes Place house also allowed extended visits by Clarke's family members. Now that he no longer *had* to leave Sri Lanka, there was no reason to limit family gatherings to England. Thus Clarke's eighty-two-year-old mother, Nora, had come to visit for the winter. Unfortunately, she broke her hip at the Polonuhra Resthouse while sightseeing 130 miles away from Colombo.

"The last 3 weeks have been dominated by her operation, convalescence etc.," Clarke wrote to Tom Craven on December 29. "However she came home today and is in good spirits, and with some difficulty I've managed to arrange full-time nursing."

Nora Clarke was on the mend as 1975 began, and the beginning of the year had no pressing deadlines for Clarke. He was thinking about visiting his peaceful retreat on the south coast when he heard some interesting news: his old diving partner, Mike Wilson, had left his wife, Liz, to become a monk [Siva Swami]. He had not seen either of them for two years.

The Wilsons had moved into their own home for more space when the children came along in the early 1960s. Later in that decade there had been a falling-out between Mike Wilson and Clarke. Wilson always depended on Clarke for the venture capital to fund his various projects, but he proved to be financially irresponsible, spending and wasting a lot of money. This had been going on for several years before there was a confrontation.

The blowup actually occurred between Hector Ekanayake (who had become protective, especially after Clarke's paralysis) and freewheeling Mike Wilson.

"I can remember the falling-out," says Clarke. "It was a trivial thing, really, but it was the last straw. Mike wanted to borrow an inflatable boat, but Hector wouldn't lend it to him because he believed that Mike wouldn't return it."

That day the line was drawn and the relationship changed irrevocably. What once was a close relationship became a distant one.

Next to arrive from England in early 1975 was Clarke's brother Fred.

"Fred arrived last Sunday for a five-week holiday," Clarke wrote to Craven in March. "However, within 24 hours or so Mum's hip gave way completely and they could do nothing for her here. We had a terrible two or three days getting a flight with stretcher and Nurse back to London, and she should be operated on tomorrow for a complete hip rebuild."

"That's when Arthur decided that she wouldn't be able to live out there," says Fred Clarke, "and that I'd have to take over the looking after her. And that's when I decided to sell up in London and come down to Somerset."

Considering the stronger presence of family and home in Clarke's life, it is not surprising that the novel he completed during this period, which was published in England in September 1975 and in the United States in early 1976, seemed marked by more-than-usual concern for characterization. In *Imperial Earth*, Clarke attempted to portray the strange environment of Saturn's moon, Titan, which was home to the fictional Makenzie clan. Clarke went on to describe a United States of America three hundred years in the future, in 2276, during its quincentennial celebration, and how odd much of it appeared to the hero, Duncan Makenzie, who had lived his entire life on Titan. Duncan's visit to Earth also involves the fascinating technology of cloning (a hot topic in the mid-1970s) to create the next Makenzie generation that would govern Titan.

"This book has more plot and human interest than Clarke's previous opus *Rendezvous with Rama*" wrote the reviewer at the *Washington Post*. Gerald Jonas wrote in the *New York Times* that the novel showed Clarke "at the height of his powers." Clarke is, says Jonas, "clearly less interested in 'what happens next' than he is in describing a society in which sex has finally been freed from shame or guilt, in which near disaster and the lessons of space colonization have taught man to live in partnership with nature, in which visitors from one planet must gradually accustom themselves to the gravity of another planet, and so on."

Clarke admits that he has always been more interested in things and ideas than in people, but he is still sensitive to the criticism that his characters lack depth and has tried to compensate. What pleased him immensely was that another novel was behind him—"after 20 years work, on and off, and almost the whole of '74 behind the typewriter." He even thought for a while that *Imperial Earth* would be "the big one": the best and most successful of his works.

Clarke took advantage of having finished *Imperial Earth* and being able to stay in Sri Lanka as he wished by spending much of 1975 pursuing interests and business other than writing.

"I am now taking things very easy," he wrote to Tom Craven in April, "basking in the warm afterglow of completing *Imperial Earth*. Both U.K. and U.S. publishers are delighted with it and I am pretty sure it's the best thing I have ever done.

"I am now leading a very quiet life—doing a lot of reading, playing with Hal Jr. [his computer]—hardly going out except for two hours of hectic table-tennis every day at the local club. I can now beat (almost) everybody in sight."

Clarke also bragged to Sam Youd about how little he was writing.

"Since I delivered 'Imperial Earth' to Gollancz and Harcourt Brace Jovanovich at the end of '74, I have written exactly 1,000 words—a book review for the *New York Times*! And that's *all* I intend to do this year," he wrote to Sam in June 1975.

The *New York Times* review covered two UFO books (*"UFO'S Explained* by Philip J. Klass and *The UFO Controversy in America* by David Michael Jacob"] and appeared in late July.

"Klass is a complete skeptic," wrote Clarke. "Jacobs thinks that there may be a hard core of phenomena still unexplained by contemporary science."

The *New York Times* agreed to print a footnote Clarke requested. The footnote, with a mix of Clarke's humor and opinion, rather succinctly stated his position on UFOs.

It read, in part, "He believes that UFOs need a few decades of benign neglect, and threatens to sue *The Times* if it forwards any correspondence relating to this review."

"I am happy to say that the *Times* kept its side of the bargain, and I never received a single letter," says Clarke.

The one lesson so far learned from UFOs, according to Clarke: "They tell us absolutely nothing about intelligence elsewhere; but they do prove how rare it is on Earth."

The review was reprinted in *The View from Serendip*, a collection of nonfiction pieces published in 1977. In a short introduction, Clarke wrote:

"I am no longer interested in any further books, or letters, *about* UFO's.

"But I am still interested in UFO's themselves.

"Mildly."

Arthur C. Clarke's basic position on UFOs hasn't really changed since. Show him one, and he'll give it his complete attention.

This period in the mid-1970s served as a personal turning point for Clarke. He finished a book that had been gestating in his mind for twenty years. He adopted a more relaxed attitude toward his writing. And he settled into the new home on Barnes Place. It was now the Lunar Age that Arthur C. Clarke was living in—one of his earliest and most persistent dreams had come true.

As 1973 came to a close, and Clarke and company were settling in to the new, spacious home, the *Skylab 4* crew continued to orbit overhead in much smaller quarters. Only five years after Clarke's more sophisticated version appeared in the film *2001*, a *real* space station (primitive though it be) was circling planet Earth. That it was made and converted from leftover Apollo hardware made it no less a historic first. The *Skylab 4* mission, the longest of three manned Skylab flights, began on November 16, 1973. It would keep flying right through Christmas and into the New Year, finally returning to Earth on February 8, 1974.

Arthur C. Clarke may not have been able to see *Skylab 4* overhead at his new home, but a year and a half later modern technology was definitely in evidence at Barnes Place. A large satellite dish—a manifestation of Clarke's own vision of thirty years earlier—had been erected on the upper-level terrace.

It was Wernher von Braun who first advised Clarke on the possibility of obtaining a satellite dish from the Indian government to receive signals from the ATS-6 satellite. Sri Lanka, then, in its own modest way, could participate in India's Satellite Instructional Television Experiment (SITE), which began in 1975.

Von Braun was the man who, more than any other person, gave the United States the Saturn rocket that took the first men to the moon. After the Apollo program ended in the early seventies, he became vice president at Fairchild Industries. Fairchild built the ATS-6.

"The best solution for you," wrote von Braun in the summer of 1974, "would be to get a hold of one complete Indian village installation. It consists of Antenna, UHF adapter and TV set (plus plug-in power connects). Several thousand of these installations are in production in India proper, so the task is to syphon one off for you."

Von Braun added that he would be glad to take the matter up with the head of the Indian space program, Dr. Satish Dhawan.

"I think they will agree with us," said von Braun, "that they could not possibly deprive the inventor of the geosynchronous satellite of the fruits of his own labors!"

The bureaucratic wheels began to turn, and Clarke received a letter from the director of India's Department of Space in April 1975 indicating that the necessary clearances from the Sri Lankan authorities had to be initiated before he could obtain a ground station for "demonstration purposes."

A few more months of red tape, and then six Indian engineers arrived at Clarke's home to install his earth station.

"Lanka's link with unique TV venture" was the headline in the *Ceylon Daily News* on August twelfth. "India's gesture to Arthur Clarke, World's first private home to have reception unit."

Yash Pal, director of the Space Applications Centre in Ahmadabad, India, wrote to Clarke telling him that he would have installed a "specially made community receiving station to enable you to directly participate in the realisation of your dream of many years ago, because Sri Lanka is far from the beam centre, and in order to provide you with a proper signal, we have fabricated a 15-foot diameter antenna instead of the normal 10-foot one and we have also made a special low-noise converter."

The front-page photo showed the six Indian engineers standing in front of the erected satellite dish on Clarke's balcony at Barnes Place. Clarke stood to the right of them, wrapped in one of his favorite batik sarongs, his right hand holding on to one of the ribs of the satellite dish.

It was the only privately owned Earth satellite station in the world, and Clarke's home had the only TV set on the island of Sri Lanka in 1975.

A few days later Clarke wrote to Yash Pal expressing his gratitude, commending the engineers, and telling him how he was spreading the good news.

"I am now inviting the Prime Minister, Cabinet, leading government officials etc., to come and see the programmes. Although I shall be leaving Sri Lanka for two months on 20 August, I will make arrangements for continued viewing during my absence." And, he added, he'd promote India's innovative program wherever he spoke, including his upcoming appearance at the Nobel Institute Space Symposium in September.

Clarke promised to accommodate a limited number of people at his home to view the Indian educational programs. This "limited" number, however, proved very difficult to control.

"House now looks like Jodrell Bank," he wrote to Tom Craven on August 11. "Getting dozens of visitors a day and it will increase." He was right about that.

Hugh Downs remembers Clarke telling him how hard it was to accommodate all the viewers who came to Barnes Place.

"He told me it was the most expensive gift he ever received," says Downs, "because everybody came there to see the programs, and he'd have to serve them drinks. He was buying liquor by the barrel to serve the people who dropped in on him. A wonderful gift, but it cost a lot."

By 1975 there had been other global changes significant to Arthur C. Clarke. Early in the year he received the news that *Rendezvous with Rama* had been sold to the Russians.

"Am delighted," he wrote to Tom Craven, "to hear that *Rama* is the *first* English novel that the Russians have bought under the new copyright agreement." Andrew Nurnberg, the agent who made the sale, sold the Clarke novel while visiting Moscow to sell scientific books. The deal was made with the Mir (Peace) Publishing House and took about eighteen months to complete.

"I consider it a breakthrough for writers in the West," wrote Nurnberg. "The Russians will pay in sterling at 9 to 10 percent of the retail price. They will sell 50,000 copies in hardback at 70 kopecks each, so Clarke should collect 1,944 pounds ($4,654). It certainly will be financially worthwhile."

When the Russian sale was announced, Fred Clarke said that it was an important introduction to a market, even if it represented only "a drop in the ocean."

"Arthur's books have been published in the Soviet Union before, but only for blocked rubles, which could only be spent there. As Arthur never visited Russia, he never had any benefit from it," said Fred.

The euphoria was somewhat dampened, however, when Clarke read that the Russians take out ninety percent in tax. "If this is so," he wrote to Sam Youd in June, "they certainly won't have any more books of mine, and of course, they won't be able to pirate them now."

The Russian tax turned out to be thirty percent of the advance. Other charges and commissions added another twenty percent.

Another product of detente was one of two important events in July 1975 that took Clarke out of Sri Lanka for most of the month. It was the launch and rendezvous of Russia's *Soyuz 19* and *Apollo 18* for the first superpower linkup in orbit.

Both launches for the Apollo-Soyuz Test Project were successful on July 15. The Russians roared skyward first, about seven hours before *Apollo 18* left the pad at Cape Kennedy. Clarke was in

Florida and witnessed the U.S. launch. Afterward he went to the CBS studios at the cape and, along with Neil Armstrong, helped Walter Cronkite with the coverage.

"Neil Armstrong and I waited while President Ford gave long-winded replies to Walter. I think we finally had a minute each on camera."

The day after the U.S. launch, Clarke flew to New York to be at the CBS studios with Walter Cronkite for the actual linkup in orbit on July 17. His long-standing and consistent support of international cooperation in space exploration made this a sweet launch for him. Once more his vision was being realized.

The second event that took Clarke away from home was his appearance before the House of Representatives Committee on Space Science and Applications, with Chairman Don Fugua. The hearings were focused on the future of the American space program, and Clarke appeared on July 24.

"I was both flattered and apprehensive," he admitted to the committee members. "It was quite one thing to write inspirational prose about the wonders of space exploration in the centuries to come, but it would be quite another to answer even the friendliest interrogator wanting to know 'Yes—but exactly *what* should we be doing in fiscal seventy-seven?'"

Ten witnesses in all gave their testimony. They included James Fletcher, NASA administrator; Norman Cousins, editor of *Saturday Review*; Carl Sagan of Cornell; and Gerard O'Neill of Princeton. Other authorities such as Isaac Asimov, Bruce Murray, Bernard Oliver, John Pierce, Edward Teller, and Wernher von Braun presented written contributions.

True to form, Clarke praised and promoted his beautiful island of Sri Lanka and mentioned his recently completed, though still unpublished, novel *Imperial Earth*, whose future hero actually addresses the U.S. Congress. He read the portion of his novel in which the protagonist, who has had his expenses paid from Titan, speaks to Congress on July 4, 2276. The character's speech even includes some historical perspectives on early centennials, the one celebrated in 1976, for example, which was then a future event (about a year away) for Clarke and the committee members.

"'In 1976, the conquest of interplanetary space was about to begin,'" Clarke read from his novel. "'By that time, the first men had already reached the Moon, using techniques which today seem unbelievably primitive. Although all historians now agree that the Apollo project marked the United States' supreme achievement, and its greatest moment of triumph, it was inspired by political motives that seem ludicrous—indeed, incomprehensible—to our modern minds.'"

He next spoke about technological forecasting and how important timing was to development of a technology that was both possible and desirable. "[I]t can be disastrous," he said, "to be a premature pioneer." And he went on to mention the *Great Eastern* steamship of the middle nineteenth century or the Comet jetliner of the twentieth.

"I have always been more interested in the spectacular possibilities of the distant future, and not the practical problems of the day after tomorrow," he told the committee members. "Indeed, I've summed this up in the warning that if you take me *too* seriously, you'll go broke—but if you don't take me seriously *enough*, your children will go broke."

He spoke of various applications satellites—communications, weather, Earth resources—and the difficulty of getting the public to understand their importance and to support them. He told the committee about the ongoing ATS-6 direct broadcast satellite experiment. And he spoke of his strong conviction that the communications revolution would change forever the geopolitical realities of the planet.

"What we are seeing now—largely as a result of space technology—is the establishment of supernational, global-service organisations in which all governments, in their own sheer self-interest, will simply *have* to cooperate. Intelsat is the obvious prototype," he told them.

Clarke next spoke to Congress about the space shuttle, which wouldn't fly until 1981, and stated how important it was to the future of space exploration. "It's unfortunate that the shuttle, once touted as the DC-3 of space, has now been degraded for fiscal and other reasons to the DC-1½." He believed it would provide "the final convincing demonstration of the need for men in space, not just on occasional sorties but as full-time workers."

Projecting further into the future, Clarke talked about an advanced propulsion system based on research "that is going on at the moment to trigger fusion reactions with laser pulses. . . . One can imagine microspheres of hydrogen-deuterium being zapped several times a second during the climb through the atmosphere, and at more leisurely intervals thereafter."

And for the more distant future he summarized for the committee members the incredible idea of someday laying a cable from a geostationary satellite high above the Earth all the way down to the surface—a concept that both the Americans and the Russians originated separately.

"And then, in principle, one could send payloads up the cable by simple mechanical means. An electric elevator to space, or a Streetcar Named Heaven . . . ," he said two years before he began writing *The Fountains of Paradise*, his novel incorporating the concept.

The committee hearings were winding down. Clarke's cosmic eloquence was in top form when he made his closing remarks.

"It is true that we must cherish and conserve the treasures of this fragile Earth, which we have so shamefully wasted. But if we come to our senses in time, we may yet have a splendid and inspiring role to play, on a stage wider and more marvelous than ever dreamed of by any poet or dramatist of the past. For it may be that the old astrologers had the truth exactly reversed, when they believed that the stars controlled the destinies of men.

"The time may come when men control the destinies of stars."

Once more he effectively used one of the great and most famous Clarke quotes.

Just a year before he addressed Congress, Clarke made another trip, this one timed so that he could, in person, continue the tradition of throwing a few good-natured insults at Isaac Asimov and receiving a few in return. Asimov would be in London on June 14 to address the British chapter of Mensa (all of whose members have high IQs).

Asimov and Clarke had been gleefully trading insults for more than two decades, ever since they met at the Hydra Club in New York City the week before Clarke was married in June 1953. A year earlier they had met again when Asimov was on the *Canberra*, the sister ship of the *Cunard Adventurer*, both of which were setting sail for the 1973 total eclipse. It was a unique relationship between two of the world's great science fiction writers and science popularizers.

Said Asimov, "I love Arthur and I'm sure he loves me, and

when we do meet we have a lot of fun. There's no jealousy what-soever, because in the science fiction field or the literary field it's an open-ended game. If I sell a story, that doesn't mean that Arthur Clarke can't sell a story, and vice versa. So my success does not depend on his failure, and vice versa. We both are very pleased with our mutual success, and there's no reason whatsoever to be jealous."

The June 1974 occasion of Asimov's visit to England took their exchange of friendly insults to new heights.

"I spent several days composing an impromptu collection of carefully contrived insults," says Clarke, "duly delivered in the Commonwealth Hall, London, on 14 June. Isaac had no warning; nevertheless, . . . *his* riposte gave as good as he received."

"When he introduced me in London," related Asimov, "he was extremely funny, and I made up my mind that when I got up and answered him, I too would say things at his expense. And we've been doing it ever since."

The battle of wits began with Clarke's opening remarks. "Well, Isaac—I've lost my bet. There *are* more than five people here. . . .

"I'm not going to waste any time *introducing* Isaac Asimov. That would be as pointless as introducing the equator, which indeed, he's coming to resemble more and more closely."

Asimov's amazing prolificacy was the next target for Clarke's insults, and he told the audience that he had discovered, through his "private plumber's unit" in Manhattan, some of Asimov's forth-coming titles, including "Asimov's Guide to Cricket," "The Asimov Exercise Book," and "Asimov's Kama-Sutra."

"It's an awesome output—and it's not true, as some have suggested, that Isaac is actually a robot himself. If you want proof, ask any of the thirty young ladies at the Globe last Wednesday what they had to do to get his autograph."

After estimating that Asimov's prolific output at that time was responsible for deforestation to the extent of "5.7 times ten to the sixteenth microhectares," Clarke introduced his friend to the London audience.

Without much time for preparation ("He was also very funny, and he was spontaneous," says Clarke), Asimov answered in kind, suggesting that Clarke knowingly gives the worst kind of introduc-tions—long and clever ones.

"Let me tell you the kind of guy Arthur is. When he met me on the *Canberra* and he saw that I was perfectly at ease and had overcome my fear of traveling and was standing there with nothing between myself and the sea but some thin steel, he said, 'Isaac, at great expense I have persuaded the captain of this ship to show *The Poseidon Adventure.*'" The high-IQ audience loved these childlike antics, and the applause was heartening.

Clarke enjoyed all of this; it was "great fun," he said. He even got the transcripts of the meeting and put together a short piece, "Introducing Isaac Asimov," which appeared in the *Magazine of Fantasy and Science Fiction* in early 1975. It was, Clarke wrote to Tom Craven, "done *con amore* with a perfumed hatchet."

Fifteen years later, in the summer of 1989, one of the more memorable international insults flew around the planet. *Time* magazine, in its coverage of an airplane crash in Iowa that year, reported that one of the passengers had been reading an Arthur C. Clarke novel in the last half hour before the fatal crash.

"I sent the *Time* article to Isaac, saying that the man should have been reading an Asimov novel because that would have put him to sleep. Soon I got a letter back from Asimov saying, 'Oh no, the passenger should have been reading an Arthur Clarke novel; then death would have been a merciful release!'"

Clarke has even gotten some points in when he was simply passing on information, like a review of one of Asimov's books.

"Arthur cut it out carefully and mailed it to me, just in case I might miss it otherwise," said Asimov. "Someone gave me a bad, bad review for a collection of science essays called *The Relativity of Wrong,* which began, 'This is a book which never should have been written.'" Asimov chuckles. "That's typical of Arthur. I would do the same for him, believe me," Asimov said, laughing.

Their witty insults were unpredictable, but on one matter Asimov and Clarke came to a mutual agreement upon which they could both depend. It had to do with their writing status: who did what best?

Clarke, in part jest, decided to put to rest any rumors of rivalry that might be circulating. Originally it was a verbal agreement between Clarke and Asimov, spoken inside a Manhattan taxi. This was in the early 1970s, and they were racing down Park Avenue to some now-forgotten dinner or meeting.

"I do remember saying to Arthur that I was perfectly willing to maintain that he was the best science fiction writer if he would maintain that I was the best science writer, and he said, 'Done.'

"After Sputnik," said Asimov, "I decided it was patriotic to write on science, but it was something I wanted to do anyway. I was tired of writing fiction. I'm still tired of writing fiction, but I've got to. Fiction is much more difficult. Writing novels is the hardest thing," he admitted just a few weeks before his seventieth birthday.

Asimov was less than optimistic about renegotiating the Clarke-Asimov Treaty. "I don't want to let go of 'the best science writer' business," he said. And so the treaty stood unchanged from when it first appeared as the dedication to Clarke's 1972 essay collection, *Report on Planet Three and Other Speculations*:

"In accordance with the terms of the Clarke-Asimov Treaty, the second-best science writer dedicates this book to the second- · best science-fiction writer."

Asimov said, "When anyone asks me who my favorite science fiction writer is, they always say, 'other than yourself.' And I always say Arthur C. Clarke. He's supposed to say I'm the best science writer. God knows if he does."

"On the whole I've kept my side of the treaty," Clarke says. Both he and Asimov have acknowledged that it's always been a treaty between their two rather substantial egos, and they recognize that there's plenty of young talent out there.

"If people were to take votes as to who was the best science fiction writer these days," said Asimov, "it's quite possible that neither Clarke nor I would win."

This is not to suggest that either of their famous egos was ever in jeopardy of deflation. Asimov reflected on their respective egos.

"I don't think anybody begrudges Arthur his ego. If he thinks he's hot stuff, we've got to admit he is hot stuff. The guys who are offended are the guys who think they are hot stuff and aren't. As I frequently say about myself, people say I'm immodest, but no one says I'm a liar.

"My ego refers only to my writing," admitted Asimov. "I'm very proud of my writing. But not necessarily of me. When it comes to me, I know my faults and failings, and I make no big deal about it. As far as I know, Arthur really has the ego people think I do, but that doesn't stop him from being lovable."

"The one thing Isaac and I have in common," says Clarke, "is that we're almost as good as we think we are."

Just days after Isaac Asimov's death in April 1992, Arthur C.

Clarke made his feelings known when he reflected on the contributions his friend had made to the world:

"Many years ago, when introducing Isaac Asimov to a Mensa meeting in London, I said, 'Ladies and gentlemen—there is only one Isaac Asimov.' Now there is no Isaac Asimov, and the world is a much poorer place.

"Isaac must have been one of the greatest educators who ever lived, with his almost five hundred books on virtually every aspect of science and culture. His country has lost him at its moment of direst need, for he was a powerful force against the evils that seem about to overwhelm it (and much of western society). He stood for knowledge against superstition, tolerance against bigotry, kindness against cruelty—above all, peace against war. His was one of the most effective voices against the 'new age' nitwits and fundamentalist fanatics who may now be a greater menace than the paper bear of communism ever was.

"Isaac's fiction was as important as his nonfiction, because it spread the same ideas on an even wider scale. He virtually invented the science of robotics—and named it before it was born. Without preaching, he showed that knowledge was better than ignorance and that there were other defenses against violence than violence itself.

"Finally, and not least, he was great fun. He will be sorely missed by thousands of friends and millions of admirers."

It was a pity that there was no radar to guide one across the trackless seas of life. Every man had to find his own way, steered by some secret compass of the soul.

Glide Path *(1963)*

24
PERTURBATIONS IN TIME

The second half of the 1970s seemed to be a period of winding down for Arthur C. Clarke. It was a domestic period, marked by the only year, 1978, Clarke had ever spent entirely in Sri Lanka. Clarke himself actually confessed to resting on his laurels during this time. Those laurels were, in truth, plenty, and these years also were marked by celebrations—of Clarke as the father of modern communications and even as the "grandfather" of science fiction. Sadly, as his immortality seemed ensured, Clarke was also forced to confront human mortality.

In a year that would be dominated by U.S. bicentennial festivities, there was also a significant centennial to celebrate. Bell Telephone Company and the Massachusetts Institute of Technology marked the hundredth anniversary of the invention of the telephone with a special program of symposia in March 1976.

Dr. Jerome Weisner, then president of MIT, asked Clarke if he would deliver the keynote address.

"Since your remarkable forecast of communication satellites," wrote Weisner, "you have been recognized around the world as one of the principal figures in the shaping of modern communication.

It would seem most appropriate for you to open the second century of telephony with some thoughts about where it is likely to take mankind."

Even though Clarke was accepting very few speaking engagements, he was happy to travel to Boston to accept the offer. Having a couple of days free before his presentation, Clarke was able to see old friends like John Pierce and meet Dr. Edwin Land, the man who invented the Polaroid Land Camera—"one of the greatest living Americans," Clarke called him. He also had a reunion with Bert Fowler, a buddy from the radar days of World War II, who was on hand for the communications festivities when, after lunch, speakers from the various workshops were giving their summaries prior to Clarke's lecture.

"They were held in the Kresge Auditorium at MIT," Fowler says, "and the room was only fifteen to twenty percent filled when the experts spoke on their sessions. Then, about ten minutes before Arthur was scheduled to speak, I became aware that the room had quietly filled up, and about five minutes before the appointed hour, every seat was taken. There were people seated in the aisles, and they were lined up several deep along the sides and the back of the auditorium.

"The group that filled up the auditorium was mainly young people," says Fowler. "And before that time I had never realized (I probably had taken Arthur too casually) what a cult figure he had become."

Bert Fowler repeats a particular phrase President Jerome Weisner used to introduce Arthur C. Clarke. "He said, 'Our next speaker is the only one I know who can be unambiguously introduced by a four-digit number—2001.' And then there was a standing ovation."

In his speech Clarke spoke of an ideal communications console, a "comsole," whereby "one could have face-to-face interaction with anyone, anywhere on Earth, and send or receive any type of information." The comsole could bring forth information at the speed of light from the great libraries of the world. It also would be a sophisticated robot secretary and could have advanced voice recognition capability.

Clarke also spoke on the philosophy of communications: "For man is the communicating animal; he demands news, information, entertainment, almost as much as food. In fact, as a functioning human being, he can survive much longer without food—even without water!—than without information, as experiments in sensory deprivation have shown."

The search for signals from extraterrestrial intelligence—which looked at communications on an interstellar scale—was Clarke's last topic before his concluding remarks.

"For we can now say, in the widest possible meaning of the phrase, that the purpose of human life is information processing," Clarke told the MIT audience, following up with the begged question: "'Well, what is the purpose of information processing?'"

"I'm glad you asked me that."

And with that cliff-hanger ending, his speech celebrating the centennial of the birth of the telephone was over. In August, he was delighted to hear from his good friend in Washington, Fred Durant, who sent him a copy of the *Congressional Record* in which Senator Jacob Javits read his MIT speech.

Back home across the world, the Padukka earth station was officially opened in Sri Lanka in early May. Finally there would be satellite facilities in Sri Lanka that were not located at Clarke's home. This visionary from Somerset was always plugged into the world at large; the new earth station simply meant he would have an even greater capacity to communicate.

Clarke's stature as communications prophet was further affirmed when AT&T asked him to do twelve minutes of television commercials that would appear first on the NBC Bell System Family Theatre's two-hour primetime presentation of *The Man in the Iron Mask* starring Richard Chamberlain.

Clarke was in good and playful humor when he wrote to Tom Craven, whose film company would shoot the ads, in late October. "Can't you persuade them [AT&T] to change it to THE MAN IN THE RUBBER MASK and shoot it underwater? Much bigger draw," he jested before getting down to business.

"I suggest you let me have, a.s.a.p., outlines of what they want me to say & I'll turn them into my own words."

The AT&T commercials with Arthur C. Clarke were the brainchild of Bob Olsen, vice president and creative director of N. W. Ayer advertising agency.

"Olsen's idea was actually quite bold," wrote Tom Craven about the project. "He would devote nearly six minutes of prime commercial time during the two-hour special to Arthur Clarke prophesying about the future of telecommunications. The theme of the evening's six commercials was technological progress leading to the development of new frontiers in telecommunications by the year 2076."

The shoot took place during the first few days in December at three different locations in Sri Lanka: Polonnaruwa, the ancient capital of Sri Lanka, with its beautiful (although eroded) Buddhist temple called Watadage; Sigiriya (meaning "Lion Rock" in Sinhalese), one of Asia's most photographed archaeological sites; and Black Rock Shrine, where three huge sculptures, including a large reclining Buddha, form a temple.

The last shoot was back in Colombo at Clarke's home. The crew was tired from the long drive back, and they gathered around the big table in the dining hall for tea and sandwiches.

There was even some unexpected live entertainment when two snake charmers showed up at the front door, and Hector's fiancée, Valerie Fuller, offered to invite them and their cobras and monkeys into the garden for a show.

"By the time the final trill of the snake charmer's flute sounded," Craven recalled, "the sun had outlined the huge [dish] antenna on the porch roof outside Arthur's bedroom. It made a good setting for his opening statement, so we filmed several hours until weariness and waning light made us fold our tripods for the day."

When *The Man in the Iron Mask* aired on January 17, 1977, Clarke was introduced to the vast television audience as "the author of *2001: A Space Odyssey*, the man who predicted telecommunications via satellite."

"The Bell System knows that I like thinking about the future," Clarke began, standing on his balcony next to his satellite dish, "and the second century of the telephone has just begun, so later in the program I'm going to stick my neck out and speculate about the future of telecommunications one hundred years from now, in the year 2076."

The locale then changed to Polonnaruwa. Clarke spoke standing in front of the huge reclining Buddha.

"Five hundred years before Columbus, this was the ancient capital of Ceylon—one of the great cities of the world. Engineers and artists of genius labored here, men as brilliant as any alive today. But they lacked something that we now take for granted. They could not speak to each other beyond the range of a shout.

"Like almost all men before the nineteenth century, the builders of this city lived in a tiny, isolated world. And then, just a hundred years ago, Alexander Graham Bell changed the whole pattern of society. And yet the communication revolution is only just beginning. Our grandchildren will wonder how we ever managed to run our world with such clumsy, primitive tools. For they will have face-to-face contact with anyone anywhere on Earth, at any time. They will have instant access to all the visual arts of mankind."

Clarke went on to describe his vision of a positive future:

"All the knowledge of mankind will be available at the touch of a fingertip through the global electronic library. We'll even approach the old science fiction dream of teleportation. You'll be able to send a life-sized, three-dimensional image of yourself to anywhere in the world.

"Technology is not an end in itself. It exists to provide us with what we want. It is our servant, not our master."

This was an important message. What's more, it reached one of Arthur C. Clarke's largest, all-at-one-time audiences ever— twenty-five million American homes.

Arthur C. Clarke was also being lauded during the late seventies for his visionary contributions to space exploration.

After speaking at MIT, Clarke traveled to Washington, D.C., to participate in celebrations of the fiftieth anniversary of Robert Goddard's first-in-the-world flight of a liquid-propelled rocket. At the Museum of Natural History's Gem Room, which held some of the most beautiful gems in the world, including the famous Hope Diamond, Fred Durant, then assistant director, astronautics, of the new National Air and Space Museum, asked the gathered guests, "Do you realize that *all* this collection wouldn't pay for my latest exhibit?" The exhibit he had just installed in the great hall of the new museum was the second complete Skylab—the one that had not flown. Clarke, who had spoken of such developments years before, guessed that it was worth between a quarter and a half *billion* dollars, "enough to buy at least a hundred Hope diamonds—even assuming that there was no discount for quantity."

Another part of Clarke's dream came true that summer. Mar-

tian history was made when the planetary explorers *Viking 1* and
2 arrived on the red planet during July and August and the *Viking
1* lander settled onto the rust-colored sands on July 20, 1976. A
quarter of a century had passed since Clarke's novel *The Sands of
Mars* was first published. Clarke was thrilled. Man's machines
were scouting Mars for the manned missions that would someday
follow.

And there were the more practical aspects of Viking technology that Clarke reminded us about, such as how the state-of-the-
art hardware could easily be adapted to important remote-sensing
satellites in orbit above planet Earth.

"In a very important and fundamental way, when we study
Mars we are also studying our own world," says Clarke, "and what
it may teach us about our planet may one day be a matter of life
and death."

He was referring to the discovery of dried-up riverbeds on
Mars, which meant that large-scale climatic changes had occurred
there over time. Where and how had all the water gone? By finding
the answers, science could conceivably predict and avoid such an
epochal calamity on planet Earth.

Clarke wrote to his friend Tom Craven, "I am hard at work (to
my considerable surprise) on the new novel [*Fountains of Paradise*]." He went on to describe the Non-Aligned Conference taking
place in Colombo.

"You wouldn't recognize Colombo. I expect to meet Mrs. In-
dira Gandhi next week, but on the whole I am lying low."

"They cleaned up the city," says Clarke, "they built a highway
from the airport into the city, and they built the earth satellite
station, which for the first time linked the country to the rest of
the world. And the Chinese built a beautiful international conference hall."

A Tokyo lecture, "Managing the Universe," took Clarke to
Japan in late September for a conference put on by the Dentsu
Advertising Agency, one of the largest in the world. "I wanted to
see Japan again," he says to explain why he accepted this rare
speaking engagement, "and the date worked well with my sched-
ule." While in Japan, Clarke had the opportunity to meet Edward
Heath, British prime minister in the early 1970s and, along with
Harrison Salisbury, the other speaker at the conference.

"'Managing the Universe' was mostly off the cuff," he told Craven, "though v. carefully prepared. I did write the opening statement to give time for it to be translated into classical Japanese. I used about 100 NASA ERTS slides [Earth Resources Technology Satellite; later known as Landsat], which made a terrific impact."

In mid-October 1977 Clarke was back in Boston to be acknowledged for his part in the dramatic developments in spaceflight during his lifetime. He was to receive the Bradford Washburn Award from the Museum of Science, given "to recognize an outstanding contribution toward public understanding of science, appreciation of its fascination, and of the vital role it plays in all our lives."

At the press conference following the award ceremony, Clarke emphasized the tremendous changes that had taken place since the late 1930s: "I saw the subject of spaceflight go through a complete cycle. One, it's utter nonsense, don't waste my time. Two, it's possible, but isn't worth doing. Three, I said it was a good idea all along. Now in some ways we're back to square one again. But to be fair, we have made some progress. We may have only gone back to square two."

More kudos followed, and Clarke was sought widely to speak on how the human race could get beyond "square two." Also in October he spoke before the "Congressional Clearinghouse on the Future," where the topic under discussion was energy for the future—a major preoccupation because of the decade's oil shortages.

The following year, Clarke wrote to Tom Craven, "I've been appointed the Chancellor of the new Technical University here. I still haven't been officially notified, but it's definite. I'm not sure whether this is a life sentence, or whether I'll get time off for good behavior."

This appointment—at the newly created University of Moratuwa, formerly the University of Colombo, an engineering campus of two thousand students—came from the president of Sri Lanka, J. R. Jayawardene, and Clarke received it with "flattered alarm." Why? "My occupation of 'resting on my laurels' has been jeopardised," he wrote good-humoredly to Sam Youd in January 1979.

Clarke had just turned sixty-one, and "resting on his laurels" during 1978 had probably provided him with a much-needed and well-deserved respite. His sixtieth had not been the happiest of birthdays. He had made it, but two of his dearest friends had not.

AT&T had been pleased with the ratings *The Man in the Iron Mask* had earned in January 1977, and there was even some talk about producing more ads for another television special. But the first order of business was to produce new ones that would run when *Iron Mask* was telecast again in the summer.

Bob Olsen and Tom Craven asked Clarke to commit to making the initial introduction and several shorter ones to lead into each of the commercials. The idea of shooting some of it at Stonehenge was also discussed. Clarke replied to Craven's letter in mid-June.

"The big problem is that I am committed to Bucky Fuller's birthday in Bali on 12th of July! So that the earliest I could get to London is the last week in July, and I must return to Colombo by about 10th of August at the latest. I have to take off to Prague on 24th September and before then will have to write my Congressional speech and do as much work as possible on the novel. . . . "

Clarke's friend Fuller, whose path he often crossed on the lecture and conference trail, would be eighty-two years old, and it was one birthday celebration Clarke didn't want to miss. Unfortunately, fate took a painful turn.

"I was going to Bucky's birthday party in July 1977—he had a big party in Indonesia—but that was just a week after Leslie Ekanayake was killed. Hector's youngest brother. I can't forget that. It is the greatest sadness I have ever known. We all were devastated. We never got over it. I cancelled the trip, of course.

"Leslie had had a row with his girl friend, I think, and probably wasn't driving carefully. He was on a motorbike, coming back from seeing her. A bus overtaking on the wrong side of the road went right into him. On July the 4th, '77. That's why I never go to independence day ceremonies, [not] for quite a few years. He was killed a week before his thirtieth birthday."

Leslie Ekanayake had become like a son to Clarke in many ways—the son he'd never had.

"There were ten in the family, I think," recalls Clarke, "and Leslie was the youngest and the best. He was the sweetest and best person I have ever known in my life, and his radiant and compassionate spirit completely transcended his rather plain appearance. He was the only man who ever said to me (several times) 'I love you' without the slightest hint of embarrassment or mawkishness."

"Leslie was also perhaps the most widely loved person I have ever known," Clarke wrote to Sam Youd. "Hundreds came to see him while we were waiting for his brother and sister in New York to get here for the funeral."

The grief was deep and long-lasting. Clarke had lost a son. He wrote and called many of his friends for support. "We are now picking up the pieces of our lives," he told Tom Craven less than a week after the funeral. "Leslie's presence was everywhere; among those who came to pay their respects were weeping beggars, and an Ambassador to the Court of St. James."

More than a year later, in December 1978, he wrote to Sam Youd: "I don't think we'll ever recover from the loss; it still seems like yesterday."

Almost eight years after Leslie's death a friend accompanied Clarke to the cemetery and recalls the scene. "He took me to Leslie's grave the day after we arrived in Sri Lanka. A photograph of Leslie was etched into the headstone of the grave. He cried like a baby at the grave and told me, 'This is where I will be buried, next to Leslie.'"

Clarke later named his big house on Barnes Place "Leslie's House" in memory of his "only perfect friend of a lifetime. . . ."

In September, death struck another person close to Clarke. Val Cleaver died unexpectedly.

"For forty years he had been my closest friend in the U.K.," Clarke wrote to Sam Youd, "and our professional as well as social lives were inextricably intertwined. Now that he's gone, I simply don't feel like visiting the U.K., or going to the London cinemas and theatres which will always remind me of him. (The last night we met, we saw EQUUS.)"

Clarke had had the utmost confidence and trust in Val Cleaver's professional opinion, which he solicited whenever he completed a manuscript. In fact he concluded his preface to *The Exploration of Space* with an expression of gratitude to "A.V. Cleaver for his careful reading of the MS. and his many valuable, and frequently pungent, suggestions and criticisms."

Perhaps as part of his recovery from painful losses, Clarke did not leave his adopted homeland in 1978.

"I've become more and more reluctant to leave Sri Lanka," he wrote to Sam Youd, ". . . and as I have everything here that I need, I hardly ever go out—except for a couple of hours to a local club each afternoon to play table-tennis.

"Underwater Safaris I leave entirely to my Sinhalese friend Hector Ekanayake and his Australian fiancée Valerie, who share the house with me. . . . The company is doing very well—we're now building a couple of 28-foot dive boats to extend our operations. Among Hector's clients were the entire Apollo 12 team when they got back from the moon."

Of his creative output, Clarke wrote, "Professionally: the completion of the two books I've been working on for almost twenty years has cleaned out the cupboards in a way I'd never have believed possible. There's simply nothing more I want to write, fiction or nonfiction. And I don't have to if I don't want to."

Honors came from the other side of the Atlantic as well. King's College, Clarke's alma mater, made him a fellow in 1977. It was, he wrote to Sam Youd, "about my first UK recognition! That middle C makes everyone assume I'm American, dammit."

He explains: "I can't think of any English writer who has a first name and then an initial. It seems that it's a specifically American custom. The reason I used that form was because the pulps were specifically American. I still get annoyed when people just refer to me as A. C. Clarke or A. Clarke—even more annoying. Arthur Clarke's OK. But I regard myself as Arthur C. Clarke. Art: only Americans. But that doesn't bother me."

He bragged to one interviewer that he hadn't used a typewriter since January 1978 and confessed to a secret, humorous fantasy. "I'm thinking of taking the typewriter down to the reef and photographing it surrounded by fish," he told Malcolm Kirk, the interviewer/photographer for *Omni* magazine.

"And at last I have time for a secret ambition I never dreamed I'd really achieve (I'll still need another five years. . .). I'm learning to play the piano!!" He had his first piano lesson on September 5 and stayed with it.

"I spend a half an hour a day on the piano and may appear in public around the year 2001!" Clarke wrote to Tom Craven in December.

At the beginning of 1979 there was good news from his British literary agent.

"I've just sold the UK paperback rights of *Fountains* for a record sum—it will pay for the Hovercraft that I've now definitely ordered."

"I had thought that *Imperial Earth* would be the big one," Clarke had written to Sam Youd. "But it turned out that *The Fountains of Paradise* was *the* book, and the one I'll be remembered by, if at all. . . ."

"It's the most ambitious thing I have ever done," Clarke told Martin Walker from *The Guardian*. "Everything is in it: Buddhist philosophy, ancient history, the ultimate space transport system. It's my magnum opus. . . . Two main locales, both in Ceylon, awe-inspiring places. One of them is Adam's Peak, sacred to every religion. Christians and Moslems say it's Adam's footstep on the summit, Buddhists say it must be Buddha's mark, and the Hindus say the footprint is that of the god Shiva."

Clarke was especially pleased with *Fountains* because his beloved tropical island played such an important part in the novel. And he was fascinated by how the concept of the "space elevator" had evolved separately, first in Russia and then in the United States, and what its real future potential might be. As he had explained at the 1975 congressional hearings, in theory it could offer an inexpensive and safe method of reaching space—an alternative to the costly and polluting chemical rockets that we still depend on today.

Clarke in fact devoted several pages at the end of the novel (in "Sources and Acknowledgments") to detailing the history of the idea, and he would deliver a major paper on the subject in Germany later in the year.

In 1982, during his first visit to the Soviet Union, Clarke finally had an opportunity to meet the Russian originator of the space elevator concept. "Among those waiting for us," he recalled, "I was delighted to meet Yuri Artsutanov, inventor of the 'space elevator' (theme of *The Fountains of Paradise*—my very last book, as I'd been claiming ever since 1977). He seems a shy, modest person, and I hope all the publicity (the cameras invaded his apartment when I was there) hasn't upset his life."

The theme of space elevators was also the topic of an introduction Clarke wrote in January for another science fiction writer's book—Charles Sheffield's *The Web Between the Worlds*. Such a contribution to another writer's work was a rare act for Clarke. That *Fountains of Paradise* and this book, published just months

later, shared a major technological concept was purely coincidental, but there was concern that some people might misinterpret
Sheffield's paperback novel as plagiarism. Clarke's introduction set
the record straight.

"A clear case of plagiarism? No—merely an idea whose time
has come. And I'm astonished that it hasn't come sooner. . . .

"Anyone reading our two books will quickly see that the
parallels were dictated by the fundamental mechanics of the subject—though in one major respect we evolved totally different
solutions. Dr. Sheffield's method of anchoring his 'Beanstalk' is
hair-raising, and I don't believe it would work."

Clarke introduced his latest technological concept—the space
elevator—to millions of *Time* magazine readers in a piece titled
"The Best Is Yet to Come" in the July 16, 1979, issue, which *Time*
asked him to write to mark the tenth anniversary of the first
manned landing on the moon.

"Today's comsats demonstrate how an object can remain
poised over a fixed spot on the equator by matching its speed to
the turning earth, 22,320 miles below," he wrote. "Now imagine a
cable, linking the satellite to the ground. Payloads could be
hoisted up it by purely mechanical means, reaching orbit without
any use of rocket power. The cost of operations could be reduced
to a tiny fraction of today's values."

The same basic message about a new transportation system to
space, although much amplified and accompanied with technical
details, was presented by Clarke to the 30th Congress of the
International Astronautical Federation, which met in Munich,
Germany in September 1979.

Clarke's ability to deliver such messages through fiction as
well as nonfiction no doubt was a factor in moving a *Publishers
Weekly* interviewer to write, in 1976, that Arthur C. Clarke could
"easily be regarded as the grandfather of contemporary science
fiction if only he weren't so sprightly, [and he] sees the present as
'the golden age' of the genre. Then he adds, with that touch of
playful facetiousness that so often occurs in his work: 'There have
been many golden ages, of course, but up to now they've all been
only 12-carat.'"

Asked about his current reading habits, Clarke replied that he
reads anything that sounds interesting to him.

"Maybe a quarter of it is good stuff—which I suppose means about 1 or 2% of everything that's published.

"In a way I'm sorry for this new generation of science fiction readers. When I was young you could read everything that was written—there were maybe two hardcover books a year, and the rest was the magazine stuff."

He was a firm believer in traditional storytelling, he told his interviewer.

"I'm often accused of being a reactionary old-timer, with no interest in stylistic innovation. And it's true I still think in linear terms. In *Rendezvous with Rama*, for instance, I was trying to prove that the traditional adventure story can still carry everything I want to say. In that sense Conan Doyle's *The Lost World* is a model of what I mean."

And why is the science fiction genre so popular? he was asked. "The young today are looking to expand their minds," he replied, concluding the interview, "and good science fiction is the only genuine consciousness-expanding drug there is."

Apparently many others agree with him. Perhaps uniquely among genre fiction, science fiction engenders high enthusiasm from all involved, from the readers to the publishers. An example:

While tending to literary business in New York in early October 1977, Lester and Judy-Lynn del Rey invited Clarke and Isaac Asimov over for supper one evening. Judy-Lynn was genuinely excited about having Clarke and Asimov—two of the world's best and best-known writers of science and science fiction—over at the same time. If only Robert Heinlein were there too, she thought. She decided on the next best thing.

"Let's call Bob," she said and went to her bedroom phone and dialed the number. He was home, and everyone had a turn and spoke with Heinlein.

"That's the only time I can recall that Heinlein, Clarke, and I were on a conference call," said Asimov, whose exceptional memory brought forth a portion of the talk with Heinlein.

"I said, 'Come on fellows. We've been the *big three* now for decades, and people are getting tired of it. Don't you think, in order to give a break to the other writers, that one of you two (since you're older than I am) should step aside?' And Heinlein said: 'Fuck the other writers!'"

The same evening Asimov penned a limerick for Clarke that is still hanging on his office wall:

Old Arthur C. Clarke of Sri Lanka
Now sits in the Sun sipping Sanka
Enjoying his ease
Excepting when he's
Receiving pleased notes from his banker.

Less than a minute to go now. It's like a door closing with a great light behind it, a curved door, hanging up there in space. The moon has almost completely covered the Sun. The last light is beginning to go. Just a tiny narrow thread of light—that's all. Going . . . going. Gone.
Filming total eclipse at Palam, India, February 1980

25
TRANSITS, ECLIPSES

In February 1980 Nora Clarke—mother of Arthur, Fred, Mary, and Michael—died at her home, Dene Court, in Somerset.

Clarke couldn't return to England in time. Nor could he have faced it well had he gone. "He had said his good-byes to her at their last meeting," says Fred, "for we knew the end was not far away. Yorkshire TV had arranged a tight schedule, and I saw no reason to hold up everything until he could have got back to England. Nor would Mother have expected it under the circumstances."

The day Nora Clarke was buried, her eldest son was in Hyderabad, India, filming the "Arthur C. Clarke's Mysterious World" series with the Yorkshire Television crew. The two men responsible for the series, John Fairley and Simon Welfare, had first met Clarke in the 1970s, when they were filming a Yorkshire Television documentary, "Arthur C. Clarke: The 2001 Ideas of the Prophet of the Space Age," produced and directed by Michael Deakin. (Deakin, by the way, remains the most active filmmaker of Clarke's work after all these years, with plans and rights to film many of the classic stories. In 1990 he created a screenplay of *A Fall of Moondust* for the television market, but model-making and special effects costs were deemed prohibitively high, so it is not likely to be aired anytime soon.) Clarke described the "Mysterious World" series as a "13-part series on various scientific and other mysteries. They are writing the script and doing all the research; I'll vet, edit and narrate."

Fred Clarke wrote to his brother on February 15 about their mother's passing. "For the last four days she was completely out of pain and at peace. She slipped quietly away. There were two people beside her all the time."

Clarke wrote a brief letter to Tom Craven about Nora's passing. "Mother died just before I left for India—it was really a great relief as she had failed badly and her life was becoming a misery to herself and all around."

Nora Clarke was gone, but her indomitable spirit remained. All four of her children—reared alone by her after her husband died more than forty years earlier—were well and prospering. And Ballifants, their childhood farm, remained in the family, with her youngest son, Michael, running it as a dairy farm.

The day after checking in to the Hyderabad Bantarra Hotel on February 15, 1980, Clarke, Fairley, and the Yorkshire Television crew filmed the total eclipse of the sun in nearby Palam. This became the opening sequence for the series.

"There's the corona!" Clarke exclaimed as the camera captured solar totality. "The most glorious sight—a great crown of light—the solar corona. There are streams of light stretching out around it, and very bright bursts of flame near the edge itself . . . I can't see any stars, just Venus and little Mercury."

Much of 1980 and early 1981 were likewise dominated by TV and film projects—and the sea.

While in London on September 10 Clarke delivered the Second Annual *Omni* Lecture, "Towards the Space Elevator," at the Royal Institute. The next day he and Kathy Keeton, *Omni*'s president, flew to Goonhilly Downs, to the satellite earth station on the Cornwall coast, to shoot some television ads for the magazine. Ridley Scott, director of the 1979 film *Alien*, directed the two commercials, one of which opened with a view of the Atlantic Ocean and pounding surf.

"Here in the sea," spoke Clarke, "billions of years ago, life began an odyssey that would reach across space and time. . . . I know that even the sea is not eternal, but the life it spawned will survive, for man's destiny lies among the stars."

As Clarke spoke, a white doorway appeared on the beach with the breaking waves in the background. Clarke then stepped off camera. The door opened, and there was Arthur C. Clarke standing by the same white door and ocean scene. As he spoke about man's destiny among the stars, the door opened once more. This time it was filled with stars—intimations of the Star Gate in *2001*.

The timing of his career, Clarke realized, was serendipitous, coinciding as it did with the new mass media of television and paperback book publishing. His messages about science and technology were sharply enhanced and amplified by the very technology he spread the good news about. He was one of the very first writers to appear in both of these media on a regular basis after World War II, and they spread his published work and ideas to hundreds of thousands, then millions, of people.

Communications satellite technology had come a long way since the launch of *Early Bird*, the world's first commercial communications satellite, on April 6, 1965, when its capacity was a modest 240 telephone circuits or one TV channel. Fifteen years later, after being launched successfully on an Atlas Centaur rocket from Cape Kennedy and placed in a geostationary orbit on December 4, 1980, *Intelsat V* had the capacity to handle simultaneously twelve thousand telephone circuits (fifty times that of *Early Bird*) *and* two TV links. Capacity would be more than doubled again in 1989 with the launch of *Intelsat VI*.

The movie *Beddegama* (*Village in the Jungle*), in which Clarke had a bit part, opened in Colombo in February 1981. Filmed in Sri Lanka during the summer of 1979, it was based on Leonard Woolf's 1913 book *The Village in the Jungle*. Clarke played Woolf as a young magistrate in Ceylon, dressed in Edwardian colonial clothing. The scenes were shot in the actual courtroom over which Woolf presided.

"As I sat on the bench in my borrowed judicial robes," Clarke wrote, "I was not in the least conscious of acting a role; even the camera and lights did not break the spell. The courtroom was a time machine that had carried me back to the beginning of the century." American producer Julia Phillips descended on Barnes Place with a movie script in hand about this time. She had an impressive track record, with such successful credits as

Close Encounters of the Third Kind, The Sting, and *Taxi Driver.*

"When I made it clear I wasn't interested (even for ¼ million)," Clarke wrote to Tom Craven, "she cheerfully left with *five* other projects—we'll see what happens. Meanwhile I'm waiting to hear what Yorkshire TV wants me to do next."

The series "Arthur C. Clarke's Mysterious World" had been very successful worldwide, and in 1981 there was serious talk of a sequel—which did become reality three years later, as "Arthur C. Clarke's World of Strange Powers."

Just a few weeks before Clarke's friend Walter Cronkite arrived with a CBS television crew to film a feature for "Walter Cronkite's Universe," the maiden test flight mission of the space shuttle was flown. Launch date: April 12, 1981. Commander John Young and pilot Robert Crippen flew the *Columbia* for thirty-six orbits above the Earth and tested all the systems. They successfully landed at Edwards Air Force Base in California on April 14. The first reusable spaceship was also "the world's greatest flying machine" according to Commander Young, and history was made.

Walter Cronkite, his wife, Betsy, and the CBS crew arrived in Colombo in May.

"I remember the visit to his home quite well," says Cronkite. "Betsy kept talking about snake charmers, and so Arthur produced one for us at the house. Brought a guy, someone he knew around town, out one lunchtime. So we had this snake charmer out on the lawn with the snakes coming out of his basket and the whole bit while we ate lunch."

There was, of course, a ride on Clarke's famous Hovercraft.

"We've got video footage showing Walter riding on the Hovercraft and driving into the camera with it," says Clarke. "That's how the program started."

"We just scooted around the yard a little bit," Cronkite says. "It was at his house, right in his backyard. Great fun. I've had a lot of experimental vehicles and enjoyed running them. I kind of wish I'd become a test engineer. I like that sort of thing. And so it was great fun with that machine of his, although I regretted that our time in it wasn't as extensive as I would have liked."

The feature for the "Universe" series, aired on July 14, 1981, was produced by Jody Perkins. Clarke was the focus; it was simply titled "Arthur C. Clarke."

"You probably can't think of very many people who have their own Hovercraft in their backyard," Walter Cronkite told the TV audience when the show aired. "If you could think of one, you might think of Arthur C. Clarke, the famed science fiction writer, the man who conceived of the communications satellite—and therein possibly lost a billion dollars. That story and others tonight as we explore our universe."

Returning after the advertisements, Cronkite then gave the television audience some background about Arthur C. Clarke's famous concept about satellites in geostationary orbit that could provide global TV and radio coverage.

"Today," Cronkite went on, "there are clusters of satellites in Arthur's orbit, providing instant worldwide communications. For laying the cornerstone for a new era, Clarke earned the magazine's [Wireless World] standard fee, forty dollars."

The TV images shifted to Sri Lanka, showing a snake charmer, then to excerpts from the film 2001. A scene was shot at Padukka, the satellite Earth station in Sri Lanka, one of more than a hundred ground stations that form the Intelsat network. This shot led into Clarke's predictions about future communications and one of his most famous future tools, the Dick Tracy wristwatch telephone, "where you can tune in and talk to anyone through a satellite. . . . And that's going to transform human society, when anywhere in the world you've got to communicate instantly to anyone."

Clarke closed with his famous evolutionary analogy, where man's climb into space is compared with life's climb onto land from the sea a half billion years ago.

A few weeks after Cronkite and company had left Sri Lanka, Clarke was in Paris, addressing the UNESCO Conference on the International Programme for the Development of Communications (IPDC). He was the Sri Lankan delegate, and his talk, "New Communications and the Developing World," summarized what new communications hardware and services would be available in the next ten years. (It was later reprinted in his 1984 collection of speeches and essays 1984: Spring—A Choice of Futures.)

During his presentation he mentioned the recent Cronkite visit and related it to new technology.

"Last month I had the pleasure of showing my old friend Walter Cronkite around Sri Lanka while we filmed one of his 'Universe' programs. I say 'filmed,' but actually we were using electronic cameras, and it was wonderful to view what we had shot within minutes instead of days.

"However, even the electronic cameraman still has to get his cassettes through an obstacle course of postal authorities and customs officials and censors. But not for much longer; very soon he will need only a small collapsible dish, about the shape and size of a beach umbrella, and he'll be able to beam his pictures up to the nearest satellite, and straight to home. . . ."

More than thirty nations were represented at the conference at the UNESCO headquarters in Paris that June.

"I sat next to the Russians and opposite the Americans," recalled Clarke, "and had a lot of fun with both.

"UNESCO has been severely, and not always fairly, criticized in many quarters for its assumed attitude towards the free flow of communications—which is what this conference was all about. So I seized the opportunity to point out that it didn't matter *what* the politicians said or did; the issue had already been settled by the engineers.

"Rather to my surprise, the speech was applauded by *all* the delegates. Obviously, some of them hadn't understood what I was saying. . . ."

Clarke also spoke about the marvels of future "electronic educators"—hand-held microprocessing machines that would provide instant access to the information of an entire library and tutoring in any subject. They would be adaptable, through a wide variety of plug-in programs, to many teaching and learning situations. If the future comes down to what H. G. Wells envisioned as a "race between education and catastrophe" (a remark that Clarke sometimes quotes), then such microteaching machines could give education a real advantage in the race to solve the ever more complex problems confronting our species.

Joseph Pelton, friend and telecommunications expert, was at the conference. "This was at the height of Arthur's interest in what can be done with space technology for educational purposes, and this was the thrust of his keynote speech.

"In effect the conference was a U.S.–Sri Lankan initiative. Its purpose was to make a positive response to the need for education and information in the developing countries, rather than the negative connotation about a new world information order where there would be control and censorship of what the developed countries might send to the developing countries, and so on. There was a great deal of tension during the 1970s on that point. And Arthur was right at center stage of some of these major developments in terms of world politics."

If better and more communication between nations and individuals was what was needed for global progress, then the future was promising. Technology had put state-of-the-art hardware into space, following Arthur C. Clarke's vision of 1945, and it was improving all the time. If the global family wanted to talk more, it had all the "extraterrestrial relays" high above Earth it needed by the end of 1980. A decade later, as geopolitics changed old political divisions formed after World War II, it appeared that a lot of chatter and exchange of information had been taking place in Clarke's orbit.

When not involved in video projects during 1980 and 1981, Arthur C. Clarke was concentrating on the sea.

Colombo hosted an unusual ship in early March 1980. "I visited the *Golden Hind*, or at least the remarkable full-scale replica which sailed into Colombo Harbour," Clarke remembers. The day after this replica of Sir Francis Drake's famous ship anchored in Sri Lankan waters, Clarke's longtime friend and fellow writer Robert Heinlein and his wife, Ginny, arrived on the island, and Clarke hosted them.

"We chartered a plane and flew Bob and Ginny over Sigiriya and Adam's Peak and then on to the Great Basses Reef. Hector and Valerie were at Great Basses then, instructing thirteen Italian divers, and we flew out over the reef and, in the good old RAF tradition, bombed them with toilet paper rolls before flying back up the coast."

Colombo Harbor, always busy, had the USS *Enterprise* and the SS *Universe*, the sailing university, anchor there in late March. For the first time since he had sailed on the SS *Universe* in the spring of 1979, Clarke met with Dr. Lloyd Lewan and his colleagues who ran the educational program Semester at Sea.

They discussed future sailing schedules and how Clarke might join them again as a lecturer on upcoming voyages. The sea beckoned, and he agreed to sail the following October and give lectures to the well-heeled American students who were aboard for an adventure in learning sponsored by the Institute for Shipboard Education and the University of Colorado.

On October 18 Clarke flew to Djakarta, a port on the island of Java, where he rendezvoused with the SS *Universe*. As the ship passed through the Sunda Strait, between Java and Sumatra, the next day, it sailed by Krakatau, the famous volcano that literally blew itself out of the Pacific when it erupted in August 1883.

Clarke loved life aboard ship—especially this particular ship, whose passenger students all relished new experiences and enjoyed learning.

"He was our distinguished writer in residence," says Lewan. "Arthur would do the preparatory slide shows and lectures about Sri Lanka—its culture and history and literature. And he would do special programs. I remember one called 'UFO's and Other Nonsense.' One evening he played a tape where he introduced Asimov, and Asimov introduced him, and they spoke about science fiction. Another time he lectured on the Great Barrier Reef and his experiences there."

A videotape on exponential population growth, by a University of Colorado professor, was shown during the journey. "Arthur watched and listened," said Lewan, "and I asked him to react to it. He took the microphone, raised it up to the ceiling speaker, and the sound exponentially screeched across the room. Then he pulled it away, and the sound reduced exponentially. Then all he said was 'It's up to the human race.' Isn't that powerful?"

Clarke knew this unique traveling educational program had great value for students; he believed in it enough to give a scholarship for one student.

Says Lloyd Lewan, "I remember sitting with him at breakfast one time and saying, 'Arthur, we have a terrible time coming up with funds to put minorities on the ship.' Of course he wanted to help. The result was he gave us a full scholarship for a minority student—a black woman student from the University of Pittsburgh. He paid for it completely."

I showed him [Ambassador Vernon Walters] the dedication of ODYSSEY II, which is highly classified until I get back from Moscow. (It's going to delight and enrage my Russian friends, about 50:50.)

"Egogram," 4 April 1982

26
ODYSSEY'S RETURN

Scott Meredith and his wife, Helen, arrived in Somerset on July 1, 1981. Clarke was expecting to hear one of the greatest appeals of his agent's career. Meredith had come to England to try to convince Clarke to write a sequel to *2001*. One more book? This would take some doing.

"When it came time to force Arthur to write *2010*—and that's exactly what it amounted to—I had told Arthur that I was going to go to Sri Lanka to see him," says Meredith. "We had this visit all set, and then one of their many revolutions broke out. So we decided to meet on neutral ground, and I went over to Arthur's house in England. Arthur and Fred picked my wife and me up at Heathrow, and then we drove two hours into the countryside."

How did Scott Meredith win Clarke over? "It was a variety of things," he says. "Threats, cajoling, flattery. But most important, I think, was when I said, 'You know, Arthur, none of us know what the hell the ending of *2001* was really all about. We don't understand it, we're not sure what you meant, and you owe it to the public, and most of all, Arthur, you owe it to me.'

"Arthur was afraid, I think, to tackle *2010* because *2001* was such a success, and he was typecast. To many people," says Meredith, "he's known only for *2001: A Space Odyssey*. Of course he's done so much more than that, but that attitude, I think, was an area of terror for him.

"Well, about the third day Arthur knocked on my door at about six in the morning, waking my wife and me up. As I opened the door, thinking the house was on fire, Arthur stuck his hand out and said, 'I'll do it.' That's how the thing finally worked."

"I realized he was right," Clarke said later, referring to the enigmatic ending. "In *2001* we went to Jupiter, and the finale of the film takes place among the moons of Jupiter. When I wrote the novel, those moons were just spots of light we knew nothing whatsoever about. Well, the Voyager spacecraft went there only twelve years later. So with the new information about conditions on Europa, Io, Callisto, Ganymede, the moons of Jupiter—and Jupiter itself—that I'm able to work into the new novel [*2010*], I have a much more realistic background."

Voyager 1 encountered Jupiter and its moons in the spring of 1979 and flew on to ringed Saturn and its retinue in the fall of 1980. During the Saturn flyby, radar instruments aboard the spacecraft discovered that Titan wasn't the largest moon in the solar system after all; it had given up its title to Jupiter's Ganymede. Clarke incorporated many of the Voyager revelations into the planetary descriptions of his new novel, *2010*:

"The most extraordinary feature of the Ganymedean landscape was the presence of meandering stripes, built up from scores of parallel furrows a few kilometers apart. This grooved terrain looked as if it had been produced by armies of intoxicated ploughmen, weaving back and forth across the face of the satellite."

Such detailed descriptions would have been impossible before the Voyager flybys, and Clarke took great care to make them accurate in his second odyssey.

"You know," says Meredith, "Arthur has retired about three hundred times since 1980. He always says, 'I've retired.' But he's only done these hundred things since he's retired. He works much faster and harder in retirement."

The fact that this was only a book contract and did not involve Clarke in a movie obligation in any way helped him keep his angst to a minimum. Just a novel to write—no film, no Kubrick, and none of the big problems of *2001*. And the advance was encouraging, to understate the truth. Within a few months Meredith had negotiated a one-book contract for *2010* with the del Reys of Ballantine Books for one million dollars.

Clarke wrote *2010*, the novel, between July 1981 and March 1982. It was a concentrated effort, and luckily there were no major interruptions that ate up weeks of writing time, although Roger Caras and an ABC-TV unit arrived to film a segment for "20/20" in early August.

Caras took this opportunity to conduct a long interview with Clarke, which went beyond the scope of the "20/20" segment. During this interview Clarke revealed one of the secrets to his often successful forecasts.

"If you are an optimist, you have a better chance of making a self-fulfilling prophecy," he said. "If you say this is a wonderful world and we can make it better, then there is a chance that people will listen to you and do what you say."

The "20/20" segment began with a dawn over the Indian Ocean and a brief description of Arthur C. Clarke's adopted country that gave additional insight into his view of the cosmos.

"Many of the elements of Sri Lanka, including its mystical and religious elements, even if I don't necessarily agree with them, I respect them and I have worked them into my books," said Clarke. As he spoke, the ABC camera captured the parade of the Buddha's tooth, the Perahera, a festival in Kandy that is always held under the full moon of August.

"But I'm antimysticism," he went on. "I'm very anti the sort of lamebrains who accept anything fanciful, nonsensical like pyramid power, astrology, which is utter rubbish, much UFOlogy, flying saucers. There's so much garbage floating around and on the newsstands. This is one thing that does worry me about the present mental state of the West, not only the United States. At the same time I'm sure there are many very strange things in the universe."

In another "20/20" shot, Clarke is on the roof of his home in Colombo, looking at the moon through his telescope.

"It's just past half full, and as it happens I'm looking this very second at the two main locations at the opening of *2001*. The great Crater Clavius, which is a magnificent crater. I can see about a dozen small internal craters. This is where the moon bus took off at the beginning of *2001* to the Crater Tycho, which is just above it, a very sharply defined crater with a beautiful central peak."

Not many authors can revisit a scene from their novel and movie by peering through a telescope.

About three months after the "20/20" shooting, Clarke wrote in haste to Roger Caras, "Now working night and day on novel. Going well—getting word-processor next week to start on final version."

When "Archie"—as he christened his Archives III computer—came into his life, Clarke had produced about a hundred pages of "messy" manuscript on his electric typewriter.

"As soon as I realized what word processing could do," Clarke says, "all writing came to an abrupt halt. I was in exactly the same position as an Egyptian scribe who had spent his life carving inscriptions on granite—and suddenly discovered ink and papyrus."

After hiring someone to key the hundred pages of typescript into Archie's memory, Clarke began writing the rest of *2010* on his new dedicated word processor.

"I can honestly say that I have never touched a typewriter since that day."

He was still thrilled about his new computer in the spring of 1982 when he sent his first "Egogram" to friends.

"The marvellous thing about Archie (Archives III, 5 megabytes Winchester disk, Wordstar program) is that he has totally eliminated the drudgery (mechanical, not mental!) from writing; I could no more imagine going back to a typewriter—I've not touched one since last year—than to a slide-rule after using a pocket calculator. (That's a pretty exact analogy.) Getting rid of carbon paper (ugh!) is another bonus; it gives a wonderful sense of power to know that I have only to press a button and I can zapp off as many perfect copies as I like of any letter. (Archie's main memory can hold 1,000,000 words; the diskettes about 80,000. But the printer is rather slow—it takes almost a minute to do a 500-word page.) So now I'm writing letters again *for fun*—something I've not done since about 1939—and I don't even rule out the possibility that I may do another book every few years, if I happen to feel like it (and for no other reason)."

Clarke said that Archie had "quite literally changed my life." He was writing more, and even after the nine-month writing marathon that produced *2010: Odyssey Two*, he was generating a substantial amount of correspondence.

The new novel, he told his friends in early 1982, was unexpected. "Scott Meredith is entirely to blame (he flew over to UK and slipped something into my coffee at Dene Court)." But by April the real work was done on *2010*, and Clarke was experiencing his postdelivery euphoria.

Ballantine Books was already thinking about promotion ideas for the fall and asked Clarke to commit to promoting the book in New York, where a big publication party was planned, and in Los Angeles.

The U.S. visit was only one of several major trips in 1982. Clarke also learned that he had won the Marconi Fellowship Award and would be flying to the Netherlands for the ceremonies in June. After this, he would fly to Moscow—his first visit to the Soviet Union, arranged by his Russian publisher. Summer lecture commitments would also take him to Vienna and Geneva.

In his speech accepting the Marconi award—granted to individuals who "have made a significant contribution to the advancement of the technology of communications through discoveries, inventions or innovations in the physical or information sciences or engineering"—Clarke told his distinguished audience how he had come to write his famous *Wireless World* article in 1945 when he was serving as a radar officer in the Royal Air Force. "So communications and astronautics were inextricably entangled in my mind, with results that now seem inevitable," he said, modestly emphasizing that if he hadn't first proposed geostationary relays, someone else soon would have.

"My efforts to promote and publicize the idea may have been much more important than conceiving it," he went on, again emphasizing the important practical roles of scientists like John Pierce and Harold Rosen, whom he considered the "true fathers of satellite communications."

"The world needs uninhibited thinkers not afraid of far-out speculation; it also needs hardheaded, conservative engineers who can make their dreams come true. They complement each other, and progress is impossible without both."

His Royal Highness Prince Claus presented Clarke with the unique trophy, consisting of "two orthogonal brass rings, with plastic threads radiating down to them from a circular ring at the top—I assume they represent radio waves beamed somewhere!"

The award was accompanied by a thirty-five-thousand-dollar grant, with which Clarke proposed to establish a Developing

World Communications Centre, in cooperation with the government of Sri Lanka, at the University of Moratuwa. (Two years later, in 1984, the Arthur C. Clarke Centre for Modern Technologies was created by an Act of the Parliament in Sri Lanka.)

Clarke flew on to Moscow on June 14, arriving in the evening. He was met at the airport by the counsellor of the Sri Lanka Embassy, Casie Chetty, and three Russians: Vasili Zaharchenko, editor of *Tekhnika Molodezhi* magazine; Oleg Bitov, translator of Arthur's last two books published in Russia (*Rendezvous with Rama* and *Fountains of Paradise*); and his interpreter and guide, Svetlana Prokhorova.

"Though it was now late evening, there was still plenty of light (something I couldn't grow accustomed to after two decades near the equator), so we made a quick trip to Red Square for the usual photos at Lenin's tomb. Then to the huge Ukrania Hotel, where I slept well and woke up to the good news that the Falklands war was over." (Clarke had his Sony radio, and with some difficulty he could get news from BBC's English service.)

The Moscow Space Park, with its impressive displays of spacecraft, was Clarke's first stop the following day. Mounted outside was a huge Vostok rocket.

His interpreter and an official photographer next accompanied Clarke to Star Village (*Zvezdny Gorodok*), some fifty kilometers from Moscow. Clarke voluntarily handed over his camera before they entered, but it was given back as soon as they were inside, and he was able to photograph whatever he wanted.

At the entrance to the administrative building, Clarke met his good friend Alexei Leonov, cosmonaut and general, and a TV crew. Leonov was the first human ever to "walk" in space, and he also was Russian commander of the 1975 Apollo-Soyuz mission with the United States.

"We greeted each other with bear hugs, and he introduced me to two other cosmonauts I'd met before—Vitaliy Sevastyanov and Valery Lyakov, whom I'd recently taken for a spin in my Hovercraft."

Clarke was next introduced to General Georgi T. Beregovoy, commanding officer of Star Village and onetime pilot for the *Soyuz 3* mission. The general gave an unexpected lecture, illustrated with his own sketches, about mankind harming the environment. After this, Clarke and Leonov exchanged gifts—a set of British

Interplanetary Society ties for Leonov and a volume of space art authored by Leonov and fellow artist Andrei Sokolov (*Life Among Stars*) for Clarke.

Then Leonov took Clarke to see the film *Our Yuri*, which his host explained had never been screened elsewhere. It showed the cosmonaut's training as well as his family life. Clarke found it "deeply moving."

After the movie, they visited Soyuz-Salyut trainers and crawled inside to be filmed and interviewed by the TV crew.

"I was also inserted, with great hilarity, into an EVA suit and then filmed grinning inanely through the visor," said Clarke.

Still followed by the TV crew, they proceeded to the Gagarin memorial and then on to Gagarin's own office. It was exactly as Gagarin had left it, on March 27, 1968, the day he died when his jet trainer crashed. They had stopped the clock to record his time of death.

"I heard the crash," Leonov told Clarke sadly. "We never found exactly what happened."

Clarke was then given a fragment of the jet trainer in which the first man to orbit planet Earth had been killed and a commemorative medal struck in 1981 on the twentieth anniversary of Gagarin's historic flight.

It wasn't until Clarke was a guest for dinner at Alexei and Svetlana Leonov's apartment that the subject of his not-yet-published new novel, *2010: Odyssey Two*, came up.

Between toasts, and with the family parrot Lolita occasionally orbiting the room, Clarke told Leonov some exciting news.

"I revealed that most of the action in *2010: Odyssey Two* takes place aboard the spaceship *Cosmonaut Alexei Leonov*. This obviously delighted Alexei, and now most of the Soviet Union has heard, via TV, his ebullient reaction: 'Then it must be a good ship!'"

The ultimate compliment delivered, Clarke was still not finished. Through his translator, he expressed his hope to Leonov that the joint mission to Jupiter in the new novel, where Americans and Russians work together and become friends, might in its own small way foster friendship between the two nations. But, he continued, genuine understanding must be based on honesty, and he had to be honest and warn him: "[T]here were some aspects of the book that would not be well received in the Soviet Union. In particular, the plasma propulsion system for *Leonov* was being invented right now [in the novel], by Russia's most famous scientist, whose moving appeals for peace I greatly admired. He has plenty of time on his hands, being exiled in Gorky. . . .

"Alexei gave a wry smile, and we parted affectionately." Clarke did not, however, reveal his controversial dedication to *2010* at this time. "I felt it tactless to spell out in detail."

The dedication read:

Dedicated, with respectful admiration, to two great Russians, both depicted herein:

General Alexei Leonov—Cosmonaut, Hero of the
Soviet Union, Artist
and
Academician Andrei Sakharov—Scientist,
Nobel Laureate, Humanist.

Before he left for the Sheremetyevo-2 airport, Clarke got a surprise call from Alexei Leonov wishing him a good flight. Leonov was on his way to the launch site for the next manned Russian mission—the flight of *Soyuz T-6* on June 24, which would rendezvous and dock with *Salyut 7*.

Clarke's interpreter paid him what she considered to be a compliment before he left the hotel. "You're not a bit like an Englishman," said Svetlana Prokhorova with a subtle smile and a twinkle in her eye.

Clarke had been in Russia for a week, and he would never forget it. Perhaps in some small way he had brought his vision of a global family closer to reality.

When Clarke returned to Colombo on June 21, he found the galleys of *2010* waiting for him—"with an editorial request that all corrections be phoned to New York within forty-eight hours."

Archie had been upgraded with a modem during the first half of 1982, so while the text of *2010* was sent to New York on a disk, the corrections would be sent via satellite and international telephone circuits.

"It was a great thrill when, after several false tries, I succeeded in sending a short file called ODYCOR from Colombo to New

York," says Clarke, who ended his back-of-the-book acknowledgments in *2010: Odyssey Two* with that fact: "Last-minute corrections were transmitted through the Padukka Earth Station and the Indian Ocean Intelsat V."

Not long after he had cleared away the backlog of correspondence and chores, Clarke was off to Europe to participate in two important conferences.

First Clarke was a Sri Lanka delegate to the Second United Nations Conference on the Exploration and Peaceful Uses of Outer Space (UNISPACE 82), held in Vienna in early August. His speech, "Space Flight—Imagination and Reality," intentionally avoided any politically sensitive issues, but before leaving the podium Clarke did quote a well-known phrase from *Prelude to Space*: "We will take no frontiers into space." This succinct statement reflected his unwavering conviction that no territorial disputes should be exported to orbit. Although the agenda didn't include the militarization of space as a topic, it was on the minds of all present. In his opening address, the secretary general of the United Nations mentioned the urgent need to prevent a new arms race in space.

Clarke's talk was a well-wrought overview of space fantasies and science fiction dating from Lucian of Samos in A.D. 160 all the way to his own *2010: Odyssey Two*. He described and compared means of propulsion over the centuries and even dug out the first use of the "spacegun" launcher, made famous by Jules Verne, from a 1728 book, *A Trip to the Moon*, by the obscure Irish writer Murtagh McDermot.

Propulsion concepts evolved from the supernatural to the scientific, and Clarke scrutinized the early ones for science and the modern ones for superstition. Only since 1925 had rockets for spaceflight received any serious attention.

"It is hard to believe," he said, "that this pioneering era is only half a century old, and that a mere forty years after the flight of the first liquid-fueled rocket in 1926, men were preparing to go to the Moon."

While visiting the UNISPACE 82 exhibits Clarke took special notice of *Landsat D* images shown for the first time. The same technology, but even more sophisticated, was having a revolutionary impact on reconnaissance and treaty verification of the superpowers. This and closely related subjects were what he would be discussing in Geneva.

On August 31 Clarke delivered his speech "War and Peace in the Space Age" at the meeting of the UN Committee on Disarmament.

"My Geneva speech was probably the most important thing I've ever done," Clarke told a journalist a few months later. "I'm very proud of that speech. I also had lunch with the American, Soviet, and Chinese ambassadors, at the same table. They told me I should have been a diplomat—which I'm not sure is a compliment."

Clarke spoke in his speech of the complexities and fuzzy lines between military and peaceful uses of technology. For example, scientific satellites that detect minute irregularities in the Earth's gravitational field have been extremely important to those who design intercontinental missiles. Citing several real-world examples, Clarke made the case that the missile numbers and other military counts can be misleading and can actually result in dangerous and wasteful policy decisions.

"The importance of halting this arms race before it gets truly under way will be emphasized when one realizes that these planned ASATs [antisatellite weapons] are only the primitive precursors of systems now being contemplated."

Clarke went on to describe an early "Star Wars" vision, put forth by General D. O. Graham in his "High Frontier" study, where dozens of orbital fortresses are put into space to intercept enemy ICBMs—at a cost of hundreds of billions of dollars. This was more than a half year before President Reagan gave his pro-"Star Wars" speech in the spring of 1983.

"The two superpowers," said Clarke, "are both led by intelligent and responsible men, yet they sometimes appear like small boys standing in a pool of gasoline—each trying to acquire more matches than the other, when a single one is more than sufficient."

His was an eloquent plea for reason, intelligence, and well-weighed decisions. Clarke was against "Star Wars" technology and deployment even before the press had borrowed the Lucas film title or heard of its euphemistic acronym, SDI (strategic defense initiative). Space was international. It should be a place for cooperation, not conflict, for the challenges of exploration, not war.

Perhaps Clarke's speech in Geneva made such an outcome a bit more likely. Less than a month later, back in Sri Lanka, he was delighted to learn that his speech had been placed in the *Congres-*

sional Record (on September 21, 1982) by Representative George E. Brown of California. It all helped; it all added up.

The official publication date for *2010: Odyssey Two* was set for November 15, 1982, and Clarke agreed to do a two-city promotional tour—New York and Los Angeles—for Ballantine Books.

The famous Rainbow Room on top of the RCA Building in Rockefeller Plaza was the site of the publication party hosted by Ballantine. This was probably the largest-ever gathering of Clarke's friends and publishing colleagues, and he was happy to see them all. The guest list included the Ballantines, the Asimovs, Gioia Marconi Braga, the del Reys, the Durants, Peter Gimbel, Marjorie May, Frederik Pohl, Kerry O'Quinn, James Randi, Bernie Shir-Cliff, and dozens more—as many as a hundred people.

"We were all in the cocktail lounge on the south side of the Rainbow Room," recalls Fred Durant. "I remember looking south toward the Empire State Building and beyond. It was a beautiful view, and we watched the lights of Manhattan come on that evening."

Lester del Rey recalls the part he played in the final plot of *2010*: "I did manage to get Arthur to save HAL in 2010. He was going to kill him off again. And I wrote him a letter saying, 'For God's sake, let's change this nonsense about killing HAL off in 2010.' Scott [Meredith] agreed and sent a note off with my letter, telling Arthur he'd better pay attention. The public liked HAL. The letter included a limerick I wrote, to the tune of 'Daisy, Daisy':

"Arthur, Arthur, give me a chance please do
"I've been murdered all for your volume 2
"Though I hate to cause commotion,
"You'll win my deep devotion,
"If you revise my sad demise, and the story'll be stronger too."

Clarke did pay attention, agreed, and HAL survived through the entire novel.

There was only a rumor about a film version of *2010* at this time. A few days earlier Clarke had told a *Washington Post* reporter what he'd told Stanley Kubrick when he'd passed through London en route to New York.

"I called Stanley on the way over here and said, 'Your job is to stop anybody making it so I won't be bothered.'" Clarke was at least half serious at this point. He went on to tell the reporter that

Left: The famous sacred mountain, Adam's Peak, in Sri Lanka was an important inspiration and setting for The Fountains of Paradise.

Below: Buckminster Fuller visiting Clarke at his home in Sri Lanka in early 1978.

Above: Robert and Ginny Heinlein visiting Clarke in Sri Lanka in 1980.

Below: Tom Craven and Clarke take a ride on air in the Hover Hawk.

Left: Walter Cronkite and Clarke take a break during the filming of a segment for the CBS "Universe" series in 1981.

Below: Scott Meredith and Clarke toast to their agreement on 2010: Odyssey Two—a book Clarke had yet to write.

Above: Promoting 2010 on the "Today" show in 1982.

Below: At the Hollywood premiere of 2010, December 1984. Left to right: director Peter Hyams, Clarke, Ray Bradbury, and Gene Roddenberry.

Above: Alexei Leonov hosts Clarke at Star City, USSR, June 1982.

Below: Steven Spielberg and Harrison Ford visited Clarke in May 1983 after filming Indiana Jones and the Temple of Doom *in Sri Lanka. Left to right: Valerie and Cherene Ekanayake, Spielberg, Ford, and Clarke.*

Clarke and the Ekanayakes, his extended family, Minehead, England, July 1992. Clockwise from left: Hector, Valerie, Cherene, Tamara, Clarke, and Melinda. (Courtesy Charles Adams)

Above: Clarke meeting Queen Elizabeth and Prince Philip at the British High Commissioner's home in Colombo, Sri Lanka, in the early 1980s.

Below: Clarke meeting with Prince Sultan in Riyadh, Saudi Arabia, November 1989, as an honored guest at the Fifth Planetary Congress of the Association of Space Explorers.

Clarke relaxing after a 100-foot dive off the coast of Sri Lanka in March 1992.

too many movies like *Close Encounters* and *E.T.* (and he loved them, make no mistake) made the reality of space travel, as seen in TV news coverage, disappointing for many people as compared to the "over-glamorizing" that takes place on the silver screen. But after being interviewed by Bryant Gumbel on NBC's "Today," Clarke and his assistant, Steven Jongeward, flew to Los Angeles for a week of promotional activities, personal and institutional visits, and some movie talk with the top brass at MGM.

"There was a big lunch with Freddie Fields [then vicechairman of MGM], Douglas Trumbull, and all the heads of MGM," recalls Jongeward. "And I think Louie Blau [Stanley Kubrick's lawyer and agent] was there. It was held in the executive dining room. They also took major publicity shots in front of the Irving Thalberg Building with Arthur and Freddie Fields and Doug Trumbull. They were certainly trying to woo Doug Trumbull since he was involved with the original. Then, a year later, Peter Hyams was in charge of MGM. The movie deal was set; only some of the players changed."

Says Scott Meredith, "The *2010* book contract had nothing to do with the movie deal, of course, movie rights having been reserved for Arthur, with the movie deal made after the book was completed. We submitted first to MGM because they'd made *2001*, and they tried first to get the rights under the usual movie contract 'sequels' clause, which allows them to acquire author-written sequels for a percentage of the amount paid for the previous movie. We said, 'Absolutely not—this is a brand-new and major property, and it's got to be a major new deal.'

"There was a lot of fighting back and forth with various executives of MGM, and then they finally capitulated and said, 'Let's make a new deal.' Freddie Fields had an apartment in New York, so he flew in and I drove in, and we spent a couple of hours in the apartment and made our deal.

"There were no negotiations with Stanley or Lou Blau on the *2010* movie. Of course, I kept Lou informed of all the negotiations between myself and MGM and with Freddie Fields, and Lou was able to step in at just the right time to finalize things for the footage and Stanley's fees for the productions."

Amid his radio, TV, and bookstore appearances, Clarke finally met author David Lasser, fifty-one years after he'd bought the book *The Conquest of Space*, a major influence on him when he was growing up. "It was a heartfelt meeting," recalls Steven Jongeward, "as if the two of them had known each other for a long time."

Clarke flew out of Los Angeles on November 24. Three days later he was back in Colombo at Barnes Place, where he was greeted by family, pets, and staff. His new computer friend, Archie, awaited his commands. It was Archie, after all, who had persuaded him to come out of retirement by eliminating much of the mechanical drudgery of writing. Thanks to Archie, writing had become fun again for Arthur C. Clarke.

*So is it absurdly optimistic to hope that, by Columbus Day
1992, the United States and the Soviet Union will have
emerged from their long winter of sterile confrontation?*
Video Presentation to U.S. Senate, Committee on
Foreign Relations, September 13, 1984

27
WORLD
TELECOMMUNICATIONS YEAR

If there was a recurring and consistent theme to Arthur C. Clarke's
life in 1983, it was his active involvement in the global telecommunications revolution that was continuing to gain momentum on
planet Earth. Indeed 1983 had been declared World Telecommunications Year, and on February 12 Intelsat celebrated its tenth
anniversary. As for his part, Clarke addressed the United Nations
in the spring, communicated with the director of the film *2010* via
a computer modem, and had dish antennas installed at his home
and at the new technology center in Sri Lanka that would bear his
name.

The successful launch in January of the IRAS (infrared astronomical satellite) mission kicked off the year. The event had
special significance for Clarke because it encompassed two of his
lifelong pursuits: astronomy and international cooperation. The
IRAS satellite conducted the first all-sky survey to search for
cosmic objects emitting infrared radiation, and it eventually pin-
pointed the positions and intensities of more than two hundred
thousand of them, including the disk around the star Beta Pic-
toris—a possible solar system. The mission was a joint effort of
the Netherlands, the United Kingdom, and the United States.

While the IRAS was going through its orientation exercises in orbit, Clarke was busy digging through his corpus of work for early technical essays that would become *Ascent to Orbit: The Technical Writings of Arthur C. Clarke*, published by John Wiley and Sons. This was one example of the type of work Clarke concentrated on during this period: adding new words to old—but still relevant—work. He also compiled, edited, and annotated a collection of essays that included his 1981 UNESCO address. *Spring of '84* had been Clarke's working title, but Judy-Lynn del Rey at Ballantine Books decided on *1984: Spring—A Choice of Futures*. "Don't blame me for that title," Clarke told would-be readers elsewhere. "I wanted to call it something completely different."

Another recycled book was a special illustrated volume of his shorter fiction, *The Sentinel*, published in quality paperback format. With short introductions added to each story, it was the first volume in a new Berkley Books series, Masterworks of Science Fiction and Fantasy.

The fact that Clarke's video work was also timeless was affirmed when, in early 1983, he wrote to Tom Craven, "PBS has finally taken MYSTERIOUS WORLD." At about the same time, three years after talk of a sequel to that TV series had begun, Simon Welfare, John Fairley, and Yorkshire TV were making plans to film "Arthur C. Clarke's World of Strange Powers" and publish the tie-in book. Although the filming of the thirteen-part series would not take place until 1984, Clarke spent June and July of 1983 revising and finalizing the scripts and editing the spin-off book, also released in 1984.

"At a generous assessment, approximately half this book is nonsense," he wrote in the foreword. "Unfortunately, I don't know *which* half; and neither, despite all claims to the contrary, does anyone else." He went on to tell the reader that the book (and the TV series on which it was based) nevertheless contained nonsense of the "very highest quality. . . . Anyone studying it can hardly fail to be entertained, amused, sometimes saddened, and always instructed. It teaches a great deal about human psychology and the motives controlling the behaviour of even the most intelligent and rational members of that peculiar species, *H. sapiens.*"

Clarke thus wholeheartedly lent his support to the project as a mixed offering of entertainment and education, while also letting his audience know of his healthy skepticism with good humor.

In the epilogue, he produced a validity scale for strange powers, from +5 ("Certainly true") to −4 ("Certainly untrue") and went on to rate poltergeists as +2 ("Possible—worth investigating") and reincarnation as −2 ("Almost certainly untrue").

"Human judgment must stop at −3; only God can go to −4," he wrote, concluding that if half his readers thought of him as a stubborn skeptic and half as a credulous dupe, he would feel he had done his job well.

The Arthur C. Clarke revival trend extended to films as well. By mid-1983 the MGM/UA movie project *2010: Odyssey Two* was heating up. It was about this time that director Peter Hyams first approached Clarke about becoming involved in the project—after he had already spoken to Stanley Kubrick about it.

"I was filled with all kinds of reservations," admits Hyams. "The first two people I wanted to contact were Arthur Clarke and Stanley Kubrick. I had a long conversation with Stanley and told him what was going on. If it met with his approval, I would do the film; and if it didn't, I wouldn't. I certainly would not have thought of doing the film if I had not gotten the blessing of Kubrick. He's one of my idols; simply one of the greatest talents that's ever walked the Earth.

"He more or less said, 'Sure. Go do it. I don't care.' And another time he said, 'Don't be afraid. Just go do your own movie.'

"Then I called Arthur, who was a bit prickly when we first started to speak. He was a bit off-putting. I kind of said, 'OK.' Then I spoke to him later and said, 'Look, Mr. Clarke. I've been asked to do this film, and it appears now that I'm going to do this film. There are two ways it can be done. It can be done with you. Or it can be done not with you. I cannot conceive of doing it the second way, and I would really love to have you become an integral part of the whole process.'"

Ever since Clarke had given up his grueling twice-a-year lecture circuit in the 1970s, his primary consideration in taking on any project was whether he could do it without leaving Columbo. He knew he no longer had the energy or the time for a collaboration requiring the lengthy (three-year) total immersion of *2001*. But in 1983 he had his state-of-the-art, instantaneous electronic mail capability.

"It might be fun to see what could be done with the new

electronic facilities," Clarke wrote at the time. "Moreover, I did have a certain responsibility in the matter, and would like to know just what was going on in Culver City, California. . . .

"But this time, thanks to the new technology, I would be in complete control of the situation. Sitting quietly in my Colombo home, I could do as much or as little work as I liked. I knew nothing about Peter Hyams (though I had been quite impressed by his previous films *Capricorn One* and *Outland*, despite certain reservations), and if I didn't like the guy, I could always pull the plug on him."

Recalls Peter Hyams, "All of a sudden Arthur did a 180-degree turn and became very sweet. I think he had seen a couple of my films. Then we began this fairly cumbersome business of me calling him and discussing a whole bunch of changes that were made from the book. The film followed certain parts of the book fairly closely and then deviated a great deal in others—its structure and its politics. Large sections of the book were not dealt with, and a whole new section was written for the film—about the Russians and Americans—that had nothing to do with the book. I wanted to set it in a time of enormous conflict between the superpowers. I first discussed that with him, and then we began to talk more and more. Finally we set up the computer link and worked that way."

As soon as Clarke knew he could stay put and still be as involved as he wished by using his new electronic toys, he had what he wanted and was happy.

"Peter and I started looking at the available systems," wrote Clarke, "and shortly thereafter I received news that a Kaypro II was on the way to me."

Before their new modem link was established, Hyams remembers quite vividly one regular transpacific telephone conversation with Clarke that occurred on August 30, 1983.

"There was a thirteen-and-a-half-hour time difference," says Hyams, "and while I was talking to Arthur in Sri Lanka—it was late evening in Los Angeles—the coverage of the night launch of space shuttle *Challenger* came on my television set.

"Just the idea of talking to somebody in Sri Lanka, least of all Arthur C. Clarke, about a film like *2010* while the space shuttle *Challenger* was launched at night for the first time—I was just overwhelmed by it all, and I started to cry.

"I don't know, somehow the relationship changed then. He

became somebody very dear and very important to me and unbelievably helpful. And somebody with this extraordinary touch of a poet in him. I guess the writing, the communication by writing brought it out in him. He became someone I cared for enormously. And it became my mission to make a film that he liked more than anybody."

Along with the Kaypro Clarke received a Hayes Smart Modem, which was installed for him. He and Peter Hyams then began to send messages to one another over the international direct-dial telephone lines at the speed of light. They began communicating electronically on a daily basis about script problems on *2010* in mid-September and discussed such matters as the spaceship *Leonov's* design, its propulsion, and Jupiter images and help from JPL, among other things. They continued right into the spring of 1984, when Hyams's shooting schedule took over and the modem mail flow dramatically fell off, although even then the link was used quite regularly by Steven Jongeward, Arthur's onetime assistant, who was now working for Peter Hyams and MGM.

Just as Clarke's electronic Hollywood connection was up and running in September 1983, obligations for the Arthur C. Clarke Centre for Modern Technologies, which was being initiated with Clarke's Marconi Award funds, were also increasing. The inauguration of the centre was planned for late November, along with its first symposium, the subject of which was space communication. In conjunction with the inaugural activities a U.S. team from the private satellite industry was scheduled to arrive and set up three satellite dish antennae—a generous donation to the man who first envisioned global communications via satellite and to his adopted island.

In late spring Clarke had attended the first board meeting of the newly formed U.S. Foundation for the Arthur C. Clarke Centre for Modern Technologies, an offshoot of the ACC Centre in Sri Lanka.

"When I learned about the creation of the Clarke Centre in Sri Lanka, which I thought was an excellent idea," says Joseph Pelton, then of Intelsat, "it occurred to me that some sort of U.S. foundation to support it was important. And I went to Fred Durant first, and he agreed, and we put together a board and invited a number of people to participate. Then we convinced John McLucas to be the chairman."

Among other things discussed at the first board meeting was

the upcoming White House press release announcing the creation of the foundation.

The White House release, dated June 23, 1983, read in part:

"A number of the top communications leaders in the United States, as part of the World Communications Year Observances, are launching a new U S Foundation to support THE ARTHUR CLARKE CENTRE for modern technologies, being established in Colombo, Sri Lanka.

"Joseph N. Pelton, managing director of the U S Council, in his White House announcement of the new foundation, explained: 'The new U S Foundation will seek to strengthen the educational, training and R and D programs at the new CLARKE CENTRE.' The prime objective of this CLARKE CENTRE, in fact, will be 'To share the technology with developing countries, particularly in the Asia/Pacific region. This will be done by training technicians, engineers and scientists in "High tech" areas; by R and D programs in new technology appropriate to developing countries; and, possibly, initiating new joint ventures between developing and developed countries.' Projected areas for such new joint ventures might be: earth station manufacturing, ocean thermal energy conversion, and tele-education offerings via satellite."

Preparations for the inauguration of the centre went forth during the first three weeks of November, and the contractors pushed themselves to complete the centre's first modest building in time for the ceremony. Built with some government support as well as the Marconi Award funds, it was erected just across from the campus of the University of Moratuwa, some ten miles south of Colombo.

The site soon received one of the three satellite dishes that were donated and erected by a group of Americans from the then-booming private satellite industry. Robert Cooper, publisher of Coop's Satellite Digest, was the prime mover and organizer of the trip, and he was accompanied by several other industry leaders, company presidents, family members, and assorted colleagues (more than twenty in all), who arrived in Colombo in early November to begin installing the satellite dishes.

Besides erecting the twenty-five-foot dish at the Arthur C. Clarke Centre, Bob Cooper and the others installed a fifteen-foot dish at Clarke's home, on his roof terrace, and another thirty-foot dish at the University of Moratuwa. To accomplish this task before the end of November, they often worked through the night.

All three dish antennae were TVRO (TV Receive-Only) earth stations.

"This was not only a gift of extraordinary generosity, for which I shall always be grateful," Clarke wrote to friends at the time, "but an incredible feat of organisation and expertise. Ever since then we have been receiving superb pictures from Russian, Indian and Chinese comsats. (Intelsats? My lawyers have advised me to take the Fifth Amendment.)"

Father Lee Lubbers, a Jesuit priest from Creighton University in Omaha, having met most of the satellite industry people at various trade shows, eventually approached Clarke through that network to ask him to be a consultant for his educational satellites broadcasting enterprise. SCOLA is a nonprofit organization that retransmits foreign news programs from all over the world to more than five hundred colleges, universities, and primary and secondary schools in North America. Lubbers began the SCOLA service in August 1981 with three homemade dishes made with wooden frames and window screen.

Clarke's commitment to educational satellite broadcasting was strong, and he agreed to be a consultant. Among other things, Clarke eventually did a seven-minute voice-over for SCOLA video promotion.

Lee Lubbers arrived at Barnes Place one day in September 1983, ahead of the main contingent. Upon his arrival he was escorted into Clarke's study.

"He stepped out from behind his desk," says Lubbers, "and dashed across the room with his right hand extended to shake hands, all the while saying (as though he were protesting dramatically that I was going to convert him before he could reach the other end of the room), 'I am an atheist.' Well, you can define *atheist* any way you want. I'm not sure that he even meant he was an atheist. Most of us don't really know what we're talking about, unless we profess to belong to some camp. It might have been an invitation to dialogue. It certainly was an invitation to friendship, I think. I look upon his anticlerical stance as being very friendly and as coming from a person who is very secure about himself and his own image and can afford to do things like that.

"I said something to the effect that 'Well, as long as you're a good one'—something like that. Of course Arthur had plenty of time to prepare for that moment. I had sent a telegram at least a week and a half earlier telling him I was arriving about a week in advance of the other Americans because I was coming from a different route.

"Actually Arthur is very conscious of spiritual values, and I think that he really feels a deep appetite for the kind of spiritual needs that he obviously has. He is, I think, a very deeply spiritual and sensitive human being. While he doesn't have much use for organized religion, I think that's a kind of cultural thing and an accidental thing too. If you're left out of a certain part of society, where you've set yourself apart into a different society, it's very easy to feel left out. I think he does feel left out, and I think he could have, and probably could yet again, very well fit into some kind of a religious cultural context. I think he really feels the need of belonging to a community.

"Arthur has built for himself a stance that has a lot of ego in it, and I think he realizes that it's kind of hollow. He's growing enormously as a human being. He's doing everything right. He lives like a monk, really."

The official inauguration ceremony of the Arthur C. Clarke Centre took place on November 25, 1983, at the University of Moratuwa. The secretary of the Ministry of Higher Education, as well as the deans and professors of the university, gathered at the vice chancellor's office. There they formed a procession and walked to the Arthur C. Clarke Centre, where the invited guests were seated in the pavilion.

Besides the speeches, the traditional ceremonial customs were carried out.

"At the opening of any new building, there is a pot of milk with a fire built under it," says Cyril Ponnamperuma, who would be appointed the first director of the centre by the president of Sri Lanka in 1984. "And if the milk boils over very fast, it is a good omen." The milk did boil over quickly that day.

Five days later, the Inaugural Symposium of the Arthur C. Clarke Centre was held at James George Hall, University of Moratuwa. Chancellor Clarke delivered the keynote address, which was followed by more technical presentations.

The following week Clarke saw television coverage of the opening of the centre. There he was, Chancellor Clarke, dressed in his purple robes, standing in front of the centre's large satellite dish.

In contrast to this dignified portrait is another memento Clarke has of 1983. Six months earlier he had had a brief visit from two of Hollywood's most famous men—Steven Spielberg and Harrison Ford. "We only met briefly," says Clarke. "They just dropped in on their way to the airport when they finished shooting *Indiana Jones and the Temple of Doom* here."

Before they left, a few pictures were taken. There they were— Clarke, Ford, Spielberg, Hector's wife, Valerie, and three-year-old daughter Cherene (holding an E.T. doll)—standing in Clarke's study, Clarke's forearm resting on Harrison Ford's shoulder.

"I was wearing a genuine E.T. T-shirt," Clarke recalls, laughing with childlike glee.

To those who have seen Arthur C. Clarke as chancellor or Clarke as he appeared when he spoke at the United Nations on World Telecommunications Day, that picture presents an incongruous image indeed. The UN event, held on May 17, 1983, was organized by the same group that was funding a three-part television documentary on the communications revolution, "The Messengers," directed by David Kennard. Kennard, who filmed the UN speech as part of this project, was a senior producer on Carl Sagan's "Cosmos." Two weeks earlier he had been in Sri Lanka, working with Clarke and filming some segments for this series.

To befit the occasion, Clarke checked into the Waldorf Astoria. Somehow his favorite Hotel Chelsea did not quite complement this august event.

"I was invited to give the keynote address at the United Nations headquarters," says Clarke, "and it was a great privilege to stand in the shadow of history and speak from the podium of the General Assembly Chamber itself, although I did not actually address the General Assembly. It was also a weird feeling to stand there on that famous rostrum and see so many of my friends sitting at desks still bearing the names of the UN's 150-plus disputatious members."

"What most impressed me was the sharp contrast of seeing Arthur in Sri Lanka and then a few days later in the General Assembly," said David Kennard.

"Once Arthur knows you, he's a tremendously informal guy, and while we were filming I saw Arthur in every sort of sloppy beachwear. He is a kind of benign slob in terms of his dress. He is at his happiest being a sort of beaming shambles. His style suggests that he's never seen a decent tailor in his life.

"So the single thing I remember on that day of the United Nations speech was to see Arthur in a suit! Suddenly there he was in this extraordinarily natty gentleman's suit and a tied tie looking like an ambassador from the finest nation on Earth. When he saw us and the film crew, he gave me a big wink and said, 'I bet you didn't recognize me, did you?' And I said, 'Well, quite honestly, no.' He's so boyish. Given half a chance, Arthur will have this strange little twinkle, this impish grin, and a twinkle in his eye. And he'll always get the good little one-line gag out."

Clarke's UN speech, "Beyond the Global Village," contained no gags as such, but it was given in the afternoon after lunch, so the audience was in receptive good humor. And Clarke did deliver a few humorous anecdotes from the history of communications as openers. He told one about the chief engineer of the British Post Office who was not impressed when he heard the news of Alexander Graham Bell's invention. Clarke repeated the chief engineer's response: " 'The Americans', he said loftily, 'have need of the telephone—but we do not. We have plenty of messenger boys. . . .' "

Clarke spoke about the telecommunications revolution in the developed and undeveloped nations and what it meant to the future of planet Earth—including a prediction that the wristwatch telephone would be coming into general use by 1997. "They will give you direct access to most of the human race, through the invisible networks girdling our planet.

"The long-heralded Global Village is almost upon us, but it will last for only a flickering moment in the history of Mankind. Before we even realise that it has come, it will be superseded—by the Global Family." The audience applauded, and Clarke relished the ovation.

In Washington, D.C., next, Clarke participated in other World Telecommunications Year events. Joseph Pelton recalls one event at which he spoke.

"He gave a brief speech at George Washington University in the Lisner Auditorium," says Pelton. "This was another event sponsored by the U.S. Committee for the World Telecommunications Year. John McLucas and I introduced him, and it was a packed house. He only spoke a few sentences, saying how delighted he was to be there and thanking his hosts. He then agreed to a short question-and-answer period.

"I remember one lady in particular asked, 'Arthur, what is the greatest invention of the twentieth century?' And Arthur, without any hesitation, said, and this is a paraphrase of course, 'Well, the greatest invention of the twentieth century is just happening now, and it hasn't really entirely happened, but it will have happened by the end of the twentieth century. It is artificial intelligence. With artificial intelligence we are going to be able to do almost everything that we have envisioned and conceived of and need to do—be it interstellar space travel or finding extraterrestrial life or what-have-you. And it will be ultimately the most practical and important technology—not only for the twentieth century, but maybe ever—in terms of the evolution of mankind.'

"And I think everybody was impressed by that, because they were expecting him to say something like electronics or space travel or such."

The explosive development of artificial intelligence and expert systems in the late twentieth century, coupled with advances in information technology, would, Clarke knew, have a far-reaching influence on human society and profoundly transform the world in the twenty-first century. His 1945 vision of global communications foresaw a vital feature of this future revolution. As the final countdown to the new century began in the 1990s, it seemed certain that his legacy would be more than a literary one.

The United Nations Organization is the last hope of Mankind. . . . It is therefore necessary to consider in what way the rocket can be used as an instrument of world peace rather than regional security.

"The Rocket and the Future of Warfare,"
March 1946

28
NINETEEN EIGHTY-FOUR

The only Big Brother in Arthur C. Clarke's life as 1984 began was the large listening ear out on his terrace—the fifteen-foot satellite dish donated by Hero Communications. Because it was a receive-only antenna, there was no need to fear any invasion of his privacy as the character Winston did in George Orwell's classic novel *1984*.

His own personal Earth Station was perhaps the largest technological toy with which he'd ever had the pleasure of playing. The first program he received was a cricket match held in India, broadcast from a Russian satellite. In mid-January he wrote to Peter Hyams, "I feel very happy—after weeks of hunting I've located and identified eight of the twelve Comsats in my sky, though I can only get good TV from three (two Russian, one Indian). I've also been able to peek at Intelsat newsfeeds. No wonder I've had no time to think about writing . . . but doubtless my subconscious is bubbling away."

Back in Hollywood, Hyams was frantically preparing to start shooting *2010: Odyssey Two* in February. He had signed Roy

Scheider (*The French Connection, Jaws,* and *All that Jazz*) for the lead role in late 1983. Other than that, however, things at the MGM/UA studios were in a state of creative chaos.

When Hyams sent Clarke the film script of *2010,* Clarke responded with approval on the day shooting was to begin, although he couldn't resist having a little fun: "I felt like playing a few tricks on you—like a message from my secretary saying that I was last seen heading for the airport carrying a gun. But being the day it is and the delicate condition you are in, I'll say right away that it's a splendid job and you have brilliantly chiselled out the basic elements of the novel, besides adding quite a few of your own. I laughed—and cried—in all the right places."

Meanwhile, at the studio: "Federal and state inspectors are hovering around the Esther Williams tank . . . trying to determine if it is suitable for our dolphin," Hyams transmitted to Clarke in January as he worked out the problems for the dolphin-in-domicile scene with Roy Scheider. "It turns out that you have to bring over three dolphins so that no one will get lonely."

While Hyams and his MGM team struggled to capture the future on film, the future that Clarke had envisioned was unfolding before him. Less than two weeks before the shooting of *2010* began, President Ronald Reagan initiated the U.S. space station program during his State of the Union address on January 25. At the same time, space shuttle *Challenger* was orbiting the Earth with a crew of five.

"Do you realise," Clarke wrote to Hyams at the beginning of February, "that during the next few days the shuttle crew will be performing, for the first time, what we showed in *2001*—a nontethered EVA [extravehicular activity]?"

On February 7 astronaut Bruce McCandless successfully completed the first untethered space walk, using the manned maneuvering unit (MMU) for the first time. He was a human satellite, orbiting planet Earth at more than seventeen thousand miles an hour. Many times Clarke had imagined and written about a variety of similar mind-boggling experiences in his fiction, where a character finds himself alone and isolated, floating above a planet or marooned on its surface. In fact one of Clarke's favorite stories, "Transit of Earth," tells of a lone survivor on a Mars expedition who is marooned on the red planet. The story's narrator, Evans, is doomed, running out of oxygen to breathe, but he continues to collect scientific data on the Earth's transit across the face of the sun before he dies.

On May 11, 1984, that rare astronomical event in "Transit of Earth" actually took place in the solar system. It was, Clarke wrote to his friends, "exactly as described—but without a human spectator. We'll have to wait until 2084." An observer on Mars who had the appropriate equipment and filters could have seen the Earth's tiny disk move across the face of the sun just as it was described in the story.

While Hyams and crew struggled to create an illusion of the future in Hollywood, Clarke reveled in the future that he'd brought to Sri Lanka. As described by friend Elmer Gertz, a well-known Chicago attorney and champion of literary freedom and civil rights, who wrote a series of pieces about his world cruise for the *Chicago Sun-Times*, "Clarke's residence is next door to the Iraqi Embassy. I don't know which place is more elaborate— Clarke's or the ambassador's. The Clarke home is like Merlin's castle—spacious, with every convenience, and a beautiful garden.

"He has just about every device that can bring the world to him instantaneously. In the space of moments, we watched a television program going on in Moscow, then other programs in every part of the world. We observed him communicating with the same dazzling speed with his associates in Hollywood in connection with his new film. . . ."

In April, Clarke took the first of two trips to the United States that he would make during that ominous year. He would pass the remaining months in what had become his usual pursuits—public speaking, lecturing, seeing friends, and writing. In New York, he attended the annual meeting of the American Association for the Advancement of Science, where he met, among others, Charles Pellegrino, colleague of Robert Ballard and the man who would become an important resource for Clarke's 1990 novel about the *Titanic*, *The Ghost from the Grand Banks*. Also in the works during that trip was the Arthur C. Clarke Foundation of the U.S., dedicated to promoting and funding technical and academic training in the sciences in the Third World. Out of the association of people who helped establish the foundation—Joe Pelton, Naren Chitty, Fred Durant, John McLucas, Todd Hawley,

Bob Richards, and Peter Diamandis—eventually grew the International Space University, whose mission was to educate people of all nations in the space sciences, emphasizing space ventures as international efforts.

September took Clarke to Rome to attend the Study Week "The Impact of Space Exploration on Mankind," organized by the Pontifical Academy of Science, where he also had an audience with Pope John Paul II. Clarke memorialized the brief encounter by sending friend Father Lee Lubbers a sheet of mounted photos to which Clarke had added little balloons holding words supposedly spoken by the pope: "How nice to meet at last" on the photo of the two shaking hands and "What—*another* book?" on the shot of Clarke handing the pope a copy of *Ascent to Orbit*, his collected scientific articles. Says Lubbers: "This kind of thing amuses Arthur. At the same time he's self-conscious about stuff like that."

The main foci of 1984 for Clarke would be stardom—and Star Wars. Fame had attended Clarke for a number of years and had accrued to him as a result of many different facets of his productive, creative life. It was during this year, however, with the whole world waiting anxiously for the long-anticipated sequel to *2001*, that Clarke's renown seemed to blossom into stardom. With it came both privilege and pitfalls.

A photo session after Clarke's spring telecommunications talk at George Washington University easily drew one hundred fans who were lined up with books (most were copies of his latest novel, *2010*) for the author to autograph. He had dealt with most of the line but then suddenly felt woozy; he couldn't go on.

"He was physically exhausted," says Todd Hawley, "and had stomach pains. He almost fainted, but Fred Durant cut off the line and took him behind the stage curtain. The remaining people were terribly disappointed. One man in particular, a senior NASA person, had an early Clarke novel, *The City and the Stars*, which he had had for almost thirty years. This book, the man claimed, had changed his life and motivated him to a career in the space agency. But Arthur's protectors firmly said no; he was too shaky to sign even one more book. It was a terrible disappointment for the man."

In the heat of the *2010* publicity, the pressure on Clarke from publisher and agent to commit to future odyssey works was strong. Clarke submitted—but on his own terms.

"In an extraordinary show of faith in his publisher and in his forthcoming works," read the Ballantine publicity release, "Clarke has asked for an advance of 10¢ on SONGS [*The Songs of Distant Earth*] and, in consideration of probable inflation, an advance of $1.00 for *20,001* [*The Final Odyssey*].

"Clarke further explained that he had originally intended to ask for 1¢ for the first book, but realized that the sum would not be easily divisible to enable him to pay the 10% commission to his agent, Scott Meredith. Clarke upped the advance to 10¢."

"The token figure was agreed upon," says Meredith, "because Arthur was reluctant to accept any money for *20,001*, which he wasn't sure he'd ever actually write. I persuaded Arthur that money had to pass hands on any book he might do, so that token initial payment (the total advances were well into the seven figures, of course) was agreed to. . . .

"What Arthur then ended up writing wasn't the concluding book to the *2001* saga that del Rey had been expecting from *20,001*, but rather another intermediate volume in *2061*. Del Rey wanted and wants to have whatever moral suasion results from having *20,001* under contract, and a separate contract was then struck up for *2061* after delivery, for a seven-figure advance, so technically, the second half of that old two-book deal remains unfulfilled."

"If I don't deliver, of course," Clarke wrote to Stanley Kubrick, "I'll cheerfully refund the advances; if I do, some slightly larger amounts will be forthcoming. Meanwhile I'm proud to have brought back the dime novel. . . ."

For the moment, everyone was happy, especially Scott Meredith, who knew how much his penny would be worth in a few more years.

After signing the book contracts Clarke headed west but reached the MGM studios toward the end of the *2010* shooting, too late to see the main sets. "When Arthur came to visit the set of *2010*," says Peter Hyams, whom Clarke was meeting for the first time, "he was wonderful and I was like a great puppy."

One of the more memorable events while on the West Coast was a lunch with several Apollo astronauts he knew (Edwin "Buzz" Aldrin, Alan Bean, and Charles "Pete" Conrad) arranged and hosted by his friend and onetime deputy administrator of NASA, George Mueller.

A few days later Clarke and the film crew were in Washington, where they were going to shoot a scene in front of the White House. Hyams had a surprise gift for Clarke: a cameo part! "I did a Hitchcock for *2010*," says Clarke.

"It was only a one-day shooting," recalls Fred Durant. "They had the area cordoned off on the north part of the Ellipse. It was the scene where Roy Scheider, playing Floyd, is sitting on a bench in front of the White House explaining to the head of NASA, played by James McEachin, why they must go on the mission. Arthur was two benches away, feeding the pigeons. They were specially trained pigeons, by the way, brought in for the scene, and Pip and I provided the brown paper bag he used as a prop."

One persistent rumor, officially denied by MGM's publicity department, was that one of the lead actors made an "impolite gesture" with his body as President Reagan flew overhead in the presidential helicopter that was preparing to land. The rumor came from several (here unidentified) sources and included claims that at least one camera was rolling at the time and that still photographs actually exist.

Says one source: "We had to stop shooting when Ronnie flew overhead in his helicopter and landed behind us. We knew it was going to happen while we were filming the park bench scene. I think there's a memorandum from [the actor] to the publicity department saying, 'You keep talking while I get out of town.'"

The slang word for the rumored body gesture is *mooning*. Clarke's response to the story: "I was feeding pigeons and didn't notice."

Clarke left town too—but voluntarily. Back in Sri Lanka, he was able to shift his focus to domestic matters. While household problems arose as they do everywhere, Clarke obviously basked in the company of the family he had gathered around him. In a newsy letter sent to Tom Craven in July, Clarke said that all was well, "apart from the usual domestic crises (maid fired, cook's sister vanished so he's distraught and will probably poison us). The little girls are gorgeous—and we've also acquired a ridgeback and bull mastiff puppy to keep Ravi company. He's cute, but already I have to fight for my breakfast. But we won't need to buy a pony for Cherene when he grows up."

When he returned to the United States in mid-November, he had almost a month to spend in the Los Angeles area before the long-awaited premiere of *2010*. Quickly it became obvious that the three-and-a-half weeks would not be spent in leisure.

"When you're in a production line of TV interviews, it's very hard to stop them," says Clarke about the *2010* promotional blitz. "These interviews are totally blurred together. I don't think I can remember a single interview. I did thirty in one day."

December 7 finally arrived. The premiere was held at the Village Theater in Westwood. The Ekanayake family—Hector, Valerie, Cherene, and Tamara—arrived in time for the event, and so did Fred and Pip Durant. Because of his frenzied schedule, Clarke himself doesn't recall much about the event—with one exception: "I couldn't believe how bald Sean Connery was," he said, "when I saw him in the foyer."

Connery was late and almost didn't get in. Todd Hawley was with Arthur in the foyer before the film started.

"There was this person with his face pressed against the door glass tapping on it, and it was Sean Connery," recalls Hawley. "I walked over and let Connery in, and Arthur was surprised to see him. Connery probably showed up out of courtesy to Hyams, because he had starred in Hyams's *Outlander*."

Everyone enjoyed themselves, even the *New York Times* critic, Vincent Canby, who wrote that "'2010' is a perfectly adequate—though not really comparable—sequel to Stanley Kubrick's witty, mind-bending science-fiction classic, '2001: A Space Odyssey.' . . ."

Canby went on to say that the film, unlike most sequels, avoided the tacky, but never quite escaped the feel of something made by "clever copyists who . . . do their work well and efficiently though without the excitement of truly original inspiration and lunatic risk. . . .

"Mr. Hyams and Mr. Clarke carefully avoid the sort of poetic and—to some—maddening ambiguities that forever separate the Kubrick film from all that came before and all that have come after." It was a positive and fair review, and no one had cause for serious complaint.

The morning after the premiere Clarke invited Ray Bradbury and Robert Bloch for breakfast, but Bloch couldn't make it that early. He did arrive just before they finished, however, and the threesome left the hotel together and were photographed out front by the doorman.

"Then Ray pedaled away," recalls Bloch, "and Arthur said, 'Come with me. I've got something to show you.' So he popped me into a limo, and we went down to a place in Culver City, about a mile away from MGM. This was where all the special effects had been done for *2010*. He, as always, was fascinated with the technology. We went through the whole place, and he showed me what they had done and how they had done it.

"What he wanted to show me particularly was the space child, the baby, operated by remote control, some kind of wind pressure. It was rubberized, a beautifully done thing, and he was fascinated by it, and he knew I would be too. I looked at it, and I said, 'Arthur, it looks just like you!'"

Any good story lends itself to screen adaptation, and Arthur C. Clarke has plenty of good stories. The fact that more of them have not been translated to film is related mainly to the high costs of the necessary special effects. Still, future moviegoers probably will be able to see Clarke's works brought to film or television.

A couple of months before the *2010* premiere, Bob Swarthe and Susan Marie Phillips arrived in Colombo from Los Angeles to scout Sigiriya and Adam's Peak, among other locations. As partners and coproducers, they held the film rights to *The Fountains of Paradise*. While that film adaptation has been in the gestation stages for several years, Swarthe hopes it will reach the screen by the mid-1990s.

In August 1984 Clarke videotaped a presentation that was shown before the U.S. Senate Foreign Relations Committee on September 17, 1984. His video speech was followed by an in-person presentation by General Thomas Stafford, the American commander of the 1975 Apollo-Soyuz Test Project—the only rendezvous in space between a U.S. and USSR spacecraft in the twentieth century.

Cooperation between the two superpowers in future space missions has been one of Clarke's important and consistent themes over the years. In the second half of his speech he advocated a joint American/Russian mission to Mars (and at the same time got in a good plug for his latest novel and the movie adapted from it).

"As you doubtless know," he told the senators, "the novel *2010: Odyssey Two* describes a joint US–USSR mission—though to Jupiter, not Mars!—and at this very moment Peter Hyams is filming it at MGM/UA."

He went on to confess that he was currently in disgrace in the

Soviet Union (an exaggeration) because someone "has noted the extraordinary coincidence that all seven Russians in *2010* are named after well-known dissidents."

Clarke named his presentation "A Martian Odyssey," a title he admittedly borrowed from the American science fiction writer Stanley Weinbaum, whose 1934 story by that name became his best remembered.

Before addressing the subject of cooperative space missions (what he called "technological decency"), Clarke opened his fifteen-minute video with a discussion of his views on Strategic Defense Initiative (SDI; "Star Wars") weaponry (in one context referred to as "technological obscenities").

"I have also talked with many of the experts involved—hawks, doves, and those who, like myself, might be classified as anxious falcons," he said, before telling the senators that, yes, he believed that ICBMs could be intercepted and destroyed by projectile or beam weapons but that a 90 percent success rate would be astonishing: "I doubt if any informed person really believes that such a figure is possible." But if it were, he went on—if nine out of ten missiles were effectively stopped—the remaining ones that got through would unleash a destructive power equivalent to a World War II every ten seconds: "The result would make 'The Day After' look like an optimistic exercise in wishful thinking."

The cost of a manned Mars mission, hopefully a joint venture between the United States and Russia, would be less than *just* the research into anti-ICBM systems, he told the senators, and actual deployment costs would be "orders of magnitude greater."

"I am not so naive as to imagine that this could be achieved without excruciating difficulty, and major changes in the present political climate. But those changes *have* to be made, sooner or later, and I commend your Committee for its courage in recognising this fact."

Four months later, following the well-received premiere of *2010*, Clarke found himself in a more conservative setting. A group of approximately forty people met at the home of writer Larry Niven in Tarzana, California. It was Saturday, December 8, and they were all members of the Citizens Advisory Council on National Space Policy, a group organized in 1980 by Jerry Pournelle. The membership consisted of scientists, professors, and aerospace and military men who advocated and promoted a space defense posture for the United States. Most of them were politically conservative and were strong proponents of the military concepts that would become popularly known as "Star Wars" and formally designated as the Strategic Defense Initiative (SDI). Portions of President Reagan's Star Wars speech of March 1983, in fact, originated from a similar meeting of the council in 1982.

"About fifty of the top experts in the country were in the room," says Jerry Pournelle. "They were not just space enthusiasts, but people like Max Hunter, General Daniel O. Graham [author of *High Frontier*], Lowell Wood, Edward Teller's chief deputy, and so on.

"Arthur arrived at about eleven o'clock in the morning, when the formal meeting was still going on. He was not a member of the organization, but he had been invited and was there on his own behalf, and I introduced him.

"Well, Arthur had published this article in which he had said that no idea was ever dumber [than SDI] because there were extremely simple ways to destroy this thing. Almost everybody there had read it. So, he walked into the room and looked at Max Hunter and said, 'I think I'm in trouble.' And Max said, 'Why?' And Arthur says, 'Because I learned all I know about orbital mechanics from you, Max.' And Max said, 'You didn't learn enough, Arthur.'"

The article in question was "War and Peace in the Space Age," first published in *Analog Science Fiction/Science Fact* in March 1982. Two years later it was reprinted in the collection of essays *1984: Spring*. The pro-SDI group objected to what Arthur presented as an "absurdly cheap and simple" means of destroying such SDI laser fortresses in orbit.

"Assume that there's an unfriendly object in a two-hour orbit—that's about seventeen hundred kilometers up. To destroy it, you launch your counterweapon into exactly the same orbit—*but in the opposite direction*. And you do it on the other side of the Earth from your target, so you won't be detected.

"Your warhead is rather cheap; it's a bucket of nails."

Clarke was telling people that any multibillion-dollar orbiting SDI system could easily be knocked out by launching a bucket of nails in a retrograde orbit to the Star Wars hardware.

Says Jerry Pournelle, "This doesn't turn out to be true. It doesn't work for the simple reason that space is big, very big. As a matter of fact, if you just take cross-sectional areas of the orbits of the objects and a bucket of nails, you will discover it's not true."

Several of the people there pointed out this position to Clarke, telling him that his understanding of celestial mechanics was somewhat less than perfect. It was not a heated discussion or debate at this time, although at one point the word *imbecile* was used against him.

While there were no doubt other criticisms of the article (Clarke also referred to General Daniel O. Graham's *High Frontier* study as a "horrifying description of the next phase of space warfare . . . "), the main criticism was focused on Clarke's proposed method of destroying the orbiting laser stations.

"As far as this technical discussion was concerned," says Pournelle, "Arthur had no defense. He asked several questions, and at the end of it he admitted, 'I clearly was wrong.'"

"I certainly have a more open mind [now] about the bucket of nails concept," Clarke said recently. "Even if it isn't viable, I'm sure it will scare the hell out of any manned fortresses. But even if these systems can work—and I think the reflecting mirrors and the laser stuff is utter nonsense for decades at any rate—they may be a bad idea because of their destabilizing influence."

Soon after the formal session had ended and everyone had broken for lunch, a confrontation took place between Arthur C. Clarke and Robert Heinlein—what friends later called the "bloodbath sequence" or the "battle of the Titans."

Heinlein had said nothing during the meeting itself, but he soon made up for it. Unfortunately, he had taken Clarke's skeptical remarks personally.

"Arthur had made some statements about what the United States ought to do about strategic defense, weapons in space, foreign policy, and so forth," recalls G. Harry Stine, who became acquainted with both men in the early 1950s. "And Robert Heinlein lit into him verbally. He just took Arthur apart. And all of us just sat there.

"I've never seen Arthur defensive. He really just sat there too. He made a few rather semidefensive comments, but he basically just almost withered from the scathing verbal attack from Heinlein. And after his blistering attack, Heinlein wouldn't talk to him.

"I think what shocked Arthur as it shocked us was the fact that Robert Heinlein did this in public, among his own peers and Arthur's peers."

"He accused me of typically British arrogance," says Clarke, "and he really was vicious. It really hurt me. I was very sad about it."

Science fiction writer Gregory Benford recalls that when Clarke stated his reservations about the very idea of strategic defense, Heinlein chose not to argue about it as a technical problem but rather to say something like "Look, this is a matter of the defense of the United States, and you're not assisting the United States, and therefore you really don't have call to have an opinion about it." Heinlein continued in that vein, saying that if he were visiting England or Sri Lanka, he would not tell those people how to run their country.

At some point Clarke said that he had doubts about it as a moral issue. This outraged Heinlein, who then loudly told Clarke that *he* had no moral right to frame a moral argument about something in which he had no stake. This was a matter of national sovereignty, and Arthur C. Clarke was not a citizen.

"Heinlein was always big on freedom and the balance with responsibility," says Gregory Benford. "I mean that's what *Starship Troopers* is all about. You don't get to vote unless you fight. And similarly, you don't get an opinion unless your skin is personally risked."

After the Heinlein blast, people had lunch and conversations continued—at a normal volume. Clarke spoke to several of the group and then spent a lot of time talking to General Graham. When that conversation ended, he said to the general, "Well, you may be right." This was hardly a ringing endorsement of the general's SDI advocacy.

Later, when the meeting was breaking up, Clarke approached Heinlein and said, "I can't help the British, but I'll try to do something about the arrogance." That's the last time he ever saw Robert Heinlein, who died in May 1988.

Jerry Pournelle walked Clarke out to the car. "He looked at me, and he said, 'I know that Robert thinks I am, but I'm really not inflexible, and I don't really believe I'm infallible.'" And with those parting words, he was driven back to the Beverly Wilshire.

Months later friends said that the two "Titans" had reconciled their differences. As far as it went, this was a tribute to their long-standing friendship.

"Usually," says Benford, "if you violated Heinlein's standards, you went into Coventry. That didn't happen to Arthur, and they patched things up. Robert told me the last time I saw him that they had exchanged some letters and had ironed out their positions. Heinlein said to me, 'Arthur changed his position; I didn't.' Which I would gather, is the case," says Benford. "Arthur's always been a very friendly and gregarious person—not the recluse type that most prominent SF writers are. The amount of withdrawal you see among well-known SF writers is really an unexplained phenomenon. They tend to be hermitlike. But not Arthur, even though he lives in Sri Lanka."

Robert Heinlein did not change his position—there's no doubt about that in Clarke's or anyone else's mind. "And I wasn't quite so arrogant about mine after that," Clarke says. "I'm prepared to admit that there are certain aspects of SDI that made sense and, in fact, that may still do so. What I was attacking was the utter nonsense about putting an umbrella over the United States. That was the version I was attacking. You couldn't even put an umbrella over a missile site. You could put a leaky roof over it, which might be worth doing."

The reconciliation between Clarke and Heinlein was at arm's length and not complete, it turns out.

"I did send notes to him," Clarke says, "and Ginny acknowledged them. I do remember one thing. I came across a photograph of two bull elephants in a Congo scene, sort of butting each other, and I sent it to him and said, 'Does this remind you of anything?'" Clarke laughs, then turns serious again. "I imagine he probably would have responded himself eventually, but it wasn't to be, and of course we never discussed or mentioned SDI again."

In a short tribute for a Heinlein memorial volume in September 1990, Clarke said that he was not resentful about the verbal attack. "I realised that Bob was ailing and his behavior was not typical of one of the most courteous people I have ever known." He then bid a final farewell to his friend.

"Goodbye, Bob, and thank you for the influence you had on my life and career. And thank you too, Ginny, for looking after him so well and so long."

It was a song for all exiles, and it spoke as clearly to those who were sundered from Earth by a dozen generations as to the voyagers to whom its fields and cities still seemed only weeks away.
"The Songs of Distant Earth" (1958, short story)

29
A NEAR AND DISTANT EARTH

The first spacecraft launched in 1985, *Sakigake*, was one of two Japanese probes bound for that famous celestial vagabond, Comet Halley. It reached escape velocity from planet Earth on January 7, and fifteen months later flew past the comet and measured the solar wind in its vicinity.

While this "made-in-Japan" spacecraft began its cosmic journey through the solar system, beauty queen Miss Japan was being filmed under water in the Indian Ocean with Arthur C. Clarke. The shoot took place at Coral Gardens, Hikkaduwa, about fifty miles due south of Colombo, where a new hotel complex had been built a few years earlier. The footage was for a program that would inaugurate Japanese satellite television.

In early 1985 Arthur was in London to attend the royal charity premiere of *2010*. It was, he told friends, "only the promise of meeting Princess Di" that brought him back to the United Kingdom so early in the year. "I did my best," he deadpanned, "to put Prince Charles and Princess Diana at their ease." He was very pleased that his cameo part was noticed. "Everything went splendidly, and Princess Di made my evening by recognizing me in the White House scene."

Later in the month, across the Atlantic, another famous person referred to the space cadet from Somerset, but Clarke wasn't there to hear him.

President Ronald Reagan gave a speech before the National Space Club on March 29, 1985, at the Shoreham Hotel in Washington, D.C. The president was presented with the Goddard Award on this occasion.

"Dr. Goddard persevered for decades of intense research and development," said the president. "And as so often happens, his genius was not apparent to many until after his success.

"Arthur C. Clarke, distinguished author of science and fiction, says ideas often have three stages of reaction—first, 'it's crazy and don't waste my time.' Second, 'it's possible, but it's not worth doing.' And finally, 'I've always said it was a good idea.'"

The audience laughed and applauded. It was a lighthearted speech, with the president's usual share of one-liners. It was also appropriate to mention Clarke, who had taken Goddard's dream, mixed it with his own, and retold it thousands of times, with many variations and new plots, to readers and audiences around the planet. Clarke was, in a real sense, Goddard's protégé, his messenger to the masses. For fifty years, from the time he was a lanky, bespectacled farm boy, Arthur C. Clarke had been spreading the word about rockets and space travel and our future in space. President Reagan's association of Clarke with Goddard was cosmic justice from a high station.

In May, Clarke was invited to face the friendly Washington crowd in person and speak at the MIT Club there, but he wasn't feeling that well (he noticed regularly that he had less energy), and he also had a French television crew in Sri Lanka to keep happy. They were filming a biographical piece: *Star-Glider: Portrait of Arthur Clarke*. As a compromise he packaged his electronic image and speech in a thirty-minute videocassette, which he titled *Visions of Space*, and sent it to Washington, D.C., to stand in for him.

There he was, wearing a bright blue shirt, sitting at his desk, with books and more books filling his office shelves in the background. Script in hand, he spoke of the deep and treacherous gravitational well of Earth and how difficult it was for us to climb out of it into space. He spoke of various propulsion systems, including the recent British single-stage-to-orbit, oxygen-collecting ramjet design "based on an engine that's still secret."

He spoke of nuclear propulsion and the canceled Project Orion, of his electromagnetic slingshot launch concept for the moon, of colonies in space and multigenerational starships, and of the possibility of communicating with or meeting extraterrestrial beings.

During the first six months of 1985 almost all of Clarke's writing efforts were focused on his interstellar novel, *The Songs of Distant Earth*, the early notes for which he had composed some thirty years before. Although he had made several attempts to get on a regular writing schedule in late 1983 and 1984, little progress was made on the novel before 1985.

In his *Visions of Space* video Clarke quoted a person he loved to quote, the British geneticist J. B. S. Haldane, who many years before had told him that "the human race had obviously been designed for interstellar—yes, interstellar—travel, because by accelerating at a comfortable 1 g for one year you get to the speed of light. An interesting coincidence!" And in a letter to Clarke dated January 8, 1964, as Haldane lay dying of cancer in London, he raised yet another intriguing possibility: "I suggest the following hypothesis: Interstellar travel occurs on a vast scale. Cosmic rays are merely the exhausts of rockets."

The interstellar travel of *The Songs of Distant Earth* was predicated on the realities of future science, not on a "Star Trek" propulsion fantasy like "warp speed." To bring the human and cosmic time scales into harmony without abusing the universal laws of physics and human life spans, Clarke relied on a future science of hibernation (as he did in *2001* and *2010*), where the human body was suspended in time during the long voyages between planets or stars. This grand master of hard science fiction did not have to compromise scientific realities to move his characters from star to star.

In his new novel the interstellar voyage to the planet Oceana, located fifty light-years away from Earth, took five hundred years traveling at ten percent of the speed of light. This was a reasonable propulsion system projected from the technology of the late twentieth century. As a matter of fact, the feasibility of such a starship had already been confirmed in the 1970s by the British Interplanetary Society's detailed report, *Project Daedalus*. (The study was dedicated to the memory of Clarke's dear friend, Val Cleaver, who had given it constructive encouragement until his death.)

Back on Earth, global distances continued to be bridged at the speed of light. On June 28 Clarke participated in the first United States Information Agency's Worldnet global linkup. From London, Prime Minister Margaret Thatcher emphasized that communication satellites were a British invention.

"In view of the UK's current deplorable space record, she's now been reminded of this," Clarke told friends.

In Sri Lanka, the Arthur C. Clarke Centre for Modern Technologies was bridging the technological gap for students in the small nation.

"What was important at that time," says the center's first director, Cyril Ponnamperuma, "was the feeling that here was a country in the Third World wanting to move into the twenty-first century, wanting to build an awareness of future technology—advanced communications, computers, and so on. And during my directorship what I really wanted to do was set the programs in place and bring the people together.

"One of the first important things we did in 1985 was to set up a program for bright young people. On a national and competitive basis, we selected twenty-five, and they came to the centre six or seven Saturdays in a row. One Saturday they were exposed to computers, the next weekend to communications, the next Saturday to robotics, and so on. Out of that eventually came the Young Astronomers' Association and the Computer Society of Sri Lanka. These were the first important teaching activities at the centre."

The political situation in Sri Lanka in August was unstable, however, with violence flaring up in northern and northeastern areas of the island, and the Underwater Safaris business near Trincomalee was closed down because of the conflict.

"All the hotels there have been robbed and some even blown up," Clarke wrote to Michael Craven, who had been at the helm of the family film company since his father's death in August 1984. "Just heard that the terrorists have stolen one of our 18-foot boats."

He also told Craven that he was looking forward to a holiday in England, "now that I have finished the novel [*The Songs of Distant Earth*] I have been working on for thirty years."

"We went down to Minehead and saw Aunt Nellie who was then in a nursing home," says Fred Clarke of his brother's late-summer trip home. "She had a lot to do with bringing Arthur up, of course. Probably more than Mother did, who was so tied up with the farm."

"My last memory of Nellie was in the park at Minehead, during our September visit," says Clarke.

Three months later, on December 30, Aunt Nellie died in her ninety-fourth year. She was "the last of her generation," Clarke says, "and my strongest remaining tie with England was broken."

Clarke had already had bad news about someone else close to him. After returning from his fifth annual voyage on the SS *Universe* on October 28, he had discovered the news that he relayed two days later to Michael Craven in New York:

"My publisher Judy-Lynn del Rey is desperately ill and may well be dead by now (she has had a brain clot and has been in a coma for over a week)."

Del Rey remained unconscious for months and never recovered. She died in early 1986. The following year Clarke dedicated *2061: Odyssey Three* to her: "To the memory of Judy-Lynn del Rey, editor extraordinary, who bought this book for one dollar—but never knew if she got her money's worth."

One of the last books Judy-Lynn del Rey ever edited was *The Songs of Distant Earth*, published in May 1986. She was a great editor in the genre and would be deeply missed.

After the examination, the doctors told Arthur he had only fifteen months to live. . . .
                                    Fred Clarke, speaking of July 1986

"My objection to organized religion is the premature conclusion to ultimate truth it represents."
                                    Playboy *interview (July 1986)*

30
BORROWED TIME

In his December 1985 Christmas message, Arthur C. Clarke told friends that his next novel, the one he had "been tinkering with for a quarter century, *The Songs of Distant Earth*," would be published the following May. In a playful mood, he went on talking about himself in the third person: "As he's convinced that it will make him famous, he's decided (again) to do no more writing, and now spends his time sorting videotapes, reading computer magazines, coping with mail and visitors. However, if *Galileo* reaches Jupiter according to schedule on 11 December 1988, he *may* start thinking about *Odyssey Three.*"

All bets were off when the *Challenger* tragedy occurred on January 28, 1986. The future of the entire U.S. space program, manned and unmanned, was in doubt, and the mission of spacecraft *Galileo* was delayed for years.

Scott Meredith knew he'd have to come up with something special to get Clarke motivated again. As it happened, the well-known film producer Peter Guber (*The Color Purple, The Deep, Midnight Express*) wanted to do a Clarke film. Meredith called Clarke in early 1986 to tell him of Guber's interest and to persuade him to listen to the proposal. Clarke listened, but with a skeptical ear.

"I groaned inwardly when Scott went on to say that Peter had a friend with a brilliant idea he'd like me to develop into a screenplay," Clarke wrote in the late eighties.

Peter Guber wanted to fly to Sri Lanka with his friend and discuss the project. Clarke began to warm to the possible collaboration when he learned more about Guber's friend. His name was Gentry Lee, and his credentials impressed even Arthur C. Clarke. He worked at the Jet Propulsion Laboratory and was chief engineer on the stalled Project Galileo. Before that he had been director of mission planning for the Viking Mars landers. He also had been Carl Sagan's partner in the company that produced the "Cosmos" television series and in fact had been manager for the entire production.

Guber and Lee flew into Colombo on February 12, 1986, checked into their hotel, and went out to Barnes Place to meet Arthur C. Clarke.

"The first day we went out to see him," says Lee, "Arthur was probably thinking to himself, What are these people here trying to get me to do? On top of that, when Arthur's at home he can be easily distracted. Often there are interruptions, and sometimes he has a hard time focusing on anything.

"After the first five or ten minutes of conversation with Peter and me, one of the help walked in and needed to borrow a hundred rupees. Arthur interrupted the conversation to give this guy a hundred rupees—about four bucks or something like that.

"Well, Peter Guber is one of the most focused people you'll ever meet in your life," continues Lee, "and he could not believe that Arthur interrupted the conversation for such a trivial matter. He took me aside and said, 'He's a lunatic. I fly halfway around the world to talk to this guy, and he's worried about giving some little guy four dollars.'

"Peter was going to go home. He was going to go home immediately. I assured Peter that if he would just be patient, everything would work out well in the long run. And it did. All in all, I thought the meetings went very well. Arthur was willing to do most anything except go through the intensity of another *2001*."

Thus began the literary collaboration between Arthur C. Clarke and Gentry Lee. For the next several weeks Clarke worked on story elements and eventually produced a four-thousand-word outline that became the foundation for their film script treatment for Guber. Then Gentry Lee again traveled to Sri Lanka to work with Clarke on the treatment, and they began the creative process of working out the plot and characters and backgrounds. It was during this first working session together on the movie script that they realized that they were well on their way to a novel. As a result they later agreed to coauthorship and to a division of labor. Scott Meredith sold the project to Warner Books, and they were off and running.

Cradle, written by early 1987, was the first book produced by their joint efforts. It never got to the silver screen, however. Warner bought the film rights, but, says Lee, "Their writers wrote an absolutely ghastly screenplay, and eventually the studio abandoned the deal."

Several critics had similar responses to the novel when it was published in August 1988. "When is an Arthur C. Clarke novel not an Arthur C. Clarke novel? When it's co-written by someone called Gentry Lee and entitled *Cradle*," wrote one reviewer who referred to the work as a "ludicrous hybrid."

Another reviewer wondered in print "why Arthur C. Clarke, who can write intelligent and suspenseful novels when he wants to (e.g., *Rendezvous with Rama*), should have got himself involved with this leaden piece of self-parody."

While the first collaborative work between Clarke and Lee was not well received in some quarters, their friendship and working relationship were unscathed.

Their general attitude about the criticism was that some of it was justified; theirs was a new working relationship, after all. Book buyers and reviewers, they had assumed, would understand that a coauthored novel by Clarke and Lee was an entirely different entity from an Arthur C. Clarke novel.

The response to *Cradle*, however, told them that their assumption was wrong. They underestimated the audience expectations of a novel bearing the name Arthur C. Clarke, even though Gentry Lee's name also appeared (in lower position and in smaller type) on the book jacket. For readers it became an identity crisis of authorship. This was not what many of them expected, and for some the standards of truth in advertising had been violated.

One result of the criticism was that they agreed to play down the explicit sex in what became their next effort together, *Rama II*. Such sexual descriptions were so foreign to Arthur C. Clarke's fiction that it was another dead giveaway that it was Lee's apprenticeship prose, not Clarke's. Despite these efforts, negative reader and critic responses continued to one degree or another for the *Rama* sequels in the early 1990s.

Some of the reaction no doubt came from established writers who resented the fact that Gentry Lee, who was not a professional writer but a space scientist, hitched his name to Arthur C. Clarke's and received half the seven-figure advance for a three-book contract.

"The Clarke-Lee collaboration," wrote Clarke, "is much like thousands of other coauthorships, but during the past few years Scott has got me involved in several more unusual deals. It hasn't been very difficult, because curiosity is my most abiding characteristic, and I tend to agree with the British nobleman who told his son: 'Try everything once—except incest and folk-dancing.'"

Another project the Scott Meredith Agency handled, a more straightforward use of Clarke's name, was a series of six paperbacks, published by Byron Preiss/Avon Books and written by Paul Preuss: *Arthur C. Clarke's Venus Prime V.*

"They are loosely based on short stories of mine, and in each case I have contributed an afterword," says Clarke. "But the novels themselves, as is clearly stated, are all written by Paul Preuss, and I did not agree to the project until I had read some of his excellent fiction (and nonfiction).

"The use of an author's name on projects with which he is only marginally—or not at all—connected is known as 'franchising' and is of course well known in the fields of sport and entertainment. Literary agent Richard Curtis, biting the hand that feeds him, has wittily termed the practice 'strip-mining an author'; perhaps it is better than mind-stripping, a torture much practiced in Hollywood's gilded gulags."

Clarke had a less fortunate experience with another "unusual deal" made during the mid-1980s. In 1986 he was putting the finishing touches on and adding his editorial stamp of approval to a book of essays (and slick visuals) about the future by *Omni* magazine writers. The previous year he had edited this anthology and written its introduction. It was *Arthur C. Clarke's July 10, 2019*, an idea conceived by Robert Weil, then an editor at the magazine.

"I got very excited about the idea of taking one day in the life of the future—the fiftieth anniversary of the Apollo moon landing—and writing a book about it," says Weil. Clarke also thought it was a great idea when he saw the proposal and agreed to lend his name to it. This was all Weil needed; he sold it immediately to Macmillan in 1985.

When the book was finally published in late 1986, however, Clarke was disturbed that Macmillan was marketing it as if it were *his* book and not the work of several writers whose chapters he'd overseen and finally approved. In a very short list of acknowledgments, various people were thanked for their contributions, but a reader would be hard-pressed to know that they were the actual writers of the book.

The publisher was trading on the Clarke name, which in itself was not a problem—that's what Macmillan had bought, after all. Clarke, however, objected to the way the group authorship was hidden from the reader.

"To add insult to injury (and the many distinguished contributors were undoubtedly injured)," Clarke wrote later, "I was never sent the final proofs, so didn't know what happened until it was too late. (Almost equally annoying were the stupid sub-sub-editorial mistakes that I never had a chance of correcting.)"

Earlier on he had agreed to promote the book on ABC's "Good Morning America" via satellite link, but he canceled when he realized the publisher was promoting *2019* as if it were his book.

Fortunately, a celestial event that had occurred in April 1986 spurred Clarke on to a new solo effort. He saw Comet Halley from his rooftop for the first time. His fourteen-inch Celestron, with its binocular eyepieces, provided the view despite the city lights. Later he saw the comet's featherlike tail spread across the stars.

"I realised that its next appearance, in 2061, would provide a splendid opportunity for a third *Space Odyssey*." Comet Halley thus made its important appearance in Clarke's novel in progress, *2061: Odyssey Three*.

On May 26 of the same year, *The Songs of Distant Earth* was published in the United States. Besides admirably fulfilling the requirements of hard science fiction, the novel tells the story of a love affair between a man and a woman put up against the vast impersonal gulfs of space and time and future generations. Thematically, as in much of Clarke's fiction, there is the quest for a purpose and the immortality of the species in contrast to the certain death of the individual. The loneliness of man is intensified by the immensity of cosmic space and the finiteness of human time. Even if the survival of *Homo sapiens* is assured through interstellar travel, are not individuals doomed even as they embrace in love and light to keep the fall of night at bay? Clarke's "songs of distant earth" are not as joyous and uplifting as we might first expect. Always present in the novel is the feeling of insurmountable separation across the voids of space, time, and death.

"I tried to write a lyrical book; I wanted to make people cry," Clarke told John Cunningham of *The Guardian*. "I'm rather tired of critics going on about the lack of characterisation, and my rather flat prose."

Most reviewers believed he succeeded. "In his 70th year, he's written a novel to prove to the critics he cares as much about human beings as scientific concepts," wrote Cunningham.

This interstellar novel was a blueprint for utopia, a "cosmic yet essentially serene tale," wrote another reviewer, which rewarded him the more he thought about it.

Ian Watson, a British writer and reviewer, believed it could change the way we view reality. "*The Songs of Distant Earth*," he wrote, "is certainly a novel to hand to any adolescent SF fan, to make them think and feel differently about the universe, the future, and fellow life." The novel remains a favorite of Clarke's to this day.

In July 1986 more than four million readers of *Playboy* read the featured Arthur C. Clarke interview: "a candid conversation about the future of space travel—and about sex, immortality and '2001'—with the witty dean of science-fiction writers."

Ken Kelley, the interviewer, had visited Sri Lanka for a week and a half, interviewing Clarke several times and also hanging about to absorb his unique lifestyle and character.

Clarke's prolific output was discussed (his opus numbers were over six hundred in the fall of 1985 when the interview was conducted), and then they talked about the difference between extrapolation and prediction. Clarke had always emphasized that

he was extrapolating, not predicting, but Kelley got him to admit
that sometimes when he extrapolates he is trying to predict. Then
the interviewer brought up some of the earlier Clarke predictions
that had turned out wrong: that Clarke himself would go to the
moon by 1980 (stated in 1966); that mankind would have landed
on other planets by 1980 (also said in 1966); and that actual
colonization of other planets would take place by the year 2000
(same 1966 interview).

"You're trying to pin me to the wall," Clarke protested, "and
believe me, it's a tough job being a prognosticator—for instance,
the success of Apollo and then trying to recover from the imme-
diate-post-Apollo emotions. I remember standing next to Vice
President Spiro Agnew, just after he'd seen the Apollo Two leave,
and hearing him say, 'Now we must go to Mars.' It seemed quite
reasonable that we'd be on Mars during this century. And we
would have if the momentum had continued."

The *Odyssey* trilogy was discussed, including the mysterious
monolith: "I like to think of the monolith as a sort of cosmic Swiss
army knife—it does whatever it *wants* to do," Clarke told his
interviewer. His slightly changing position on SDI/"Star Wars"
came up ("Reagan's Star Wars may turn out to be a stroke of
political genius, even if his motivations and political conclusions
are quite wrong . . ."), but he was steadfast in his conviction that
the long-term solutions were diplomatic ones.

About the *Challenger* accident early in 1986: "The [final]
shuttle is simply the wrong system. It was designed, then
redesigned by Congress," Clarke said, convinced that budgetary
cuts created some of the problems that may have ultimately resulted in the accident. But he still believed, as he had stated before
the *Challenger* explosion, that catastrophes were inevitable in such
complex systems.

Toward the end of the interview the conversation turned to
sex—a topic that Clarke rarely talks about in public.

Some school boards in the United States banned *Imperial
Earth* because of references to a homosexual relationship the
protagonist, Duncan Makenzie, had when he was young. When
Kelley used the word *lover* Clarke thought the word was too
strong.

"They'd just mucked around as boys," he said, adding that

there was "a whiff of that in *Rendezvous with Rama*, too. I guess I get more and more daring as I get older."

Kelley then asked Clarke what he meant by that.

"I guess I just don't give a damn anymore," he replied. There was a pause. "Maybe that isn't true, actually. One of my problems now is that I'm not just a private citizen anymore. I have to keep up certain standards, or at least pretend to, so I don't shock too many people."

Bisexuality was discussed. "I think Freud said something to the effect that we're *all* polymorphously perverse, you know. And, of course, we are," Clarke said, adding (when asked) that he had had bisexual experiences.

"Who hasn't? Good God! If anyone had ever told me that he hadn't, I'd have told him he was lying. But then, of course, people tend to 'forget' their encounters. I don't want to go into detail about my own life, but I just want it to be noted that I have a rather relaxed sympathetic attitude about it—and that's something I've not really said out loud before. Let's move on."

The novel *2010* also briefly alludes to bisexuality, when Heywood Floyd questions his own motivation for talking to one of the crew members about a relationship that was causing some stress in another member of the crew.

"So the intervention had been worthwhile, whatever the impulse behind it. Even if, as Floyd sometimes ruefully suspected, it was no more than the secret envy that normal homo- or heterosexuals feel, if completely honest with themselves, toward cheerfully well-adjusted polymorphs."

The Ghost from the Grand Banks (1990) briefly describes a lesbian relationship between Edith Craig and her psychiatrist's nurse. It also describes a bordello, "the Villa," near Gatwick Airport, and a somewhat unusual case history of one of its clients, "O.G.," a successful engineer who enjoys various forms of bondage.

Alfred C. Kinsey's study *Sexual Behavior in the Human Male*, first published in 1948, had a tremendous influence on Clarke when he was in his early thirties. This landmark study allowed him to gain an objective perspective on his own sexuality, and this became very important to him.

One friend remembers Clarke coming into the White Horse pub in London one evening with a copy of the Kinsey report and being much more effervescent than usual. Apparently the book had given him a new confidence in his own sexuality; he could compare himself with all the people whom Kinsey had interviewed.

Had Kinsey included the United Kingdom in his data base, Clarke would have been ready to help.

"At one time I kept a chart of the number of times I masturbated! And when Kinsey published his results, I was astonished at how feeble Americans were," Clarke says, laughing.

During the same month that the *Playboy* interview appeared, Clarke went to London to attend an H. G. Wells Symposium and then on to Bishops Lydeard to visit family. During the trip he was not feeling well.

"I'm walking with difficulty, and tiring easily," he wrote to friends. Because of these symptoms, he decided to get a complete checkup at London's National Hospital for Nervous Diseases.

"Arthur was having difficulty walking and balancing," says brother Fred, "and so he arranged to have a checkup. Hector went with him to the hospital. After the examination, the doctors told Arthur he had only fifteen months to live. Their diagnosis was that he had amyotrophic lateral sclerosis, commonly known as Lou Gehrig's disease in the United States. It is a degenerative motor neuron disease of the spinal cord and brain.

"The first time I really saw Arthur," says Fred, "was when he came out of the hospital. And Hector was livid because they had told Arthur. Hector was furious. He believed that you never tell a person that sort of thing, no matter what the situation is. Some people would break up immediately.

"It depends on the doctor, of course, whether a patient is told or not," says Fred. "In this case the doctor thought Arthur was the sort who would really want to know.

"When I saw him, he was very subdued and obviously not too happy about things. But after the initial shock, Arthur more or less said, damn it, he'd got an enormous amount he wanted to do, and if he's only got fifteen months to do it, he'd better whack into it. And he did whack into it, and the next year he produced four books.

"Eighteen months later he was still writing, and all the horrible things they told him might happen hadn't happened to him. Of course they had told him all the things he should do to keep it under control—what diets to take and what exercises to do, which he very religiously did. He carried on working intensely and produced an enormous amount of work, which might have been the saving grace. If he had been the sort to say, 'Oh my God, I'm going to die in fifteen months,' he probably would have.

"By the end of eighteen months and all this work behind him, and able to walk better than he could before, he thought, Well, I better have a second opinion. With the help of his friends in Washington, a complete and thorough examination was set up for the summer of 1988 at Johns Hopkins."

Soon after the London diagnosis, Clarke updated his friends. "Saw Neuro-specialists who gave gloomy diagnosis. Rather depressed until I reminded myself (a) I'm not a baseball player so my career will be, if anything, assisted (b) my two typing fingers will be the last to go (3) a high-tech wheelchair might be fun to play with. (Stephen Hawking is now a source of much inspiration.) Started taking intensive physiotherapy in an attempt to prove the experts wrong."

Not surprisingly, Clarke did prove them wrong. He worked hard on his body. His physiotherapist was first-class, and Clarke received treatment three times a week. He considered himself in better physical and mental shape than he'd been in for years.

"The only problem is my undercarriage—sometimes I can walk perfectly normally, but at other times I limp badly," he wrote to Roger Caras in late October. "I still don't need to use a stick and may graduate directly to a hi-tech wheelchair (solar powered, computer controlled, video etc.)."

When science fiction's own magazine *Locus* reported Clarke as "frail-looking" in September (from seeing him in London in July), he was mildly miffed and wrote a letter to Charlie Brown, the editor, saying that a more accurate description would be "clumsy."

"I'm now glad to say that, since my return to Colombo, daily physiotherapy and massive vitamin inputs have restored my mobility almost to normal. (How many *Locus* readers can walk across the room, *backwards*, balancing the Ray Bradbury omnibus on their head?) My personal physician gives me until 2001; then he'll take an option on 2010. Frankly, I've not felt so well for years and am now involved in about twenty projects, including two movies and a novel [*2061: Odyssey Three*]. If I *am* eventually incapacitated I'll get wired into a word-processor—and then, Isaac, look out!"

Throughout the rest of 1986, Clarke continued to play table tennis at the Otters Club for an hour or more each day and was beating all his opponents, at least some of the time.

"Arthur gets a charge out of seeing and talking with people there," says Gentry Lee. "He's eccentric, lovable, humorous—*puckish* is a good adjective, and not one that most people would think of—while he challenges and plays table tennis with the young people."

Fit as he claimed to be, he decided to play it safe and cancel all engagements with one exception—the Nehru Memorial Lecture in the fall—because he considered it a true honor and the travel was not too strenuous.

Clarke's personal physician, Dr. Theva Buell, traveled with him to New Delhi, where he delivered the lecture "Space Wars and Space Peace" (the variant title on the printed text itself was "Star Wars and Star Peace") on November 13. His address gave an overview of some of the SDI scenarios and discussed what he believed to be some of the inherent problems of such systems, including their destabilizing influence. The last half of his lecture emphasized the peaceful uses of space such as reconnaissance satellites that had no offensive capability ("Peacesats") and helped to build international trust.

Concluding, he spoke of his vision of the global family, brought together by the telecommunications revolution; "its loyalties and interests will transcend all the ancient frontiers," he said. And speaking of the age of the dinosaurs and their extinction, he said, "Intelligence, not armor, was to inherit the Earth. May it do so once again."

Prime Minister Rajiv Gandhi then arranged a special flight to Agra and the Taj Mahal. Although Clarke taxed his strength with a long walk through the gardens there, he said it was well worth it.

"Incredibly, the Taj Mahal is *not* over-rated," he later wrote to friends. It was "a pretty good finale to the 35 years of globe-trotting."

The last month of 1986 gave Clarke an opportunity to reflect on the year that soon would be history. It was a year of major setbacks: the space shuttle program was grounded indefinitely after the worst space disaster in history, and Arthur C. Clarke was diagnosed with a terminal illness.

But the positive notes were there also. He was still alive and feeling reasonably healthy as the New Year approached—no matter what the doctors said. It was also natural to think of one's legacy after being diagnosed as terminally ill. Such thoughts no doubt motivated him to establish in 1986 the annual Arthur C. Clarke Award, sponsored by the Science Fiction Foundation of Britain and given for the best science fiction novel published in the United Kingdom. Margaret Atwood won the award and its thousand-pound cash prize for the first year for *The Handmaid's Tale*.

Much of Clarke's good work would remain, even if *he* didn't last out the decade. But that thought of legacy, perhaps positive from an immense Stapledonian perspective, didn't offer much emotional comfort. Instead he went to his work. It was always there for him. That is what Arthur C. Clarke put up against the fall of night.

*My great-grandfather Arthur Heal barely missed the century
mark, dying in the year I was born and passing on his name
to me. . . . We farm boys have good genes.*
                          Arthur C. Clarke's July 20, 2019 (1986)

31
THREESCORE AND TEN

As Arthur C. Clarke approached the age of seventy, his opus
number climbed toward seven hundred—a body of work that most
writers would be ecstatic to produce in a lifetime. Perhaps Clarke
really was feeling the urgency imposed by age and ill health. Or
maybe it was simply that the muse would no longer be denied.
Whatever his motivations, in early 1987 he had apparently forgotten his protestations—pronouncements, delivered intermittently
through the 1970s, that he would write no more—and was hard at
work at the keyboard of his portable Kaypro 2000.

The major work in progress was *2061: Odyssey Three*, and he
continued to devote most of his time to it. "I hid out in a hotel
near Galle recently and did 10,000 words of ODYSSEY III on it in
four days," he wrote to Roger Caras in early May.

When he finished the book not long afterward, Clarke began
to itch for a new project, and by the end of July he had begun his
rather chatty work on early science fiction and science fiction
writers who appeared in the pulp magazines of the late 1920s and
1930s. These early stories had stirred Clarke's fantasies and fired
his imagination, so this work was pure nostalgia for him. What his

memory couldn't bring forth his personal library could. He began writing on July 30, 1987, and completed the manuscript on November 13 after a consistent daily effort. *Astounding Days: A Science Fictional Autobiography*, was "Gratefully and affectionately dedicated to the memories of Harry Bates/F. Orlin Tremaine/ John W. Campbell."

When it was published in Great Britain in May 1989, Clarke's longtime American friend Isaac Asimov wrote a review for the *Observer* titled "King Arthur's Heavenly Nostalgia." While the review was a friendly piece, it was not blatant puff: "The contents deal almost entirely with the authors and stories of the first 15 years of that magazine, the period that culminated in what will always be the Golden Age (to science fiction people of my age and Arthur's) under John W. Campbell."

The review expresses Asimov's genuine appreciation of and love for his friend: "Clarke is incapable of nastiness or captiousness. He discusses stories that in some cases were sub-literary, but does not use his own mastery of the field to sneer at them and reduce them to literary rubble. He remembers them as he enjoyed them at the time. His concern is not with their literary values, but with their ideas. . . ."

With a second book behind him that year, Clarke's own endless store of ideas began to foment a new novel. "I was once again beginning to feel those nagging guilt pains that assail an author when he's not Working On A Project," he wrote in 1989.

The result of this literary restlessness was an outline for a sequel to his much praised novel *Rendezvous with Rama*. Here's what happened.

Gentry Lee arrived in Sri Lanka in late July 1987 for the final working session on *Cradle*.

"We were halfway through *Cradle*," recalls Lee, "and Arthur had not made much comment to me at all. I didn't know whether he thought it was good or bad, but everybody assured me he thought it was fine, given the amount of experience I had had. . . .

"We were finishing up the novel, sitting in his library, and he gave me his schedule for the next year. One of the things on it was a sequel to *Rendezvous with Rama*, and it said '(with collaborator).' And I knew what he was doing. He was playing a game—that was his way of asking me if I wanted to collaborate with him on the sequel."

Lee was thrilled, of course, and they discussed how they would approach it. What with Lee's expertise in the space sciences, this would be an ideal project on which to collaborate.

First they brainstormed and produced an outline, which was then sent on to Scott Meredith.

"In a remarkably short time Scott had sold a whole package to Bantam's Lou Aronica," wrote Clarke. It was originally defined as a sequel to *Rendezvous with Rama*, plus two other books, which were not named at that time. Ultimately the two other books were sequels to *Rama II: The Garden of Rama* and *Rama Revealed*, written from 1989 to 1991. That Clarke and Lee got along and worked well together was more than half the battle. They genuinely enjoyed one another, and Lee willingly traveled halfway around the world for working sessions with Clarke and enjoyed the travel and the different culture of Sri Lanka—at least when things were not out of control.

Political unrest had been heating up in Sri Lanka all year. In their spring 1987 correspondence Roger Caras had expressed concern for Clarke's safety because of recent violence. There had been two massacres in the east and random killing at a bus station. Caras pleaded with his friend to get out while he could—before he too became a victim. "You can't live with your head in a bag," said Caras.

"The situation is indeed tragic, yet it's amazing how things continue normally," Clarke replied, adding that he had been taking some action by shipping some files and important books back to his brother Fred for the "Clarkives."

"And," he told Caras, "we have a pied-à-terre in Australia." Hector Ekanayake's wife, Valerie, was Australian, the girls half Australian; it would be a logical place for the family to live if things went from bad to worse in Sri Lanka. With this in mind, an apartment was purchased in Brisbane, to be leased in the meantime, in case the family was forced to escape the country.

Toward the end of Gentry Lee's July 1987 visit things got rougher in Sri Lanka. It was not even safe in the streets of Colombo.

"When I was there in '87," says Lee, "the Sri Lankan government had just signed an agreement with India to allow Indian troops to come into the country and help control the separatist Tamils—the Hindu minority who were trying to secede. Because of this agreement with India, another group of Ceylonese extremists and terrorists, the Sinhalese People's Liberation Front (JVP), had gone wild and burned down the state building in Colombo and a lot of other things. I was over at Arthur's house, and things got very uncomfortable in the city. I had to make my way back to the Meridian Hotel in downtown Colombo, where I was staying, and I saw all sorts of terrible things along the way. We were stopped once by a soldier who'd stuck his machine gun into my chest in the back seat of the car.

"Just as I went in the front door of the hotel, shots rang out. I went up to the second floor, where the foreigners who had courage were sitting out by the swimming pool, leaning over and watching some Sri Lankan gunmen shoot down a couple of students who were trying to burn a bus right outside. They slapped a curfew on the whole town, and I had to bribe a taxi driver to get me out of Colombo to the airport to get home.

"Now that the JVP has been [temporarily] destroyed, it's just the conflict between the Sinhalese and the Tamils again."

Lee was back in Sri Lanka in January 1988 for another work session with Clarke.

"We holed up in a beach hotel with my KAYPRO 2000 portable and produced a 10k word treatment of RAMA II—as well as the outline of RAMA III," Clarke told friends in his newsy "Egogram."

When people ask Lee how he and Clarke work together, he tells them, "'The creative process we do together, and then I do the writing process with Arthur looking over my shoulder.' Then they say, 'Well, that doesn't sound like he's doing that much.' And I say, 'You don't understand that the creative process is where the ideas, the great sweeping interactions between character and situation, get developed. You couldn't have two people doing the writing process—it would be disjointed.'

"It's not as if there's a left brain mechanism where we follow a structure," says Lee. "It's literally sitting down after the BBC news, staring around at the palm trees in a southern Sri Lankan resort, and just saying, 'Well, what do you think about this?' Then my job is to weave these things together.

"The next day I'd say to him, 'OK, if you put this thing together that you talked about and this thing that we both talked about and these in the story, then we'll have a first quarter of the novel that looks like this.' Then he'll say, 'No, no, that won't work for the following reasons. And by the way, last night I had a dream about such and such, and that reminded me of such and such,' and then he says that 'somehow that ought to fit into the story, but I just can't see how.' And I get all excited and I'll jump up and I'll say, 'That's great! Suppose we put that in this piece' and so on. And now all of a sudden we're working in the back third of the novel, whereas we had thought that morning we were going to work on the first quarter.

"A lot of people misunderstood what we were doing by breaking the novel into parts and actually thought that Arthur had written some of them and that I had written others. It was amusing to us that people would spend time (particularly the Japanese, who like to analyze everything) trying to figure out who contributed what in *Cradle*.

"We both admitted that *Cradle* was on the one hand very good for a first collaboration and on the second hand not quite as good as we thought it ought to be.

"Arthur was a little bit uncomfortable after *Cradle* came out because there were things that I did in the writing process that were not consistent with his personality—the explicit sexuality, for one. . . . I admit the sex was overdone.

"When we began *Rama II*, I went to Arthur and said, 'I know you've been a little embarrassed by all this,' and he never gave me a bad time about it. He would laughingly say when people would give him a hard time, 'Well, that's my friend Gentry.' So in *Rama II* we pushed the sex into the background.

"I love working with Arthur," says Lee. "Not only is he a mentor, but he is a friend and even a surrogate father at times. We have a great time together."

It was a happy partnership, with Lee handling all the communications between publisher and editor and agent ("so that Arthur wouldn't be battered"). This helped Clarke achieve his lifelong goal of avoiding the mundane "mechanics of life," as he said, and gave him more time for creative endeavors and play—his specialty in childhood and adulthood.

Of course for Arthur C. Clarke, the self-proclaimed perpetual nineteen-year-old, the point at which childhood ended and adulthood began is difficult to identify. When he celebrated his seventieth birthday on December 16, 1987, his new age seemed rather unreal to him. "I still don't believe it," he told friends afterward.

He entertained special visitors for the occasion.

"My old friend, the ECHO and TELSTAR pioneer Dr. John Pierce, arrived with his new wife Brenda to receive the 2nd Arthur Clarke Award. President Jayewardene cut the cake, and we all took part in a Colombo-Washington live panel discussion via USIA's WORLDNET with Fred Durant (Arthur Clarke Foundation), Todd Hawley (International Space University), Joseph Pelton (INTEL-SAT)."

This Clarke award, not to be confused with that given for science fiction, recognizes "vision and achievement in global communications." The first one went to Dr. John McLucas, chairman of the International Space Year, 1992, and onetime Comsat vice-president and secretary of the U.S. Air Force.

"We went to the award ceremony in his red Mercedes, with the little flag flying on the left front fender, showing that he was Chancellor of the University of Moratuwa," recalls Pierce. "It was quite a colorful ceremony. We all traipsed in covered with flowers. There was a sort of band of antique instruments, and they lit this huge candlelike lamp—all very colorful.

"My wife and I were there about ten days. After we'd been there a couple of days and had gotten to know Sinhalese a little bit, my wife asked Arthur, 'Is there a word corresponding to *mañana* in Sinhalese?' And he said, 'Yes, but it doesn't have the same sense of urgency.' We left a few days after his birthday."

Dr. Cyril Ponnamperuma, first director of the Clarke Centre, was also there, and he brought a birthday surprise: a felicitation volume, with messages from the famous and not-so-famous friends of Arthur C. Clarke.

"It was my privilege to gather this bouquet for you," Ponnamperuma wrote in *his* birthday letter to Clarke. "The outpouring of affection, appreciation, and admiration from world leaders in the art and technology of communication is a powerful testament. Your preeminent position in the 'Global Village' which you helped to forge from the babel of sounds on planet Earth is recorded for posterity."

There were letters from Neil Armstrong, Isaac Asimov, Walter Cronkite, Norman Mailer, Gene Roddenberry, Carl Sagan, Ted

Turner, and many others. An impressive verbal outpouring for Clarke's seventieth—what he jokingly called "embarrassingly fulsome messages."

Back in Great Britain, Fred and Michael Clarke represented their older brother in yet another ceremony. The mayor of Minehead unveiled a plaque at the old Clarke house at 13 Blenheim Road. "All this," said Clarke, "gave me a distinctly posthumous sensation."

The release of *2061: Odyssey Three* in the fall of 1987 was an extra present for Clarke's seventieth birthday. The last of the odysseys (so far!) was quite an accomplishment for someone who, according to the London doctors, was lucky to be alive.

And Clarke was not just alive but youthful—a condition he attributes to the company of his extended family. "Having young people around me, particularly these delightful little girls [Hector and Valerie Ekanayake's daughters], just makes me feel young, you see. Just the other day, Tamara, the middle one, left a little note that I found on my desk, which said, 'I love you, and I hope you love me.' Those little things happen and brighten my days."

When the little girls' father, Hector Ekanayake, turned forty-eight on January 14, 1988, Clarke forgot all about it. But when Cherene turned eight on January 11, Clarke bought her present early: "a tiny bundle of fluff I've named Dainty, after one of the cairn terriers Mother had at the farm half a century ago. This Dainty is one of the most engaging puppies I've ever known—and bullies Rikki though he's about fifty times her size."

At the age of seventy, Arthur C. Clarke had no reason to fear the onslaught of a second childhood. He had never left his first—an advantage to any creative person.

That advantage aside, Clarke's adult accomplishments—up to and during 1987—were many. He had seen, albeit from long distance, the International Space University, which was established in large part because of his inspiration and encouragement of "the gang of three" (Todd Hawley, Peter Diamandis, and Bob Richards), hold its April 1987 Founding Conference. He had received the Tenth Charles A. Lindbergh Award, one of his highest honors, given to recognize an individual whose lifetime's work has contributed to the balance of technological advancement and preservation of the environment. Describing the reenactment of the historic landing held during the Paris award ceremonies, Clarke said, "I was at the Le Bourget Airport watching a perfect replica of the *Spirit of St. Louis* land exactly sixty years later, while a Concorde took off on the next runway!"

In conflict with his willing spirit, unfortunately, Clarke's ailing body made trips like that to Paris persistently taxing. Although he felt reasonably fit in the spring of 1987, his walking was either difficult or normal, depending on what day you asked. While he was in Paris, Clarke's doctor friends, Susott and di Pietro, flew in from New York to look after him. And a year later, before boarding the *Queen Elizabeth II* to sail to see the total eclipse on March 18, 1988, Clarke wrote to friends, "I look forward to giving a few talks and meeting interesting people on what may very well be my last trip outside Sri Lanka. Although I still think I've a fair chance of seeing 2001, even before my current disability travelling was becoming too time- and energy-consuming, while telecommunications and visitors steadily reduced its importance to me."

As much as Clarke wanted to remain in Sri Lanka in the summer of 1988, his physical condition warranted outside medical attention. But it took some real behind-the-scenes maneuvering by several people to get him to leave home.

"We had a visit by a chap named Michael Snowden," says Clarke, "the only one I know of a vanishing species, of which Percival Lowell is a prototype—a gentleman astronomer. Michael travels around the world, living where he pleases. These days all a professional astronomer needs is a desk and a computer, and he can work anywhere he likes.

"Michael got very friendly with us during his visits to Sri Lanka. When he visited Barnes Place in 1988, he noticed my health and was worried about my mental and physical deterioration.

"Well, it so happens that Michael and Jay Keyworth (President Reagan's science adviser for six years) are best friends. They were college roommates together. In fact, Michael is godfather to Keyworth's son, George Jr. So Michael wrote Keyworth and told him about my declining health. And then Keyworth wrote to Valerie and Hector behind my back.

"I was quite willing to go, really, but I just didn't have the strength because of some kind of pneumonia which I had for the whole of 1988. It just knocked me out. I was getting treatment in Colombo, but there wasn't much improvement. I began to think that it may be the moist environment, some kind of allergy. I'm in a closed air-conditioned room, and the carpets mildew. This was my state when Jay made the necessary arrangements for me to fly to the United States and have a thorough, several-day examination at Johns Hopkins Hospital in Baltimore."

The examination would confirm or refute the 1986 London diagnosis of Lou Gehrig's disease. Hector Ekanayake accompanied Clarke on the trip, which took them through England as usual before they flew on to the United States. They were in London for four days. Even though Clarke was in a wheelchair, there was one media event he was eager to participate in—a videotaping session with Dr. Stephen Hawking in a London studio and (via satellite link) Carl Sagan at Cornell University in Ithaca, New York.

The discussion ("God, the Universe and Everything Else") never aired as intended, but there's little question that it will air (or certainly portions thereof) at some future date. The narrator, Magnus Magnusson, introduced this trinity of intellect.

"Tonight: The time before time began. The universe, black holes, God, and the laws of science. Professor Stephen Hawking, Dr. Carl Sagan, and Arthur C. Clarke discuss the mysteries man faces as he starts to explore the stars."

Besides freewheeling discussions among Clarke, Hawking, and Sagan about the universe (its beginning and its ending), unified field theory, extraterrestrial life, and interstellar travel, the narrator asked Clarke to do some computer doodling with what mathematicians call a Mandelbrot Set, named in honor of a French scientist working for IBM. It is a mathematical equation that leads toward the infinite, making the universe visual.

"You can use the computer as microscope," said Clarke, "and you can continue that process forever. Some of the images are incredibly beautiful and are going to have a great impact on artistic design in the next decade or so. I found what looked like black holes, and I'd like to show them to you."

Clarke zoomed in on the screen, magnified the image about a thousand times, and came to a so-called black hole. The original picture he had shown the audience was now about five hundred feet across, and the screen was showing a detail from it. After the next magnification the original Mandelbrot Set's image would be about ten million miles wide.

"This is black hole number three," said Clarke. "And this one took me twenty-two hours of computing. The day before I left Sri Lanka, I had the computer running all night. I'm rather proud of this one because on this scale that original little picture you saw is the width of the orbit of Mars. So you understand that no human being has ever seen that picture pattern before, simply because of probabilities.

"You can go on forever and ever," he continued. "Now I would like to ask Stephen this question. Is the real universe also infinite in detail? I mean we know we have molecules, atoms, electrons, protons, subatomic right down to the quarks so far, but does it continue forever and ever, or is there a limit, is there a basement to the real universe?"

Stephen Hawking's computer-driven voice synthesizer answered to the will of its owner.

"We will discover new structures when we look at the universe on smaller and smaller scales," Hawking said, "but in the case of the universe, there seems to be a limiting scale. It is called Planck length, and this is about a million billion billion times smaller than an inch. This means that there is a limit to how complex the universe can be. It also means that a universe could be destroyed by a theory that is fairly simple at least on scales of the Planck length. I just hope that we are smart enough to find it."

Clarke, of course, was about to embark on a fantastic voyage closer to home—into his own ailing body—and he and Ekanayake flew into Dulles Airport outside of Washington, D.C., on July 13. John McLucas was there to meet them.

"He was sitting in a wheelchair," recalls McLucas, "which they had ready for him as soon as he got off the plane. I met him in the area where you meet international visitors, and then we managed to get the car as close to the exit as we could. He was quite preoccupied with his malady and about how there seemed to be some difference in the medical views. But he was looking forward to the diagnosis by the Johns Hopkins team."

McLucas drove Clarke and Ekanayake to Baltimore, where they checked into the Johns Hopkins Inn, just across the street from the hospital. The testing began the next day under the direction of Dr. Daniel B. Drachman, director of the Neuromuscular Unit at Johns Hopkins.

"I was somewhat unprepared for the sight that originally greeted me when he arrived in our clinic," recalled Drachman. "He had come from the front entrance of Johns Hopkins via wheel-chair. He was being wheeled by Hector and was sitting in the chair wearing what I can only describe as a 'team jacket' and peaked sort of baseball cap. This unassuming appearance was entirely consistent with his compliant behavior as a patient."

The entire evaluation process took about a week, and Dr. Drachman knew nothing about the 1986 London diagnosis of amyotrophic lateral sclerosis until his last meeting with Clarke.

"He was very coy about that," said Drachman. "He didn't even tell me about the earlier diagnosis of ALS until after we had done all our tests and electromyography and biopsy. The electromyography in fact showed that he had very long-standing, quite old muscle denervation—the muscle had lost its nerve supply a long time previously.

"I insisted that he hold still for a biopsy, and that really gave it away. That showed very striking features of so-called target fibers. These are characteristic of old denervation—an attempt of the nerves to resupply the muscles. So having seen that and all other test data, I simply put it together and decided he had old polio."

After the medical tests were completed, Clarke and Ekanayake left Baltimore and checked into the Holiday Inn at Chevy Chase, conveniently located near the Durants' home. Here Clarke rested quietly and recuperated from the biopsy surgery on his leg. He was cheerful enough, and he was eager to hear the full and formal test results from Dr. Drachman.

"Just as I was summarizing all the results for him during our last meeting and telling him I thought he had a case of postpolio syndrome, he pulled out this earlier diagnosis and confronted me with the fact that the London doctor had made this other diagnosis, which, although it's hard to say, may have been made a bit casually. The diagnosis of ALS, since it carries with it such a dire prognosis, should be made only when you're absolutely sure. It doesn't do anybody any good to know early on. I am very circumspect about making that diagnosis. But with Arthur, I felt very fortunate to be able to bring him good news.

"Arthur's immediate reaction to the good news that he did not have ALS was an expression of relief that he would live till the year 2001. The second reaction was a rather mischievous satisfaction regarding the misdiagnosis by my British colleague."

Dr. Drachman judged Clarke a "terrific patient." "People who are well known or celebrated can be terrible patients," he said. "They can be very demanding or directing. They can ruin their medical care. Arthur was quite the opposite. He was compliant but not passive. He went along. He was trusting. He was very modest in a funny way. That really is a characteristic of his—that he has a curious combination of modesty and the opposite.

"He has a very open approach to everything, and he's constantly—I can't quite say astonished—intrigued by new impressions. He's always amused and always quite open to new ideas—an intellectual curiosity."

Later Clarke told friends in a newsy letter, "The Johns Hopkins specialists diagnosed something much less serious [than ALS]—the recently discovered Post-Polio Syndrome. This was both a relief and a surprise, since my complete paralysis in 1962 had been attributed to a spinal injury. The prognosis now is that instead of having already used up most of an ALS victim's usual 2–5 years of survival, I have a good chance of seeing 2001, even if from a wheelchair (which, I have discovered, is the secret ingredient required for painless transit through today's over-crowded airports)."

Clarke wasn't completely immobilized during his stay at Johns Hopkins. On July 19 he went to Hughes Network Systems to be taped as part of the twenty-fifth anniversary of the first synchronous satellite, *Syncom 2*, in orbit in July 1963. After checking into his motel, he continued to rest and received a few close friends and visitors each day as his leg healed. He made hundreds of phone calls to friends and colleagues in the United States and spoke to all but a few whom he couldn't reach or track down. And he saw many of his Washington friends at a cocktail party hosted by the Durants for him on July 24.

Shortly before he left the United States, Clarke, Durant, Ekanayake, and writer Gregory Benford visited the National Air and Space Museum. "He was much on the up when I saw him at the museum," says Benford, "just days after his good medical news. Among other things, we talked about contemporary science fiction and both agreed that it doesn't take very much of a long perspective, that the recent fashion has been very near future with somewhat repetitive themes. We started talking about *Against the Fall of Night*, and at some point I noted that his early novel had been written before the discovery of DNA—that biology really had been left out of the entire story.

"He then told me that he had deliberately fixed on the city in the desert in which biology had no rule, in part, because he'd never known anything about biology and was interested in the metaphor machines. And I said that it would be fun to look back at that and see if his early novel couldn't be reconciled with the world as we know it, because science had learned so much since he wrote it. He said that, yes, it would be a fun project, and I told him that I'd talk to my agent about it. That's how *Beyond the Fall of Night*, published in 1990, got started."

Actually, as was Clarke's pattern, he had been ruminating several ideas over 1987 and 1988. References to Bob Ballard and icebergs in his preeclipse letter indicated the incubation period for *The Ghost from the Grand Banks* had already begun. And the fact that the need for a separate contract for *2061* had left the second half of Clarke's 1984 two-book contract technically unfulfilled meant that his subconscious was probably already germinating *20,001*.

"I had a nice chat with the queen."
Arthur C. Clarke, October 1989

32
NEW LEASE ON LIFE

The summer of 1988 had brought Arthur C. Clarke a reprieve. No longer burdened by the threat of terminal illness, he was able to look beyond the upcoming decade to the new century—and a new millennium. He did so with characteristic relish, but also with hard-won realism—and his innate wry sense of humor.

Toward the end of April 1989 Clarke learned that the paperback edition of *2061: Odyssey Three* was on the *New York Times* bestseller list. When a friend asked, "Does the thrill remain for you?" he answered, "Not really. It didn't give quite as much thrill as my finding out I'd lost two pound weight, which is what I'm trying to do."

Clarke continued his recuperation from surgery in London and at Dene Court with Fred and Babbs Clarke for a week or so in early August. They drove Clarke to Minehead to see the house where he was born, and the owner's son took them through and showed them the grounds. When Clarke saw the garden hut in the backyard, he was flooded with memories of changing into his bathing suit there as a young boy before following the well-worn path down to the Minehead beach. More memories were called up, and new ones etched, when all four children of Charles and Nora Clarke were able to meet for a rare family luncheon.

Back in Colombo late in the month, Clarke was "full of energy and feeling about ten years younger," he wrote to friends. "Which is just as well, since to my amazement I am involved with four-teen (yes, 14) books and my first TV fiction series—A FALL OF MOONDUST."

By the fall of that year Clarke was feeling so young that, when representatives of the International Space University visited Sri Lanka and investigated the possibility of a future ISU campus there, even the possibility of a space shuttle ride to an orbiting campus of ISU in the early twenty-first century didn't seem all that outrageous.

As the new year began, unfortunately, the political situation in Arthur C. Clarke's corner of planet Earth was extremely unsta-ble. The terrorist Sinhalese People's Liberation Front was indis-criminately killing innocent people. In March, Clarke wrote to Willie Mendis, his longtime friend who was serving in Washing-ton as the minister of technology transfer at the Embassy of Sri Lanka. A mutual colleague, the vice chancellor of the University of Colombo, had recently been murdered in cold blood right in his office.

"I'm sorry to say that the situation here is still very gloomy as far as the University is concerned, and of course, you'll have heard about poor Stanley Wijesundara's murder.

"I dropped into the campus two days ago, and had a few words with Patu [Dr. Patuwathawithane, Arthur's vice chancellor at the University of Moratuwa]—he has received threats. For that matter, so have we, but we don't take them seriously."

The fact that Clarke was playing down such threats greatly concerned many of his friends, including Roger Caras. But before the year was out, Clarke's attitude would change.

In the meantime, March brought visits from two men who represented the major interests in his life—telecommunications and writing—and who pointed up the incredible range of Clarke's influence, both past and present.

When Joe Pelton, then director of policy planning for Intelsat, checked into the Intercontinental Hotel early in the month for lectures and other business, the manager offered him a suite for the price of a regular room. With all the political unrest cutting into tourism, said the manager, there were suites to spare. He then asked for a favor.

Someone in the Sri Lankan government had decided that receive-only satellite dishes would no longer be allowed, probably on the grounds that foreign information was somehow corrupting the citizens and undermining the government. The hotel manager told Pelton that the government had ordered the Intercontinental, other hotels, and businesses to take down their earth stations and reexport them. This was impossible to do, the manager explained, because the dishes were built at the Arthur C. Clarke Centre in Moratuwa just a few miles down the road. How could he reexport something that had never been imported?

Pelton had a meeting scheduled with the man who was in charge of international communications in Sri Lanka, Bernard Rodrigo, and he promised to bring up the matter then. As it happened, Rodrigo had a receiving dish at home and thought they were beneficial technology for Sri Lanka. He didn't even know why such a policy was in place.

He discovered that his own colleagues had come up with the restriction without his knowledge, and after a meeting the government policy was reversed—receive-only earth stations would be allowed after all, and the Arthur C. Clarke Centre for Modern Technologies could assemble them.

"Arthur was pleased as punch that this had come out of my visit," says Pelton. "He said he was going to inform President Premadasa about this and emphasize how valuable the centre can be to help create new and good government policy. The idea that he could help stimulate a more progressive policy in science and technology really excited him."

The government's decision to allow satellite reception bore fruit in early 1990, when Clarke attended a meeting at the Presidential Secretariat. Ted Turner and CNN had offered Sri Lanka five to ten minutes of free airtime each month on their "World Report" program. Clarke knew it was a wonderful opportunity, and he persuaded the decision makers that it would be good for the country. The Arthur C. Clarke Centre also officially began to act as the distributor for CNN in Sri Lanka in 1990.

It was not Clarke's first encounter with Ted Turner. In 1987 Turner wrote to Clarke to thank him for participating in the UN's "The Day of Five Billion" population program for global telecast.

"I'm looking forward to your participation in 'The Day of Six Billion,'" wrote Turner, "which should roughly coincide with the year of your first major odyssey."

Three years earlier the two men had met in person at the Beverly Wilshire Hotel, where Clarke walked up to Turner, held out his hand, and announced, "Oh, hello, Ted, you owe me ten percent of your income."

In mid-March, fellow British writer John Brunner arrived. Besides being considered one of the most influential British science fiction writers of the last thirty years, Brunner publishes mainstream fiction and poetry and is internationally known for his work.

During his visit to Sri Lanka, Brunner spent time with Clarke at Barnes Place, peering through Clarke's superb optics at the moon and southern constellations and talking literature. Brunner describes the influence Clarke's early work had on him:

"I read 'Rescue Party' when it first came out in 1946, and I remember going back and reading it again a few days later. It was an inspirational kind of story, very upbeat at a time when the world was in the shadow of the atomic bomb and there were an awful lot of downbeat stories in the magazines. When I first ran across it, it was very inspiring. And of all the novels, I still have to say that *Childhood's End* made the biggest impact on me, and I'm pretty certain that the majority of his fans were turned on to his work by the scope and range of that book."

Clarke was getting stronger all the time. Back to playing table tennis, he said, "It's a good sign that I'll live," and soon he was a fierce competitor again. By early April he was directing his mental energies toward getting started again on his new novel, a solo effort.

The novel had been gestating in his imagination for several years. He often discussed the latest technology and methods for raising the *Titanic* with his friend Charles Pellegrino, who had worked with Robert Ballard during the reconnaissance made by the submersible *Alvin* in 1986. In one of his letters to Clarke, Pellegrino admitted that he had very mixed emotions about actually raising the *Titanic*, even though he had been trying to figure out how it could be done for years.

"I told him I just wished the whole thing would go away with an avalanche on the Grand Banks—then no one ever would be

New Lease on Life 363

able to raise the ship again," says Pellegrino, whose misgivings about disturbing the gravesite of more than fifteen hundred people are shared by many.

The sinking of the *Titanic*, even though it occurred five years before Arthur C. Clarke was born, has always haunted him. One of the very first stories he ever wrote, in fact, "Icebergs in Space," was based on the *Titanic*.

"It must have been written around 1930, when I was at Ballifants and attending Huish's Grammar School in Taunton," says Clarke. This opus Clarke affectionately refers to as "a luckily long-lost epic. I am happy to say no copy survived."

On the collaboration front, Gentry Lee traveled to Sri Lanka in June to work with Clarke on some last-minute corrections on *Rama II*, but primarily they brainstormed and plotted for its sequel—*The Garden of Rama*—and Lee flew back to California with its detailed outline in his valise. The second *Rama* was on schedule for publication in December 1989.

Meanwhile, the civil war in Sri Lanka continued unabated. Everything was on strike—buses, hospitals, trains, and telephones—but in the midst of the crisis Clarke received some good news from England.

"The word came directly from His Excellency David Gladstone (the British high commissioner to Sri Lanka), confidentially, as it was not to be announced," Clarke recalls. "He delivered the news in person to my house."

The *London Times* and other newspapers of June 17, 1989, announced the queen's birthday honors. And there, under the rank commander of the British Empire (CBE) was "Dr. Arthur Charles Clarke, for service to British cultural interests in Sri Lanka." This honor, which was to be presented by the queen herself in October, was given in recognition of what Clarke had done for his adopted island of Sri Lanka—not for his literary accomplishments.

"I'd been waiting a rather long time," said Clarke with a chuckle, "and I was wondering if some of the powers didn't like me because it had been so long."

As the civil war worsened in Colombo, Clarke and Hector Ekanayake soon began to make plans for the fall trip to the United Kingdom. Since Valerie was pregnant, they wouldn't be able to pack up and get out before then, which would have been a reassuring option under the dangerous and unpredictable conditions in

Colombo. Their anxiety increased as the situation went from bad to worse.

In mid-July antigovernment terrorists stopped three buses in eastern Sri Lanka and gunned down at least thirty-five Muslim passengers in cold blood. During a two-day period of intensive fighting between the Tamil rebels and government troops at this time, almost 150 people were killed. It was frightening and heart-breaking.

Valerie and Hector Ekanayake's third daughter was born on August 6, 1989. While the birth enabled Clarke and Ekanayake to set a departure date, the ever-changing political situation kept things uncertain. By September 9 even the hospitals in Colombo were closed down. "It's a nightmare," said Clarke. "They've been killing the doctors. People are dying. The doctors are being killed for treating patients—while they're treating them. If you're sick, you can't go to the hospital. It's almost like Cambodia."

Everyone believed that this was really it, that anarchy and the forces of destruction and death had come to Colombo to stay. Clarke and the family began to have serious doubts about contin-uing to live in Sri Lanka.

"We're making contingency plans to leave the country now," he said in early September, "and after thirty years, it's a hell of a job. Everything will have to be abandoned; we can't take it with us."

President Premadasa brought together all political parties and ethnic groups for talks in mid-September. An agreement between Sri Lanka and India to remove the Indian troops that had been asked to come and disarm the militant Tamils in 1987 was close at hand. Over the two-year period the JVP terrorists had used the presence of the Indian troops to rally others to their cause. Their actions and the backlash had left some five thousand people dead since 1987. Their avowed goal was nothing less than to bring down the government. They did not care how many innocent people were killed in the process.

The first session of the assembly provoked more violence from the radicals, including a bomb and several fires in govern-ment buildings. More than a dozen bodies were also found in the outskirts of Colombo.

It was in this context of violence and anxiety that Arthur C. Clarke seriously began making plans to flee the island he had fallen in love with some three decades earlier. He refused to leave the house during this period, but kept very busy transferring his computer files onto disks so that he could carry them to England.

When friends called, he would tell them that he couldn't talk and that he would call them when he could. "I'm in a Salman Rushdie mode," he would say and then try to give them basic information such as his arrival date in London with an elaborate code using various chapter or part titles in books from his library.

"I hope no one listening in understands either," he would tell them when the communications of the makeshift code system would break down. "I'm sure this is totally unnecessary, but you know, one gets a little bit paranoiac."

Finally, on September 23, Clarke and Ekanayake arrived at Gatwick Airport in London. Besides meeting with dozens of friends, his publishers, and agents during his stay in the city, Clarke had thorough physical examinations—one at the hospital and another by Daniel Drachman, who was in London with his wife. Both confirmed that Clarke was recovering.

"He was in much better physical condition than when I saw him in August of 1988," said Gregory Benford, who met with Clarke on October 11 to discuss *Beyond the Fall of Night*. "He can walk short distances, 200 meters at a go, which is a vast improvement over the wheelchair he was in a year earlier. . . . Throughout Arthur was quick, spontaneous, brimming with news."

It was also in October that Clarke saw a special friend and colleague—Stanley Kubrick. "I had a most interesting day with Stanley and managed to escape by the skin of my teeth," he says mischievously. "He wanted me to work on his next movie! No way, of course. And then he said, 'Well, you're here for two weeks with nothing to do. Why don't you come in and work for me?'" Clarke laughs at what he thinks was an absurd (and perhaps frightening?) proposition.

"I had a long interview with Godfrey Smith from the Sunday *Times*," Clarke says, despite the fact that the word in London was "No interviews or press conferences." "He's a very good writer."

Writing aside, Smith thought Clarke's oral tradition was lacking. "Clarke is a hard man to interview," he wrote. "Ask him about his recent illness, and he will whip out a bulletin about it. Ask him about his writing, and he will give you a print-out summary of his 70 books, 500 articles, nine contracts for future books, and film or television options on four more. Then good nature and an unflagging interest in the way the world is going get him talking." "Still using his season ticket for tomorrow," the headline read. The interview led off with the news of Clarke's being honored by the queen on the following Wednesday. It went on to relate another upcoming event: Clarke's being honored by the most exclusive club in the world, whose members are veteran astronauts and cosmonauts—the Association of Space Explorers.

About Clarke, Smith wrote: "He is 71, an amiable, bespectacled, gangling man, slightly reminiscent of a numerate P. G. Wodehouse. There is, however, nothing remotely goofy about the brain or wit behind those mild glasses."

Clarke's first few weeks in England were leisurely and not too hard on him physically, but the last two weeks showed no mercy. Besides the audience with Queen Elizabeth, Clarke and Gentry Lee had a five-part Japanese television show, "The Future with Arthur C. Clarke," to shoot at Fred Clarke's home, Dene Court, and only a few days to do it all. During this homecoming Clarke searched and found his early journals "in their little iron box."

"I have about thirty volumes, beginning on 4 December 1938," Clarke told a friend. "Right up to now. It's the best part of three or four or five million words, I imagine. Minute detail. There's no way I'm going to do anything about it. And no one looks at them until fifty years after my death."

The big day at Buckingham Palace, Clarke's audience with the queen, finally arrived: Wednesday, October 25, 1989. He was allowed to bring two guests, so brother Fred and Hector Ekanayake accompanied him. Clarke donned his morning dress and top hat for the ceremonies, while his guests wore suits.

A journalist from *Figaro* was still interviewing Clarke when the hired limo arrived to take them to Buckingham Palace. Instead of breaking off the interview, Clarke kindly allowed her to accompany them on their ride through London before saying good-bye to her at the palace gates. They arrived at about 10:00 A.M. and were directed into the reception area, at which time Clarke went off to be briefed.

Unknown to him, his early fan and longtime friend Ian Macauley was also at Buckingham Palace that Wednesday. Macauley, an editor at the *New York Times* for many years, and Clarke had kept in touch and met in London and New York whenever their schedules permitted.

"I got into the palace with my press credentials," says Macauley, "sat down, and watched the whole ceremony.

"Of course it was very boring because we had 150 people getting awards, and it took two-and-one-half hours.

"There were two people who received the most attention from the queen. Arthur was one of them, and the other was the British consul from San Francisco, who received an award for promoting British products in California.

"Each person would march up, wait behind twenty paces, and then move up as their name was called. And then the queen would have a word with them. If they are knighted, of course, they kneel and the Queen dubs them. But if they're not getting knighted, just getting awards as is the case with the CBE, they bow slightly, and she presents the award and says a few words. In Arthur's case, the insignia of the CBE was on a ribbon and placed around his neck."

"I had a nice chat with the queen," Clarke told friends later. For her part, after noting that he was from Sri Lanka, Queen Elizabeth mentioned the problems and turmoil there. Clarke reminded her that they had met during her last visit to Sri Lanka and expressed how sad the current political situation was.

After the ceremony, Macauley worked his way over to Clarke and company.

"He was totally flabbergasted that I got in," says Macauley, "because he only had the two tickets for Fred and Hector. And he was elated when he saw me.

"We walked from the ballroom in Buckingham Palace, down the grand staircase, until we got to the palace entrance. He leaned on Fred and me to support him. He was exhausted and weak, but happy that the ceremony went well."

The next day Clarke fainted. He was complaining of vertigo and had the doctor in, who treated him for fatigue. Macauley noticed that Clarke seemed very tired and not too responsive and sometimes had lapses of memory.

"On the Saturday after the ceremony, October 28, he had an autograph-signing party at the Forbidden Planet Bookstore. It was sponsored by the publisher Victor Gollancz to promote the British publication (a month or so earlier than the U.S. edition) of *Rama II*.

'Fred and I were there with Arthur," says Macauley. "About two hundred fans showed up to have books signed. Two new books, *Rama II* and *Astounding Days*, were on sale. One fan showed up with his entire collection—about a hundred books—and Arthur had to refuse to sign them all. But throughout the signing session, Arthur was very tired and would sometimes nod off just like that—probably fatigue more than anything else."

That evening the two Clarke brothers attended a reunion of Clarke's old RAF group at the St. Ermyns Hotel. Arthur enjoyed himself as much as he could, although he was still exhausted.

Clarke and Hector Ekanayake flew back to Sri Lanka on October 31. Clarke had to work on the speech he would deliver at Riyadh, Saudi Arabia, the following month.

By the time they returned from England, the violence in Sri Lanka had subsided. Government troops had crushed the terrorists and regained control over most of the trouble areas. The contingency plans to move out of the country were put on the back burner—and that was a tremendous relief. Besides his personal safety being more assured, Clarke no longer had to face the anxiety-producing prospect of moving halfway around the planet tons of books, furnishings, computers, and other equipment—the accumulated possessions of thirty-five years of living on the tear-shaped island in the Indian Ocean.

Ten days—that's all Clarke had at home before he was off to Saudi Arabia for the Fifth Planetary Congress of the Association of Space Explorers, where he would be one of two honored guests. (Imaginative spaceflights of the mind don't count as membership credentials; only veteran real-life space travelers are eligible. Clarke's presence there was, of course, high status for someone who hadn't yet flown in orbit.) The other guest was Yash Pal, his good friend from India, who was the congress's keynote speaker and was honored for his experimental work in educational TV—the SITE program in rural India in the 1970s. In all more than fifty astronauts and cosmonauts attended from the United States, the Soviet Union, and a dozen other countries.

"As we checked in," Clarke recalls, "I was delighted to meet Alexei Leonov in the lobby—'My old friend!' he cried as we embraced. When I produced the video-cassette of *2010: Odyssey Two* which I'd planned to show him, I found it wasn't necessary: 'Best film I ever saw!' he declared."

Host astronaut Prince Sultan (payload specialist on the space shuttle *Discovery* flight in June 1985) gave the opening speech, followed by Rusty Schweickart and Alexei Leonov, who gave brief speeches before everyone fell out and socialized.

At the Tuwaiq Palace (actually a modern art gallery) the same afternoon, Clarke met Prince Sultan for the first time and chatted with many others. "I toured round in a wheelchair," says Clarke, "without which I would not have been able to cope."

Clarke was unable to avoid the press. "Began to feel I'm a celebrity," he said after being filmed and photographed constantly.

The first session of the congress, whose theme was "Space for Earth," was held Sunday morning, November 12. Yash Pal described how a storm a decade earlier had killed ten thousand people, whereas only twenty-five had lost their lives in a more recent but equally violent storm—because of active weather satellites.

That evening at the King Faisal Foundation, Clarke gave his lecture, "The Colours of Infinity: Exploring the Fractal Universe," the same subject that plays such an important role in his 1990 novel *The Ghost from the Grand Banks*. Clarke thought it was one of the most distinguished audiences he had ever addressed.

"Besides Prince Sultan, there were at least thirty astronauts and cosmonauts," he says. "I showed slides from the Mandelbrot Set, extracts from 'Nothing But Zooms,' and my 1988 videotaped discussion with Stephen Hawking, when I showed him some black holes I'd found in the M-Set."

In his suite, on Sunday, Clarke turned on the television and found, lo and behold, that *2010* was being shown. "It was weird to hear conversation about the spaceship *Alexei Leonov* when Alexei himself is here in the same hotel," Clarke wrote later in a newsy letter to friends. "But they've billed the movie as 'The Year We Make Contact' starring Helen Mirren! (I was unable to find who was responsible for this absurdity, still less get it corrected.)"

Perhaps the most memorable event, though, was a desert feast Monday evening. From the hotel a bus drove everyone about an hour into the desert twilight.

"Just before nightfall, we reached a huge tent set up in the middle of nowhere. It was an artificial oasis—with carpets, camels, horses—and a beautiful but deadly-looking falcon, which several of us handled rather nervously."

When a group of bedouin dancers began to perform, they were

soon joined by the astronauts and cosmonauts, who were in Arab dress. Clarke was asked to join by air force captain Hussein, which he did, all the while wearing the same flight jacket that Roy Scheider had worn on screen in *2010*, with its *Leonov* spaceship patch and other American and Soviet flight patches.

The fact that Clarke joined in no doubt encouraged his friend Alexei Leonov to participate.

"The three of us orbited together for five minutes—on the sand (I wouldn't have dared risk it on marble). Great fun."

Clarke couldn't get over the fact that he had danced in the desert with the first man on Earth to walk in space. A glorious full moon illuminated the scene.

The feast was held in another huge tent. There was whole roasted sheep and a variety of Arab sweetmeats to choose from.

The next morning began with an hour-and-a-half international video conference, with two-way video links among Riyadh, New York, Washington, D.C., and Atlanta. Moderated by Prince Sultan, its participants were Dr. Yash Pal of India; West German astronaut Ulf Merbold; U.S. astronaut and founding member of the Association of Space Explorers, Rusty Schweickart; Alexei Leonov of the Soviet Union; Georgi Ivanov of Bulgaria; and Arthur C. Clarke of Sri Lanka.

After the questions and answers flew back and forth to the satellites in geostationary orbit for more than an hour, Clarke spoke of the tremendous dividends all of us were getting from applications satellites, including those for weather and communications.

"Whether we become a multi-planet species with unlimited horizons," he concluded, "or are forever confined to Earth will be decided in the twenty-first century amid the vast plains, rugged canyons and lofty mountains of Mars."

After accepting "the A.S.E.'s Special Achievements Award (a massive medal weighing about 6 pounds)," Clarke spoke about a 1939 in-print controversy between the British Interplanetary Society and the BBC magazine *The Listener* about space travel. He quoted a few choice portions of the text, including one from the skeptics, who described in detail "the horrible things that would happen to any humans foolish enough to attempt space travel." It was a reminder of the nonsense early space enthusiasts had to put up with, and the audience loved it.

Clarke's last two days in Saudi Arabia included a pleasant mix of experiences: a visit to the recently built Space Research Institute, where he inspected the Landsat/Spot equipment; a farewell dinner during which he spoke with Yash Pal and his wife as well as several Soviet cosmonauts; a local TV interview; a visit to the palace and a conversation with Prince Sultan and his English-born wife; and then dinner with new friend Nasr Al-Sahhaf (a man who earned four college degrees in different subjects before he was twenty-five) and Dr. Jim Wise, an ex-NASA psychologist who told Clarke "that his PhD thesis had been directly inspired by the docking sequence in *2001!*"

This, of course, Clarke loved: "Must tell Stanley Kubrick," he said.

Leaving such good times behind was done with reluctance, but the next day Clarke and entourage flew back to Colombo.

"Not sure that it hadn't all been a dream," Clarke mused after he was back home in Sri Lanka.

"I want to take things easy for about a month and relax completely," he told a friend upon his return, adding, "I'm determined not to budge until I finish the *Titanic* novel." So Saudi Arabia would be Clarke's last international hop of the decade.

Clarke was also disheartened by some bad news. Rodney Jonklaas had died while he was out of the country. Although the two men had remained close friends, even after their business association ended, their respective commitments didn't allow for their spending much time together—"more so Arthur who is very much a 'writerholic'," wrote Jonklaas early in 1989.

On another unhappy note, at the end of December the *Washington Post* printed "Rama Redux," written by novelist Gregory Feeley, a very negative review of *Rama II*, which had just been released in the United States. That it was soon balanced out by more positive (although shorter) reviews in the *New York Times* (which praised a few of the characters as being more interesting than those of Clarke's other novels) and elsewhere did not deflect the impact of this hard-hitting piece.

"Readers may welcome Clarke's newfound prolificity, even with the proviso of partnership with his unknown (and previously unpublished) collaborator. They should be warned: There is good reason to hold the gravest doubts as to the extent of Clarke's contribution to this exploitative and amateurishly written book."

Feeley went on to write that *Rama II* was "abominably written" and that "the sensibility of the book is simply not that of Arthur C. Clarke, nor is it one to which he might plausibly have made a major contribution. The handling of religious matters is simply the most obvious: Clarke is a famously secular atheist, while *Rama II* was plainly written by a Roman Catholic."

The reviewer closed by saying he couldn't imagine "any lover of Clarke's fiction who would not feel cheated by this subcontracting job. . . . If I paid for my copy, I would be in a rage."

Because this devastating review appeared on December 31, Clarke did not see it until early 1990. This was a blessing in disguise, because he was getting up to speed again on his solo effort—a genuine all-Clarke novel, *The Ghost from the Grand Banks*.

As he stared into the blue infinity that had swallowed his son, the stars seemed suddenly very close. "Give us another hundred years," he whispered, "and we'll face you with clean hands and hearts—whatever shapes you be."

The Deep Range *(1957)*

33
TOWARD 20,001

"I'm working hard on the *Titanic* novel," Clarke said in early January 1990. "I've started, and it's going quite well. A third has been written for nearly a year, and it's entirely plotted. It's just a question of sitting down and writing it. If I'm left alone, I can complete it in three months."

Arthur C. Clarke was never left alone, however. That's why he loved to tell people he was a "failed recluse." During intensive writing periods he was only partly successful in avoiding the "mechanics of life," including the demands of the daily influx of mail, most of which was handled by assistants with form-letter replies. But there were also plenty of letters that required personal (and often lengthy) responses. No matter how much he tried to focus his energies on the project at hand, some of these demands would penetrate the defenses and command his attention.

In fact, some unfinished Russian business from 1982 bobbed up to the surface and required some correspondence early in 1990. It had to do with the controversy over publication of portions of the novel *2010: Odyssey Two* in Russia, the discovery that many of the characters' names in the novel were those of Russian dissidents, and the discovery's aftermath.

In 1984 the Russian magazine *Tekhnika Molodezhi* ("Technology for Youth") had published two excerpts from the novel *2010*, and even these were printed with considerable omissions. But the fact that several characters had the same last names as Russian dissidents had not been noticed by the magazine's editor, Vasili Zaharchenko. Then much of the world press noticed these names. Editor Zaharchenko was in big trouble; he was summarily dismissed after working for the magazine for forty years.

The novel was then banned in the Soviet Union. According to the Soviet censors the publication of those portions in *Tekhnika Molodezhi* was "a gross blunder which happened due to the loss of vigilance by Zaharchenko V.D., Editor-in-Chief, as well as due to the unprincipled positions of other staff members of the magazine." Some of the staff members were also severely reprimanded.

Six years later two Soviet officials from the Russian Embassy in Sri Lanka visited Barnes Place and presented Clarke with a November 1989 copy of *Tekhnika Molodezhi*. The issue contained a complete translation of *2010: Odyssey Two*, along with an honest commentary on what had happened in 1984, which in part stated:

"Today, all these accusations seem to be ridiculous. . . . The attitude toward 'dissidents' has radically changed.

"The decision on the novel by Arthur Clarke was one of the last 'flights' of the stagnation period in our ideology, demonstrating the paradoxical inability of the administrative guidance in literature."

Clarke's hope, stated in the end-of-book acknowledgments (and apologies) in *2061: Odyssey Three* (1987), that "the subscribers to *Tekhnika Molodezhi* can read the installments of 2010 that so mysteriously disappeared . . ." had actually been fulfilled.

"The last thing I'd intended," Clarke wrote to Vasili Zaharchenko in January 1990, "was for the names of the dissidents to be a 'time bomb'—in fact, I regarded it as little more than a mild joke or a gentle criticism (which shows how I had misjudged the situation). Had I dreamed of the consequences, I would have alerted you immediately—as it was, I felt certain that you would recognize the names and either: (1) decide they didn't matter; or (2) change them. In fact, when I received your last letter at the time saying you had 'sanitised' the novel, I assumed all these matters had been taken care of."

Zaharchenko detailed the misfortunes that had befallen him

as a result of the incident, and he asked Clarke for help. Clarke replied that he would be more than happy to do some television segments with him in Sri Lanka and also assist him with a book on space art that he was compiling.

The novel's Russian publication was welcomed by everyone. *2010: Odyssey Two* became a small literary bridge between the West and the East at a time when the USSR was undergoing a revolution—one that might help the world become a global village.

By the end of January, with his assistant sick in the hospital, Clarke was fighting to get back to the *Titanic* novel, but too many distractions made it all but impossible.

The political situation in Sri Lanka was still dangerously unstable, especially in the north and the east of the country. "I'm afraid all the best people are going," Clarke wrote to Willie Mendis in Washington, "and psychologically it's very depressing."

"I'm being bombed out by visitors and mail," Clarke noted on a more mundane level. "I've received more than thirty books and magazines in a day—and not enough time to physically sort them out, let alone read them."

He continued fighting for every minute he could get and in late January did manage to write some of chapter ten, "The Isle of the Dead," named after Arnold Boecklin's famous nineteenth-century painting. It was, Clarke said, a key element in his new novel. Clarke also loved Sergey Rachmaninoff's symphonic poem, *The Island of Death*, which was based on the Basel painter's work.

By early February he was in the swim again, "working night and day on the novel," and hoping to complete it by March. He had polished the first thirty thousand words and had actually written the novel's conclusion.

"I've been writing whatever I've wanted to write—bits of the book that interest me at the moment. Then I'll link them together later. It's like a jigsaw puzzle, but it's going very very fast. This isn't my usual approach," he confessed. "Most of my books have been linear, but this has been like a mosaic."

Despite his complaints about daily distractions, Clarke met his goal of completing *The Ghost from the Grand Banks* in late February 1990 and sent floppy disks off to Scott Meredith and his brother Fred Clarke in early March.

Although there was no contract in place, Bantam had the

option, and in early April Clarke learned of the splendid deal that had been negotiated by the Scott Meredith Literary Agency.

"Everybody loves it, and some of them say it's the best thing I've ever done," he told a friend. "It's my first contemporary novel and is completely different from anything else. It begins in 1977 and goes up to 2012. It starts with Howard Hughes and the *Glomar Explorer*. Bantam is rushing it through to bring it out at Christmas."

Published in December in the United States as planned, the novel received several lukewarm reviews, which pointed out that some of the plot elements had been created only to allow Clarke to lecture about number theory. The cast of characters, one writer said, were "mainly technical wizards with flat personalities—the most interesting character is a 50-ton-octopus—but then no one reads a Clarke story to find out about human nature."

Ever since the early 1950s, reviewers and critics have pointed out the weak fictional characters in Clarke's novels and his apparent inability (or unwillingness) to describe in-depth human relationships. At least one Clarke expert suggests that this weakness does not come from any lack of technique but rather from underdeveloped traits in his own personality. Clarke had confronted this criticism with his 1986 novel, *The Songs of Distant Earth*, in which he'd spent more effort developing characters. He was in part successful, especially when compared to earlier fiction. But in *The Ghost from the Grand Banks* he again neglected character development. The characters were lightly sketched and did not offer readers much with which to identify and empathize. One notable exception was the character of Edith Craig, who was compulsively searching for her dead daughter among the fractal images on her computer screen.

Kirkus Reviews closed its review of *Ghost*, "Average Clarke, more emotional than usual, with excellent extrapolation of future technologies." A reviewer in *Locus* magazine wrote that the novel was a "fast and pleasant read," but nevertheless was "a latticework book, a sketch of a larger, deeper work, resonant but not dense." A British reviewer said it was "vintage Clarke, with all the virtues and weaknesses that we have come to expect from this Grandmaster."

The best came last. Writing for the *New York Times*, Gerald Jonas called the novel "sunny" and its author "a happy man."

Clarke, he wrote, "sees the universe as a marvelous toy, coquettishly begging to be understood yet always mocking our success with some deeper mystery. . . . [H]is ability to keep a story moving ahead while teaching us what we must know to follow narrative logic wherever it leads is the very essence of his art. He only makes it look easy."

In spite of the surrounding tumult, many of the projects that, all told, made this such a productive period for Clarke came to fruition in 1990. He did, indeed, make it look easy. Once his manuscript for *The Ghost from the Grand Banks* had left his house in March, he could decide what to write next. He said yes to a few prefaces for worthy projects, one of which was a major volume for MIT, with top computer scientists in the field: *Technology 2001*. When they told Clarke that he was the only person who could write the preface, he believed them, enjoyed the flattery, and wrote the short piece in early March.

Michael Deakin, film producer and president of Griffin Productions, arrived in Colombo in March to work with Clarke in making final revisions on the television script for *A Fall of Moondust*. It was, regretfully, turned down by Universal later in the year. Deakin visited again in the fall, and they worked together on the "Deplorable Inventions" TV series together. Clarke could do as little or as much as he liked for this project, which suited him just fine. He wasn't even obligated to introduce the programs, although as of early 1992, with the project not yet in production, he thought he probably would do so.

Another volume of Clarke's short pieces, *Tales from Planet Earth*, was published in June. It was produced in a handsome quality paperback edition and illustrated by the artist Michael Whelan. Clarke also wrote short introductions to each of the fourteen stories, placing them in time and in the context of his other work. Most of them were originally written in the 1950s and 1960s, but the last piece, "On Golden Seas," was from 1986.

"It was written as a reaction to the mountains of literature I'd read on the strategic defense initiative," Clarke says, and he summarized how it had made its way into the White House and the inner sanctums of SDI research.

July 1990 brought forth the sequel to *Against the Fall of Night* that had begun as a conversation with Gregory Benford two years earlier. If ever there was a lifelong literary project for Arthur C.

Clarke, it was this book, which he'd begun to write as an adolescent in the 1930s. *Beyond the Fall of Night,* published by Ace
Putnam, is made up of Clarke's original novel (Part I) and Benford's
sequel (Part II).

"It was a voyage of discovery," said Clarke after reading Benford's sequel. "It's particularly interesting to see how some of the
concepts of this half-century-old story are now in the forefront of
modern science: I am especially fond of the 'Black Sun,' which is an
obvious description of the now extremely popular Black Holes."

Several reviewers concentrated on the differences in style
between Clarke's original and Benford's sequel. At least one writer
believed that the two halves didn't fit and that both good works
suffered as a result. Of course science fiction buffs were pleased to
have these two authors in the same volume.

Revolutionary events in the real world led Clarke to his next
major literary project, a nonfiction book on telecommunications—
past, present, and future—and how they have changed (and would
continue to change) the planet.

The "global village," especially the Eastern European branch,
was going through some major changes in the fall of 1989. Clarke
believed, as did many others, that these geopolitical shifts could
eventually evolve into a new world order of international cooperation and interdependence. Perhaps his long-standing vision of a
cooperative global family was in the process of being realized. He
hoped this was true.

Clarke chose a catchy title for his telecommunications tome:
How the World Was One: Beyond the Global Village. The contract
was negotiated with Bantam, and Clarke signed on the dotted line
on August 10, 1990; publication date, June 15, 1992.

"This has turned out to be a much bigger project than I
planned," he wrote to friends in September. "It will also be my
longest book (possibly 150,000 words). It may also be one of my
most important, since it's covering the whole history of telecommunications, from the invention of the telegraph, up to the fibre
optic revolution."

An advance review printed in spring 1992 noted that half
the book came from *Voices Across the Sea,* published thirty-five
years earlier, but stated that "few authors bear repeating as well
as this renowned writer of science fiction and fact." The review
went on to say that "Clarke made his reputation by crafting imag-

ination into vision" and called his latest book a "vintage offering."

In October Gentry Lee submitted the manuscript of *The Garden of Rama*—the third collaborative novel he and Clarke had written—to Bantam. Lee worked on the revisions suggested by editor Lou Aronica through year's end. The novel was published in the fall of 1991 and received a warmer reception than *Rama II*. The *Locus* reviewer wrote, "It is not often that collaborations produce a work that not only exceeds what each author might achieve on his own, but which must be recognized as a genuine achievement."

Simon Welfare and John Fairley, Clarke's coauthors for a new anthology, *Arthur C. Clarke's Century of Mysteries*, had not yet delivered their material as of mid-December. "I'm still waiting, but have written an introduction and one essay that can be used somewhere in the text."

The essay, "The Mona Lisa of Mars," was about the controversial image on the Martian surface that some people believed to be an ancient alien artifact. Clarke's old colleague Richard Hoagland, who had been a science adviser to CBS during the Apollo coverage, was a strong and relentless advocate of this possibility. He persuaded enough people in Washington, including some congressmen who had influence with top NASA brass, to retarget the Mars Observer spacecraft so that it would scrutinize the site with its remote sensing instruments. (Clarke gave Hoagland credit for thinking of Jupiter's moon Europa as a possible abode for life, a key plot factor in his *2061: Odyssey Three*.)

Clarke's views on the subject were consistent with those of a good scientist and similar to those he held on UFOs. He needed some real evidence—not just suggestive shapes seen in images taken from an orbiting spacecraft above the Martian surface. "The Mona Lisa of Mars" was the last piece Arthur C. Clarke would write in 1990 and was written some fifty-five years after he'd penned his first known story about the red planet, "Mars," in 1935.

In December, Arthur C. Clarke celebrated a fruitful year and his seventy-third birthday with a modest birthday party at Barnes Place.

"Quite a big cake was made," says cousin John Clarke, "in the shape of an oceanliner, but it didn't have the right number of funnels for the *Titanic*. When Arthur cut the first slice, he said, 'This is where the iceberg went.'

"Later in the morning a bunch of people from the Arthur Clarke Centre came with another cake for him before everyone headed off for the award ceremonies in the afternoon."

The Third Arthur C. Clarke Award for achievement in global communications was presented to Dr. Harold Rosen by President Premadasa. Rosen, a vice president at Hughes Aircraft Company, had developed the Comsat hardware that Clarke envisioned in his 1945 global geostationary satellite system published in *Wireless World*. The two men have known one another since the pioneering days of communication satellites in the late fifties and early sixties.

In his introductory remarks the president praised Arthur C. Clarke and the award:

"Our tribute to you is not really for your birthday alone. We salute your achievements. Even more, we esteem your humanity. For us, you have no age. You belong to all ages. The conventional chronology of time has no meaning for men of vision. Arthur is such a visionary."

* * *

As we approach the new millennium, the crew of spaceship Earth is cooperating more than it has in the past, believes Arthur C. Clarke, his lifelong optimism about humanity's future again holding sway.

"I used to say mankind has a fifty-one percent chance of survival; I'd put the figure now at a solid fifty-five percent."

He is also optimistic about his personal future, now believing that he will fulfill his dream of seeing the year 2001. He will be eighty-three years old when New Year's Day, 2001, comes to pass.

"There's been a lot of talk about immortality and the extension of the human life span," Clarke said in the early 1980s. "I have a feeling that our life span is about right, because our brains begin to wear out, let's say around about a hundred years. If we can keep good health for that period of time, I think most people will settle for that. The idea of immortality I find horrifying, even though I've written all about it." Clarke paused and reflected a few seconds.

"I don't feel that I am the person that was alive fifty years ago. I feel very little feeling towards that person. I am a different person now. So immortality, in the sense of you, yourself, as you are now, being able to exist forever is a contradiction, I think."

Arthur C. Clarke's first seventy-five orbits around the sun indicate that he enjoys life, ever keeping busy, making no distinction between work and recreation. When asked what new work, fiction and nonfiction, readers can expect in the future, Clarke paused to consider his reply.

"*The Ghost from the Grand Banks* will almost certainly be my last novel; certainly there won't be one for years," he says. This statement is, of course, suspect considering his literary history of "last" novels.

"If I'm still fit and the *Galileo* spacecraft does something spectacular in '95, there may be a final odyssey," he adds, covering all the bases.

When asked how he might view his work from the perspective of one hundred or five hundred years in the future, Clarke hedges and says he hasn't the faintest idea.

"I don't think I'm a sufficiently detached and unbiased observer. I've often said that on occasion I've had delusions of significance," he ends with a chuckle. About all he will commit to regarding his work a hundred years from now is the likelihood that his 1945 *Wireless World* paper on communications satellites will be referred to in a footnote in the textbooks of the period.

Of course, Clarke is right about his lack of detachment regarding his own work. Back in early 1938 he confessed to his friend Sam Youd that he didn't see any reason to believe that he had "any great literary ability" but that he could probably do better than most of the pulp writers if he spent enough time perfecting his style. He added that he didn't have the time to devote to writing seriously. Science fiction fans, of course, are happy that he was mistaken.

"He is the greatest living science fiction writer," wrote Gregory Benford, "in part because he stands in a tradition that began with Julian Huxley, J. D. Bernal, and of course Olaf Stapledon and goes through Freeman Dyson and Clarke himself. The cool, distant, analytical thinking patterns apply to immense perspectives, and that's a discernible, intellectual English tradition.

"Stapledon, whom Clarke idolized, dragged the conflicts of his era into far-future visions, attributing Marxist—indeed, Stalinist—

dynamics to even alien, insectoid races. This riddles some of Stapledon's work with anachronisms.

"Clarke never loses his bearings this way, and his work will probably wear well.

"Arthur is also the most read science fiction writer in the world, and his British agent has the numbers to prove it."

Lester del Rey, who ran the leading science fiction and fantasy publishing imprint for Ballantine Books until 1992, has known Clarke for forty years and harks back to his first visits to the United States in the early 1950s.

"I have never heard of anyone," says del Rey, "looking at the bulk of Arthur's work, saying they didn't like it. He's had his share of bad reviews, but they never take his total work apart and knock it. There is a humanity and often an innocence to Arthur's work. And although he doesn't generally draw characters well in his books, he draws the race of man well."

Longtime friend Isaac Asimov wrote in 1989: "In his social thinking he is humane, liberal and gently skeptical, a fact entirely admirable in his outlook on the world. . . . You will find Clarke in this book [*Astounding Days: A Science Fictional Autobiography*] as he is—utterly free of any trace of modesty. But he is so artless in his appreciation of himself that you will not be offended. Rather, the book will endear him to you."

Science fiction has in part been defined as the last refuge of the morality tale, and British writer John Brunner believes that much of Clarke's work, where rationality and intelligence usually prevail, fits well into this definition.

"In the context of a science fiction story the hero is the man who knows what's going on. And I see this over and over and over in Arthur's books, as well as in Heinlein's and Asimov's. The person who has the knowledge and understands is the person you can rely on, and he appears in all kinds of guises. After all, in *Childhood's End*, he's Karellen, the alien delegate from the stars. He's the only one who knows what's going on.

"'The Star' is the most emotionally charged story Arthur ever wrote," says Brunner. "It's the only work of his that I have ever read which I could imagine him crying over when he finished. And it's strictly abstract. But you can feel your way into the person who has just discovered he has got to give up his lifelong faith. Because if he's going to believe in an unjust God, he doesn't want to. That's a terrific piece of work. It's certainly the one that hits—and hurts."

Fellow writer Frederik Pohl, who also bought some of Clarke's work as an editor in the 1950s, judges him "a very graceful and dependable writer."

"Science fiction novels last forever, and I am confident that Arthur's work will be read in the next century," says Pohl when asked—a rather safe prediction that even Clarke himself declines to make. "And Arthur is a significant figure in the twentieth century because of what he has done—the writing and everything else.

"I owe Arthur for a quotation I've used many times for years. A long time ago he was interviewed by some fans who published a symposium of what writers thought about this and that. They asked Arthur why he wrote science fiction, and he said, 'Because no other literature concerns itself with reality.' I agree. I agree that science fiction is the literature of change, and change is the biggest reality we all face."

Eric S. Rabkin of the University of Michigan, a Clarke scholar, points out that much of his work is not the hard science fiction for which he is so well known.

"Hard SF seems to be stylistic trope for Clarke," says Rabkin, "rather than the heart of the matter. His early story [1949] *The Lion of Comarre* is not hard science fiction at all, and the same can be said for the book that runs throughout his career, *Against the Fall of Night*, which in its final version became *The City and the Stars*. And if you look at the end of *Imperial Earth*, he has an 'Additional Note' in which he points out that several experts found fault with the genetics of his novel. He more or less says in response, 'I'm a writer, and I can do whatever I want.'"

Two fundamental themes occur repeatedly in Clarke's work, Rabkin observes. One is that the world has somehow stagnated and an essentially adolescent character somehow has to reinvigorate the world. This story gets told again and again—*Childhood's End*, *The Lion of Comarre*, *The City and the Stars*, *The Deep Range*, and *Dolphin Island*.

The other recurrent theme is the human race's confrontation with its own relative insignificance.

"This happens in his two greatest books," says Rabkin, "*2001* and *Rendezvous with Rama*. In *2001* we confront our own insignificance, but it turns out that although we are insignificant, we don't have to stay insignificant. The monolith has control over human evolution, and its Star-Child is 'master of the world.'

"With *Rendezvous with Rama* he has us confront the universe, and we stay insignificant. And that's his boldest book. All its technical detail—its hard science fiction—becomes thematically crucial. In a sense, what it leaves you with is a recognition that no matter how complete and accurate our understanding of the physical objects of the world may be, we still don't have the answers to the deepest issues. We explore scientific fact in this novel, but the narrative does not allow us to make a leap of faith from scientific fact to dominance of the universe.

"In the other novels, however, he seems to be saying, 'Not only do we know how to calculate orbits, but we're also the soul of the universe.'

"It's as if Clarke is of two conflicting minds. There's this conscious mind that appreciates classical mechanics—the old-fashioned kind of science that's entirely deterministic. The early novels such as *Earthlight*, *Prelude to Space*, *The Sands of Mars*, and *Islands in the Sky* all have lots of classical mechanics in them. Such science may be complicated to some of his readers, but in mathematical terms, conceptual terms, and in ethical terms it's as simple as you can get.

"Then, on a lower level, thinking in Freudian and Jungian terms, Clarke seems to want the ability to dissolve himself into something great and powerful that is of the order of importance of the universe as a whole. I think that's what links the sky and the sea for him, which constantly resonate in his work. He never gets onto the ground, physically, in a happy way. It's always in the sky or in the ocean. These are both realms in which he can dissolve himself. Like the Overmind in *Childhood's End*. By joining the Overmind, he can occupy all of space at once. That's what Clarke wants to do. Somehow get to the heart of this huge web of reality that's everything."

Perhaps it is in this elusive heart of reality that Arthur C. Clarke has been seeking what he lost in his youth, that eclipsed aspect of his own identity, his life's black hole, created by his long-missed father, whose death and absence during his adolescence had a powerful, mostly unconscious, effect on him. Indeed his father's long illness and early death may have been a primary motivation for his endless explorations, be they on the printed page or around the planet. This interpretation may help to explain why Clarke has said more than once that writing is a hole in his life. His creative quest may be an attempt, on one level, to fill in that hole deep inside himself.

An insurmountable distance often separates father and son in Clarke novels (*Childhood's End, The Deep Range, 2010, Imperial Earth*, and *The Songs of Distant Earth* are examples).

"The starship *Magellan* was still no more than a few light-hours distant when Kumar Lorenson was born, but his father was already sleeping and did not hear the news until three hundred year later," Clarke wrote in *The Songs of Distant Earth*.

"He wept to think that his dreamless slumber had spanned the entire lifetime of his first child. . . ."

At a crucial time in Clarke's early development he discovered the work of Olaf Stapledon, his most influential literary mentor.

"Stapledon's influence on Clarke was considerable," continues Rabkin, "and he's admitted this. In *Last and First Men* the happiest humans of all are those that have a group mind. The whole book is based on the possibility of telepathic intercommunications, and it seems to me that at the age of thirteen Clarke was really bowled over by this. Stapledon's book was published at the beginning of the Depression. The whole world was fragmented. The recovery from the Great War was a false recovery. Political tensions and nationalism were on the rise everywhere.

"So here's this impressionable lad who's feeling what everyone else is feeling in the early thirties [*as well as* the loss of his father], and suddenly he reads this book and says, 'Everything has its place in this grand scheme of things, and you can lose your individuality if you wish, submerge it into this great whole.'

"Clarke has an obvious desire to construct a world in which some kind of higher benign order makes clear the centrality and importance of humanity. He really does seem to want to believe there's something higher and that it cares for us. This desire appears in his work in various ways, but in all of them it can be recognized as a statement of faith, not a statement of scientific fact."

Such a quest for faith appears throughout much of Arthur C. Clarke's fiction, and this continuing search, which takes many forms in his work, is one of the foremost reasons that his novels have permanent value.

As the quincentennial of Columbus's discovery of the New World is celebrated in 1992, along with the activities of the International Space Year (and Clarke's seventy-fifth birthday), it is fitting to acknowledge that Arthur C. Clarke is one of this century's great explorers in the realm of ideas and possibilities. His life's work—the voluminous literature, the lectures, the Hollywood and documentary films—has been devoted to searching for the future of the human race and its place in the ever-mysterious and boundless universe of space and time. In a real sense Clarke is a Columbus of the future, and his spaceship is his mind.

"In projecting our ideas into the future," he said, "much of the technology that exists now is going to be around for the next hundred years. But about every ten years there will come along something completely unexpected, like the transistor and its successors, which will bring in a new dimension."

It is the future evolution of artificial intelligence and its relationship with the human mind that Clarke believes will have the most profound effect on *Homo sapiens* and our descendants. He has gone on record that the development of AI is the most important breakthrough in the twentieth century. As the third millennium rushes to become the present, the potential and actual capability of this revolutionary technology expands explosively. Clarke believes that ultimately—in context of the evolution of *Homo sapiens* to its next level (*Homo electronicus?*)—it may be the most important technology ever.

"One day we may be able to enter into temporary unions with any sufficiently sophisticated machines, thus being able not merely to control but to *become* a spaceship or a submarine or a TV network," he writes. "The thrill that can be obtained from driving a racing car or flying an aeroplane may be only a pale ghost of the excitement our great-grandchildren may know, when the individual human consciousness is free to roam at will from machine to machine, through all the reaches of sea and sky and space." (Readers of *2010* will immediately think of David Bowman's superhuman flights in the chapters "Homecoming" and "Fires in the Deep.")

This pure and powerful mentality, free from physical limitations, appears in many of Clarke's novels. It represents transcendence over human limitations and a more complete knowledge of the universe and ultimate reality. In *The City and the Stars,*

Callitrax says that the conception of a pure mentality was "common among many of Earth's ancient religious faiths, and it seems strange that an idea which had no rational origin should finally become one of the greatest goals of science."

When will the artificial intelligence of computers attain the level of human intelligence?

"Not by 2001," Clarke believes, "but certainly by 2100. And their intelligence and insight will, of course, continue to grow and expand after that. This may lead to some very interesting things. I think man is a transitional species, to be supplanted by some new life form that includes computer technology."

Does Clarke dare extrapolate into the far future? In his fiction, of course, he gives himself more freedom of time and space than in his nonfiction forecasting.

Will humanity or its future evolutionary progeny have made contact (physical or electromagnetic) with other intelligent life in the universe by 20,001? Not even with this eighteen thousand years' leeway will Arthur C. Clarke make a commitment to when this event (arguably the most important one in the history of our species) might occur—even though his most famous novel puts it at 2001.

When he created his "Chart of the Future" at the end of *Profiles of the Future,* and revised it in 1984, Clarke put "First Contact" as occurring sometime *beyond* 2100. He is convinced, after looking at what has happened in the last 150 years, "that no imagination can hope to look beyond the year 2100." He therefore limits his credible "real world" forecasts to a hundred years to retain any reasonable probability and value. But as the twentieth century has shown, planet Earth can undergo great changes in a mere century.

And while he hesitates to give any forecasting odds as to the likelihood of contact with alien life forms, he is willing to put some numbers on the probability of extraterrestrials existing in our vast and wondrous universe.

"I think there's a ninety-nine percent chance of life all over the universe and a ninety percent chance of intelligent life being all over the place as well. The most likely scenario for contact is reception of a radio signal of some sort. Next most likely would be detection or interception of astroengineering or physical artifacts. And they might land tomorrow on the White House lawn.

"This is the wild card," said Clarke. "This is one future of fate we can do absolutely nothing to control."

Clarke confesses he *wants* to believe that there is life elsewhere in the universe, "because it's very lonely if there's nobody else out there. But we haven't the slightest evidence for such existence. There's only statistical argument, and it's very tantalizing."

"The fact that we have not yet found the slightest evidence for life—much less intelligence—beyond this Earth does not surprise or disappoint me in the least," he said. "Our technology must still be laughably primitive; we may well be like jungle savages listening for the throbbing of tom-toms, while the ether around them carries more words per second than they could utter in a lifetime."

"One of the great lessons of modern science is that millennia are only moments," wrote Clarke, referring to the cosmic scale and the life cycles of stars and galaxies—and perhaps the universe itself. He admits to being skeptical about finding answers to the great questions and problems of existence that humans have debated for thousands of years. And the reason he is skeptical is that such questions will not likely be answered in such short time scales. He doubts that "we will really know much about the universe while we are still crawling around in the playpen of the solar system."

Make no mistake: Arthur C. Clarke has had a lot of fun playing. He has said more than once that he writes because it's fun—adding that he also likes to eat. Having "great fun" (one of his more common expressions) extends to all his explorations, cerebral and geographical—not just to his writing craft. He is somewhat coy about any deeper driving forces in his life.

"Actually, my motivation and aim in life is very simple," Clarke lightly confessed in 1990. "It's been expressed by a famous remark of a British prime minister (Stanley Baldwin, I think), who was talking about the newspaper world of Fleet Street in London and comparing its advantages with those of another profession: the privilege of the harlot throughout the ages, which is power without responsibility. I recently told the president of Sri Lanka that this was my goal and I'd now achieved it."

Of course Arthur C. Clarke's responsibility has been self-imposed, and when it comes to work and worthy causes, he's a tough taskmaster. On the other hand he doesn't really think of himself as having any great amount of power. So while he may want "power without responsibility" and has casually claimed success, his actual circumstances may be closer to the reverse: responsibility without power. In appraising himself, however, he plays down this all-too-familiar adult dilemma.

"I thought of my epitaph the other day," he said recently. 'He never grew up, but he never stopped growing.' It occurred to me that it was quite appropriate. Not that I thought it was for any imminent use."

SOURCES

The sources for this biography have been divided into two sections. First, there is a list of selected interviews, with alphabetized names and dates, from which came interview quotes that *actually appear* in the text. The only exceptions are for those few people who have been interviewed many times. For such serial interviews, inclusive dates covering all conversations are given. In such cases, the reader will know in what general period of time the interviews took place, but not the specific dates.

Second, there is a section of notes for all print, audio, and video sources. All quotes are listed by chapter and text page. Each note is keyed to quoted words or a phrase that appears on a specific page in the text.

The interview list and the endnotes will enable the reader to find the spoken or written source for any quoted material.

SELECTED INTERVIEWS

Forrest Ackerman (26 March 1989)
Brian Aldiss (30 March 1989)
Isaac Asimov (5 December 1989)

Betty Ballantine (22 May 1989)
Ian Ballantine (22 May 1989)
Joel Banow (6 February 1990)
Gregory Benford (17 and 21 November 1989)
Louis Blau (10 December 1989)
Robert Bloch (8 April 1989)
Ray Bradbury (6 December 1989)
John Brunner (15 January 1990)
Roger Caras (19 September 1989, 31 May 1990, and other telephone
     interviews)
Arthur C. Clarke (31 July 1988 to 9 May 1992)
Fred Clarke (23 March 1989 to 9 May 1992)
John Clarke (31 December 1990)
Michael Clarke (2 August 1990)
Michael Craven (4 April 1989)
Walter Cronkite (5 April 1990)
Lester del Rey (2 December 1989)
Hugh Downs (15 February 1990)
Daniel Drachman (31 October 1990)
Olga Druce (16 March 1989, 16 May 1989, and other telephone
     interviews)
Fred Durant (8 July 1989 and 1 July 1990)
David Fowke (28 June 1989)
Bert Fowler (19 March 1989)
James Gunn (22 January 1990)
Todd Hawley (13 September 1990)
Dick Hoagland (30 December 1989)
Leonard Hobbs (6 April 1989)
Peter Hyams (19 June 1990)
Dick Jenvey (4 April 1989)
Dot Jones (25 July 1989)
Steven Jongeward (26 June 1990 and other telephone interviews)
Kathy Keeton (4 April 1989)
David Kennard (9 August 1990)
Dick Kriegel (15 March 1989)
David Kyle (23 March 1989, 6 June 1989, and other telephone inter-
     views)
Gentry Lee (13 August 1990, 9 October 1990, and other telephone
     interviews)
Lloyd Lewan (18 April 1990)
Ray Lovejoy (21 December 1989)
Lee Lubbers (21 November 1989)

Ian Macauley (6 August 1989, 30 October 1989, and other telephone
    interviews)
Marjorie May (17 May 1989)
Marilyn Mayfield (24 July 1989)
John McLucas (27 September 1990)
Scott Meredith (28 March 1989)
Harry Morrin (28 July 1990)
Sam Moskowitz (7 February 1989)
George Mueller (25 March 1989)
Julian Muller (23 January 1990)
Kerry O'Quinn (27 February 1990)
Fred Ordway (1 October 1989)
Thomas Paine (8 September 1989)
Charles Pellegrino (10 November 1990)
Joseph Pelton (25 March 1989 and 4 June 1990)
John Pierce (21 February 1989)
Bobby Pleass (31 March 1989)
Frederik Pohl (17 March 1989 and 22 April 1989)
Cyril Ponnamperuma (9 September 1990)
Jerry Pournelle (11 September 1990)
Eric Rabkin (7 December 1990)
Gene Roddenberry (22 January 1990)
Carl Sagan (20 February 1990)
Bernard Shir-Cliff (11 July 1989)
Ken Slater (26 January 1990)
Harry Stine (11 March 1989)
Eric Taylor (22 February 1990)
Joan Temple (8 February 1989)
Pat Weaver (7 February 1990)
Robert Weil (1 September 1990)

ENDNOTES
Chapter 1

Page 3. **"The price ..."**: Nora Clarke, *My Four Feet on the Ground*
    (London: Rocket Publishing Company, 1978), 59.
Page 4. **"or, better still, hovering ... "**: Arthur C. Clarke, "Of
    Sand and Stars," in *1984: Spring—A Choice of Futures* (New
    York: Ballantine Books, 1984), 152.
Page 4. **"Underfoot, the sand ..."**: Arthur C. Clarke, *The Nine
    Billion Names of God* (New York: New American Library, 1967),
    243.

Page 4. **"Beyond the sea wall . . . "**: *Ibid.*
Page 4. **"but he was a solitary . . ."**: *Ibid.*, 244.
Page 5. **"I can still hear . . ."**: Arthur C. Clarke, *Astounding Days* (prepublication manuscript), 2–3.
Page 5. **"a weird beast, a stegosaur . . ."**: Shirley Thomas, ed., *Men in Space*, vol. 1 (Philadelphia: Chilton Book Company, 1968), 14.
Page 8. **"More than his father . . ."**: Arthur C. Clarke, *Glide Path* (New York: New American Library, 1987), 181.

Chapter 2

Page 11. **"His first telescope . . ."**: Letter, Mary Clarke Mcclean to author (4 July 1990).
Page 11. **"It came as a great surprise . . ."**: Thomas, *Men in Space*, vol. 1, 14.
Page 13. **"First there were balsa . . ."**: Fred Clarke, "Foreheads in the Air" (unpublished manuscript, received July 1989), 68.
Page 14. **"I remember listening to music . . ."**: *Ibid.*, 71 ff.

Chapter 3

Page 17. **"I read that March 1930 . . ."**: Arthur C. Clarke, *Astounding Days* (New York: Bantam Books, 1990), 11–12.
Page 17. **"I'd save up all my spare . . ."**: Shirley Thomas, ed., *Men in Space*, vol. 8 (Philadelphia: Chilton Book Company, 1968), 15.
Page 18. **"There were heartbreaking . . ."**: *Ibid.*
Page 19. **"[T]he stories brimmed . . ."**: Arthur C. Clarke, "Of Sand and Stars," in *1984: Spring*, 154.
Page 21. **"Our houses are built . . ."**: Arthur C. Clarke, "News from the Torrid Zone" (*Huish Magazine 22*, Christmas 1933), 34–35.
Page 23. **"As the rocket rose . . ."**: Fred Clarke, "Foreheads in the Air," 68.
Page 24. **"Please could you send . . ."**: Letter, Arthur C. Clarke to L. J. Johnson, in L. J. Johnson, "No Air to Push Against" (unpublished manuscript).

Chapter 4

Page 26. **"I quickly realised . . ."**: Arthur C. Clarke, *Astounding Days"* (prepublication manuscript), 167–168.

Page 27. **"Today, of course, it is famous . . ."**: Arthur C. Clarke, *Ascent to Orbit* (New York: John Wiley & Sons, 1984), 207.

Page 28. **"The British Interplanetary Society . . . "**: Arthur C. Clarke, brochure for BIS public relations and membership drive (London: BIS, ca. 1938–39).

Page 29. **"I have four short stories . . . "**: Letter, Arthur C. Clarke to Sam Youd (10 October 1937).

Page 29. **"At the moment . . . "**: *Ibid.* (17 January 1938).

Page 30. **"I don't want . . . "**: *Ibid.* (28 January 1938).

Page 30. **"I maintain . . . "**: *Ibid.* (14 May 1938).

Page 30. **For there was hardly room . . . "**: William Temple, "The British Fan in His Natural Haunts" (London: *Novae Terrae*, June 1938), 15–16.

Page 32. **"I beheld a tallish . . . "**: *Ibid.*, 17.

Page 32. **I can thank science fiction . . . "**: Arthur C. Clarke, *Astounding Days*, 173.

Page 33. **"We have plenty of space here . . . "**: Letter, Arthur C. Clarke to Sam Youd (2 July 1938).

Page 33. **"The huge Moon photo . . . "**: William Temple, "The Saga of the Flat" (London: copy of manuscript, ca. 1946).

Page 34. **"'Maurice came,' Temple recalled . . . "**: William Temple, "The Saga of the Flat."

Page 34. **"The meetings were often . . . "**: Letter, William Temple to author (23 February 1989), 8.

Page 35. **"One night we returning . . . "**: William Temple, "The Saga of the Flat."

Page 35. **"We were a group . . . "**: Letter, William Temple to author (23 February 1989).

Page 36. **"tall fellow with the quiet . . . "**: William F. Temple, "The Flat Truth" in *Gargoyle* (April 1940).

Page 36. **"I think we succeeded . . ."**: Letter, William Temple to author (22 April 1989).

Page 36. **"The cover of the March . . . "**: William Temple, "Publicity Staggers on," *Bulletin of the British Interplanetary Society* (London: March 1939), 10.

Page 37. **"I fell to examining . . . "**: William F. Temple, "Chingford Chiaroscuro (A Layman's First Experimental Meeting)," *Bulletin of the British Interplanetary Society* (September 1938).

Page 37. **"Sometimes when it was . . . "**: William Temple, *Bulletin of the British Interplanetary Society* (January 1939), 3.

Page 37. **"The theory of . . . "**: Arthur C. Clarke, "Memoirs of an

Astronaut (Retired)," in *Voices from the Sky* (New York, Harper and Row, 1965), 171.

Page 38. **"Here Messrs. Edwards . . . "**: William F. Temple, "Chingford Chiaroscuro" (September 1938).

Page 38. **" 'Soon,' reported Temple, . . . "**: *Ibid.*

Page 40. **"Excuse me, sir . . . "**: Arthur C. Clarke, *Voices from the Sky*, 169–170.

Page 41. **"With present-day materials . . . "**: Arthur C. Clarke, "Into Space," *Chequer-Board* (October 1937).

Page 42. **"We used to . . . "**: Letter, William Temple to author (23 February 1989).

Page 42. **"Here I sat out the Blitz . . . "**: Arthur C. Clarke, *Astounding Days* (prepublication manuscript), 129.

Chapter 5

Page 43. **"I determined to go . . . "**: Arthur C. Clarke, *Ascent to Orbit*, 25.

Page 44. **"how to behave . . . "**: Arthur C. Clarke, *Glide Path*, 23.

Page 44. **"It was near Aldgate . . . "**: Arthur C. Clarke, *Astounding Days* (prepublication manuscript), 128–129.

Page 45. **"One day we were . . . "**: Arthur C. Clarke, *Ascent to Orbit*, 26.

Page 45. **"When he discovered . . . "**: *Ibid.*

Page 45. **"I suspect that . . . "**: Letter, Barry King to author (23 February 1989).

Page 47. **"The idea's extremely simple . . . "**: Arthur C. Clarke, *Glide Path*, 38.

Page 48. **"found the American scientists . . . "**: Arthur C. Clarke, *Ascent to Orbit*, 33.

Page 48. **"I can still remember . . . "**: Arthur C. Clarke, MIT speech (March 1976).

Page 49. **"I soon decided he . . . "**: Neal Jolley (unpublished manuscript, spring 1989), 49.

Page 50. **"We were now very much . . . "**: Arthur C. Clarke, *Ascent to Orbit*, 33.

Page 51. **"The scene might have come . . . "**: *Ibid.*, 32.

Page 51. **"The hissing roar . . . "**: Arthur C. Clarke, *Glide Path*, 205.

Page 52. **"The pilot was unable . . . "**: Arthur C. Clarke, *Ascent to Orbit*, 34.

Page 52. **"Luis's brainchild . . . "**: Arthur C. Clarke, MIT speech (March 1976).

Page 53. **"Started typing out . . . "**: Arthur C. Clarke, private journal entry (July 2–6, 1945).

Page 56. **"[O]nce I had got the idea . . . "**: Arthur C. Clarke, "Introduction" (*The Beginnings of Satellite Communications* by John R. Pierce), vi.

Page 57. **"For in my heart of hearts . . . "**: Arthur C. Clarke, *Voices from the Sky*, 126.

Chapter 6

Page 59. **"I was swiftly rejected . . . "**: Arthur C. Clarke, *Ascent to Orbit*, 69.

Page 62. **"This, I thought . . . "**: Arthur C. Clarke, *1984: Spring*, 180.

Page 63. **"It would only be fair . . . "**: Letter, Arthur C. Clarke to C. S. Lewis, in A. N. Wilson, *C. S. Lewis: A Biography* (New York: W. W. Norton, 1990), 177–178.

Page 63. **"I hope I should not be . . . "**: *Ibid.*

Page 63. **"Needless to say . . . "**: Arthur C. Clarke, *Voices from the Sky*, 175–176.

Page 66. **"I decided to devote . . . "**: Arthur C. Clarke, *Ascent to Orbit*, 83.

Page 66. **"Unlike most of my . . . "**: Arthur C. Clarke, *The Sentinel* (New York: Berkley Books, 1986), 117.

Page 67. **"Luckily I escaped . . . "**: Arthur C. Clarke, *Ascent to Orbit*, 83.

Page 67. **"My job was to . . . "**: *Ibid.*, 117–118.

Page 69. **"When I was in high school . . . "**: Carl Sagan, "In Praise of Arthur C. Clarke" (*The Planetary Report*, No. 3, 1983), 3.

Page 69. **"Never in my wildest . . . "**: Arthur C. Clarke, *Interplanetary Flight* (New York: Berkley Books, 1985), xi.

Page 70. **"After terrifying my wife . . . "**: "Green on the Screen," Fred Clarke, *Fred Clarke's Cameos* (17 January 1986).

Page 71. **"It is also widely recognized . . . "**: Arthur C. Clarke, *Ascent to Orbit*, 175–176.

Page 71. **"You called on me . . . "**: Letter, Wernher von Braun to Arthur C. Clarke (30 August 1951).

Page 73. **"All these weeks . . . "**: Arthur C. Clarke, *The Sands of Mars* (New York: New American Library, 1974), 71.

Page 73. **"I am agreeably surprised . . . "**: *Ibid.*, v.

Chapter 7

Page 76. **"in a moment of wild . . . "**: Clifton Fadiman, "Introduction," *Across the Sea of Stars* (New York: Harcourt, Brace & Company, 1959), 151–152.

Page 79. **"His hand had gone . . . "**: Arthur C. Clarke, *The Other Side of the Sky* (New York: New American Library, 1959), 98.

Page 79. **"watching the performance . . . "**: Arthur C. Clarke, "'Ego' Visits America," ASFO (fanzine), edited by Ian Macauley (January 1953).

Page 83. **"I have a theory . . . "**: *Ibid.*

Page 84. **"I met Arthur . . . "**: Bill MacQuitty, "Clarke of Ceylon" (unpublished manuscript, received fall 1989).

Chapter 8

Page 88. **"I submitted it to . . . "**: Arthur C. Clarke, *The Sentinel*, 41.

Page 91. **"There was a mist . . . "**: Arthur C. Clarke, *Childhood's End* (New York: Ballantine Books, 1953), 187.

Page 92. **"I was carrying . . . "**: Arthur C. Clarke, *The Deep Range* (New York: New American Library, 1958), ix–x.

Page 92. **"a fair-sized alligator . . . "**: *Ibid.*

Page 96. **"'A boy needs his father . . . '"**: Arthur C. Clarke, *2010: Odyssey Two* (New York: Ballantine Books, 1982), 302.

Page 99. **"In *Childhood's End* . . . "**: Basil Davenport, *New York Times Book Review* (23 August 1953), 19.

Page 103. **"There was Dr. Wernher von Braun . . . "**: Arthur C. Clarke, *The Making of a Moon* (New York: Harper & Brothers, 1957), 39–40.

Page 104. **"If you want to continue . . . "**: Arthur C. Clarke, *Christian Science Monitor* (10 February 1972), 10.

Page 104. **"I can still remember . . . "**: Arthur C. Clarke, *The View from Serendip* (New York: Ballantine Books, 1978), 116.

Chapter 9

Page 105. **"I now realise . . . "**: Arthur C. Clarke, "Ceylon," *True*, 39.

Page 106. **"A good deal of . . . "**: Arthur C. Clarke, *The View from Serendip*, 2–3.

Page 106. **"I spent the first 3 . . . "**: Letter, Arthur C. Clarke, "Report to the Globe (First and Probably Last Report)" (27 December 1954), 2.

Page 106. **"In particular, certain developments ... "**: Arthur C. Clarke, *The City and the Stars* (New York: New American Library, 1957), vii.

Page 107. **"He's accumulated some stunning ... "**: "Report to the Globe."

Page 108. **"We spent a couple ... "**: *Ibid.*

Page 108. **"first big shark ... "**: Letter, Arthur C. Clarke to Val Cleaver (1 January 1955).

Page 109. **"We had planned ... "**: Arthur C. Clarke, *The Coast of Coral* (New York: Harper & Row, 1956), 65.

Page 109. **"We are just going ... "**: Letter, Arthur C. Clarke to Val Cleaver (7 May 1955).

Page 110. **"I was to see ... "**: Arthur C. Clarke, *Coast of Coral*, 26.

Page 110. **"I did not enjoy ... "**: *Ibid.*, 125.

Page 112. **"We now have some ... "**: Letter, Arthur C. Clarke to Val Cleaver (2 August 1955).

Page 113. **"Harper's are very ... "**: *Ibid.* (24 September 1955).

Page 114. **"Saying that I am ... "**: *Ibid.*

Chapter 10

Page 115. **"Both Mike and I ... "**: Letter, Arthur C. Clarke to Val Cleaver (16 October 1955).

Page 116. **"We knew that the earlier ... "**: Arthur C. Clarke, with Mike Wilson, *The Reefs of Taprobane: Underwater Adventurers Around Ceylon* (New York: Harper & Brothers, 1957), 12.

Page 117. **"a small but pleasant apartment ... "**: *Ibid.*, 15.

Page 118. **"Mike also seems happy ... "**: Letter, Arthur C. Clarke to Val Cleaver (7 February 1956).

Page 119. **"We had the satisfaction ... "**: Arthur C. Clarke, *Reefs of Taprobane*, 33.

Page 122. **"The contrast between here ... "**: Letter, Arthur C. Clarke to Val Cleaver (6 April 1956).

Page 122. **"Hector was working ... "**: Fax, Arthur C. Clarke to author (2 June 1990).

Page 123. **"spoilt by silly ... "**: Letter, Arthur C. Clarke to Val Cleaver (16 June 1956).

Chapter 11

Page 125. **"I hope to sit ... "**: Letter, Arthur C. Clarke to Val Cleaver (16 September 1956).

Page 126. **"No other form of literature ... "**: Arthur C. Clarke, speech to the 1956 World Science Fiction Convention (2 September 1956).

Page 130. **"For some reason, at the beginning . . . "**: Arthur C. Clarke, *The Sentinel*, 254.

Chapter 12

Page 133. **"In my 1958 season . . . "**: Arthur C. Clarke, *The Challenge of the Spaceship* (New York: Harper & Brothers, 1959), 160.

Page 136. **"It is hard to believe . . . "**: *Ibid.*, 164, 210, 165, 166, 180, 181, 179.

Page 137. **"About 200 people . . . "**: Letter, Arthur C. Clarke to Sam Youd (10 July 1958).

Page 137. **"We are just floating . . . "**: *Ibid.* (13 August 1958).

Page 137. **"As he was leaving . . . "**: *Ibid.* (21 September 1958).

Page 138. **"I'm getting quite reactionary . . . "**: *Ibid.* (13 August 1958).

Page 138. **"Should the Soviet Union . . . "**: Letter, Arthur C. Clarke to Val Cleaver (23 February 1959).

Page 139. **"I was to preside . . . "**: Elmer Gertz, *Chicago Sun-Times* (15 April 1984).

Page 139. **"I was about to switch . . . "**: Arthur C. Clarke, *The Treasure of the Great Reef*, revised ed. (New York: Ballantine Books, 1974), 259.

Page 140. **"But the struggle . . . "**: Arthur C. Clarke, *Treasure* (Harper & Row, 1964), 18.

Page 141. **"We had sharks . . . "**: Letter, Arthur C. Clarke to Val Cleaver (13 May 1959).

Page 141. **"Usually Ali Baba . . . "**: Arthur C. Clarke, *Treasure*, 25.

Page 142. **"Writing the script . . . "**: Arthur C. Clarke, "Sri Lanka and Me" (*Millimeter*, March 1977), 41.

Page 142. **"The first draft . . . "**: Letter, Arthur C. Clarke to Val Cleaver (17 September 1959).

Page 143. **"Our new house . . . "**: *Ibid.* (20 November 1959).

Page 143. **"I hope to be . . . "**: *Ibid.* (29 September 1959).

Chapter 13

Page 145. **"Mixing fact and fiction . . . "**: Letter, Arthur C. Clarke to Val Cleaver (14 April 1960).

Page 145. **"We'll be using America's . . . "**: Arthur C. Clarke, "I Remember Babylon," in *The Nine Billion Names of God*, 33.

Page 145. **"Only a few years after . . . "**: *Ibid.*, 22–23.

Page 146. **"*GLIDE PATH* abandoned . . . "**: Letter, Arthur C. Clarke to Val Cleaver (28 February 1960).

Page 147. **"It varies in a way . . . "**: *Ibid.* (14 April 1960).

Page 147. **"quite a tough piece . . . "**: *Ibid.* (13 June 1990).

Page 148. **"All hell has broken loose . . . "**: *Ibid.* (24 August 1960).

Page 148. **"That means I've gambled . . . "**: *Ibid.*

Page 148. **"And any moment . . . "**: *Ibid.*

Page 148. **"I decided to . . . "**: *Ibid.* (17 October 1960).

Chapter 14

Page 151. **"I am pretty firm . . . "**: Letters, Arthur C. Clarke to Val Cleaver (7 January 1961, 14 January 1961, 16 March 1961).

Page 153. **"After a very few lessons . . . "**: Arthur C. Clarke, *The Treasure of the Great Reef* (New York: Harper & Row, 1964), 32.

Page 154. **"They were thinking . . . "**: Arthur C. Clarke, with Mike Wilson, *Indian Ocean Adventure* (New York: Harper & Row, 1961), 100.

Page 154. **"After we got to . . . "**: Arthur C. Clarke, *Treasure*, 38–39.

Page 155. **"Well, Mike has done . . . "**: Letter, Arthur C. Clarke to Val Cleaver (26 March 1961).

Page 156. **"Well, the Russians . . . "**: *Ibid.* (15 June 1961).

Page 157. **"I was pleased that . . . "**: *Ibid.* (16 May 1961).

Page 157. **"Mike and Liz got married . . . "**: Letter, Arthur C. Clarke to Sam Youd (ca. June 1961).

Page 158. **"I'm sorry to say . . . "**: *Ibid.* (26 June 1961).

Page 158. **"We met at his Fourteenth . . . "**: Fax, Arthur C. Clarke to author (June 1990).

Page 160. **"I was walking back . . . "**: Arthur C. Clarke, Opus 729, prepublication manuscript for "Close Encounters with Cosmonauts" (*OMNI*, October 1989, Russian edition).

Page 160. **"Why doesn't your film . . . "**: Arthur C. Clarke, *Treasure*, 81.

Chapter 15

Page 162. **"Leaving one store . . . "**: Arthur C. Clarke, *Treasure*, 86.

Page 163. **"I was almost completely . . . "**: *Ibid.*, 86–87.

Page 163. **"A plastic collar fastened . . . "**: *Ibid.*, 88.

Page 165. **"I wrote a couple . . . "**: *Ibid.*

Page 165. **"Though he never stopped . . . "**: Arthur C. Clarke, *Dolphin Island* (New York: Ace Books, 1987), 154.

Page 165. **"*Ran mutu Duwa* turned out . . . "**: Arthur C. Clarke, *Treasure*, 89.

Chapter 16

Page 168. **"all of us a chance . . . "**: Isaac Asimov, *The New York Times Book Review* (15 April 1963), 22.

Page 170. **"Though Mike had pressed me . . . "**: Arthur C. Clarke, *The Treasure of the Great Reef*, 115.

Page 170. **"I very quickly recognised . . . "**: Arthur C. Clarke, *Treasure*, 127, 128, 134–136.

Page 173. **"the further we try . . . "**: Arthur C. Clarke, with R. A. Smith, *The Exploration of the Moon* (New York: Harper's & Son, 1954), 112.

Page 174. **"Meanwhile I remain . . . "**: Letter, Arthur C. Clarke to Sam Youd (24 October 1963).

Chapter 17

Page 176. **"FRIGHTFULLY INTERESTED IN WORKING . . . "**: Jerome Agel, editor, *The Making of Kubrick's 2001* (New American Library, 1970), 11.

Page 177. **"He wanted to do the proverbial . . . "**: Arthur C. Clarke, *Report on Planet Three and Other Speculations* (New York: Berkley Books, 1985), 234–236.

Page 178. **"I am continually annoyed . . . "**: Arthur C. Clarke, *The Sentinel*, 117.

Page 178. **"I was happy to find . . . "**: Arthur C. Clarke, *Report on Planet Three*, 236.

Page 179. **"We talked for eight . . . "**: *Ibid.*

Page 179. **"I was working at Time-Life . . . "**: *Ibid.*, 237.

Page 180. **"He proposed that . . . "**: *Ibid.*, 239.

Page 180. **"In theory, therefore . . . "**: Arthur C. Clarke, *The Lost Worlds of 2001* (New York: New American Library, 1972), 31.

Page 181. **"I felt that when . . . "**: *Ibid.*, 32.

Page 181. **"Stan's a fascinating . . . "**: Letter, Arthur C. Clarke to Sam Youd (19 June 1964).

Page 181. **"We shook hands . . . "**: Arthur C. Clarke, *Report on Planet Three*, 238.

Page 182. **"Stanley was in some danger . . . "**: Arthur C. Clarke, *The Lost Worlds of 2001*, 29.

Page 183. **"They had no idea . . . "**: Carl Sagan, *The Cosmic Connection* (New York: Dell Books, 1975), 182.

Page 184. **"Just bought a ream of paper . . . "**: Letter, Arthur C. Clarke to Sam Youd (19 June 1964).

Page 184. **"Stanley installed me . . . "**: Arthur C. Clarke, *Report on Planet Three*, 239–240.

Page 185. **"The merging of our streams . . . "**: *Ibid.*

Page 185. **"Across the gulf of centuries . . . "**: Arthur C. Clarke, *The Challenge of the Spaceship* (New York: Harper & Brothers, 1959), 213.

Page 185. **"We set out . . . "**: Arthur C. Clarke, *Report on Planet Three*, 243.

Page 185. **"MGM doesn't know . . . "**: *Ibid.*

Page 186. **"This was typical . . . "**: *Ibid.*, 239.

Page 186. **"Stanley decided . . . "**: *Ibid.*

Page 188. **"My primary job . . . "**: Arthur C. Clarke, *Lost Worlds*, 36.

Page 190. **"equally divided between . . . "**: *Ibid.*, 37.

Page 190. **"suddenly realised how the novel . . . "**: Arthur C. Clarke, *Lost Worlds*, 38.

Page 190. **"The ending was altered . . . "**: Agel, editor, *The Making of Kubrick's 2001*, end of photo session.

Page 190. **"Bowman will regress . . . "**: Arthur C. Clarke, *Lost Worlds*, 37.

Page 191. **"After all, Odysseus . . . "**: *Ibid.*

Page 191. **"happened to remark . . . "**: *Ibid.*, 39.

Page 192. **"He called to say . . . "**: *Ibid.*

Chapter 18

Page 193. **"About a hundred technicians . . . "**: Arthur C. Clarke, *Lost Worlds*, 41.

Page 194. **"I got quite scared . . . "**: *Ibid.*, 45.

Page 194. **"I have never seen . . . "**: Andrew Sarris, *Village Voice* (May 1979).

Page 194. **"Stan spliced together . . . "**: Arthur C. Clarke, *Lost Worlds*, 45.

Page 195. **"[This would] make them highly suited . . . "**: Arthur C. Clarke, "Explorations in Tomorrow," in *Man and the*

Future, James Gunn, ed. (Lawrence, Kansas: University Press of Kansas, 1967), 263.

Page 196. **"I cabled Stanley . . . "**: Arthur C. Clarke, *Lost Worlds*, 46–47.

Page 197. **"I gather that there . . . "**: Letter, Arthur C. Clarke to Sam Youd (12 September 1966).

Page 197. **"He keeps promising . . . "**: *Ibid.* (1 December 1966).

Page 197. **"It was a very sad period . . . "**: Arthur C. Clarke, *Lost Worlds*, 46.

Page 198. **"The 2001 novel contract . . . "**: Letter, Arthur C. Clarke to Sam Youd (June [no day] 1967).

Page 198. **"I had to invent . . . "**: Jerome Agel, ed., *The Making of Kubrick's 2001*, 351, ff.

Page 200. **"Keir Dullea, dressed . . . "**: Jeremy Bernstein, *A Comprehensible World* (New York: Random House, 1967), 241.

Page 201. **"Maybe the company can . . . "**: *Ibid.*

Page 202. **"It is the year 2001 . . . "**: *The Making of 2001* (New York: Thomas Craven Film Corp., 1966).

Page 203. **"I tried to work things . . . "**: Agel, *The Making of Kubrick's 2001*, photo section.

Page 203. **"banal to the point of extinction . . . "**: *Ibid.*, 299.

Page 204. **"There are certain areas . . . "**: *Ibid.*, photo section.

Page 204. **"This is what makes 2001 . . . "**: *Ibid.*

Page 204. **"2001: A Space Odyssey is about man's . . . "**: *Ibid.*, front matter.

Page 204. **"Stan and I used . . . "**: Letter, Arthur C. Clarke to Sam Youd (2 August 1968).

Page 205. **"I can still recall . . . "**: Arthur C. Clarke, *Astounding Days*, 21.

Page 205. **"It's hard to find anything . . . "**: Agel, *The Making of Kubrick's 2001*, photo section.

Page 206. **"the longest flash forward . . . "**: Arthur C. Clarke, *Lost Worlds*, 51–52.

Page 206. **"(ugh!) My 50th!!! . . . "**: Letter, Arthur C. Clarke to Sam Youd (21 October 1967).

Page 206. **"I feel pretty relaxed . . . "**: *Ibid.*

Page 207. **"I think it just affected . . . "**: Agel, *The Making of Kubrick's 2001*, 170.

Page 208. **"Well, that's the end of . . . "**: *Ibid.*, photo section.

Page 208. **"dazzles the eyes and gnaws . . . "**: *Life* (5 April 1968), 27.

Page 209. **"They were plotting . . . "**: *Ibid.*, 34.

Page 209. **"Whenever the thunder . . . "**: Agel, *The Making of Kubrick's 2001*, 229.

Page 209. **"I have seen . . . "**: *Ibid.*, 329.

Page 210. **"I still stand by . . . "**: Arthur C. Clarke, *Report on Planet Three and Other Speculations*, 245.

Page 210. **"Now I feel I've been . . . "**: Agel, *The Making of Kubrick's 2001*, photo section.

Page 210. **"It was a particularly . . . "**: postcard, Neil Armstrong to author (May 1989).

Page 210. **"I remember thinking . . . "**: Agel, *The Making of Kubrick's 2001*, photo section.

Page 212. **"I always used to tell people . . . "**: *Ibid.*

Page 212. **"[t]he book does something . . . "**: Arthur C. Clarke, *Lost Worlds*, 257.

Page 212. **"After seeing *Space Odyssey* . . . "**: Agel, *The Making of Kubrick's 2001*, 309.

Page 212. **"since the motion picture . . . "**: *Ibid.*, 256.

Page 213. **"I tore up . . . "**: Arthur C. Clarke, *Astounding Days* (prepublication manuscript), 58.

Page 214. **"As an artist . . . "**: Agel, *The Making of Kubrick's 2001*, photo section.

Chapter 19

Page 215. **"When I published . . . "**: Arthur C. Clarke, *The View from Serendip*, 70.

Page 217. **"I am sitting glued . . . "**: Letter, Arthur C. Clarke to Tom Craven (24 December 1968).

Page 218. **"How many people have powerful . . . "**: Arthur C. Clarke, quoted in the *Ceylon Observer* (27 December 1968).

Page 219. **"The SF Symposium was only . . . "**: Frederik Pohl, *The Way the Future Was* (New York: Ballantine Books, 1978), 301.

Chapter 20

Page 223. **"Then you'll be able to tune . . . "**: CBS transcript, "The Communications Explosion," broadcast 29 January 1967.

Page 225. **"I hadn't cried for twenty years . . . "**: Jeremy Bernstein, "Profiles: Out of the Ego Chamber," *The New Yorker* 45 (9 August 1969), 40.

Page 225. **"Well, it is one of the most thrilling . . . "**:

0:56:20PM 7/20/69: The historic conquest of the moon as reported to the American people by CBS News over the CBS Television Network, 21–22.

Page 228. **"Yes, I'm always running . . . "**: *Ibid.*, 59–60.

Page 229. **"When the *Eagle* landed . . . "**: Fax, Arthur C. Clarke to author (20 April 1990).

Page 229. **"We're going out indefinitely . . . "**: CBS, 7/20/69, 107.

Page 230. **"Now the moon has yielded . . . "**: *Ibid.*, 129.

Chapter 21

Page 232. **"I had to check . . . "**: Letter, Arthur C. Clarke to Tom Craven (14 January 1970).

Page 233. **"I begged him . . . "**: Arthur C. Clarke, "Ceylon: An Adventurer's Retreat," in *True* (April 1972).

Page 233. **"They liked it so much . . . "**: Letter, Arthur C. Clarke to Sam Youd (25 April 1970).

Page 233. **"For it may be that . . . "**: Arthur C. Clarke, "Epilogue: Beyond Apollo," in *First on the Moon* (Boston: Little, Brown, and Company, 1970), 419.

Page 234. **"That's what I *intended* . . . "**: Arthur C. Clarke, *Imperial Earth* (New York: Ballantine Books, 1976), 128.

Page 236. **"Besides this house . . . "**: Letter, Arthur C. Clarke to Sam Youd (21 December 1970).

Page 236. **"I have a long-standing . . . "**: Dialogue between Arthur C. Clarke and Alan Watts in "At the Interface: Technology and Mysticism," *Playboy* (19 January 1971), 94–97, 130 ff.

Page 237. **"Over the previous decade . . . "**: Arthur C. Clarke, *The Sentinel*, 207.

Page 237. **"island of 13 million . . . "**: Arthur C. Clarke, *The Treasure of the Great Reef*, rev. ed., 254–255.

Page 239. **"When I was a boy . . . "**: Letter, Joseph Allen to Arthur C. Clarke (September 1984).

Page 239. **"We are here . . . "**: audio transcript from film coverage of the event, Thomas Craven Films, Inc., August 1971.

Page 239. **"Do we have the imagination . . . "**: Arthur C. Clarke, speech, State Department, August 1971.

Page 240. **"It was Edgar Rice Burroughs . . . "**: Arthur C. Clarke et al. *Mars and the Mind of Man* (New York: Harper & Row, 1973), 27–28.

Chapter 22

Page 244. **"It has often been suggested . . . "**: Arthur C. Clarke, *Report on Planet Three*, 133.

Page 244. **"This statement by a spokesman . . . "**: Saul Bellow, "Literature in the Age of Technology," in *Technology and the Frontiers of Knowledge* (Garden City, New York: Doubleday, 1975), 4.

Page 245. **"I count it as noble . . . "**: Arthur C. Clarke, *View from Serendip*, 187.

Page 245. **"enjoyed none more . . . "**: Letter, Joseph Allen to Arthur C. Clarke (ca. spring 1973).

Page 245. **"We should build them . . . "**: Arthur C. Clarke, *View from Serendip*, 126.

Page 246. **"The TV coverage . . . "**: Arthur C. Clarke, "The Last Revolution," speech given at Goddard Dinner (Washington, D.C., 14 March 1972).

Page 247. **"I was tempted to give . . . "**: Arthur C. Clarke, *The Wind from the Sun* (New York: Harcourt Brace Jovanovich, 1972), vii–viii.

Page 248. **"That was very nearly . . . "**: Fax, Arthur C. Clarke to author (27 February 1990).

Page 248. **"I went up a hundred meters . . . "**: *Ibid.* (20 March 1990).

Page 249. **"I stood in the back . . . "**: Kerry O'Quinn, "Rendezvous with Clarke," *Starlog* (December 1983), 4.

Page 251. **"Science fiction is often called . . . "**: Interview, Arthur C. Clarke and Alice Turner, *Publishers Weekly* (10 September 1973).

Page 251. **"story-telling of the highest order . . . "**: *New York Times* (22 August 1973), 35.

Chapter 23

Page 254. **"It will be hell . . . "**: Letter, Arthur C. Clarke to Tom Craven (3 December 1973).

Page 255. **"Still fighting to get . . . "**: *Ibid.* (21 December 1973).

Page 258. **"This book has more plot . . . "**: Joseph McLellan, *Washington Post* (23 January 1976), c-4.

Page 258. **"at the height of his . . . "**: Gerald Jonas, *New York Times Book Review* (18 January 1976), 20.

Page 258. **"after 20 years work ... "**: Letter, Arthur C. Clarke to Roger Caras (23 January 1975).

Page 258. **"I am now taking things ... "**: Letter, Arthur C. Clarke to Tom Craven (21 April 1975).

Page 258. **"Since I delivered ... "**: Letter, Arthur C. Clarke to Sam Youd (20 June 1975).

Page 259. **"He believes ... "**: Arthur C. Clarke, *View from Serendip*, 161.

Page 260. **"The best solution for you ... "**: Letter, Wernher von Braun to Arthur C. Clarke (5 August 1974).

Page 261. **"India's gesture to Arthur Clarke ... "**: *Ceylon Daily News* (12 August 1975).

Page 261. **"I am now inviting ... "**: Letter, Arthur C. Clarke to Yash Pal (11 August 1975).

Page 262. **"Am delighted to hear ... "**: Letter, Arthur C. Clarke to Tom Craven (18 February 1975).

Page 262. **"I consider it a breakthrough ... "**: *Christian Science Monitor* (28 May 1975).

Page 262. **"If this is so ... "**: Letter, Arthur C. Clarke to Sam Youd (20 June 1975).

Page 263. **"Neil Armstrong and I waited ... "**: Fax, Arthur C. Clarke to author (20 March 1990).

Page 263. **"I was both flattered ... "**: Arthur C. Clarke, *View from Serendip*, 189–215.

Page 266. **"I spent several days ... "**: *Ibid.*, 137.

Page 266. **"Well, Isaac ... "**: *Ibid.*, 138.

Page 266. **"It's an awesome output ... "**: *Ibid.*, 140, 143.

Page 267. **"done *con amore* ... "**: Letter, Arthur C. Clarke to Tom Craven (29 December 1974).

Page 269. **"Many years ago ... "**: Arthur C. Clarke, "Goodbye Isaac" (Colombo, Sri Lanka, 7 April 1992).

Chapter 24

Page 270. **"Since your remarkable forecast ... "**: Letter, Jerome Weisner to Arthur C. Clarke (21 October 1975).

Page 271. **"one could have face-to-face ... "**: Arthur C. Clarke, *The View from Serendip*, 219, 221, 239, 217.

Page 272. **"Can't you persuade them ... "**: Letter, Arthur C. Clarke to Tom Craven (28 October 1976).

Page 272. **"Olsen's idea was ... "**: Tom Craven, *Millimeter* (March 1977), 78.

Page 273. **"The Bell System knows . . . "**: script, *The Making of 2076* (Thomas Craven Films, 1976).

Page 275. **"In a very important . . . "**: Arthur C. Clarke, *Spaceflight*, Vol. 18, No. 12 (British Interplanetary Society, December 1976), 429–431.

Page 275. **"I am hard at work . . . "**: Letters, Arthur C. Clarke to Tom Craven (13 August 1976, 9 October 1976, 28 October 1976).

Page 277. **"The big problem is . . . "**: Letter, Arthur C. Clarke to Tom Craven (16 June 1977).

Page 277. **"Leslie had had a row . . . "**: Letter, Arthur C. Clarke to Roger Caras (13 July 1977).

Page 278. **"Leslie was also perhaps . . . "**: Letter, Arthur C. Clarke to Sam Youd (3 December 1978).

Page 278. **"For forty years he . . . "**: *Ibid.*

Page 278. **"I've become more and more . . . "**: *Ibid.*

Page 279. **"I'm thinking of taking . . . "**: Malcolm Kirk, *OMNI* interview (March 1979), 102.

Page 279. **"And at last I have . . . "**: Letter, Arthur C. Clarke to Sam Youd (3 December 1978).

Page 280. **"It's the most ambitious . . . "**: Martin Walker, "The Man with Space for Development," *Guardian* (30 August 1978), 8.

Page 281. **"A clear case of plagiarism . . . "**: Arthur C. Clarke, *1984: Spring*, 210.

Page 281. **"Today's comsats demonstrate . . . "**: *Ibid.*, 98.

Page 281. **"easily be regarded as the grandfather . . . "**: *Publisher Weekly* (14 June 1976).

Page 283. **"Old Arthur C. Clarke . . . "**: Fax, Arthur C. Clarke to author (summer 1991).

Chapter 25

Page 285. **"For the last four days . . . "**: Letter, Fred Clarke to Arthur C. Clarke (15 February 1980).

Page 285. **"Mother died . . . "**: Letter, Arthur C. Clarke to Tom Craven (10 March 1980).

Page 285. **"There's the corona! . . . "**: Arthur C. Clarke, audio from *Arthur C. Clarke's Mysterious World: The Journey Begins* (Pacific Arts Video, 1989).

Page 285. **"Here in the sea . . . "**: Arthur C. Clarke, soundtrack from *OMNI* TV ad, 1980.

Page 286. **"As I sat on the bench . . . "**: Arthur C. Clarke, *1984: Spring*, 195.

Page 287. **"When I made it clear . . . "**: Letter, Arthur C. Clarke to Tom Craven (March 1981).

Page 287. **"You probably can't think . . . "**: Walter Cronkite, CBS transcript, vol. III, number 5 (May 1981).

Page 288. **"Last month I had . . . "**: Arthur C. Clarke, *1984: Spring*, 24.

Page 289. **"I sat next to the Russians . . . "**: Arthur C. Clarke, "New Communications Technologies and the Developing World," in *Analog Science Fiction/Science Fact* (December 1983), 36–37.

Chapter 26

Page 293. **"I realized he was right . . . "**: Interview with Roger Caras, "Our Man in the Future," *Science Digest* (March 1982), 95.

Page 294. **"If you are an optimist . . . "**: *Ibid.*, 95.

Page 294. **"Many of the elements . . . "**: ABC News, *20/20: Arthur C. Clarke Transcript.*

Page 294. **"It's just past half full . . . "**: *Ibid.*

Page 295. **"Now working night . . . "**: Letter, Arthur C. Clarke to Roger Caras (16 November 1981).

Page 295. **"I can honestly say . . . "**: Arthur C. Clarke and Peter Hyams, *The Odyssey File* (New York: Ballantine Books, 1984), xv.

Page 295. **"The marvelous thing . . . "**: Arthur C. Clarke, "Egogram 1" (6 April 1982).

Page 296. **"Scott Meredith is entirely . . . "**: *Ibid.*

Page 296. **"have made a significant . . . "**: Arthur C. Clarke, *Ascent to Orbit*, 3.

Page 296. **"two orthogonal brass rings . . . "**: Fax, Arthur C. Clarke to author (5 July 1990).

Page 297. **"Though it was now late . . . "**: Arthur C. Clarke, "Egogram 2" (27 June 1982).

Page 297. **"We greeted each other . . . "**: Arthur C. Clarke, *1984: Spring*, 38–39.

Page 298. **"I was also inserted . . . "**: *Ibid.*

Page 298. **"[T]here were some aspects . . . "**: *Ibid.*

Page 299. **"You're not a bit like . . . "**: Arthur C. Clarke, "Egogram 2" (27 June 1982).

Page 299. **"It was a great thrill . . . "**: Arthur C. Clarke, *2010: Odyssey Two*, 335.

Page 300. **"It is hard to believe . . . "**: Arthur C. Clarke, *1984: Spring*, 107.

Page 301. **"My Geneva speech . . . "**: Marcia Gauger, "Arthur C. Clarke Spins Tales of Outer Space . . . " *People* (20 December 1982).

Page 301. **"The importance of halting . . . "**: Arthur C. Clarke, *1984: Spring*, 53, 56.

Page 302. **"I called Stanley . . . "**: Interview, Arthur C. Clarke and the *Washington Post* (November 1982).

Page 303. **"There was a lot of fighting . . . "**: Letter, Scott Meredith to author (16 March 1990).

Chapter 27

Page 306. **"Don't blame me . . . "**: Arthur C. Clarke, *Ascent to Orbit*, 213.

Page 306. **"At a generous assessment . . . "**: Arthur C. Clarke, John Fairley, Simon Welfare, *Arthur C. Clarke's World of Strange Powers* (New York: Putnam, 1984).

Page 307. **"Human judgment must . . . "**: *Ibid.*, 243.

Page 307. **"It might be fun . . . "**: Arthur C. Clarke and Peter Hyams, *The Odyssey File* (New York: Ballantine Books, 1985), xvi, xvii.

Page 308. **"Peter and I started . . . "**: *Ibid.*

Page 310. **"A number of the top . . . "**: press release, White House (23 June 1983).

Page 311. **"This was not only . . . "**: Arthur C. Clarke, "Egogram" (1983).

Page 313. **"I was invited . . . "**: Arthur C. Clarke, *Ascent to Orbit*, 213.

Page 314. **"The Americans . . . "**: *Ibid.*, 221.

Chapter 28

Page 316. **"I feel very happy . . . "**: Arthur C. Clarke and Peter Hyams, *The Odyssey File*, 100.

Page 318. **"Clarke's residence is next door . . . "**: Elmer Gertz, *Chicago Sun-Times* (15 April 1984), 6–7.

Page 320. **"In an extraordinary show of faith . . . "**: press release, Press Syndicate, A Media Service of Book Communications Systems, no date.

Page 320. **"The token figure . . . "**: Letter, Scott Meredith to author (28 June 1990).

Page 320. **"If I don't deliver . . . "**: Letter, Arthur C. Clarke to Stanley Kubrick (12 July 1984).

Page 321. **"I was feeding pigeons . . . "**: Arthur C. Clarke, "Egogram, 1984."

Page 321. **"apart from the usual . . . "**: Letter, Arthur C. Clarke to Tom Craven (12 July 1984).

Page 322. **" '2010' is a perfectly adequate . . . "**: Vincent Canby, *New York Times* (7 December 1984).

Page 323. **"As you doubtless know . . . "**: Video presentation, "A Martian Odyssey." Audio transcript (17 September 1984).

Page 324. **"I have also talked . . . "**: *Ibid.*

Page 325. **"Assume that there's an unfriendly . . . "**: Arthur C. Clarke, *1984: Spring*, 55.

Page 328. **"I realised that Bob . . . "**: Arthur C. Clarke, "Tribute to R.A.H." (prepublication manuscript, 5 September 1990).

Chapter 29

Page 329. **"I did my best . . . "**: Letter, Arthur C. Clarke to Ian Macauley (May 1985).

Page 330. **"Dr. Goddard persevered . . . "**: President Ronald Reagan, speech before the National Space Club (29 March 1985).

Page 330. **"based on an engine . . . "**: Roger Caras, "Our Man in the Future," *Science Digest* (March 1982), 58.

Page 332. **"In view of the UK's . . . "**: Arthur C. Clarke, "Egogram 1985."

Page 332. **"All the hotels there . . . "**: Letter, Arthur C. Clarke to Michael Craven (14 July 1985).

Page 333. **"My publisher Judy-Lynn . . . "**: *Ibid.* (30 October 1985).

Chapter 30

Page 334. **"been tinkering with . . . "**: Arthur C. Clarke, "85 Update."

Page 335. **"I groaned inwardly . . . "**: Arthur C. Clarke and Gentry Lee, *RAMA II* (New York: Bantam Books, 1989), v–vi.

Page 336. **"When is an Arthur C. Clarke novel . . . "**: Review, "Bookends" (26 October 1988).

Page 337. **"The Clarke-Lee collaboration . . . "**: Arthur C.

Clarke, "Coauthors and Other Nuisances" (unpublished manuscript, received fall 1990).

Page 338. **"To add insult . . . "**: *Ibid.*.

Page 338. **"I realised that its next . . . "**: *The Guardian* (9 August 1986).

Page 339. **"I tried to write . . . "**: *Ibid.*

Page 339. ***"The Songs of Distant Earth . . ."***: review, Ian Watson, "Today" (3 July 1986).

Page 340. **"You're trying to pin me . . . "**: Interview, Ken Kelley for *Playboy* (August 1986), 57, 66 ff.

Page 341. **"So the intervention . . . "**: Arthur C. Clarke, *2010: Odyssey Two*, 164.

Page 343. **"Saw Neuro-specialists . . . "**: Arthur C. Clarke, "Egogram '86."

Page 343. **"The only problem . . . "**: Letter, Arthur C. Clarke to Roger Caras (20 October 1986).

Page 343. **"I'm now glad to say . . . "**: Letter, Arthur C. Clarke to Charles N. Brown (6 October 1986).

Page 344. **"its loyalties and interests will transcend . . . "**: Arthur C. Clarke, speech, Nehru Memorial Address, New Delhi (13 November 1986).

Chapter 31

Page 346. **"I hid out in a hotel . . . "**: Letter, Arthur C. Clarke to Roger Caras (11 May 1987).

Page 347. **"The contents deal almost . . . "**: Review, Isaac Asimov for *The Observer* (7 May 1989).

Page 347. **"I was once again . . . "**: Arthur C. Clarke and Gentry Lee, *RAMA II*, viii.

Page 351. **"I still don't believe . . . "**: Arthur C. Clarke, "Egogram 1987."

Page 351. **"It was my privilege . . . "**: Letter, Cyril Ponnamperuma to Arthur C. Clarke (16 December 1987).

Page 352. **"All this gave me . . . "**: Arthur C. Clarke, "Egogram 1988."

Page 352. **"Having young people around me . . . "**: *Ibid.*

Page 354. **"Tonight: The time before time . . . "**: "God, the Universe and Everything Else" (copy of transcript, July 1988), 25, 30, 31.

Page 355. **"I was somewhat unprepared . . . "**: Letter, Daniel Drachman, M.D., to author (13 November 1990).

Page 357. **"The Johns Hopkins specialists . . . "**: Arthur C. Clarke, "Bulletin from Baltimore or: A Medical Odyssey" (August 1988).

Chapter 32

Page 360. **"full of energy . . . "**: "Bulletin from Baltimore."

Page 360. **"I'm sorry to say . . . "**: Letter, Arthur C. Clarke to Willie Mendis (22 March 1989).

Page 363. **"It must have been written . . . "**: Fax, Arthur C. Clarke to author (13 December 1990).

Page 363. **"The word came directly . . . "**: Fax, Arthur C. Clarke to author (29 November 1990).

Page 365. **"Clarke is a hard man . . . "**: Interview, Godfrey Smith and Arthur C. Clarke, *Sunday Times* (22 October 1989).

Page 367. **"I had a nice chat . . . "**: Fax, Arthur C. Clarke to Scott Meredith Literary Agency (26 October 1989).

Page 370. **"Whether we become a multi-planet . . . "**: Transcript, satellite video conference between Riyadh, New York City, Washington, D.C., and Atlanta (November 1989), 24.

Page 371. **"more so Arthur who is . . . "**: Letter, Rodney Jonklaas to author (6 April 1989).

Page 371. **"Readers may welcome Clarke's . . . "**: Review, Gregory Feeley, "Rama Redux," *Washington Post* (31 December 1989).

Chapter 33

Page 374. **"a gross blunder . . ."**: *Tekhnika Molodezhi* (November 1989).

Page 374. **"The last thing I'd intended . . . "**: Letter, Arthur C. Clarke to Vasili Zacharchenko (January 1990).

Page 375. **"I'm afraid all the best . . . "**: Letter, Arthur C. Clarke to Willie Mendis (Summer 1989).

Page 376. **"mainly technical wizards . . . "**: Review, John Sladek for the *Washington Post* (25 November 1990).

Page 376. **"vintage Clarke . . . "**: Review, Dan Chow for *Locus* (October 1990), 22.

Page 377. **"sees the universe . . . "**: Jonas, *New York Times Book Review* (3 February 1991), 33.

Page 377. **"It was written as a reaction . . . "**: Arthur C. Clarke, "On Golden Seas," in *Tales from Planet Earth* (New York: Bantam, 1990), 299.

Page 378. **"It was a voyage of discovery . . . "**: Arthur C. Clarke and Gregory Benford, *Beyond the Fall of Night* (New York: Ace/ Putnam, 1990), xi.

Page 380. **"Our tribute to you . . . "**: *Colombo Daily News* (17 December 1990), 12.

Page 380. **"I used to say mankind . . . "**: Prepublication interview transcript (received June 1990), Bob Frost and Arthur C. Clarke.

Page 380. **"There's been a lot of talk . . . "**: Interview, Roger Caras and Arthur C. Clarke for ABC's *20/20*, unpublished transcript (September 1981), 114.

Page 381. **"any great literary ability . . . "**: Letter, Arthur C. Clarke to Sam Youd (28 January 1938).

Page 381. **"He is the greatest living science fiction . . . "**: Gregory Benford, "Arthur C. Clarke: The Prophet Vindicated," in *Lan's Lantern*, No. 28 (1989), 4–5.

Page 386. **"In projecting our ideas . . . "**: Interview, Roger Caras and Arthur C. Clarke for ABC's *20/20*, unpublished transcript (September 1981), 92.

Page 386. **"One day we may be able . . . "**: Arthur C. Clarke, *Profiles of the Future* (New York: Holt, Rinehart and Winston, 1984), 242.

Page 387. **"Not by 2001 . . . "**: Prepublication interview transcript (received June 1990), Bob Frost and Arthur C. Clarke.

Page 387. **"I think there's a ninety-nine percent chance . . . "**: Arthur C. Clarke, *Omni* (October 1989), 8.

Page 388. **"because it's a very lonely . . . "**: Arthur C. Clarke, *Los Angeles Times* (1 December 1982), 15.

Page 388. **"One of the great lessons . . . "**: Arthur C. Clarke, "Credo," prepublication manuscript, Opus 735 (30 July 1989), 4, 5, 10.

Page 388. **"Actually, my motivation and aim . . . "**: Fax, Arthur C. Clarke to author (18 January 1991), 2.

INDEX